KEYNESIANISM, MONETARISM AND THE CRISIS OF THE STATE

Keynesianism, Monetarism and the Crisis of the State

SIMON CLARKE
Senior Lecturer in Sociology
University of Warwick

EDWARD ELGAR

Published by
Edward Elgar Publishing Limited
Gower House
Croft Road
Aldershot
Hants GU11 3HR
England

Gower Publishing Company
Old Post Road
Brookfield
Vermont 05036
USA

HB
99.7
.C55
1988

ISBN 1–85278–010–X

Printed in Great Britain at the University Press, Cambridge

Contents

Chapter 1

Introduction

The challenge of monetarism

Over the past decade Keynesian full employment policies have been abandoned in one country after another, to be replaced by monetarist policies that place a premium on price stability. The monetarist counter-revolution has not only abandoned the Keynesian commitment to full employment, but more fundamentally has challenged the Keynesian conception of the role of the state in the regulation of capitalism, returning to the pre-Keynesian emphasis on the primary role of money and the market. How are we to understand this development, and what is its significance?

Monetarists would claim that their triumph simply reflects the failure of Keynesianism and the correctness of their point of view: a new sense of realism has replaced the Keynesian fantasy of universal plenty, a popular demand for freedom has arisen to challenge the tyranny of the state. Many Keynesians, by contrast, see monetarism as a reactionary throwback, a misguided academic theory that has been pressed by doctrinaire economists on bigoted and narrow-minded politicians. But to see monetarism as the triumph of either rationality or irrationality is to attribute too much coherence and too much power to theories that serve more to legitimate than to guide political practice. The ideas of monetarism are important, but their importance is ideological, in giving coherence and direction to political forces which have deeper roots.

The most popular explanations for the rise of monetarism look

1

for these roots in political developments. The triumph of monetarism is commonly explained by the political failures of the left, that opened the way for the populist ideology of the New Right, manifested most dramatically in the rise of 'Thatcherism' and 'Reaganism'.[1] The appropriate response of the left is then supposed to be a political response, to regain the ideological initiative. The left has to develop a new politics and a new ideology, that will address the popular hopes and fears to which the New Right speaks, and rebuild a united movement that will win the hearts and minds of the people.

The problem with this approach is that the rise of monetarism cannot be explained in terms of purely political developments. 'Thatcherism' and 'Reaganism' are only variations on a theme that has been played around the world. Moreover the rise of monetarism has not been specifically tied to the rise of the New Right. In Britain it was under a Labour government, and most particularly from 1976, that monetarist policies began to be pursued and Keynesian objectives abandoned. Moreover the turn to monetarism under Labour did not only involve a turn to monetarist economic policies and objectives. The Callaghan government played all the New Right tunes, however off-key, attacking the trades unions, extolling the virtues of the family, pandering to racism, tightening the administration of social security, stressing its commitment to 'law and order', launching the 'Great Debate' on education. Although in Britain Thatcher replaced Callaghan, in Southern Europe, Australia and New Zealand social democratic governments have taken it upon themselves to carry through the monetarist revolution, in the guise of a 'politics of austerity', while social democratic parties around the world have capitulated to a 'new realism'. Thus monetarist policies have been forced on governments of very different political and ideological persuasions, although policies that have in some cases been adopted only under the force of circumstances have in others been espoused enthusiastically. While social democratic governments submit to the power of money in the name of realism, right-wing governments proclaim its power as that of a moral principle. These differences are important, but to stress the

---

[1] The most influential version of this explanation on the British left has been that proposed in the pages of *Marxism Today*, and particularly in Stuart Hall and Martin Jacques, eds. , *The Politics of Thatcherism*, Lawrence and Wishart, London, 1983.

distinctiveness of the variations is to ignore the underlying theme. The rise of monetarism cannot be explained in terms of contingent political developments, in terms of personalities and political factions of the right and the left, for these developments are systematic, to be observed throughout the capitalist world. These political developments express a deeper crisis, of which they are themselves a part.

An alternative set of explanations looks to the economic crisis to explain the rise of monetarism, seeing monetarism as a capitalist response to the crisis. There are two very different interpretations of the significance of monetarism along these lines. The first interpretation rests on an identification of Keynesianism with the interests of 'industrial capital' and monetarism with the interests of 'financial capital'. Keynesian policies involve high levels of state expenditure in support of the productive sector of the economy, state intervention in financial markets to secure cheap credit for industry, and demand-management to provide a growing market for industry, making possible a high and rising standard of living and of welfare provision for the mass of the population. Although such policies serve the general interest, as well as the particular interests of industrial capital, they do not serve the interests of bankers and financiers, who seek high interest rates and the freedom to invest their money where they can achieve the highest returns, without regard for the common good.[2]

On this interpretation the crises of the 1970s arose because the interests of financial and industrial capital came into increasingly sharp conflict with one another, these conflicts coming to a head in the form of financial crises as the freedom of mobility of financial

---

[2] For an interpretation of Britain's economic decline from this point of view see the work of Sidney Pollard, especially *The Wasting of the British Economy*, Croom Helm, London, 1982. Geoffrey Ingham, *Capitalism Divided*, Macmillan, Basingstoke, 1984, offers a sociological account. This has been a recurrent theme in *New Left Review* since Perry Anderson's manifesto, published soon after he took control of the journal, 'The Origins of the Present Crisis', *New Left Review*, 24, 1964, devastatingly criticised by Edward Thompson, 'The Peculiarities of the English', *Socialist Register 1965*, Merlin, London, 1965. Far more valuable than any of these accounts of a supposed British exceptionalism, which cannot account for the global character of the crisis, is Kees van der Pijl's *The Making of an Atlantic Ruling Class*, Verso, London, 1984, which applies a similar analysis on a global scale. I have criticised the approach, particularly in relation to the analysis of South Africa, in Simon Clarke, 'Capital, Fractions of Capital and the State', *Capital and Class*, 5, 1982.

capital threatened to undermine Keynesian industrial strategies.
The rise of monetarism reflected the victory of financial over industrial capital. Bankers exploited their financial power and their
privileged access to the state to force governments to adopt restrictive financial policies that restored financial stability and confidence, but at the expense of high interest rates and cuts in public
expenditure that drove the economy into recession. The appropriate response of the left within such a framework is to reassert
the virtues of Keynesianism within a strategy that subordinates
financial interests to the needs of national industrial regeneration,
exposing and confronting the narrow and unpatriotic self-interest
of the bankers and financiers that hides behind the ideology and
politics of monetarism.

This explanation has a superficial plausibility. The economic
crises of the 1970s, like those of previous decades, did indeed take
the form of financial crises whose resolution sacrificed the real economy on the altar of money. However on closer examination the
plausibility of the account soon breaks down. How could financial capital manage to impose policies which are so transparently
against the national interest? If Keynesian industrial strategies
could really have succeeded, if only they could subordinate financial
capital to the state, why has government after government, elected
on manifesto commitments to such strategies of national regeneration, capitulated and pursued monetarist policies? Why should
ambitious politicians drive the economy into recession if they could
so easily have adopted policies which would have brought prosperity and votes? Only the crudest of conspiracy theories could explain
such pervasive irrationality.

The problem underlying such an account is that there is no
evidence that the supposedly sharp conflict of interest between 'financial' and 'industrial' capital actually exists. Industrial capital
has no more interest than financial capital in the expansion of production for its own sake. Both forms of capital are motivated by
the one concern, profit. Only a relatively small part of the capital,
even of manufacturing companies, is tied up in plant and buildings required to carry on production, and even the apparent fixity
and immobility of those assets proves illusory when production becomes unprofitable. On the other hand, a significant proportion of
the assets commanded by the financial institutions takes the form
of loans to, and shares in, manufacturing enterprises. Moreover

the financial institutions derive the bulk of their profits not from investment of their own capital, but from concentrating the savings and bank deposits of the mass of the population, so that they do not necessarily benefit from high interest rates, their profits depending primarily on commissions and on the difference between interest paid and profits received. The profitability of financial institutions depends on a high level of demand for their loans, which in turn depends on general capitalist prosperity. When the economy goes into a recession, so that there is surplus capital available, the financiers search ever more desperately for outlets for this capital, which is diverted into ever more speculative channels. But this diversion of capital is not the cause of the shortage of funds for productive investment, but the consequence of the shortage of profitable opportunities.

The very distinction between financial and industrial capital is becoming increasingly anachronistic as accumulation on a world scale is dominated by multinational corporations, which take the form of financial holding companies, closely integrated with multinational banks and financial institutions, which move their capital freely between countries, between branches of production, and between productive and financial investments. It was these multinational corporations who closed plant, moved productive investment abroad, and diverted their funds into cash and into financial and speculative investments in the course of the crisis. Far from being the victims of the rise of monetarism, they were its driving force.

The fundamental error underlying this influential approach is its misunderstanding of the power of money. The power of money is not the power of banks and financial institutions, although it is the latter who wield the power of money, it is the power of capital in its most abstract form. Thus the conflict between the needs of the domestic economy and the interests of multinational capital is not a conflict between the interests of different fractions of capital, but between the interests of multinational capital and the needs of the mass of the population. The irrationality of monetarism is not the irrationality of economists and politicians, it is the irrationality of capitalism.

The second kind of economic explanation of the crisis sees it not as a confrontation between 'industrial' and 'financial' capital, but between capital as a whole and the working class. There are two dominant versions of this approach. On one interpretation the ris-

ing wages and high standards of welfare provision associated with
the Keynesian Welfare State represented a significant achievement
of the working class, asserting its own interests against the interests
of capital. In a period of boom capital could afford the concessions
required to finance the Keynesian welfare state, in the interests
of political and industrial peace. However the continued advance
of the working class eventually encroached on capital's profitability and precipitated, or at least intensified, a crisis of profitability.
Capital had therefore to reverse the gains of the post-war decades,
cutting state expenditure and increasing unemployment in order
to weaken the working class politically and industrially so as to restore profitability. Monetarism is the ideological mask that seeks to
conceal this capitalist counter-offensive. The appropriate response
of the left is a militant and determined counter-offensive to restore
the gains of the post-war boom and to bring capital under social
control.[3]

This approach has the merit of bringing the capitalist crisis and
the class struggle to the fore. Unfortunately it is much too simplistic. The rate of growth of wages and improvement in welfare
provision in the post-war boom had little to do with the strength
of the organised working class. Britain had probably the strongest
and most militant working class, but consistently had the lowest rates of growth of wages and welfare spending. Rather than
militancy being the cause of the profitability crisis, it is far more
plausible to argue that it was the consequence, as workers aspirations were increasingly frustrated by the inability of capitalism to
deliver the goods. More importantly, the transition from Keynesianism to monetarism does not simply involve a rise in the rate of
exploitation. Monetarism does not consist in a frontal assault on
the working class, pushing the trenches back a few hundred yards
like a Somme offensive, any more than Keynesianism represented
an unequivocal advance of the working class. If things were so sim-

---

[3] The classic expression of this position in Britain was Andrew Glyn and
Bob Sutcliffe, *Workers, British Capitalism and the Profits Squeeze*, Penguin,
Harmondsworth, 1972. An alternative version stressed labour shortages as the
source of both capital's weakness and the working class's strength. See Andrew
Glyn and John Harrison, *Britain's Economic Disaster*, Pluto, London, 1980.
Its development in relation to the state stressed the contradiction between the
'legitimation' and 'accumulation' functions of the state, the fiscal crisis of the
state precipitating a legitimation crisis. See especially Jim O'Connor, *The
Fiscal Crisis of the State*, St James Press, New York, 1973.

ple the popularity of monetarism with the working class electorate would be inconceivable. Monetarism rather involves a fundamental restructuring of the relations between capital, the working class and the state, involving not simply a shift in the balance of economic and political power, but a change in the form of the state and class relations, in which some elements of the working class gain at the expense of others.

It is this observation that underlies the second approach which sees the roots of monetarism in the capitalist crisis. In this case the crisis is not simply a crisis of profitability, it is a structural crisis, throwing the predominant institutional forms of regulation of capital accumulation into doubt. The crisis of profitability is not the result of a fall in the rate of exploitation, but of the growing barriers to accumulation presented by the exhaustion of the technological possibilities of the third industrial revolution. It is therefore a crisis of the overaccumulation of capital in relation to the outlets for its profitable employment. First, increasing industrial profits require the massive replacement of labour by machinery, which substantially increases the fixed costs of the enterprise. Second, there are limited opportunities for increasing productivity in the service sector, so that the latter acts as an increasing drag on profitability, whether services are publicly or privately provided. Third, accumulation in the metropolitan centres has run ahead of the supply of raw materials, and especially oil, leading to a sharp deterioration in their terms of international trade. The simplest version of this argument sees the class struggles that ensue from this profit squeeze primarily in economic terms.[4]

A more complex version of this analysis has recently come to prominence in the work of the French 'Regulation School'.[5] This approach interprets the Keynesian welfare state as one aspect of the systematic forms of regulation appropriate to a particular 'regime of accumulation', characterised by the dominance of 'Fordist' production, based on the rapid cheapening of consump-

---

[4] The work of Ernest Mandel, especially *Late Capitalism*, New Left Books, London, 1975, and *The Second Slump*, New Left Books, London, 1978, is the most sophisticated example.

[5] The pioneering work was Michel Aglietta, *A Theory of Capitalist Regulation*, New Left Books, London, 1979. See also Wladimir Andreff, 'The International Centralisation of Capital and the Re-ordering of World Capitalism', *Capital and Class*, 22, 1984 and Michel De Vroey, 'A Regulation Approach Interpretation of the Contemporary Crisis', *Capital and Class*, 23, 1984.

tion goods through assembly line production, with rising wages
and welfare expenditure conciliating the working class and providing capital with a growing market for its products. The crisis
is then seen as a crisis of Fordist methods of production, which
undermines the whole apparatus of Fordist regulation. The main
question raised by this analysis is whether the ensuing crisis is some
kind of terminal capitalist crisis, with monetarism representing the
last desperate response of a doomed class, or whether capitalism is
entering a new phase of post-Fordist accumulation, in which monetarism represents the attempt to construct forms of regulation
appropriate to a new regime of accumulation based on 'flexible
specialisation';[6] the application of the microelectronics revolution
to manufacture and to services; the 'commodification' of public services; the 'Japanisation' of industrial relations; the globalisation of
accumulation under the dominance of the multinational companies; and a growing segmentation of the labour force, based on the
division between core and peripheral labour, on a world scale.

The main weakness of the regulation approach is that, despite its sophistication, it tends to degenerate into a structural-
functionalist reductionism in which the forms of regulation of accumulation are determined by the social form of the labour process
and the structure of production. This weakness is most marked in
the regulation approach's treatment of money and the state.

The regulation school sees monetary disturbances not as an expression of the contradictory form of capitalist production, but only
as a symptom of an underlying crisis in the regime of accumulation.
For the regulation school the regulative role of money is function-
ally integrated into the regime of accumulation. The appropriate
relationship between the various branches of production is established by the institutionalisation of the regime of accumulation.
Once such a relationship is established, the presumption seems to
be that accumulation is confined within the limits of the market, as
the allocation of investment is determined by the tendency to the
equalisation of the rate of profit. As accumulation comes up against
the barrier of existing technology, the introduction of new methods of production breaks down the existing relation between the
branches of production. Monetary instability, in which money appears as an autonomous power, is a symptom of this breakdown in

---

[6] Michael Piore and Charles Sabel, *The Second Industrial Divide*, Basic
Books, New York, 1984.

the regime of accumulation. With the reconstitution of the regime of accumulation the regulatory role of money is once more subordinated to the institutional forms of the regime of accumulation. Thus money is seen as an instrument of regulation that expresses the social and political relations of the regime of accumulation.[7]

However much the power of money may be institutionalised within, and circumscribed by, the social and political relations of a particular 'regime of accumulation', the power of money does not derive from the institutional forms in which it appears. The power of money is the power of command over commodities and, in a capitalist society, over labour-power as a commodity. It is consequently the irreducible form, and the most abstract embodiment, of the social power of property. It is correspondingly the foundation of the capitalist mode of production, which is a form of social production defined by the appropriation of labour on the basis of property. The subordination of civil society and the state to the autonomous power of money is not, therefore, merely a symptom of the breakdown of the regime of accumulation, it is the permanent expression of the subordination of the economic, social and political reproduction of capitalist society to the reproduction of the social power of capital.

The treatment of the state in the regulation approach suffers from the same weakness as the analysis of money. The underlying model is one of successive phases of structural integration and structural disintegration of capital accumulation. In a phase of structural integration sustained accumulation is possible within the framework of the appropriate forms of regulation. As accumulation comes up against the limits of profitability within the regime of accumulation, capital seeks to develop new forms of production to increase the rate of exploitation. However these new forms of production undermine the structural integration of the regime of accumulation.

The phase of disintegration is a period in which the transformation of methods of production lays the foundations for a new regime of accumulation. However the construction of such a regime cannot be accomplished solely through the market. The task of the state is to remedy this deficiency by sponsoring the restructuring

---

[7]Aglietta has recently developed a very idiosyncratic theory of money in Michel Aglietta and André Orlean, *La Violence de la Monnaie*, PUF, Paris, 1982.

of the regime of accumulation and associated forms of regulation, including those that are a part of the state itself, to establish the structural integration on the basis of which accumulation can be renewed. Thus the state is no more an expression of the power of capital than is money. The state is merely the institution that ultimately secures the functional integration of the regime of accumulation as it imposes order onto chaos. The power of capital is diffused through the structure of the regime of accumulation, which is ultimately determined by the social form of production. Not surprisingly this approach tends to lead to very pessimistic political conclusions in confining the class struggle within the developing structure of the regime of accumulation.

The analysis of the state on the basis of the regulation approach has been developed primarily in Germany by Hirsch and Esser, who have proposed the concepts of the 'Fordist' and 'neo-Fordist' forms of the state, which define the modes of domination appropriate to the corresponding regimes of accumulation.[8] The crisis of Fordist accumulation is simultaneously a crisis of Fordist modes of domination. As capital accumulation undermines the social relations appropriate to previous forms of reproduction, it leads to monetary instability, a rise in industrial conflict and the emergence of 'new social movements'. The state responds to social disintegration in the crisis by penetrating more deeply into civil society to restructure social relations into forms appropriate to the emerging form of the regime of accumulation. This 'statification' of society in the crisis is expressed in the concept of the 'Fordist security state', which gives way to the 'neo-Fordist state' in which state regulation is achieved not through the Keynesian modes of political integration appropriate to Fordism, nor through the directly repressive mechanisms of the transitional phase, but through the state-regulated 'commodification' of civil society. Monetarism does not involve a withdrawal of the state from economic regulation, but offers new, highly differentiated and flexible forms of state regulation, appropriate to the segmentation of the working class and the greater flexibility of production characteristic of neo-Fordist accumulation. The role of the class struggle is strictly limited within this framework. It cannot overcome the structural constraints imposed by the form of

---

[8] This contribution is assessed by Werner Bonefeld, 'Reformulation of State Theory', *Capital and Class*, 33, 1988. See also Bob Jessop's reply in *Capital and Class*, 34, 1988.

accumulation, it can merely slow down or accelerate the restructuring of the regime of accumulation, and modify the balance of class forces within the regime. The only available political strategy for the left is therefore to abandon the struggle to reconstruct outdated forms of regulation and political integration in order to seek a new accommodation with capital on the basis of the new forms of accumulation.

The regulation approach is very valuable in drawing attention to the systematic character of the regulation of capital accumulation, relating the forms of regulation of capitalist production to the forms of regulation of accumulation by money and the state. However the explanatory relationships proposed are very unclear, both theoretically and empirically. Thus the approach has tended to produce impressionistic typologies of the structure of the regime of accumulation that lack any firm historical anchorage. Although the connections indicated by the regulation approach are very suggestive, it is not at all clear that the different aspects of a particular 'regime of accumulation' can be so neatly tied together in a functional whole, nor that the directions of causality are as unambiguous as indicated in the model. Moreover the structural-functionalism of the approach leads it considerably to overemphasise the coherence and stability of the 'regime of accumulation' in a period of sustained accumulation, and to exaggerate its disintegration and instability in a period of crisis, so that it loses sight of the continuities underlying the historical transformations of capitalist reproduction and of the capitalist state form. It is unable to grasp these continuities because it has no theory of money and the state as the dual forms of capitalist power, nor any conception of the contradictory character of capitalist regulation that derives from the contradictory form of capitalist production.

Money and the state

This book draws on the insights of all the approaches outlined above. My starting point is the belief that it is important to take the issues that divide monetarists and Keynesians seriously. Although monetarism and Keynesianism are undoubtedly ideological, even in their most abstract and theoretical forms, they conceal within themselves practical truths, however mystified the form in which they represent such truths. However monetarism and Keynesianism are not populist ideologies so much as ideologies of the state, giving ideological coherence to the institutional framework and policy decisions of the state. The crisis of Keynesianism and the rise of monetarism did not express a popular ideological revolution, but a crisis of the policies and institutions of the Keynesian welfare state. The Keynesian ideology was discredited because Keynesian policies became increasingly unpopular. Monetarism assumed a 'hegemonic' position because monetarist policies secured electoral endorsement.

The crisis of the Keynesian state was itself the expression of a more fundamental crisis in the accumulation of capital. This crisis appeared in the growing financial pressure faced by national governments as they attempted to maintain economic growth by expansionary Keynesian policies. However the crisis did not express a conflict of interests between financial and productive capital, but a contradiction between the popular demand for rising incomes and employment, which could only be satisfied by the growth of production, and the capitalist need to subordinate production to profit. This contradiction was not simply a matter of a decline in the rate of profit, whether as a result of the 'tendency for the rate of profit to fall' or the growing strength of the working class, but of a structural crisis of accumulation. However this structural crisis was not the result of the changing functional requirements of changes in the labour process, but of the tendency for capital accumulation to take the form of the overaccumulation and uneven development of capital. Moreover the political and ideological crisis to which the crisis of overaccumulation gave rise cannot be reduced to the unfolding of an economic or a structural logic, but was determined by the development of the class struggle within the framework of particular social, political and ideological forms.

My criticisms of the approaches outlined above are not primarily empirical, but are essentially theoretical. The immediate theoretical problem raised by the debate between monetarism and Keynesianism is that of the relation between the power of money and the power of the state. The underlying theoretical problem is the more general one of the relations between economics, politics and ideology. All the approaches outlined above are unsatisfactory in the last analysis in offering a one-dimensional analysis of the crisis of Keynesianism and the rise of monetarism, seeing it alternatively as an ideological, political or economic phenomenon, rather than offering an analysis that can grasp the complex relationship between these different dimensions of the historical process. My primary aim in this book is to develop a more adequate framework within which to grasp both the coherence and the complexity of the relationship between economics, politics and ideology in the crisis-ridden development of capitalism.

The immediate origins of this book lay in my own earlier work on the analysis of ideology. My first book in the field prepared the methodological ground, rejecting the idealism of 'structuralist' analysis in favour of an historical materialist approach to ideology.[9] The present book develops out of my analysis of the ideological dimensions of political economy, marginalist economics and modern sociology as social theories.[10] However the confrontation between Keynesianism and monetarism raises the more complex question of the political significance of economic ideology, which can only be addressed within the framework of a theory of money and the state.

The theoretical framework of my argument draws primarily on two related strands of thought that have developed over the past fifteen years, involving a re-examination of Marxist theories of money and the state. In Britain these developments have taken place primarily through the Conference of Socialist Economists.

The reconsideration of the Marxist theory of money arose out of a renewal of the debate around Marx's theory of value.[11] The central theme of the debate was the distinctiveness of Marx's labour theory of value in relation to that of Ricardo, and the conclusion was that for Marx value did not correspond to Ricardo's embodied labour, but to abstract labour that appeared in the form of money. This implied that the distinctiveness of Marx's theory lay not so much in the idea of labour as the source of value and surplus value, as in the idea of money as the most abstract form of capitalist property, and so as the supreme social power through which social

[9] Simon Clarke, *The Foundations of Structuralism*, Harvester, Brighton and Humanities, New York, 1981

[10] Simon Clarke, *Marx, Marginalism and Modern Sociology*, Macmillan, Basingstoke, 1982.

[11] See particularly Diane Elson, ed., *Value*, CSE Books, London, 1979; Sue Himmelweit and Simon Mohun, 'The Anomalies of Capital', *Capital and Class*, 6, 1978; Simon Clarke, 'The Value of Value' *Capital and Class*, 10, 1980.

reproduction is subordinated to the reproduction of capital.[12]

The reconsideration of the theory of the state was sparked off by the German 'state derivation' debate.[13] However the CSE debate also drew heavily on the reconsideration of Marx's theory of value, to move away from the German debate, which was strongly influenced by the systems theory of Jurgen Habermas and Claus Offe, and later embraced the structural-functionalism of Nicos Poulantzas and the French Regulation School.[14] This divergence arose primarily because the central substantive issues in the CSE debate were rather different from those that motivated the French and German contributions. The CSE debate was stimulated particularly by Britain's entry into the EEC, which raised the fundamental question of the relationship between the internationalisation of capital, working class struggles and the nation state. The debate then developed in relation to the issues of law and the state, raised by the growing recourse to the legal regulation of the working class through the 1970s; of the relation between money and the state, raised by the succession of financial crises confronted by Labour governments; and of the relation between the working class struggle and the state, raised by the growing conflicts around the form of the welfare state.[15] All these issues raised the question of

---

[12] The seminal paper on money was an undated, untitled, unpublished paper by John Merrington and Christian Marazzi, followed by an unpublished paper by Christian Marazzi on 'Theories of Money', that drew on the work of Toni Negri, see especially his *Marx Beyond Marx*, Bergin and Garvey, S. Hadley, Mass., 1984. A recent book that develops an analysis of the power of money within a different theoretical framework is William Reddy, *Money and Liberty in Modern Europe*, Cambridge University Press, Cambridge, 1987. Despite its idealist formulation Georg Simmel's *Philosophy of Money*, RKP, London, 1978, remains the most penetrating phenomenological exploration of the social power of money. By contrast most of the Marxist literature is remarkably sterile, particularly when set against Marx's own writings.

[13] See especially John Holloway and Sol Picciotto, *The State and Capital*, Edward Arnold, London, 1978. Bob Jessop, *The Capitalist State*, Martin Robertson, Oxford, 1982. John Holloway, 'The State as Class Practice', *Research in Political Economy*, 3, 1981.

[14] I have criticised Poulantzas's theory in Simon Clarke, 'Marxism, Sociology and the Theory of the State', *Capital and Class*, 2, 1977.

[15] The debate around the form of the welfare state was an international debate, particularly influenced by the work of Claus Offe, see especially his *Contradictions of the Welfare State*, Hutchinson, London, 1984, for his most recent position. The seminal work was probably Frances Piven and Richard A. Cloward, *Regulating the Poor*, Random House, New York, 1971. The most valuable contributions to the debate have come from feminists, who have gone

the 'form' of the state in relation to the 'forms' of class struggle, and it was this question that brought the state debate into a close relationship with the value debate.

The theoretical conclusion of the CSE contribution was that we have to look behind the institutional separation of economics, law and politics to see money, law and the state as complementary economic, legal and political forms of the power of capital. The underlying unity of these differentiated, and complementary, forms of capitalist power was explained by Marx's theory of value, the three aspects being united in capitalist property, money representing the most abstract form of capital, whose power is institutionalised in the law and enforced by the state.[16]

The methodological conclusion was to reject equally the dominant tendencies of the economistic Marxism of the Second and Third Internationals, and the complexity of post-Marxist modernism, whose sophistication was no more than a mark of its superficiality,[17] in favour of a view of Marxism as a theory of social forms. This interpretation drew particularly on Marx's *Grundrisse* and on various oppositional currents in the Marxist tradition to reaffirm Marx's famous dictum, 'men make their own history, but they do not make it just as they please; they do not make it under circumstances chosen by themselves, but under circumstances directly encountered, given and transmitted from the past'.[18] However this approach was concerned to reject the interpretation of Marx's dictum in terms of the dualism of structure and process that marks sociological interpretations of Marx. The forms of capitalist domination cannot be theorised in structural-functionalist terms, because the functional imperatives are themselves generated

---

the furthest in demystifying the forms of domination embedded in the welfare state. See especially Elizabeth Wilson, *Women and the Welfare State*, Tavistock, London, 1977 for an early contribution, and her 'Thatcherism and Women: After Seven Years', *Socialist Register 1987*, Ralph Miliband et al., eds, Merlin, London, 1987. I do not attempt to cover the detailed debates over the form of the welfare state in this book not because they are not central to my theme, but because they are relatively well known.

[16] On the analysis of the law, which I hardly touch on in this book, see Bob Fine, ed., *Capitalism and the Rule of Law*, Hutchinson, London, 1979, and the important book by Geoff Kay and James Mott, *Political Order and the Law of Labour*, Macmillan, London, 1982.

[17] Kay and Mott, op. cit. , pp. 64–7, 72–4.

[18] Karl Marx, 'The Eighteenth Brumaire', in Karl Marx and Frederick Engels, *Selected Works*, Lawrence and Wishart, London, 1968, p. 96.

by the forms of class struggle. Moreover these forms express not
the functional integration, but the profoundly contradictory character of the capitalist mode of production, so that their adequacy
is always problematic not only for the working class, but also for
capital. Thus the class struggle does not simply take place within
these forms. The forms of capitalist domination are themselves
the object of class struggle, as capital and the working class confront them as barriers to their own social reproduction. Although
the unity and complementarity of these differentiated forms can
be articulated theoretically, their development is the outcome of
a history of class struggle in and against the institutional forms
of the capitalist mode of production, whose historical resolution is
always provisional.

This approach did not lead to a systematic theoretical and historical account of the development of the forms of capitalist domination, the participants in the debate being concerned more to
analyse particular aspects of the contemporary crisis. In the meantime there was a tendency to borrow the schematic typology of the
French Regulation School to fill the gap, despite an awareness of
the theoretical weaknesses of the latter indicated above. Similarly
the gap left by the absence of an historically grounded analysis of
capitalist crises was filled by relying on the 'law of the tendency for
the rate of profit to fall', although a more adequate framework was
offered by the theory of overaccumulation, which was developed in
this context particularly by Makoto Itoh.[19]

In the absence of such an historically informed account the 'form
derivation' approach has been accused of 'economism'.[20] The focus
of such an accusation is the analysis of the relation between capital
and the state, which has been a persistent problem faced by Marxist
political theory. Although capitalists undoubtedly enjoy privileged

---

[19] Makoto Itoh, *Value and Capital*, Pluto, London, 1981. Marx's own treatment of crisis is notoriously ambiguous. In general Marxist crisis theories have
been concerned to prove or disprove the inevitability of crisis within an equilibrium theory, based on Marx's reproduction schemes or his analysis of the law
of the tendency for the rate of profit to fall, rather than exploring the historical
dynamics of overaccumulation and crisis within the kind of disequilibrium theory that dominates Marx's own work. My own analysis of overaccumulation
is similar to that of John Weeks, 'Equilibrium, Uneven Development and the
Tendency of the Rate of Profit to Fall', *Capital and Class*, 16, 1982.

[20] Jessop, op. cit. , pp. 95–6, John Solomos, 'The Marxist Theory of the
State and the Problem of Fractions', *Capital and Class*, 7, 1979.

access to state power, the capitalist character of the state certainly cannot be reduced to the political privileges of capitalists. However the political representation of capitalist interests is only one of the forms through which the relationship between the social power of capital and the political power of the state is mediated. The social power of capital is not embodied in the person of the capitalist, but in the social power of money. The fundamental theoretical problem is therefore that of the relationship between the social power of money and the political power of the state. This is equally the fundamental political and ideological problem raised by the crisis of Keynesianism and the rise of monetarism, and is the underlying theme of this book.

The relationship between the power of money and the power of the state has been a persistent theoretical, political and ideological issue since the first emergence of commerce. However the issue arose in its modern form as the penetration of capital into production subordinated social production to the rule of money and dissolved the social relations of authority and dependence that had hitherto been the basis of political power. The rise of capitalism precipitated a crisis in the political and ideological forms of the pre-capitalist state, which was resolved by the reconstitution of the state on the basis of the radical separation of the state from civil society and of the social power of money from the political power of the state. Although the crisis of the pre-capitalist state form came to a head most dramatically in the French Revolution, the reconstitution of the state was first achieved, less dramatically but more systematically, in Britain, where the erosion of pre-capitalist social relations by the penetration of capital was most complete. The construction of the liberal state form was articulated theoretically by classical political economy, which first systematically addressed the problem of the relationship between money and the state in its modern form, and which gave ideological coherence and political legitimacy to the emerging state form.

The first two chapters of the book examine the rise of political economy and the construction of the liberal state form in Britain.[21]

---

[21] Although the focus is on Britain and the presentation is historical the aim is to draw out the essential relationships from the mass of contingent historical events. In the first instance the essential relationships are taken to be those articulated by classical political economy. However the analysis is also informed by the advantages of hindsight and of comparative research, so that

Political economy legitimated the radical separation of the state from civil society on the basis of the adequacy of the market as the means by which all particular interests were subsumed under the general interest. The law of property, enforced by the state, was the means by which all members of society, capitalists and workers alike, were confined within the limits of the market, while money was merely the means of circulation, the rational instrument through which conflicting interests were reconciled. The subordination of civil society and the state to the anonymous rule of money and the law expressed not the rule of capital but the rule of reason.

Marx's critique of political economy began with his critique of its theory of money. For Marx money was not merely the means of circulation, but was also, in its developed form, the independent form of value. The subordination of social production to the power of money gave rise to antagonistic social relations of production in which the power of money confronted the direct producers in the form of capital, and in which social production was subordinated to the reproduction of capital. Money and the law were consequently the social forms through which civil society and the state were subordinated to the power of capital. In Chapter Four I build on Marx's analysis of the contradictory form of commodity money and an interpretation of his account of the capitalist tendency to overaccumulation and crisis to develop an analysis of the contradictory forms of credit money and of state money, and so of the limits of the monetary regulation of capitalist accumulation.

In Chapter Five I build on Marx's characterisation of the liberal state form to address the question of the contradictory form and the limits of the capitalist state which derive from the contradiction between the class character and the national form of the capitalist state. The class character of the state, embodied in its liberal form, requires it to secure the reproduction of capital. The national form of the state requires it to express, politically and ideologically, the national interest, against all particular interests. The reproduction of the state correspondingly requires it to resolve this contradiction. The contradiction appears to the state in the

---

the presentation, in these as in subsequent chapters, emphasises those aspects of the British experience, and of political economy, that seem to me to have a comparative significance and a contemporary resonance, although limitations of space have made it impossible to make more than gestural comparative references.

form of the social and political aspirations of the working class, to which it has to respond within the limits of its form, confining the working class within the form of the wage and the constitutional form of the state. The admission of the working class to the constitution on a national basis increases the pressure on the state to secure the sustained accumulation of domestic productive capital. However this constraint introduces a further contradiction, between the national form of the state and the global character of capital accumulation.

The remaining chapters of the book present an account of the development of the capitalist state form on the basis of the analysis of the contradictory forms of capital accumulation and the capitalist state. The capitalist state developed in the form of the nation state, within a framework of nation states, in the context of the accumulation of capital on a world scale. The accumulation of capital on a world scale, and the interaction with other nation states, defines the broad context within which particular nation states have developed, but the development of each has its own rhythm and its own harmonies and disharmonies that cannot be reduced to variations on a single theme. As in the earlier chapters the focus of the account is the British state, within the global context of overaccumulation and crisis, but again the aim is neither to provide an historical account of the British state, nor to present the British example as ideal-typical, but to draw out the theoretical, comparative, and contemporary significance of the British experience.[22]

Chapter Six explores the development of the institutional forms of industrial relations, social administration and electoral representation through which the capitalist state sought to confine the aspirations of the working class within the limits of its liberal form, and in and against which the class struggle has subsequently developed. Chapter Seven explores the contradiction between the national form of the state and the global character of accumulation to analyse the rise of imperialism that culminated in war.

---

[22] For this reason I have not cluttered the book with extensive bibliographical references to give the account a spurious scholarly authority. Any originality lies not in the empirical detail, but in interpretation. Those familiar with the literature will recognise the iconoclastic elements of my interpretation, and the degree to which I have simplified complex issues, which I hope will not be mistaken for naïvety.

Chapter Eight explores the unsuccessful inter-war attempt to re-solve the contradictions of the capitalist state form on the basis of the reconstruction of the liberal world order. Chapter Nine then turns to the ideological crisis to which this failure gave rise, a crisis that culminated in the Keynesian Revolution. Chapter Ten anal-yses the foundations of the Keynesian Welfare State in the period of post-war reconstruction and the early stages of the long boom. The Keynesian Welfare State is presented as the culmination of the attempt to resolve the contradictions of the liberal state form, rather than as a radically new form of the state, based on the rationalisation and generalisation of the systems of industrial rela-tions, social administration and electoral representation within the framework of the liberal state form and the liberalisation of the world economic system. Chapter Eleven then analyses the crisis of Keynesianism as an expression of the underlying contradiction of the capitalist state form in the face of a global crisis of overaccu-mulation. This contradiction appeared as a conflict between the power of money and the power of the state, as the institutionalised forms of class collaboration increasingly appeared as a barrier to the accumulation of capital and the aspirations of the working class, and so took the form of a class struggle over the form of the state. The rise of monetarism expressed the provisional triumph of capi-tal in this struggle as the subordination of the institutional forms of the Keynesian Welfare State to the power of money confined the aspirations of the working class within the limits of capital.

Chapter 2

The Hidden Hand and the Limits of the Capitalist State

The problem of the relationship between money and the state was the central preoccupation of Adam Smith, and, following him, of classical political economy. Indeed Smith was the first to propose the problem in its modern form, because he was the first to develop a systematic model of the economy as a sphere independent of, and prior to, the state. Before considering Smith's account we need briefly to indicate the context in which he developed his ideas.

State and economy in the eighteenth century

Although the Civil War had finally destroyed the feudal character of landed property, and the Revolution of 1688 had achieved the separation of the state from the person of the sovereign, the eighteenth century state still essentially represented the institutionalised power of the landed class, albeit a class with an increasingly capitalistic orientation. Property was the unequivocal basis of political power, and the boundaries between the state and civil society, between public and private power, were by no

21

means well-defined. The political apparatus was based on administration through institutionalised corruption and the public sanctioning of private powers. The limited franchise, and the extent of government patronage, largely insulated the government from parliamentary or popular pressure, leading to the development of a self-perpetuating political elite, drawn predominantly from the landed class, but with ties to the big metropolitan merchants and financiers, and headed by the crown.

Central government had little relevance to the mass of the population, whose only contact with it would normally be with the Customs and Excise, which had regulative duties in addition to the collection of revenue. Local administration was in the hands of persons of rank and property, whose day-to-day authority derived as much from their position in civil society as from their public office, whether in the corrupt government of the municipal corporations, or through the parishes and vestries, or, above all, as the local justices, on whom the bulk of local administration fell. The local authorities had very considerable discretion in the definition and exercise of their powers. There was very little Parliamentary supervision of local administration, while the enforcement of Parliamentary decrees was in local hands. Although the royal courts in principal had jurisdiction over the local administration, the courts were cumbersome and inefficient and largely irrelevant as a check on local power.

Although the state apparatus was firmly in the hands of the landed class, landed property was assuming an increasingly capitalist form, while the prosperity of both state and landowners depended on the growth of trade. The interest of the landed class and the state in the development of commerce gave the great merchants and financiers access to state power, above all in the formulation and implementation of the economic policies of the state. However the interest of the capitalists was not identical with that of the state and the landed class. The capitalists were interested only in their own profit, whereas the state and the landed class claimed an interest in the growth of the wealth of the nation, and in the preservation of the order and civil peace on which the security of property depended. The body of doctrines and of policies that emerged from the interplay of these conflicting considerations to provide the ideology of the state in this transitional period has come to be known as 'mercantilism'.

The theory and practice of mercantilism

The task of mercantilist economic theory was to advise the sovereign on how best to regulate the economy in order to enhance the wealth and power of the state and of its citizens. Mercantilism never constituted a coherent body of doctrine. However at the heart of mercantilist ideas was the argument that it was foreign trade alone that generated the surplus that could finance growing state activity, and above all the naval and military power of the state.

The theoretical basis of the doctrine was the idea of a surplus generated through trade. This surplus had its origin in the merchant's 'profit upon alienation', as Steuart called it, the difference between the cost of the article to the merchant and the price he received for it. Prices depended on the relation between supply and demand, so high profits depended on controlling markets in order to maintain the highest possible price differential between different markets. Profits gained from domestic trade merely redistributed wealth within the nation, so it was only foreign trade that could augment the national wealth. Success in foreign trade depended on the ability of the merchants, and of the state that backed them, to establish monopolistic control of sources of supply and of markets. Such success depended in part on the commercial skills of the merchants and on their financial resources, but more fundamentally it depended on the military power of the state, and its willingness to wage wars for commercial advantage.

Exchange was seen not so much as the exchange of commodities for one another, mediated by money as the means of exchange, as a series of exchanges of commodities for money in order to accumulate more money. Thus the primary economic role of money was to serve not as means of exchange, but as money capital. The limits to mercantile activity were set by the availability of money to serve as capital, to equip the ships and purchase the commodities to be traded. The limit to the ability of the state to maintain the naval and military forces necessary to defend its commercial interests was set by the national hoard of money that comprised its war chest. Thus the key to commercial success was the accumulation of this national hoard, which became the central objective of mercantilist policy.

The growth of commerce held out the promise of great wealth, but it also carried the risk of disruption of the social order. Trade was not seen as a productive activity, creating new wealth, it merely redistributed the wealth that had already been produced. While foreign trade provided the means to profit at the expense of foreigners, in domestic trade the merchant could only gain at the expense of the labouring and the landowning classes. The state attempted to confine trade within the limits of the existing social order through the extensive body of Tudor and Stuart legislation that sought, however ineffectively, to restrict the activity of domestic merchants by preventing usurious lending, engrossment and profiteering, and by regulating prices, wages and working conditions according to customary notions of justice and equity. Similarly the desire to maintain a favourable balance of trade, the fear of pauperism and unemployment if domestic producers were undermined by foreign competition, and the need to maintain domestic supplies of strategic materials, led to legislation, subsidies and direct state intervention to encourage domestic production and to provide protection from foreign competition.

Within the society in which mercantilism developed the identification of the mercantile interest with the national interest had a certain validity. The profits to be made in foreign trade were far greater, and far more ostentatious, than those to be made in the early forms of capitalist agriculture and manufacture, while they were far more easily taxable than was rent. Thus healthy trading profits and the accumulation of monetary reserves did make the greatest single contribution to the financial, and so military, strength of the state, and such strength was essential in a system of warring states each seeking to mobilise the political, economic and military power of the state to secure a commercial advantage. Thus the mercantilist identification of the trading interest with the national well-being had an appeal far beyond the commercial class, and mercantilist doctrines were espoused by writers and statesmen who had no commercial involvement, nor any identification with the mercantile interest.

The system of mercantilism provided the framework for the growth of capitalist enterprise between the sixteenth and the eighteenth centuries and laid the foundations for the explosive growth of capitalism in the industrial revolution. The expansion of British trade was based on the growing political, military and financial power of the state, exercised in pursuit of commercial advantage. The colonial system secured sources of supply to feed the world market, and established a system of multilateral trade lubricated by the use of gold and silver as the means of international payment. The growth of trade stimulated the commercialisation of agriculture, the expansion of domestic manufacture, the improvement of domestic and international communications and the growth of population that laid the foundations for the industrial revolution. The development of banking and the stabilisation of the monetary system provided the institutions of money and credit that financed the growth of trade and the activity of the state. The development of a regular system of taxation, primarily in the form of customs and excise, and the rationalisation of the state finances provided the state with the resources to pursue an aggressive commercial and colonial policy that, if successful, further increased commercial prosperity. Although trade was regularly disrupted by war, by financial crises and by harvest failure, the growing power and prosperity of the merchants, the landowners and the state, if not of the mass of the population, appeared to vindicate the mercantilist system.

By the middle of the eighteenth century mercantilism came up against its limits. Capital was increasingly penetrating into the sphere of production, employing wage labourers or, more generally, domestic producers working within the putting-out system, to produce for the world market. While the companies trading in colonial produce still depended on the use of the state's military and political power to secure their markets, those trading in domestic produce were increasingly competing on the basis of price and quality. For the latter the restrictions of mercantilism were at best irrelevant and at worst a barrier to the development of capitalist production and the expansion of the market.

In the first half of the eighteenth century these interests were largely reconciled. The growth of British trade was primarily at the expense of other trading nations, particularly the French and the Dutch, involving in equal proportions the export of domestic products and the re-export of colonial produce from the East and West Indies and North America. However growth of foreign trade slowed sharply after 1750 as Britain came up against the barrier of stiffer European competition. Although reexports continued to grow, until supplies were cut off by the American War, the volume of exports of British produce stagnated. On the other hand, the costs of commercial wars and the maintenance of the colonial system increased astronomically. Between 1750 and the end of the American war in 1783 central government expenditure, over 90 per cent of which in the latter year was military expenditure and debt interest, increased from 6 to 16 per cent of the Gross National Product. The slow growth of trade meant that revenues, derived largely from Customs and Excise, had not increased commensurately with expenditure. The result was that the state found it increasingly difficult to finance its expenditure. Although the burden of taxation increased by 70 per cent between 1750 and 1783, the national debt trebled over the same period, to the great profit of the emerging class of financiers. The political counterpart of the state's financial difficulty was the growing popular resistance to taxation, to financial skulduggery and to political corruption. As the century wore on the mercantilist system was increasingly discredited as it became transparently clear that it benefited only a small group of merchants and stockjobbers at great public expense. This was the context in which political economy emerged.

The challenge to mercantilism

Political economy challenged the mercantilist programme by striking at its theoretical foundations. At the heart of the challenge was the development of a completely different conception of money and exchange. By contrast with the mercantilist conception of trade as the exchange of commodities for money, in which one party gains at the expense of the other, the critics saw trade as the exchange of commodities for one another, to the mutual benefit of both parties. The aim of trade was not the accumulation of money, but the acquisition of commodities in which alone wealth consisted. This apparently small change of perspective implied a quite different conception of money. For the mercantilists the national stock of money corresponded to the accumulated profits of trade, and so constituted the national capital. Policies that regulated foreign trade in order to increase the supply of money would augment the national capital and provide the basis for the further expansion of trade. For the critics, by contrast, the national capital was not identified with a sum of money, but with the commodities that money could purchase. This changed view of money led to the fundamental distinction, absent from mercantilism, between money, seen as the means of circulation, and capital. The growth of capital corresponded to the growth of trade, and the stock of money to the needs of trade for money to serve as means of circulation. It was therefore the level of trade that determined the stock of money not, as mercantilists believed, the stock of money that determined the level of trade. This implied that restrictions on trade could only harm the national interest, which was best served by the unrestricted growth of trade.

The germs of these ideas can be traced back to the late seventeenth century, but they were first systematically developed in the middle of the eighteenth century. The new theory of money in relation to foreign trade was developed by David Hume, who saw in foreign trade the possibility of mutual advantage, and argued that money, far from being the substance of wealth, is a mere conventional unit of account, devised 'to facilitate the exchange of one commodity for another'.[1] This led Hume to develop his quantity theory of money, according to which an increase in the quantity of money, far from stimulating trade, could not increase the nation's wealth, but would merely lead to an increase in prices.

Hume's originality was not in propounding the quantity theory, but in describing the process by which the stimulus to demand provided by a rise in the quantity of money was translated into a rise in prices. According to mercantilism an increase in the supply of money, secured through a favourable balance of trade, would stimulate the domestic economy as plentiful money reduced interest rates and boosted investment. Hume's development of the quantity theory of money depended on the new view of money as a means of exchange, and the corresponding distinction between money and capital. Hume rejected the mercantilist belief that an increase in the stock of money would stimulate trade by reducing the rate of interest since the rate of interest had nothing to do with the supply of money, but was rather determined by the rate of profit on capital. An increase in the supply of money would therefore simply lead to an increase in demand, without stimulating any increase in supply. Although increased demand would lead to attempts to in-

---

[1] David Hume, 'Of Money', in *David Hume, Writings on Economics*, E. Rotwein (ed.), University of Wisconsin Press, Madison, Wisconsin, 1970, p. 33.

crease production in the affected branches of production this would merely increase the demand for labour, and so push up wages. The increase in wages would then be transmitted to other branches of production, until all prices rose.

The rise in domestic in relation to foreign prices stimulated by an increase in the domestic money supply would lead to a rise in imports and a fall in exports. Money would flow out of the country and prices fall again until the supply of money corresponded to the needs of circulation. This 'specie-flow mechanism' by which the balance of international payments regulated the supply of money in relation to the needs of domestic circulation became established as the orthodox version of the quantity theory of money in the nineteenth century. Its importance for Hume lay in the conclusion that mercantilist policies that aimed to increase the stock of money would lead to monetary instability without contributing anything to national prosperity.

The criticism of the mercantilist theory of money developed by Hume undermined the mercantilist conception of exchange and, ultimately, of the dependence of the economy on political regulation. If exchange was a transaction that benefited both parties, and profit derived not from unequal exchange but from productive investment, as Hume suggested, the conflict inherent in exchange was dissolved, and the political regulation of exchange was unnecessary. The idea of society as a political community that underlay mercantilism could be replaced by the idea of the economy as a sphere that contained the potential for harmony and prosperity within itself. The conditions for such harmony to be sustained were that exchange should be free and equal, the equality of exchange being regulated by money as the means of exchange. It fell to Adam Smith to develop these implications of Hume's conception of money and exchange.

The division of labour and the rationality of exchange

Smith's great work *The Wealth of Nations* was written primarily as an assault on the doctrines of mercantilism. Smith was concerned to demolish the mercantilist belief that money was an end, that the accumulation of wealth could be identified with the accumulation of money, and to establish instead the instrumental rationality of money as a mere means to the superior end of enhancing the material prosperity of the nation that derives from the improvement in the productive powers of labour.

For Smith the mercantilist prejudice that identified money with wealth, and the aim of economic activity as the accumulation of money, arose as a sophistical argument devised by the merchants to further their own self-interest by falsely identifying it with the national interest. The system of monopoly that hoisted their profits restrained trade and so limited the development of the productive powers of society. Smith, by contrast, following the French Physiocrats, identified wealth with production, so that the conditions most favourable to the growth of the wealth of the nation were those conducive to the most rapid growth of the productive powers of labour. Exchange was no longer seen as the means by which wealth was appropriated in the form of money. Exchange was the means by which the producer realised the fruits of his or her labour in the form of consumable commodities, with money serving merely as the means of exchange.

At the heart of Smith's critique of mercantilism was his view of money. Smith claimed that 'it is not for its own sake that men desire money, but for the sake of what they can purchase with it'.[2] The accumulation of money, far from contributing to the prosperity of the nation, constitutes a drain on the national wealth. This view of money as a mere means of exchange rests on his assertion that 'consumption is the sole end and purpose of all production', a maxim that he claimed 'is so self-evident that it would be absurd to attempt to prove it',[3] despite the fact that it was in direct contradiction to the mercantilist conception of wealth.

If money is not an end in itself, but is merely a means of exchanging one thing for another, the powers attributed to money are not inherent in money, but derive from its function as means of exchange. The rationality of money is the rationality of the system of exchange whose development it facilitates. Money is the means by which the hidden hand of the market achieves its ends, the 'great wheel of circulation' as Smith described it.

Smith regarded the development of the market as the result of

---

[2] Adam Smith, *The Wealth of Nations*, Everyman edition, Dent, London, 1910, vol. I, p. 385.
[3] ibid, vol. II, p. 155.

the propensity in human nature 'to truck, barter and exchange one thing for another',[4] a propensity rooted in the faculty of reason. Exchange made it possible for each producer to specialise according to his or her talents and so stimulated the advance of the division of labour, of productivity, and so of economic prosperity. As far as the individual economic actor was concerned each could make free judgements of the gains to be made from any particular exchange, gains rooted in the increased productivity permitted by specialisation, and so could decide whether or not to exchange accordingly. So long as the market is free, and property and the person are secure, each individual exchange that takes place will contribute to an increase in individual and social prosperity. On the other hand, any political or institutional barriers to the freedom of exchange will prevent advantageous exchanges from taking place and so will limit the extent of the division of labour and so the national wealth, even if they work to the advantage of particular individuals. The general conclusion is that free competition allows the individual to be the best judge of his or her own economic interest and provides the opportunity for each to act accordingly. Since every agent is free to decide whether or not to make an exchange, and will choose not to do so if he or she judges the exchange disadvantageous, nobody can suffer loss as a result of exchange. Since both parties gain from every exchange, the system of exchange must work to the benefit of all.

This simple model appears very convincing, and indeed has convinced generations of economists, who have followed Smith in making it their starting point. However Smith's model is developed within a very specific, and quite unrealistic, context. The model is not of a capitalist society. It is a model of a society of independent petty producers, each free to enter any branch of production, entering the market with the products of his or her own labour, and bartering them for the products of others. The example Smith gives is that of a 'tribe of hunters or shepherds' within which 'a particular person makes bows and arrows, for example, with more readiness and dexterity than any other'.[5] This fortunate person soon finds it advantageous to specialise in making bows and arrows and to exchange them for cattle and venison.

If Smith's little parable is to have any relevance to a capitalist

---

[4] ibid, vol. I, p. 12.
[5] ibid, vol. I, p. 13.

society it is necessary to establish that the introduction of money and of capital does not affect the results of the analysis, so that a capitalist society can be understood on the basis of this simple model of a barter economy.

Money and exchange

Smith's account of the emergence of money is parallel to the liberal political theorists' account of the emergence of the state. Just as the state as the form of political regulation emerged spontaneously from a mutual appreciation of the inconvenience of ad hoc alliances, so money as the form of economic regulation emerged spontaneously from a mutual appreciation of the inconvenience of barter.

Smith argued that money is simply an instrument of accounting and exchange that has no substantive economic significance. His story of the emergence of money from barter comes directly from Aristotle, and can still be found in any introductory economics textbook. With the development of exchange the inherent limitations of barter meant that 'this power of exchanging must frequently have been very much clogged and embarrassed in its operations ... In order to avoid the inconveniency of such situations, every prudent man in every period of society, after the first establishment of the division of labour, must naturally have endeavoured to manage his affairs in such a manner as to have at all times by him, besides the peculiar produce of his own industry, a certain quantity of some one commodity or another, such as he imagined few people would be likely to refuse in exchange for the produce of their own industry'.[6]

We can all appreciate the inconvenience of barter, so the rationality of money is clear to all of us. Money simply provides a means of exchange that enables the barter economy to work more efficiently. We can now sell our bows and arrows for money, and use the money to buy venison, rather than having to find a venison-owner who happens to need a new bow and arrow. The introduction of money makes no difference to the simple barter model. Money is a commodity distinguished from others only by its general exchangeability. Similarly in its role as measure of value, the

---

[6] ibid, vol. I, p. 20.

introduction of money has no substantive effects. It is simply more convenient to express exchangeable values in terms of money than in terms of labour.

In its role as measure of the value of commodities money serves to regulate production and exchange. The rise and fall of money prices in relation to the 'real prices' of commodities, that correspond to the 'trouble and toil' involved in their production, regulates the division of labour and the improvement in productivity in society. If the market is free, then supply will be spontaneously adapted to demand, and the incentive to innovation will be maintained. Any interference in the freedom of the market, however, will undermine the regulative role of money. Thus the conception of money as means of exchange, rather than as the substance of wealth, leads directly to the conception of money, rather than the state, as the appropriate means of regulation of social production and of the division of labour.

Having established the instrumental rationality of money, Smith could immediately pass on from its rational origins to the questions of its value and of the quantity required to oil the wheels of circulation.[7] For Smith money is a commodity like any other, so the value of gold and silver varies, like that of other commodities, according to the 'fertility or barrenness of the mines'.[8] 'Money prices' accordingly depend on the relation between the 'real prices' of commodities and the 'real price' of the money commodity.

In his discussion of the regulation of the quantity of money Smith followed Hume in relating the quantity of money solely and directly to the needs of exchange. However Smith made no mention of the mechanism proposed by Hume, whereby the quantity of money adapts to the needs of trade through changes in the level of domestic prices. Instead Smith argued along mercantilist lines, that if the supply of money exceeds the needs of the commerce of the nation, the balance, which cannot be employed at home, will be 'too valuable to be allowed to lie idle. It will, therefore, be sent abroad, in order to seek that profitable employment which it can-

---

[7] 'Money is ... only the instrument which men have agreed upon to facilitate the exchange of one commodity for another. It is none of the wheels of trade: It is the oil which renders the motion of the wheels more smooth and easy', Hume, op. cit., p. 33.

[8] Smith, op. cit., vol. I, p. 28.

not find at home'.[9] Hence for Smith the quantity of money will adjust spontaneously to the needs of circulation, without any of the disruption caused by inflation and deflation that marked Hume's specie-flow mechanism.

The difference between Smith and Hume becomes particularly important when it comes to the consideration of bank money, which was already well established in their native Scotland. The rise of bank money broke the simple link between changes in the money supply and the state of the balance of payments. The banks could increase the money supply simply by issuing more notes, usually by discounting bills of exchange. Within Hume's theory, if the banks expanded the note issue, the increase in the money supply would generate inflation and precipitate a drain of gold through the balance of payments, eventually forcing a contraction of the note issue as the cash reserves of the banking system were reduced.

Adam Smith, by contrast, advocated what became known as the 'real bills doctrine'. The advantage of bank money was that it freed the large sums of capital that would otherwise be tied up in coin and bullion for more productive use, gold being required only to provide the reserve to guarantee the convertibility of bank money. For Smith there was no danger of an inflationary increase in the money supply so long as bankers merely provided enough money to meet the needs of trade, and this would be assured if they simply followed sound banking principles, lending only on good trade bills. The money supply would simply expand and contract in accordance with the needs of commerce, without having any influence on prices. The interest of bankers in making only sound loans meant that the banking system could be relied upon to limit the note issue to the needs of circulation. Although Smith was the first to state this theory clearly in print, he was probably only reiterating the conventional wisdom of the bankers. However Smith's endorsement gave great authority to this view, which remained the orthodox position until the turn of the century. It was only in the course of the debates of the first half of the nineteenth century that Hume's view came to prevail.

The mercantilists had made great play of the danger of a shortage of money disrupting commerce. Smith argued that such a danger was illusory. Commerce cannot be seriously impeded by a

---

[9] ibid, vol. I, p. 259.

shortage of money. If a merchant is unable to sell all his goods, or has difficulty in extending his borrowing, it may appear that this is because of a shortage of money in the hands of his customers or his creditors. However the real problem is not a shortage of money but one of 'overtrading', often stimulated 'when the profits of trade happen to be greater than ordinary'.[10] If such overtrading is general, and gold flows out of the country, there may be some inconvenience, but there is no shortage of expedients for replacing gold and silver as means of circulation. A reversion to barter would be a most inconvenient replacement, but credit and paper-money can fill the gap, 'not only without any inconveniency, but in some cases, with some advantages'.[11] The mercantilists 'were sophistical in supposing that either to preserve or to augment the quantity of those metals required more the attention of government than to preserve or augment the quantity of any other useful commodities, which the freedom of trade, without any such attention, never fails to supply in the proper quantity'.[12]

Smith recognised the capitalist desire to accumulate wealth, and the inequality of wealth and power that is associated with such accumulation. However what the capitalist desires to accumulate is not money, but capital, money merely being a form in which capital transitorily appears. Capital is not the mercantilists' hoard of money, but the stock of means of production and subsistence that make possible productive investment. Money, accordingly, can never serve as other than means of circulation, and nobody has any interest in holding more money than is required to meet their circulation needs. However well-developed is the system of money and credit, it remains a mere convenience to facilitate circulation, with no substantive implications.

The hidden hand and the accumulation of capital

For Smith capital consisted in the means of production and subsistence, 'stock', 'accumulated in the hands of particular persons'.[13]

---

[10]ibid, vol. I, p. 383.
[11]ibid, vol. I, p. 383.
[12]ibid, vol. I, p. 379.
[13]ibid, vol. I, p. 42.

Profit is derived from the productive employment of stock. Money, by contrast, is sterile. The interest on money is not an original revenue, but 'is the compensation which the borrower pays to the lender, for the profit which he has an opportunity of making by the use of the money'.[14] It is correspondingly profit, not interest, that contributes to the net product that comprises the wealth of the nation.

Smith's demonstration of the beneficence of the hidden hand, and of the adequacy of money as the means of regulation of the division of labour, was based on the analysis of exchange between petty commodity producers. With the introduction of capital the division of labour is regulated by the allocation of capital between branches of production, and the extent of the division of labour no longer depends on the extent of the market, but on the size and employment of capital.

The growth of the wealth of the nation is limited to the growth of the capital that it employs. 'The general industry of the society never can exceed what the capital of the society can employ ... No regulation of commerce can increase the quantity of industry in any society beyond what its capital can maintain'.[15] For Smith it is not the size of profit but the rate of savings that limits the growth of the wealth of the nation. 'The industry of the society can augment only in proportion as its capital augments, and its capital can augment only in proportion to what can be gradually saved out of its revenue'.[16] The motive for saving is the principle of frugality, which fortunately prevails over the principle of expense. It just so happens, in the best of all possible worlds, that 'this frugality and good conduct ... is upon most occasions, it appears from experience, sufficient to compensate not only the private prodigality and misconduct of individuals, but the public extravagance of the government'.[17] There is, therefore, no justification for the government trying to limit private extravagance, or to divert private resources into productive investment. Indeed it is the government, the bulk of whose revenues are spent unproductively, that poses the greatest threat to productive investment.

Smith was equally opposed to the attempt of the state to regu-

---

[14] ibid, vol. I, p. 46.
[15] ibid, vol. I, pp. 397–8.
[16] ibid, vol. I, p. 402.
[17] ibid, vol. I, p. 306.

late the allocation of capital between branches of production. For Smith agricultural investment was more productive than manufacturing or trade because it set in motion the largest number of productive labourers, providing the greatest scope for developing the division of labour. In general Smith believed that capital would be appropriately allocated if freed from state direction, although to sustain the argument he was reduced to an appeal to human nature: 'That order of things which necessity imposes in general ... is, in every particular country, promoted by the natural inclinations of man ... Upon equal, or nearly equal, profits, most men will choose to employ their capitals rather in the improvement and cultivation of land than either in manufactures or foreign trade', because there the man 'has it more under his view and command'. Moreover 'the beauty of the countryside besides, the pleasures of a country life, the tranquility of mind which it promises, ... the independency which it really affords, have charms that more or less attract everybody'. Thus 'the study of his own advantage naturally, or rather necessarily, leads him to prefer that employment which is most advantageous to the society'.[18] Smith's reconciliation of the social and private rate of return to capital may be no more convincing than that of modern economists, but at least it is more picturesque!

Although Smith's analysis was hardly satisfactory, he reached his desired conclusion. 'As every individual, therefore, endeavours as much as he can both to employ his capital in the support of domestic industry, and so to direct that industry that its produce may be of the greatest value; every individual necessarily labours to render the annual revenue of the society as great as he can. He generally, indeed, neither intends to promote the public interest, nor knows how much he is promoting it. By preferring the support of domestic to that of foreign industry, he intends only his own security; and by directing that industry in such a manner as its produce may be of the greatest value, he intends only his own gain, and he is in this, as in many other cases, led by an invisible hand to promote an end which was no part of his intention. Nor is it always the worse for the society that it was no part of it. By pursuing his own interest he frequently promotes that of the society more effectually than when he really intends to promote it. I have

---

[18]ibid, vol. I, pp. 337–8, 398.

never known much good done by those who affected to trade for
the public good ....What is the species of domestic industry which
his capital can employ, and of which the produce is likely to be of
the greatest value, every individual, it is evident, can, in his local
situation, judge much better than any statesman or lawgiver can
do for him'.[19]

Capital, labour and the equality of exchange

The introduction of capital not only brings into question the regulation of the division of labour by the hidden hand, but also
the regulation of the relation between capital and labour. Smith
conceptualised the relationship between labourers, capitalists and
landowners according to the simple model of exchange based on the
division of labour, although now between the specialised factors
of production rather than between different branches of production. Land, labour and stock are the requisite means of production
that are brought together through the exchange between capitalists, labourers and landowners, whose rewards take the form of the
three revenues, profits, wages and rent.

Although Smith had a conception of land, labour and capital
as complementary factors of production, with the product 'shared'
amongst the owners of those factors, he could hardly avoid recognising the conflicts of interest between these classes, and in particular
between workers and their masters. 'What are the common wages
of labour, depends everywhere upon the contract usually made between those two parties, whose interests are by no means the same.
The workmen desire to get as much, the masters to give as little
as possible ...It is not ...difficult to foresee which of the two parties must, upon all ordinary occasions, have the advantage in the
dispute, and force the other into a compliance with their terms'.
Although Smith explained the predominance of the masters by the
fact that they are better able to combine, being fewer in number,
he also recognised the power they derive from their wealth. 'A
landlord, a farmer, a master manufacturer, a merchant, though
they did not employ a single workman, could generally live a year

---

[19]ibid, chap. I, p. 400.

or two upon the stocks which they have already acquired. Many workmen could not subsist a week'.[20]

Smith resolved the apparent conflict of interest between capitalists and workers by determining the true interests of the worker not in the admittedly unequal exchange relation between capitalist and worker, but in the dynamic context of the course of wages with the advance of the division of labour. High wages depend on the most rapid possible growth in the demand for labour, that corresponds to the most rapid possible growth of the market and of the division of labour. Thus the workers' interests are best served by the 'perfect liberty' of the market. Moreover the conflict between workers and capitalists is illusory, for high wages benefit capital too by stimulating the growth of population, the expansion of trade and the division of labour, and the industriousness of the worker.

Despite the unequal power of master and workmen, Smith insisted that the state should no more intervene in the labour market than anywhere else. The regulation of labour limits the mobility of labour, and so the ability of the labourer to seek out more favourable opportunities. Thus Smith criticised the Poor Laws primarily because of the restrictions on the mobility of labour created by the Settlement Laws that kept down agricultural wages and forced up wages in the towns. He criticised apprenticeship regulation on similar grounds. Moreover he opposed attempts to regulate wages not so much because such regulation could not benefit the working class, but because 'whenever the legislature attempts to regulate the differences between masters and their workmen, its counsellors are always the masters'. Thus Smith noted that 'when the regulation ... is in favour of the workmen, it is always just and equitable',[21] giving the Truck Acts as an example, and he stressed the role of the state in preventing combinations of employers from trying to force down wages.

The market and the state

Smith found the nature and causes of the wealth of nations to lie in the spontaneous development of the natural tendency to truck, barter and exchange. On this basis the rational pursuit of self-

[20] ibid, vol. I, pp. 58–9.
[21] ibid, vol. I, p. 129

interest alone is sufficient to secure prosperity and harmony. Production and distribution are regulated, through competitive exchange, by money. This regulation is achieved, where there is 'perfect liberty', through the rise and fall of 'market prices' above and below 'natural prices' that regulates the flow of capital into and out of different branches of production and of labour into and out of different employments. As the means of regulation money is not an external power, but the instrument of reason, the executor of the beneficence of the hidden hand.

Smith's rejection of state intervention in the market did not mean that the state had no role to play, or that political economy was indifferent to the state. On the contrary the purpose of Smith's analysis of the economic system was to define the proper role of the state. Smith argued that political economy 'considered as a branch of the science of a statesman or legislator, proposes two distinct objects: first, to provide a plentiful revenue or subsistence for the people, or more properly to enable them to provide such a revenue or subsistence for themselves; and secondly, to supply the state or commonwealth with a revenue sufficient for the public services. It proposes to enrich both the people and the sovereign'.[22]

Smith criticised vigorously the commercial, fiscal and financial policies of the state, but this did not lead him to criticise the political constitution of the contemporary state. The problem was that the capitalists had imposed their own interests on the state and diverted it from its proper tasks. What are the appropriate tasks of the state, and how should it fulfil them?

'According to the system of natural liberty, the sovereign has only three duties to attend to; three duties of great importance, indeed, but plain and intelligible to common understandings: first, the duty of protecting society from the violence and invasion of other independent societies; secondly, the duty of protecting, as far as possible, every member of the society from the injustice or oppression of every other member of it, or the duty of establishing an exact administration of justice; and, thirdly, the duty of erecting and maintaining certain public works and certain public institutions, which it can never be the interest of any individual, or small number of individuals, to erect and maintain'.[23]

'The first duty of the sovereign, that of protecting the society

---

[22]ibid, vol. I, p. 375.
[23]ibid, vol. II, pp. 180–1.

from the violence and invasion of other independent societies, can be performed only by means of a military force'. 'It is only by means of a standing army ... that the civilisation of any country can be perpetuated, or even preserved for any considerable time'. The needs of national defence also justify the navigation laws, although these impede the freedom of trade.[24]

The standing army serves to defend the society not only from external aggressors, but also from the enemy within. Such a standing army is 'dangerous to liberty ... wherever the interests of the general and that of the principal officers are not necessarily connected with the support of the constitution of the state ... But where the sovereign is himself the general, and the principal nobility and gentry of the country the chief officers of the army, where the military force of the country is placed under the command of those who have the greatest interest in the support of the civil authority, because they have themselves the greatest share of that authority, a standing army can never be dangerous to liberty. On the contrary, it may in some cases be favourable to liberty ... Where the security of the magistrate, though supported by the principal people of the country, is endangered by every popular discontent; where a small tumult is capable of bringing about in a few hours a great revolution, the whole authority of government must be employed to suppress and punish every murmur and complaint against it. To a sovereign, on the contrary, who feels himself supported, not only by the natural aristocracy of the country but by a well-regulated standing army, the rudest, the most groundless, and the most licentious remonstrances can give little disturbance. He can safely pardon or neglect them ... That degree of liberty which approaches to licentiousness can be tolerated only in countries where the sovereign is secured by a well-regulated standing army'.[25]

The second duty of the sovereign is that of the administration of justice. Justice, no less than a standing army, is directed primarily against the threat to property presented by the poor. The ignorance of the poor prevents them from appreciating the benefits that eventually accrue to them from the security of property and the freedom of exchange. They rather tend to see only the inequality of wealth and power, and to covet the property of others. Where there is little property and little inequality there is little need for a

[24] ibid, vol. II, pp. 182, 196, vol. I, p. 408.
[25] ibid, vol. II, pp. 196–7.

system of justice. The need arises with the emergence of property. 'The acquisition of valuable and extensive property . . . necessarily requires the establishment of civil government. . . . Civil govern-ment, so far as it is instituted for the security of property, is in reality instituted for the defence of the rich against the poor, or of those who have some property against those who have none at all'.[26]

The administration of justice, which secures the security of property and the person, defends the rich against the poor, but is the foundation of that 'order and good government' on which the system of natural liberty and the incentive to self-improvement depend. 'Upon the impartial administration of justice depends the liberty of every individual, the sense which he has of his own security'.[27] 'Justice . . . is the main pillar that upholds the edifice. If it is removed, the great, the immense fabric of human society . . . must in a moment crumble into atoms'[28] However Smith was not prepared to rest the stability of this pillar on so feeble a foun-dation as the consent implicit in a mythical social contract, nor even on the power and majesty of the judiciary alone. When it comes to the defence of property it is essential that relations of authority and subordination are sustained. In the last analysis the authority of the state does not rest on an implicit contract, nor on democratic consent, but on a natural respect for authority.

In the hierarchy of property and authority, from the sovereign to the lowest ranks, 'men of inferior wealth combine to defend those of superior wealth in the possession of their property, in order that men of superior wealth may combine to defend them in the posses-sion of theirs'.[29] Hence the hierarchy of authority and inequality that is sustained by the system of justice is able to rest on the con-sent of the lower orders, bred of their natural respect for authority and concern to sustain their own property against the orders be-neath them.

The political rights of the aristocracy and gentry derived, for Smith, from the fact that landed property gave them 'the greatest interest in the support of the civil authority, because they have

---

[26]ibid, vol. II, pp. 199, 203.

[27]ibid, vol. I, p. 363, vol. II, p. 210.

[28]Adam Smith, *The Theory of Moral Sentiments*, Oxford University Press, Oxford, 1976, II, ii, 3, 3–4.

[29]Smith, *Wealth of Nations*, vol. II, pp. 202, 203.

themselves the greatest share in that authority'.[30] The capitalist, on the other hand, has much less of a connection with the lower orders, and so does not enjoy any such natural authority, while the mobility of capital weakens his interest in maintaining order and good government since in the event of disorder he can simply move his capital abroad.[31] Smith, for all his attacks on the incompetence and corruption of the state, nevertheless endorsed the constitutional arrangements within which the state institutionalised the power of the landed aristocracy and gentry. The faults lay not with the constitution, but with the abuse of power by entrenched interest and faction.

The third duty of the sovereign is that of erecting and maintaining public institutions and public works which are advantageous to society, but which could never provide sufficient profit to be undertaken privately. These are 'chiefly those for facilitating the commerce of the society, and those for promoting the instruction of the people'. The former may include 'roads, bridges, navigable canals, harbours etc',[32] and the protection of trade. The duty to provide such public works might appear to give considerable discretion to the state in identifying public works and institutions advantageous to society. However for Smith the presumption was always that such works and institutions should be provided privately, for it is only where there is a direct relation between the service provided and the payment made that the entrepreneur has an incentive to meet the public need. Where public provision is essential the costs of the service should be met as far as possible by the beneficiaries.

'The institutions for the education of the youth may, in the same manner, furnish a revenue sufficient for defraying their own expense'. The payment to teachers of a salary financed by public endowments or public revenues, rather than directly by the fees of pupils, sets the interest of the teacher 'as directly in opposition to his duty as it is possible to set it' since his salary bears no relation to his exertions or to the interest of his pupils. Hence the universities have almost entirely neglected Physics, 'which is capable of making so many useful discoveries', in favour of the 'subtelties and

---

[30] ibid, vol. II, p. 197.

[31] For similar reasons Smith argued that the taxation of interest would drive capital abroad — the internationalisation of capital is hardly a new problem! Ibid., vol. II, pp. 330–1.

[32] Smith, *Wealth of Nations*, vol. II, p. 211.

sophisms' of Metaphysics, Pneumatics and Ontology.[33]

However other considerations than the interests of the pupils or the practical usefulness of knowledge come into play when we consider the public provision of education. Where the state of society does not 'naturally form' in individuals 'the abilities and virtues which that state requires ... some attention of government is necessary in order to prevent the almost entire corruption and degeneracy of the great body of the people'. This is the fate that would befall the mass of the population in civilised society, 'unless government takes some pains to prevent it'.[34] For this reason the provision of publicly subsidised education for the common people is important for the defence of the constitution.

Under all three headings Smith was quite clear that the essential duty of the sovereign is to sustain the rule of property by military force, by the administration of justice and by the provision of education and popular diversions. Smith's state is unequivocally, and without any apology, a class state. But at the same time the rule of property, and the unfettered accumulation of capital, is the condition for the most rapid growth in the prosperity of all social classes, the basis of material, moral and cultural progress, and the foundation of personal liberty.

The limits to the state

Although the market may not always function perfectly to achieve harmony, order and prosperity, the presumption must always be that the hidden hand is the best means of social regulation available. The presumption in favour of the market rests not only on Smith's analysis of the market, but also on his analysis of the state. The state suffers from two defects, self-interest and ignorance. Although the state is the embodiment of the constitution, it does not stand above society, but emerges from it as a particular institution endowed with particular powers and privileges. These powers and privileges are wielded by particular human beings, the sovereign, nobility and gentry, who are no less motivated by self-interest than are lesser mortals. However the power of the state enables them to impose their own judgements and their own self-interest on the

---

[33] ibid, vol. II, pp. 245, 246, 255.
[34] ibid, vol. II, pp. 263–4.

judgements of private individuals.

The application of the cynical principles of political economy to the state implies that the state can only be entrusted with those tasks in the proper performance of which its own interest, and that of the ruling class, coincides with the general interest. With respect to the legitimate functions of the state, to defend the realm, to protect property, and to maintain a respect for authority, their interests fortunately do correspond to the general interest. However in the administration of justice, and in more particular matters, these interests do not necessarily coincide. Hence the impartial administration of justice requires an independent judiciary, for 'when the judicial is united to the executive power, it is scarce possible that justice should not frequently be sacrificed to what is vulgarly called politics',[35] and in more particular matters the presumption must be that, whatever its faults, the hidden hand will better serve the general interest than will a government subject to the pressure of particular interests.

Even were the state constrained to act in conformity with the general interest, it could no more effectively displace the hidden hand of the market. Smith's analysis of the laws that govern the economy enlighten us as to the general principles by which the hidden hand achieves harmony and prosperity, but cannot tell us anything about the proper prices at which goods should exchange, nor the quantities in which they should be produced, nor the proper rates of wages, rent or profit, nor the proper manner in which a particular capital should be invested. Thus 'the sovereign is completely discharged from a duty ... for the proper performance of which no human wisdom or knowledge could ever be sufficient; the duty of superintending the industry of private people, and of directing it towards the employments most suitable to the interest of the society'.[36]

The principles of public finance

The limitation of the powers of the state also implies that the state must draw as few resources as possible into unproductive use, and that it must finance its activities in ways that are just and have

[35] ibid, vol. II, p. 210.
[36] ibid, vol. II, p. 180.

the least damaging impact on the progress of the nation.

Although the duties of the sovereign are limited, they are nevertheless expensive. As far as possible the costs of public provision should fall on its beneficiaries in proportion to their gain, whether from general revenue, local rates, tolls or fees. Although historically the state had derived its revenues from commercial enterprises and public lands, the proper source of the public revenue is taxation, since this relates payment to benefit. The general principles of such taxation are four. First, 'the subjects of every state ought to contribute ... in proportion to the revenue which they respectively enjoy under the protection of the state'. Second, the tax 'ought to be certain, not arbitrary'. Third, the tax ought to be levied at the time that is most convenient for the contributor. Fourth, the tax should be levied as economically as possible.[37] These continue to be the basic principles of public finance to this day.

Smith's general conclusion was that all taxation is vexatious and, because it diverts revenue from productive to unproductive employment, impedes the growth of the wealth of the nation. Thus the wealth of the nation requires not only the limitation of the powers of the state, but also the minimisation of its expenses. If taxation were the only source of revenue, political resistance to taxation would be sufficient to compel the state to minimise its expenses. However in practice the ambitions of the state have not been limited by its powers of taxation.

The limited possibilities of taxation, and the resistance of the public, have induced governments to resort to borrowing, particularly to meet the exceptional expenses of war. Moreover they have increasingly failed to make provision for the repayment of this borrowing, so that the state has come to be burdened with a growing unfunded debt. This debt can only be serviced by means of taxation that redistributes revenue from the owners of land and capital stock to the holders of the public debt, occasioning 'both the neglect of the land, and the waste or removal of capital stock'. Past experience suggests that such debts are never repaid. At best a pretended repayment has disguised public bankruptcy as the debt has been devalued by debasing, or by raising the denomination, of the coin which 'occasions a general and most pernicious subversion of the fortunes of private people, enriching in most cases the idle

---

[37] ibid, vol. II, pp. 307–8.

and profuse debtor at the expense of the industrious and frugal creditor'.[38]

The only way of avoiding the ruin of the nation by the progress of these enormous debts is to repay them, either by a considerable increase in taxation or by a considerable reduction in public expenditure. However the possibility of raising domestic taxation is limited, while 'the private interest of many powerful individuals, the confirmed prejudices of great bodies of people' [39] present obstacles to extending taxation to the colonies, in exchange for political representation, that are probably insurmountable. Yet it has been colonial wars, and the maintenance of the colonial establishment, that has largely occasioned the debts. If the colonies cannot furnish the revenues to meet the expense, Britain must cut her expenditure by abandoning her 'golden dream' and so 'endeavour to accommodate her future views and designs to the real mediocrity of her circumstances'. However there is little prospect of the state being brought to heel, for its ruinous policies are backed by powerful interests, above all those of the bankers and the merchants. It is the growth of the public debt that 'will in the long run probably ruin all the great nations of Europe'.[40]

Smith's sense of being a lonely prophet in a world dominated by dark forces could as well have been expressed by the monetarists in the early 1970s, and in almost the same words. 'To expect, indeed, that the freedom of trade should ever be entirely restored in Great Britain is as absurd as to expect that an Oceania or Utopia should ever be established in it. Not only the prejudices of the public, but what is much more unconquerable, the private interests of many individuals, irresistibly oppose it. ...master manufacturers [read 'trades unions'] set themselves against any law that is likely to increase the number of their rivals in the home market ...[and] enflame their workmen to attack with violence and outrage the proposers of any such regulation ...they have become formidable to the government, and upon many occasions intimidate the legislature'.[41]

---

[38] ibid, vol. II, pp. 410, 413.
[39] ibid, vol. II, p. 416.
[40] ibid, vol. II, pp. 430, 393.
[41] ibid, vol. I, pp. 414–5.

Chapter 3

Political Economy and the Rise of the Capitalist State

Adam Smith and the crisis of mercantilism

Smith was right in thinking that his work would have little popular appeal. Popular opposition to the corruption of the state,
to the abuse of power and, above all, to the burden of taxation,
was expressed in the voice of democratic political theory without needing any sophisticated economic theory to articulate its
grievances. Moreover Smith had considerably overestimated the
extent to which the system of mercantilism presented a barrier to
the development of capitalism. The stagnation of foreign trade
between 1750 and 1780 did not seriously inhibit economic growth
as domestic sources of expansion were mobilised, with more rapid
agricultural improvement, the beginnings of the industrial revolution, and the development of domestic financial institutions, in
the form of the country banks. The panoply of domestic protective regulations that Smith saw as such a formidable barrier to
the freedom of capital and labour simply dissolved in the face of
capitalist development, despite the resistance of the working class

(sometimes supported by sympathetic magistrates), while the Poor
Law proved an invaluable complement to the militia in maintaining order as the working class suffered the costs of industrial and
agricultural revolution. In the last two decades of the eighteenth
century outlets for the increasing production of capitalist industry
and agriculture were found not so much in domestic as in foreign
markets, taking advantage of the commercial supremacy that was
the legacy of mercantilism.

The appeal of *The Wealth of Nations* was not so much to the
forces struggling against the parasitic and corrupt state, as to the
state itself. Ironically the book was published in 1776, the year in
which the American Revolution removed the lynchpin of the colonial system. The cost of the American War provoked escalating
popular opposition, that drew increasingly radical inspiration from
the democratic principles of the rebels. The final discrediting of
the doctrines of mercantilism and the humiliation of the state with
the defeat in America precipitated an ideological crisis. Smith's
new system provided a means of resolving the crisis. The loss of
the American colonies could immediately be reinterpreted, on the
basis of Smith's theory, as a liberation from the burden of colonial
responsibility, opening up new possibilities of increasing trade by
liberalisation rather than control. The critique of the colonial system could even be used to justify the French Wars, in the name of
opening up markets to the freedom of trade. The reduction of pro-
hibitive duties could increase revenues by stimulating the growth
of trade and discouraging smuggling.

The discrediting of the colonial system, the eclectic pragmatism
of Smith's work, and his endorsement of the existing constitution,
made it easy for the principles of *The Wealth of Nations* to become established as the new political orthodoxy, and to provide
a theoretical basis for the programme of 'economical reform' that
responded to popular protest against the burden of taxation and
the corruption of the state. The enormous expansion of trade in
the wake of American independence, with exports increasing five-
fold, and the financial and political success of economical reform,
enhanced the prestige of Smith's principles. From the late 1780s
these principles came to be accepted by government as the basis
on which to determine the fiscal, commercial and financial policies
of the state, although they were always to be tempered in their
application by pragmatic consideration of the circumstances.

The espousal of the principles of free trade and economical government did not prevent the state from continuing to protect domestic industry and agriculture or from using the military, political and financial power of the state to secure commercial domination for the benefit of a wider range of capitalist interests. The East and West Indian colonies retained their importance as sources of supply and of colonial plunder, and there were few demands for their liberation. There was little opposition from capitalists to the long drawn out, and very costly, French wars at the turn of the century, which set the seal on British commercial supremacy for almost a century. Similarly there was no resistance to the use of the political and military power of the state to maintain commercial domination in North America, and later in support of the displacement of Spanish by British interests in Latin America. Tariff protection assisted the early development of important new industries. Even when the introduction of more advanced methods of production made tariff barriers anachronistic, they were maintained for revenue purposes and, despite limited liberalisation, there were few demands for their removal before the second quarter of the nineteenth century.

Economical reform and savage repression, supported by patriotic and religious chauvinism, secured the financial and political stabilisation of the state during the French Wars. Although lip-service was paid to Smith's principles, they had had little practical impact. It was the problems created by the French Wars, and particularly the problems of post-war reconstruction, that led to the adoption of a more radical anti-state ideology of laissez-faire. But again this ideology was not pressed by the capitalist class, but was adopted enthusiastically by the Tory governments of Lord Liverpool.

The Napoleonic Wars provided an enormous stimulus to capitalist development. Wartime demand gave a great boost to the growth of domestic production and the Continental blockade led to the opening up of new export markets. Agriculture too expanded rapidly during the war, particularly by increasing the area under cultivation. The enormous borrowing of the state to meet the needs of war stimulated the growth of banking and financial institutions

The ending of the war created acute difficulties. Agricultural overproduction had already appeared with a collapse of prices in 1813, and agriculture remained in depression for another twenty years. The loss of military contracts hit several industries, while inflation had weakened the competitive advantage of exporters. The financial instability associated with the enormous increase in the government debt and the suspension of convertibility in 1797 was a barrier to the growth of trade. Bouts of depression in 1816, 1819 and 1826 led to widespread distress and to increasingly menacing rural and urban unrest, which found allies among the more conservative elements of the ruling class, who saw distress and disorder as the inevitable consequence of the breakdown of the traditional society with the unfettered advance of capital.

The immediate response of the state to these problems was essentially conservative. Agricultural depression was to be alleviated by the strengthening of the Corn Laws which protected domestic agriculture from foreign competition. Disorder was met by severe repression, while the distress that fuelled disorder was alleviated by the Poor Law. The regulation of the monetary system was left to the bankers. Overall the state assumed little responsibility for economic management beyond its traditional role of securing British commercial supremacy.

Such an attitude of disengagement could not last for long. The Corn Laws were ineffective in supporting an agriculture whose problems derived from domestic overproduction as much as from foreign competition. Depression, distress and disorder led to pressure for government action. The cost of the Poor Law meant a steady rise in parish rates, on top of the increased burden of taxation required to meet government's current expenditure and the servicing of its debt. Moreover the programme of economical reform had reduced the scope for ministerial patronage, while the growth of the press and of organised public opinion brought popular pressure to bear on the government, to which the latter had increasingly to respond. The government was also under financial pressure. Monetary instability fuelled financial speculation, creating difficulties for the financing of the government debt, while political resistance prevented the government from increasing levels of taxation. It soon became clear that the political and financial stability of the government could only be secured by the more active intervention of the state to secure the conditions for the sustained growth of prosperity. It was in this context that political economy took up the challenge, going beyond Smith's critique of the commercial system to develop a theory within which the appropriate role of the state in the regulation of the economy could be considered. The leading role, in both theoretical analysis and political debate, was played by Ricardo until his death in 1823.

Classical political economy

Political economy built on the foundations that Smith laid down. The inconsistencies of Smith's analysis left a large gap between his fundamental assumptions and his conclusions, while his eclecticism provided scope for a wide range of interpretations that allowed disparate schools of thought to claim Smith as their ancestor. Smith's analysis of the quantity of money was undeveloped. His theory of wages was thin, his theories of profit and rent an eclectic mixture of physiocratic and mercantilist elements and his theory of value incoherent. It was largely in these areas that classical political economy fleshed out Smith's account. However these developments served only to reinforce Smith's conclusions about the proper relation between money and the state. Whereas Smith applied his theory to the critique of mercantilism, political economy had the more positive aim of establishing the adequate form of the liberal capitalist state.

The unifying framework of classical political economy was a view of the economy as a system of production, with exchange coordinating the division of labour by regulating the allocation of labour and capital among the various branches of production and distributing the product amongst the various social classes in the form of revenue. The normal, or 'natural' price of the product was determined by its normal cost of production, whether that be expressed in terms of labour-time, as for Ricardo, or as the sum of wages, rent and profit, as for most of the rest of the school. 'Market' prices were determined by demand and supply. However demand and supply were not independent of one another, since consumption was seen primarily as a phase in the reproduction of the system of production.

The regulation of the system of production was achieved by money which, following Smith, was seen as the means of circulation. The role of money, in permitting the fluctuation of market prices around the natural price, was to adjust the allocation of labour and capital among the various branches of production in ac-

cordance with the needs of the physical reproduction of the system
as a whole. On the whole it was presumed that these adjustments
would proceed smoothly and rapidly, so the laws of classical political economy were developed for an economy in equilibrium, in
which market prices corresponded to natural prices. To the extent
that there were barriers to the free mobility of the factors of production and so to the response of production to changing prices, such
adjustments might be delayed, and particular branches of production or particular employments might suffer more or less prolonged
distress. However such distress was not the result of monetary
dislocation, but of the existence of real barriers to adjustment.

The possibility of general overproduction was excluded by 'Say's
Law', which followed immediately from the conclusion that the
money economy worked just like a barter economy. J.-B. Say drew
out the implications of Smith's assertion that 'consumption is the
sole end and purpose of all production', so that 'it is not for its own
sake that men desire money , but for the sake of what they can
purchase with it'.[1] Say's 'law of markets' ensured the impossibility
of general overproduction since 'a product is no sooner created,
than it, from that instant, affords a market for other products to
the full extent of its own value'.[2] The consequence was that distress
and unemployment could only be a temporary problem, associated
with the structural readjustment of production to changing market
conditions. This led Malthus and Ricardo to resist demands for
the relief of distress, by the Poor Law, the expansion of credit or
public works, which would only remove the incentive for capital and
labour to seek out new opportunities for profitable employment and
so prolong the necessarily painful process of adjustment.

The theory of interest was developed to give substance to Say's
law . The rigorous distinction between money and capital meant
that the rate of interest was seen as the price of capital, and not the
price of money. The role of the rate of interest came to be seen as
that of equating savings and investment. The withdrawal of money
from circulation corresponded to an increased desire to save, which
would be accommodated by a decline in the rate of interest that
would give a stimulus to investment, so ensuring that the money
thrown back into circulation as investment always corresponded to

---

[1] Smith, op. cit., vol. II, p. 155, vol. I. , p. 385.
[2] Jean-Baptiste Say, *A Treatise on Political Economy*, C. R. Princep
(trans.), London, 1821, vol. I, p. 167.

the money withdrawn from circulation as savings. An expansion of the supply of money, by expanding the note issue, was seen as having at most a temporary impact on the rate of interest, which would be neutralised as soon as prices had risen to absorb the increased supply of money. Thus the monetary authorities could not affect the level of economic activity by intervening in the money markets to regulate the rate of interest. Demands for cheap credit, which came from distressed farmers and manufacturers, would merely stimulate inflation, while removing the pressure to redirect labour and capital to more profitable branches of production. Thus the monetary authorities should resist such pressures and regulate the currency strictly in accordance with the metallic base.

Say first integrated Smith's account of labour, land and capital as the sources of the three forms of revenue into the model of exchange. Although Smith saw wages as deriving from the sale of labour, profit and rent did not derive from the sale of any particular commodity. Profit was some kind of mark-up, that corresponded to a vaguely defined net product, while rent was pure surplus. Say integrated profit and rent into the model of exchange by developing the idea that they corresponded to the contributions of the 'productive services' of capital and land, although economists had some difficulty identifying precisely what were those contributions. Correspondingly Say proposed an 'adding up' theory of value which defined the value of a commodity as the sum of wages, rent and profit that comprised its cost of production. Say's model was very congenial in reducing the determination of these revenues to the common basis of the equality of exchange, and dispelling the uncomfortable connotations of the idea of such revenues as comprising a surplus. However such ideological considerations did not have great significance until the legitimacy of profits and rent came under serious challenge in the late 1820s. Thus Ricardo could develop his labour theory of value, that saw profit as a form of surplus labour, and rent as a deduction from profit, without imagining for one moment that his theory could be used to undermine the sanctity of private property. However it was undoubtedly these ideological implications, rather than its technical deficiencies, that lay behind the rapid abandonment of the labour theory of value, in favour of the cost of production theory, in the 1830s, although many still held to the inverse relation between wages and profits that Ricardo's theory implied.

Malthus's theory of population established a theoretical foundation for Smith's account of wages. High wages encouraged early marriage and lower infant mortality, so that population increased, low wages conversely inducing a decline in the rate of growth of population. In this way the free market would ensure that, in the long run, wages would fluctuate around the subsistence minimum. The law of population came to be complemented in the short run by the 'wages fund' doctrine, according to which the means of subsistence available to sustain the working class was fixed. Competition between the workers would ensure the equalisation of wages within the limit set by the wages fund, although the existence of 'non-competing groups' could lead to the persistence of wage differentials.

The law of population implied that any measures that sought to increase wages at the expense of rent or profits would simply lead to an increase in the population until wages were reduced to the subsistence minimum. This argument was used against the Speenhamland system of subsidising wages, which was an archetypal example of a well-intentioned policy achieving the opposite of the desired effect: 'The clear and direct tendency of the poor laws ...is not, as the legislature benevolently intended, to amend the condition of the poor, but to deteriorate the condition of both poor and rich; instead of making the poor rich, they are calculated to make the rich poor '.[3] The same argument was also used against the egalitarian schemes of cooperators and socialists. Redistribution would lead to equality, but only to an equality of misery. The only solution to the problem of the overpopulation that was the cause of low wages was the encouragement of moral restraint on the part of the working class, and the sponsorship of colonial emigration.

Classical political economy largely retained Smith's assumptions, and hardly modified his essential conclusions. Money was the adequate means of regulation of the capitalist system of production. Although inequality was a conspicuous feature of capitalist society, the laws of political economy established that the condition of the working class could not be improved by collective intervention, but only by moral restraint, prudence, sobriety and self-improvement, and by the growth of capital. Distress was a

---

[3] David Ricardo, *The Principles of Political Economy and Taxation*, Everyman edition, London, 1973, p. 61.

temporary problem, arising from the normal processes of market adjustment, the relief of which would impede the operation of the market and so intensify the problem. Cyclical fluctuations in the overall level of economic activity were the result of 'overtrading' stimulated by unwarranted monetary expansion.

Ricardo had such faith in the smooth working of the capitalist system as to regard the laws of political economy as immutable natural laws that immediately dictated policy. However such a doctrinaire approach soon proved inadequate to the political tasks that confronted the state. The failure of currency stabilisation and trade liberalisation to solve the post-war problems threatened to discredit political economy. Thus the second generation of political economists tended to take a much more pragmatic view of their task, recognising that the gap between the science of political economy and the art of statesmanship had to be bridged by political judgement. Thus political economy allied itself with utilitarianism in offering a programme for the reconstruction of the state that combined principle with pragmatism. Over the first half of the nineteenth century political economy developed from the theory that sought to limit the powers of the state into the theory that guided the rationalisation of the inherited state apparatus to create the state form appropriate to the rule of capital.

Ricardo and the problems of post-war reconstruction

The problems of post-war reconstruction focused attention on three areas: currency reform, free trade, and the regulation of the working class. On a fourth area, the need to cut taxation, the national debt, and government expenditure there was general agreement, although it was easier said than done. These issues dominated the debates around the role of the state in the regulation of the economy for the following three decades. Political economy provided a coherent theoretical framework within which to determine policy in all these areas, and in the end it was the prescriptions of political economy that prevailed.

Although the theory of political economy was based on an identification of the interests of capital, and particularly of productive capital, with the national interest, its triumph was only indirectly related to the political advance of the bourgeoisie, and time after time capitalists themselves showed little enthusiasm for the nostrums offered by the exponents of the dismal science. Although Members of Parliament were at times persuaded by the eloquence and self-confidence of the political economists, they too usually had more parochial concerns. The appeal of political economy was above all to government ministers, and later to their civil servants, for whom political economy offered a universalistic ideology that corresponded to their own pretension to stand above contending particular interests in pursuit of the general good.

The issue of currency reform centred on the responsibility of the Bank of England for the issue of paper currency. The Bullion Report of 1810 had blamed the wartime inflation on the over-issue of inconvertible notes by the Bank of England, and recommended the immediate restoration of convertibility. However the Bank had vigorously defended its policies, on the grounds of Smith's real bills doctrine that over-issue was impossible so long as the money supply was only increased by discounting sound commercial bills. Inflation was attributed to pressures in the real economy, the bank merely accommodating these pressures by meeting the legitimate demands of commerce. The opponents of the Bank noted that in accommodating inflation by expanding credit the Bank further fuelled the inflationary pressures. If the Bank pursued a competitive discount policy, and so pushed the rate of interest below the normal rate of profit, there would be no limit to the demand for money, and so to the extent of inflation and over-issue. The only solution was to restore the convertibility of the currency so that inflationary pressures would be limited by the limited supply of money, a drain on the reserves of the Bank of England forcing it to restrict credit and so limit the extent of overtrading.

Although wartime inflation had provided a powerful stimulus to the prosperity of agricultural and industrial capitalists, and monetary instability and heavy government borrowing had provided large profits for financial speculators, there was general agreement on the need to restore the stability of the currency by reestablishing convertibility. The main opposition to the return to gold derived from Birmingham, where manufacturers, hit hard by the loss of wartime contracts, agitated for policies such as the free expansion of credit, public expenditure to relieve distress, and even public works to absorb unemployment. Birmingham, whose spokesman

was the banker Thomas Attwood, continued to be the main source
of opposition to monetary orthodoxy for the next three decades.

The main problem preventing the restoration of convertibility
was that the currency was overvalued as a result of wartime inflation, and so the restoration of convertibility at the old parity could
only be accomplished after a period of deflation. The bankers' belief that inflation was not a monetary phenomenon but had real
causes, such as exceptional government expenditure, bad harvests
and war, implied that the restoration of normality would see prices
returning to their normal level, at which point convertibility could
be painlessly restored. On the other hand, it was widely believed
that any attempt to restrict credit so as to force down prices and
achieve the premature restoration of convertibility would reduce
not only prices but also income and employment and would provoke severe distress. In 1810 this consideration persuaded Parliament to reject the Bullion Report, although the expectation was
that convertibility would be re-established soon after the end of the
war as prices returned to their normal level.

Ricardo's was the main voice raised against the fears of deflation. Ricardo took up Hume's theory of the specie-flow mechanism
to show that convertibility was a sufficient condition for maintaining both the stability of the currency and the balance of international payments as domestic prices rose and fell to preserve the
international competitiveness of domestic producers. Ricardo believed that the over-issue of the currency was the only cause of an
outflow of gold, and that the contraction of the issue would restore
equilibrium by the reduction of prices smoothly and painlessly. Ricardo followed Smith in favouring the replacement of gold in circulation by a paper currency, but insisted that its issue should be
strictly regulated according to the state of the exchanges, so that its
circulation would correspond exactly to that of a metallic currency.

Ricardo's simplistic optimism, born of his stockbroker's faith
in the smoothness of market adjustment, was not widely shared.
Deflation was almost universally rejected, not least for fear of provoking further popular unrest by giving the depression an added
twist. Even capitalists in the export trades, who could expect to
benefit from lower prices and monetary stability, were very appre-
hensive of the short-term effects of deflation and currency appreciation. Those farmers and manufacturers producing for the domestic
market, who were often burdened with debt and who had already

been hard-hit by the post-war depression, were the most strongly opposed to deflation. Thus the restoration of convertibility was repeatedly postponed, until falling prices and currency appreciation with the ending of the boom in 1819 brought the issue to a head.

'Peel's Bill' of 1819 proposed the gradual restoration of convertibility over a period of four years. However the fear of deflation was still widespread, and protests against the proposal were vehement and general. Of course the problem could have been solved by a devaluation of the currency, which would have made it possible to restore convertibility without deflation, but such a proposal was unacceptable, for it would involve Parliament not simply in condoning the iniquity of inflation, but in forcing the Bank of England to abrogate the contractual obligation embodied in the law and printed on every one of its notes, and would set a precedent that future governments might use to evade the consequences of financial irresponsibility. Thus the motion for devaluation in 1819 could not even find a seconder.[4] Ricardo persuaded Parliament that action could not any longer be delayed, and that the impact of restoration would be minimal, so that the Bill was passed without recorded division, despite widespread reservations. The passage of the Bill was immediately followed by speculation against the expected appreciation of the currency, and by falling prices as the depression deepened, so that it was possible to restore convertibility in 1821.

In the event fears of the opponents of convertibility were largely confirmed following restoration, the damage being compounded by the fact that, far from stabilising the economy the mismanagement of the currency intensified the economic cycles that produced acute distress in the agricultural districts and in Midlands manufacturing. In 1819 Ricardo had estimated that a fall in prices of 5 or 6 per cent would be sufficient to establish equilibrium at the old parity. Prices actually fell 13 per cent in 1819 alone, and a further 20 per cent between 1819 and 1824. Ricardo, true to form but against all the evidence, blamed the decline in prices on mismanagement by the Bank of England. In fact the bulk of the decline was caused neither by the restoration of convertibility, nor by the Bank of England's errors, but by a European-wide depression, that was at worst intensified by monetary deflation.

The depression was widely blamed on the restoration of convert-

---

[4] Boyd Hilton, *Corn, Cash and Commerce*, Oxford University Press, Oxford, 1977, p. 47

ibility. Attwood expressed the opposition of the small Birmingham manufacturers, advocating currency reform and the free availability of credit until full employment was restored. Cobbett expressed the opposition of the farmers, who similarly called for devaluation and a reduction in the burden of taxation. The export trades saw the problem in a wider context, as reflecting a lack of purchasing power in the hands of foreigners with which to buy British goods, and advocated the abolition of British protective tariffs to open the market to foreign suppliers, having an eye especially on the South American market. It was the latter voice, particularly as it was articulated through Ricardo's Political Economy Club, to which the government listened, standing fast on the currency issue, but initiating the liberalisation of trade that made steady progress over the following twenty years. Reciprocal free trade agreements were negotiated with the major European powers over the period 1823–1830, colonial trade was relaxed and the remaining commercial monopolies abolished.

Trade liberalisation, like the currency question, met with opposition even from those who were in principle free traders. Baring, who had introduced the London Merchants' Petition calling for free trade in 1820, also led the defence of the silk industry against the removal of protection in 1824. Such apparently contradictory positions were reconciled by the argument that protection was necessary so long as domestic producers had to suffer the higher labour costs that were the result of the Corn Law. Thus the Corn Laws were made the pivot of the Free Trade case. There were signs, that worried the landowners, that the government was beginning to question the wisdom of the Corn Laws, on the grounds that they fostered price instability and popular unrest, while the squeeze on profits threatened a flight of capital abroad. However the Corn Laws, although amended, were not yet to be repealed.

Recovery in 1823 stilled urban discontent, although agriculture was still depressed and rural protest continued to simmer. The easing of urban tension raised the question of the repeal of the Combination Acts, that had been introduced in the attempt to suppress the radical agitation at the end of the eighteenth century. Political economists believed that trades unions could not increase the general level of wages, but could only benefit one group of workers at the expense of others. However most of them followed Smith in believing that moderate trades unionism could enhance competition by redressing the imbalance of power between workers and unscrupulous employers and establishing more uniform wage rates. More to the point, as far as the government was concerned, the Combination Acts had not suppressed trades unions but merely driven them underground, and into the arms of radical agitators. Thus the repeal of the Combination Acts in 1824 was above all an attempt to separate legitimate trades union activity from illegitimate political agitation. The hope that trades unions would simply disappear once they were legalised, as some political economists had predicted, was soon shattered. The rapid growth of trades unions in the boom led to further legislation in 1825 that severely restricted trade union rights.

The recovery of 1823 precipitated the first modern cycle of boom and slump. The boom was sustained by the expansion of credit by the Bank of England despite an unfavourable turn in the balance of payments, rising domestic prices and pressure on the exchanges. The boom spilled over into speculation on the stock exchange, particularly in foreign investments. The Bank of England eventually began to contract credit to restore the exchanges, but only to precipitate a crisis as the scarcity of credit undermined the solvency of traders and speculators, leading to the failure of around seventy London and country banks. The Bank of England had to step in to save the financial system from collapse, lending freely to provide liquidity to commerce and the banking system, which survived the crisis by the skin of its teeth. Nevertheless the crisis led to a wave of bankruptcies of productive and commercial capitalists who had traded on credit, and a collapse of trade and of prices.

The crisis led to renewed agitation from domestic farmers and manufacturers, who again blamed the Bank of England's contraction of the currency and the government's liberalisation policies for the crisis. Other critics blamed the crisis on the earlier overexpansion of the currency by the Bank. It was Ricardo's political economy that came worst out of the crisis, having to shoulder the blame for the full range of policies that it had inspired. The Bank of England successfully passed the buck to the country banks. The Bank's position was reflected in the restriction on the note issue of the country banks and in the Bank Charter Act of 1826, which permitted the establishment of joint-stock banks outside London and encouraged the Bank of England to set up provincial branches.

Although the Bank resisted the demands of its critics, the crisis did mark a quiet change in the policy of the Bank of England, although it was not publicly acknowledged, modifying the old orthodoxy of the real bills doctrine and partially adopting the policy that had been advocated by Ricardo of regulating the currency in accordance with the flow of gold. In stimulating the overexpansion in the boom the Bank had followed its old policy of meeting the 'legitimate demands of commerce', despite the weakening of the exchanges. In its move to contract the currency, however, the Bank had restricted credit in response to an outflow of gold, as advocated by the Ricardian theory. On the other hand, when the crisis broke the demand for gold was precipitated by domestic failures, the exchanges having already reached a balance, and the bank responded by expanding credit again to meet the needs of commerce. Thus it followed a Ricardian policy in response to a foreign drain of gold, but an accommodating policy in response to a domestic drain.

Although the banking system was stabilised in the wake of the crisis, the depression continued, particularly in agricultural districts, stimulating a renewal of political agitation. In previous depressions recovery had followed slump relatively rapidly, and had curtailed the growth of agitation. This time, however, recovery was only modest and patchy, and the pressure for reform steadily built up. The issues that lay behind the upsurge of protest were diverse, and the substantive demands of different interests were mutually contradictory, but the various strands came together over the issue of Parliamentary reform, to destroy the political monopoly of a narrow elite of landowners and financiers who subordinated their political duties to their own interests.

Political economy and constitutional reform

Political economy played a limited role in the reform agitation. Although political economists tended to be politically liberal, and to have democratic inclinations, they were not over-concerned about constitutional issues. The important consideration was that the country should have good government, and good government could be achieved within a variety of constitutional arrangements. Thus David Hume and Adam Smith had paid much less attention to the definition of particular constitutional arrangements than had earlier legal and political theorists, tempering any liberal zeal with an almost Burkean concern with the dangers of tampering with established institutions.

This was the context within which political economists approached the reform of the constitution. Although good government would tend to require a constitution with a strong democratic component to check the power of the state, the reform of the franchise was a pragmatic matter. As Ricardo had observed reassuringly, the bourgeoisie did not seek the extension of the franchise for its own sake, but only as a means to securing the good government that seemed unattainable within the existing constitution. 'It is not Universal Suffrage as an end, but as a means of good government that the partisans of that measure ask it for'.[5]

Above all else good government required the freedom and security of property. While the widest possible franchise is desirable to ensure that as many people as possible are able to defend their rights, popular ignorance, greed and envy might dispose the poorer majority of the population to abuse their numerical strength and use the state to attack property, whether by expropriation or taxation. This problem later came to be discussed euphemistically in terms of the problem of the 'tyranny of the majority', or of the 'oppression of the minority by the majority', but in the 1830s was addressed more frankly.

With a population enlightened by the truths of political economy a universal franchise would hold no fears. However the condition of the working class was such that most feared that emotion would get the better of intelligence, a fear that was confirmed not only by political radicalism but also by the popular enthusiasm for inflationism, the relief of distress and protection. Thus all but the most optimistic political economists believed that the franchise had to be restricted by a more or less stringent property qualification. Political economy could reconcile the democratic form of the constitution with its undemocratic content on the basis of its demonstration that the freedom and security of property not only served the common interest, but also the individual interest of every member of society. Since the theory of political economy established that the working class had no distinct interest, it had

---

[5] *The Works and Correspondence of David Ricardo*, (P. Sraffa ed.), Cambridge University Press, 1951, vol. V, p. 501.

no particular need for independent political representation. By the same token women had no need of independent representation since their interests were adequately represented by their fathers and husbands.

By 1832 agitation for reform had become almost irresistible, and the increasingly radical turn taken by the agitation as it mobilised the working class led Parliament to relent for fear of worse. When reform came in 1832 the franchise was extended as little as was consistent with the aspirations of the bourgeoisie. Indeed the 1832 reform was significant more for its reform of constituency boundaries than for its extension of the franchise, which in the more democratic constituencies was contracted. In 1831 3.8 per cent of the population over the age of 20 were enfranchised, in 1833 the proportion had risen to only 5.9 per cent.[6] Thus the 1832 Reform Bill did not transfer power from one class to another, but rather broadened the basis of representation of the capitalist class as the big capital of land, finance and commerce was persuaded by the threat of popular radicalism to admit the smaller capital of farming and manufacturing to a subordinate share in the constitution.

The 1832 Reform Bill settled the constitutional question for a time, but it did not resolve the substantive issues that lay behind the reform agitation. Although the various sections of the reform movement made common cause over the constitutional issue, their policy aspirations conflicted with one another, so that once represented in Parliament they did not come together to form a coherent opposition, but ranged themselves on either side of the established divisions, while the limited extension of the franchise ensured that the more radical demands of the working class and smaller farmers and manufacturers remained largely unrepresented. In fact the class composition of the House of Commons hardly changed at all, while reform left the power of the aristocracy entrenched in the Lords. The continuation of open balloting until 1872, and extensive corruption in elections, reduced but not eliminated by the Act of 1854, helped to keep Parliamentary representation in 'responsible hands', and sovereignty was still felt to lie with Parliament rather than the people. However governments had to become more responsive to the opinion of the electorate, and party organisation became more important, both inside and outside Parliament. Thus

---

[6] Peter Flora et al. , *State, Economy and Society in Western Europe 1815–75*, Macmillan, London, 1983, p. 149.

the 1832 reform ensured that henceforth the bourgeoisie would settle its differences within the constitution, united in the defence of its common class interests by the common threat of a growing working class movement.

The reformed state and economic regulation

The growing complexity of the problems facing the government, and the programme of administrative and financial reform after 1832, brought political economists into the centre of government, giving them an unprecedented opportunity to put their programme into practice. The great exponents of laissez faire in mid-Victorian Britain were centrally involved in government, as civil servants, members of Royal Commissions, and Members of Parliament.

The 1832 Reform Bill divided the reform movement, isolating the more radical elements, led by Cobbett and Attwood, who had demanded currency reform and the relief of distress. Far from meeting their demands, the reformed Parliament immediately passed the 1833 Bank Charter Act, that strengthened the grip of the Bank of England, and set in motion the reform of the Poor Laws.

Political economy had expressed the opposition of capitalists to the old Poor Laws ever since Adam Smith. The Poor Laws restricted the mobility of labour and subsidised wages, stimulating the growth of population, undermining the competitiveness of the labour market, devaluing the virtues of prudence and frugality, and eroding the incentive to work. The growing cost of the Poor Laws had made reform inevitable, but reform was resisted not only by the working class, but also by the agricultural interests for whom it secured a supply of cheap labour, and provided the institutional form through which they could maintain the paternalistic relationships on which their authority rested.

By 1832 there were few political economists who still favoured the complete abolition of the Poor Laws. Growing working class agitation made it clear that moral education, supplemented by charitable provision for the deserving poor, would be insufficient to suppress discontent. The alternative to the Poor Law was not so much education as the militia. Thus Nassau Senior, who played a leading role in the reform of the Poor Law, was ready to modify the dogmas of political economy in the light of pragmatic political considerations. The 1834 Poor Law Amendment Act was a compromise between the conflicting interests. However Senior ensured that the new Poor Law was so constructed as to impede as little as possible the operation of the labour market. The abolition of outdoor relief, the workhouse test, and the principle of 'less eligibility' were designed to ensure that recourse to the Poor Law was a last resort.

The first years of the reformed Parliament were years of industrial, but not agricultural, prosperity that quietened radical agitation, although not resistance to the implementation of the new Poor Law, particularly in the North. The course of the boom and subsequent crash closely mirrored that of the cycle ten years earlier, with the Bank of England fuelling the boom until balance of payments pressures led it to a mild restriction of credit, which precipitated a commercial crisis. Although the financial crisis of 1839 was not as severe as a decade earlier, the depression was worse as exports failed to recover and agriculture suffered a series of bad harvests.

The depression of 1839–41 stimulated a renewal of political agitation. The disparate strands of popular protest were united around the issue of the vote, expressed in the Charter drawn up in 1838, which provided the basis for popular agitation for the following decade. The demand for the vote was not an abstract demand for political rights, but the means to overthrow a constitution that still institutionalised the power of money, land and the established church. Chartism was a revolutionary working class movement in the sense that it confronted the state as the institutionalised power of the capitalist class, but the main thrust of Chartism did not lie in the mobilisation of an industrial proletariat against its employers, for the industrial proletariat was still only a minority of the working class as a whole. Although Chartist agitation in the Northern industrial towns was directed against the power of the employers, the power of capital was more generally identified with the power of land and of money.

The fact that Chartism built on the established rhetoric of radicalism and did not, on the whole, attack the employers directly meant that it could incorporate not only the radical petit bourgeoisie, but even small employers, often burdened by debt and unable to secure credit, who shared its opposition to the power of the bankers. However the increasingly revolutionary radicalism of Chartism no longer appealed to the bulk of the bourgeoisie, who looked for alternative solutions, both for their own grievances and for the economic instability that produced distress and fuelled the radicalism that threatened their own relatively privileged position. The liberal reforms of the 1840s, in response to the agitation of the Anti-Corn Law League, successfully detached the middle class from the more radical demands Chartism, culminating in the enthusiastic mobilisation of the middle class against the Chartist threat in 1848.

The currency issue was raised again by the need to renew the Charter of the Bank of England. Far from strengthening pressure for a discretionary policy of free credit, radical agitation increased fears of inflationism and ensured that it was the conservative doctrines of the 'Currency School', derived from Ricardo, that prevailed.

The Currency School saw cyclical fluctuations, that were the source of the waves of distress and disorder, as the result of financial instability that derived from the excessive discretion accorded to the Bank of England in the regulation of the currency. The over-issue of the currency in times of prosperity stimulated over-trading and speculation that could only be checked by a bout of depression. The solution was to insist that the Bank should be constrained to regulate the currency so that it operated exactly as would a metallic currency by restricting its issue to the size of its reserves of gold. This principle would remove the discretionary element from the Bank's monetary policies and prevent the emergence of cyclical fluctuations. Inflationary expansion which precipitated a drain on the Bank's gold reserves would provoke an automatic contraction of the currency until prices fell sufficiently to restore equilibrium. The Currency School was opposed by the 'Banking School', which favoured a greater degree of discretion. However the Banking School did not represent the demands of popular radicalism so much as the old banking orthodoxy, that had by now been abandoned even by the Bank of England.

The economists of the Banking School argued that the rigid regulation of the money supply would at best be unnecessary and ineffective. They insisted that an outflow of gold frequently arose from exceptional causes, such as a bad harvest, investment flows, or the disruption of foreign trade, that would be self-correcting.

To contract the currency in such circumstances would merely exaggerate the difficulties to no useful purpose. They also argued that variations in the currency had only a very indirect impact on prices, and often at the cost of considerable disruption. On the one hand, they noted that private banks had considerable latitude in the cash ratios that they maintained so could easily expand credit even when the note issue was contracting and vice versa. On the other hand, if the contraction of the currency did feed through to the contraction of credit it would only produce a fall in prices by precipitating a severe contraction of trade. The conclusion of the Banking School was that, so long as convertibility of the currency is maintained, an over-issue is impossible because circulation will only absorb banknotes to the extent that they are required to maintain circulation. The faults lay not in the orthodox principles of banking, but in the administration of those principles by the Bank of England.

The victory of the Currency School was sealed in the Bank Charter Act of 1844 which separated the banking from the issuing functions of the Bank, the confusion of which was in the past felt to have contributed to instability. The Issue Department was entitled to issue notes against securities up to £14m (the fiduciary issue) and in addition against any bullion that it might hold, buying gold and paying notes on demand at a fixed price. This ensured that the note issue would vary strictly within limits set by the flow of gold. The Banking Department was then freed from regulation, to conduct the normal banking business of taking deposits, discounting bills and extending loans. The Bank itself strongly favoured the measure not least because it freed it from responsibility for the discretionary regulation of the currency, and so from responsibility for monetary disturbances, while also freeing its banking activity from restraint. The 1844 Act continued to regulate the activity of the Bank of England until 1914.

Monetary reform might free commerce from monetary disturbances, but it could not deal with the more fundamental problem of limited export markets. Falling export prices and successive trade crises had led to increasingly insistent demands from the export trades for trade liberalisation, culminating in the formation of the Anti-Corn Law League in 1839, which was the precursor of modern popular politics in mobilising public opinion to exert political pressure within the constitution.

The issue of free trade was fundamental because, while exporters found no shortage of foreign demand for their products, their prices undercutting those of small domestic producers, foreign customers lacked the means to purchase them because their own, predominantly agricultural, products were excluded from British markets by protective tariffs. Moreover the absence of return cargoes increased shipping costs. This problem was particularly acute because the absence of developed financial institutions and stable currencies in Britain's main markets was a barrier to the stimulation of trade by the extension of credit and by foreign investment, which had repeatedly been checked by financial crises. Thus foreigners could only purchase British goods with the proceeds of their own exports, usually represented by bills of exchange drawn on London. Tariff barriers to the penetration of European and United States markets were of less immediate significance, but the fear remained that if Britain persisted with protection foreigners would retaliate by erecting further barriers of their own.

The Corn Laws were the focus of agitation, and of resistance, because they most closely affected the interests of the landed class, but the demand for trade liberalisation extended to all protective tariffs, and, through the Anti-Corn Law League, was further associated with the full range of liberal reformist demands. By the 1840s the Corn Laws had become more a symbol than an effective measure in support of domestic agriculture. The government's reluctance to liberalise trade for fear of losing revenue was soon overcome as tariff reductions were followed by such a growth of trade as hardly to affect revenues. Thus through the 1840s protection was progressively removed, culminating in the repeal of the Navigation Acts in 1849. Tariff reform was supplemented by war and diplomacy to open up the markets of Asia and to check Russian expansionism. The navy maintained the security of property on the high seas, and the gunboat in distant lands while the established colonies served as strategic bases for the maintenance of the Pax Britannica.

The administrative reform of the state

The principles of political economy were not limited in their application to the role of the state in the regulation of the banking system and in securing the freedom of trade. Political economy, allied with utilitarianism, also played a central role in the renewed bout of legal, administrative and financial reforms after 1840 that were designed to reduce the element of arbitrariness and discretion in the application of the law and the administration of government.

The unreformed state had institutionalised the power of the landed class, on the basis of its exclusive claim to represent the general interest in its attachment to the order and tranquility of society. The 1832 Reform Bill allowed other propertied interests to take their place alongside the landed interest, which thereby became merely one interest among others. However the 1832 Reform did nothing to change the administrative apparatus of the state, which remained in the hands of those of rank and property, through which they exercised their powers in their own interests. Although the Municipal Corporations Act of 1835 extended the principles of 1832 to the major towns, the powers it gave them were limited, the only requirement being to institute watch committees to supervise the police. Most local administration continued to be in the hands of the justices and of a proliferation of ad hoc local authorities, subject to little supervision or control, and exercising a considerable degree of discretion. Central government had few powers. Recruitment to the administration was still based on patronage, and administrative procedures were largely ad hoc. The system of taxation and borrowing had been regularised in the eighteenth century, to meet the financial needs of war, but there was no centralised system of control of government finances, taxes going directly to spending departments. Even the elementary step of the separation of public from private funds and the introduction of rigorous accounting for public money had only been introduced in the 1780s.

The task of the reform of government administration and finance was to transform the state from the tool of a particular class, exercising arbitrary powers within a discretionary framework, into the institutionalised representative of the general interest, imposing its authority on all particular interests on the basis of the rigorous separation of public from private powers. The general principles of reform were defined by utilitarianism, but it was political economy that gave these principles their substantive content.

For political economy the general interest was not identified with any particular interest, nor was it the sum of particular interests. The general interest was represented exclusively by the rule of law and of money which secured the formal freedom and equality of property and of exchange. In principle the powers of the state were limited to the administration of justice and the defence of the realm, which required only the establishment of the rule of law, of proper systems of taxation, and the proper regulation of the issue of the currency. However pragmatic considerations soon led political economists to recognise the need for more extensive intervention of the government, particularly in the areas of public health, education, the Poor Law, and, reluctantly, factory legislation. The task was to develop appropriate legal, administrative and financial forms through which the state could exercise its increasingly extensive powers.

The essential principles of public administration developed by utilitarianism were based on the analogy of the market, regulated by the abstract powers of money and the law. The formal equality of the market ensured that its rule applied equally to all citizens and, in that sense, was predictable. Where public administration was required to replace or supplement the rule of the market it should similarly apply equally to all citizens and be predictable in its impact. This implied the reduction to a minimum of the scope for political and administrative discretion in public administration. The ideal form of administrative intervention was not the exercise of power by public officials, but the rigid and impartial application of law and administrative regulation, subject to financial control and judicial review.

When the primary role of law and public administration had been to sanction the powers of particular forms of property, the class character of the judiciary and of the administration was essential to its role. However the increasingly active use of legislation as a means of government administration, which implied the subordination of particular powers to the abstract power of property in the form of money, meant that the discretion of public officers had to be checked by bringing them more effectively under the rule of law. This was attempted by the streamlining and strengthening of the courts that got under way in the 1830s, providing easier access to the law and a check on the capriciousness of the magistracy, and by the progressive separation of law and public administration that was pioneered in the administration of the New Poor Law. However the 'independence' of the judiciary, that was essential to its proper functioning, presented a constant barrier to the attempt to rationalise the rule of law, while the independence of public administration rapidly increased the scope for administrative discretion.

The judiciary had a dual role to play in the exercise of public authority. On the one hand, the judiciary was required to enforce the exercise of public power sanctioned by the law. On the other hand, the law was required to check administrative discretion by confining public power within the law. The former role brought the judiciary into play as an agent of the state, the latter role brought it into play as an independent check on the power of the state. These dual roles could only be fulfilled if the judiciary and the magistracy were independent of all particular interests and popular pressures, on the one hand, and independent of the state, on the other. The independence of the judiciary from popular pressure could only be secured by the recruitment of the judiciary and the magistracy from a very narrow social stratum, and its independence from the state could only be secured by its self-recruitment, which meant that the judiciary and the magistracy tended to be a self-perpetuating elite drawn from persons of rank and status. Cloaking the gentry and the younger sons of the aristocracy in the majesty of the law could not conceal their class origins or the class interests that they represented. Thus the 'independence' of the judiciary reinforced the class character of the state, but at the same time presented a barrier to its rationalisation. The same contradiction underlay the continuation of similar patterns of recruitment of the military and civil service and of local officials, and the protection of military expenditure and administrative activity from Parliamentary scrutiny and control.

Although the appropriate administrative form of the state was that of a strictly regulated and publicly accountable apparatus, whose powers derived from Parliamentary legislation, for the utilitarians and political economists Parliament was not usually the best body to draw up the rules and regulations in question, although it obviously had to approve relevant legislation and receive regular reports. The issues were frequently complicated technical issues, that required expert judgement and the evaluation of a wealth of evidence. Thus the Royal Commission began to replace the Parliamentary Select Committee as the forum within which detailed policy debate took place after 1830, while the formulation and implementation of policy was placed increasingly in the

hands of various Boards, out of which eventually developed a professional civil service. Although the new forms of administration
were gradually brought under Parliamentary control through the
mechanism of ministerial responsibility, Parliament had neither the
information nor the expertise to evaluate their activity.

The independence of the administration from Parliament was
also necessary if policies that served the general interest were to
prevail against the obstructionism of vested interests and private
prejudice. Political economy and utilitarianism offered a scientific
basis on which to evaluate policy proposals, and so legitimated the
evaluation, development and implementation of policies by experts,
out of the gaze of Parliament or the public. For example state provision for education, that was of central importance for political
economy, was bedevilled by the religious question, so that Parliament was completely by-passed in the early development of public
education. The Education Board was set up without reference to
Parliament, so had no statutory powers at all, although in practice it wielded considerable power because it administered grants-
in-aid. Similarly Chadwick used his administrative position and
political contacts to campaign long and hard against determined
Parliamentary and local opposition for the 1848 Public Health Act,
which only scraped through Parliament on the back of the cholera
scare.

The absence of any centralised system of financial accounting
and control before the last third of the nineteenth century, and
the lack of any centralised bureaucratic apparatus outside the military, meant that administration initially took the form of legal
regulation rather than bureaucratic hierarchy. The ideal form of
administration, pioneered by the administration of the New Poor
Law, was that in which a Central Board laid down the general
principles of administration to ensure rationality, uniformity and
efficiency and, through an inspectorate, superintended their implementation by local Boards, the unavoidable discretionary element
of whose activity was in the hands of elected local representatives,
so by-passing the Justices. The principle of imposing the cost of
each policy as directly as possible on its beneficiaries dictated that
each agency should have its own revenue raising powers, usually
through local rates, which also had the desirable consequence of
limiting expenditure strictly to the capacity to raise the requisite
revenue. Expenditure of national, rather than purely local, signif-

icance was assisted by central government grants, which provided
scope for greater leverage from the centre.

In practice things did not work out as simply as this, and the
first attempts to establish a rational and uniform system of public
administration had limited success. Issues that the reformers considered to be technical, were deemed by others to be intensely political, while the entrenched power of vested interests, masquerading
as the independence of the judiciary and of local administration,
presented formidable barriers to reform. Resistance to central direction meant that legislation tended to be permissive rather than
obligatory, implementation being left largely to local initiative. The
limited financial and administrative resources of the central Boards
prevented them from enforcing their policies on local authorities,
which remained largely in the hands of the locally powerful who retained a considerable degree of discretion. In practice the Boards
could often do little more than use their reports to bring problems to public attention and to propose remedies. More effective
intervention could only be achieved on the basis of political centralisation, and the development of appropriate forms of bureaucratic
administrative and financial control. However concerted opposition
from vested interests delayed the development of such a centralised
system of public administration until the last third of the nineteenth century.

The limitations of legal regulation and the rationalisation of
the structure of public administration implied the professionalisation and bureaucratisation of the civil service. Professionalisation
and the development of appropriate bureaucratic procedures took
place in some departments, most notably the Board of Trade, from
the 1820s. The new Boards, pioneered by Benthamite reformers,
similarly sought to develop efficient administrative procedures as
they were established. However the core of the civil service continued to be run on the administrative principles of the eighteenth
century, with recruitment based on patronage and political reliability rather than administrative competence. The inefficiency and
incompetence of the old-established departments was brought dramatically to public attention with the debacle of the Crimean War,
which brought the issue of professionalisation and recruitment to
a head.

The basis of reform was the Northcote-Trevelyan Report of
1853, which recommended recruitment and promotion on merit

within a hierarchical bureaucratic form of administration. However recruitment on merit by no means implied abandoning the class base of the civil service. Indeed for Gladstone 'one of the great recommendations of the change in my eyes would be its tendency to strengthen and multiply the ties between the higher classes and the possession of administrative power', and in response to the fear that competitive entry, finally introduced in 1870, would be dominated by the products of 'Eton, Harrow, Rugby and the public schools', he argued that the superior natural gifts and acquired advantages of the aristocracy, 'irrespective of book learning', would ensure their 'immense superiority'. The whole point of the reform was to separate the work of the administration 'into mechanical and intellectual, a separation which will open to the highly educated class a career and give them a command over all the higher parts of the civil service, which up to this time they have never enjoyed'.[7] In fact the reforms did broaden the class base of the civil service slightly, to include the professional middle class which had fully proved its political reliability in 1848.

The rationalisation of the law and of public administration was accompanied by a rationalisation of public finance. The fundamental principle was that public expenditure, with very few exceptions, was unproductive. This expenditure could only be financed by drawing on the net product of society that comprised profits, interest and rent, which was also the principal source of savings and investment. If savings, and so future prosperity, were not to be undermined the state had to minimise its expenditure by limiting the scope of its activity and the cost of its administration. This consideration gave added weight to the preference for legal rather than bureaucratic forms of administrative regulation.

All public expenditure should be financed out of current taxation, and taxes levied according to the principles laid down by Adam Smith. If taxes did not meet expenditure the government would have to have recourse to borrowing. However borrowing was undesirable for a number of reasons. Firstly, borrowing drew on the public's savings, directly diverting resources from productive investment to unproductive public use. Secondly, borrowing was not a substitute for taxation, but merely deferred the imposition of taxes that would have to be levied in the future to meet the

---

[7] Letter to Lord John Russell, quoted Valerie Cromwell, *Revolution or Evolution*, Longman, London, 1977, pp. 139–40.

increasing burden of interest payments, that already made up a large proportion of central government expenditure. Thirdly, there was a fear that in an emergency, particularly a war, it would be difficult to raise funds if there was a large burden of outstanding debt. Fourthly, recourse to borrowing put the government in the hands of the City. For these reasons it was believed that honest and prudent governments should aim at least to balance the annual budget, and preferably to budget for a surplus to repay the accumulated national debt. Despite these strictures the outstanding debt served an important stabilising role by providing a safe, 'gilt-edged', investment that provided the measure against which riskier investments had to justify themselves. Moreover it gave the government, through the Bank of England, some leverage in financial markets that was increasingly used as the means of implementing its monetary policies from the 1870s.

These principles of public finance had already been generally accepted by the end of the eighteenth century, although the demands of war made frequent recourse to borrowing necessary. However peacetime borrowing was scorned, and the doctrine of the balanced budget became the prime test of the moral virtue of the government. The result was that servicing the debt accounted for 40 per cent of general government expenditure in 1790, rising to over 50 per cent in 1815, and then gradually falling to 42 per cent in 1840, 18 per cent in 1890 and 7 per cent in 1910, before the First World War increased borrowing dramatically. Moreover the doctrine of the balanced budget was not merely a moral exhortation, it was seen as an essential part of the constitution itself, policed by the financial markets that followed Smith in regarding increased public borrowing as the first stage on the road to financial ruin, to be inexorably followed by debasement of the currency and national bankruptcy.

The need to finance wartime expenditure meant that an appropriate system of government borrowing was established relatively early. It took much longer to establish control over the system of revenue and expenditure, without which proper government budgeting was impossible. Taxation had largely been brought under government control during the eighteenth century, as tax farming was replaced by central government collection. However it was not until 1846 that central control was fully established with all taxes being paid into a central fund, rather than going directly to spending departments. It took still longer to bring expenditure, particularly of the defence departments, under control. In the end it was Gladstone who was the architect of the system through which the principles of political economy could be rigorously applied to the regulation of the public finances. The establishment of the Department of Exchequer and Audit in 1861 and the Public Accounts Committee of the House of Commons in 1866 were the twin pillars of administrative and political control, regulating and accounting for the flow of revenue and expenditure through the central Consolidated Fund on a continuous basis. It was only with the establishment of this regular system of accounting and financial control that government departments could be made properly accountable for their expenditure, according to the government's spending and revenue plans and projections laid down in the annual Budget and Financial Statement. It was not surprising, therefore, that individual spending departments should fight long and hard against such control. Although the Treasury had got the upper hand by the First World War, the battle continues to be fought out year by year.

The reconstruction of the state was not associated with a substantial increase in the functions of the state, the size of the administration or the levels of its expenditure. Before the 1860s local resistance to administrative centralisation meant that central government had acquired few direct administrative responsibilities. Apart from the post office, the direct responsibilities of central government did not go far beyond its responsibility for the judiciary and the military, and even where it was active, it had very few resources to implement its policies. In 1848 the Home Office, ultimately responsible, among other things, for the Factory Inspectorate, the Police and the Poor Laws, employed 24 clerks.[8]

The expansion in government administration occurred through the proliferation of local bodies, established under general or local legislation. At the same time as central government employed 29,900 civil servants, the majority in Customs and Excise (as compared with 198,000 in military service), there were about 80,000 local authorities of one kind or another.[9] The proliferation of lo-

---

[8] Gillian Sutherland, ed., *Studies in the Growth of Nineteenth Century Government*, RKP, London, 1972, p. 85.

[9] Flora et al. , op. cit. ; David Roberts, *The Victorian Origins of the British Welfare State*, Yale University Press, New Haven, 1960.

cal bodies was accompanied by a proliferation of local rates and charges, levied according to Smith's principle that the beneficiaries of a service should meet its costs. The lack of effective central supervision, and the cumbersome and partial exercise of legal regulation meant that local bodies could exercise very considerable discretion. Progressive Municipal Corporations achieved some rationalisation of local authorities, and introduced wide-ranging municipal improvements in public health, roads, housing, education and public utilities under general and local legislation. However all such initiatives came up against the barrier of vested interests, which in many cases were sufficient to keep the activity of the local administration to a minimum.

When it comes to the administrative activity of the state the astonishing thing is how little change there was in the relative size and distribution of state expenditure, and in the essential duties undertaken by the state throughout the nineteenth century. In 1790 general government expenditure accounted for 12 per cent of GDP, in 1840 it still accounted for 12 per cent, and in 1890 was down to 9 per cent. Even in absolute terms general government expenditure only increased from £23m in 1790 to £131m in 1890. If we leave debt service out of account, about half of government expenditure throughout the nineteenth century was devoted to the defence of the realm and the defence of property, the first two duties that Smith defined for the state. Apart from general administration, the next largest components of public expenditure were education, the third of Smith's essential duties of the state in maintaining the rule of property, and poor relief, which Smith decried, but which was equally a method of maintaining the necessary relations of authority and subordination. In its functions the state conformed closely to Smith's prescription throughout the nineteenth century, as it largely had in the eighteenth.

Although the functions of the state had not changed, there had been fundamental changes in the form of the state, based on the growing separation of the state from civil society, that considerably increased the power of government. Whereas the state in the eighteenth century had little relevance to the mass of the population, by the mid-nineteenth century they were embraced by a web of regulation that was still locally administered, but that was under increasingly rigorous central supervision and control. The paradox is resolved when it is realised that the power of the national state was exercised primarily through legal regulation, not through bureaucratic forms of administration. Thus John Stuart Mill could still contest, in 1862, the argument that increasing state intervention was 'an unavoidable consequence and indisputable instrument of progress' on the grounds that increased intervention had tended to take the form of new legislation, rather than 'discretionary authority, still less control'.[10]

The separation of the state from civil society, and the subordination of private to public power, did not imply that the state had assumed a role of supreme power as the central regulating agency. The need to ensure that rational policy-making was subordinated to the general interest and not subverted by self-interest, ignorance, irresponsibility or emotion informed the whole framework of constitutional, legal, financial and administrative reform. For political economy the role of the state was strictly subordinate to the roles of the law and of money in regulating social reproduction. The subordination of the state to the law and to money was institutionalised in the form of the state. The law served to check the arbitrary and discretionary exercise of state power. Political resistance to taxation, the discipline of financial markets, and the 1844 Bank Act all ensured that the government would be forced to keep public expenditure within proper limits. The need to sustain its revenues ensured that the government had an interest in the expansion of trade that, through customs and excise, provided the primary source of its revenue. The need to finance its borrowing ensured that the government had an interest in the stability and growth of financial markets. The need to meet its financial obligations ensured that it had an interest in maintaining the integrity of the currency. If this was not sufficient, the property franchise and the class basis of recruitment to the civil service, the military and the judiciary, and their protection from parliamentary control, ensured that state power would be in the hands of those who had the greatest interest in maintaining the rule of law and in limiting the ambition of the state. In short the separation of the state from civil society in no sense implied that the state stood above civil society as an independent power. However the limits on the power of the state were not limits set by particular interests or political factions, but were limits set by the abstract and universal power of the law

---

[10] John Stuart Mill, 'Centralisation', *Collected Works*, University of Toronto Press, Toronto, 1977, vol. XIX, p. 601.

and of money, by the constitution, and by the class character of recruitment to the administration.

The mid-Victorian boom

The implementation of the programme of political economy from the 1840s proved rather more successful than had been the early attempts at liberalisation in the 1820s. The 'hungry forties' was a decade of financial instability, widespread depression and mass starvation, insurrection and revolution, but gave way in the 1850s to the mid-Victorian boom. The boom was not a period of unbroken prosperity and social peace, but the contrast with the forties was startling. The continued cyclical form of boom and slump remained the one blot on the copybook of political economy.

The 1844 Bank Act was supposed to have removed the source of economic fluctuations. However things did not work out quite so smoothly in practice. A slow recovery from the crash of 1842 quickened with the railways boom in the middle of the decade, which fed growing speculation in railway shares on the stock exchange. The boom broke in 1845 in the wake of poor harvests and deteriorating export prospects, with the consequent drain of bullion and rising interest rates. However continuing investment in the railways as a result of previous speculative promotions sustained the economy until 1847, when a major financial crisis led to widespread bankruptcies. The crash focused attention yet again on the Bank of England.

The separation of its banking from its issue business under the 1844 Act had left the Bank of England free to conduct its banking business as though it were an ordinary commercial bank, so it had continued to feed the speculative boom by pursuing an increasingly aggressive discount policy, even when the exchanges became unfavourable. Eventually the drain on the reserves led the Bank to raise Bank Rate sharply and to contract its discounts, putting strong pressure on commerce. The crisis broke in October 1847, when the collapse of corn prices following an abundant harvest led to the bankruptcy of corn speculators, which spread to the banks that had financed the speculators, and then to the foreign trading companies who had maintained unfavourable positions by the heavy use of accommodation credit, finally leading to a run on the

Bank of England which was only checked when the government offered to suspend the restrictions of the Bank Act.

The crash appeared to vindicate the Banking School's insistence on the distinction between money and credit. The boom had been stimulated not by the over-issue of the currency, but by the over-expansion of bank credit that had been facilitated by the Bank's discount policy. The crash had been precipitated, just as the Banking School had warned, not by a drain on the currency reserves, but by a liquidity crisis in the banking system which led to a drain on the reserves of the Banking Department. This criticism was implicitly accepted by the Bank, which increasingly acted in crises as lender of last resort, keeping out of the discount market in a boom, but making accommodation available to maintain the liquidity of the banking system in a recession, although the Bank's obligations in this respect were not acknowledged until the 1870s. Thus the crisis was not seen as undermining the principles of monetary regulation embodied in the 1844 Act, but only as demonstrating the need for the Bank to have regard to the monetary consequences of its credit policies. In addition the crisis indicated the need for the Bank to increase the size of its gold reserves, so giving still greater importance to the expansion of exports made possible by the liberalisation of trade and fostered by aggressive commercial policies on the part of the government.

The depression that followed the crisis was very uneven in its impact. The lag between projection and construction meant that railway construction, and the related coal, iron and engineering industries, were sustained through the depression, but the export trades were severely depressed. Chartism, which had lost momentum during the economic recovery in the middle of the decade, showed renewed vigour, but was met, as before, with intense repression. Moreover the divisions within Chartism between the class-based demands of the industrial proletariat and the popular radicalism that was the basis of the wider appeal of Chartism increasingly undermined the unity of the movement.

The recovery from depression was faster and more dramatic than anyone could have anticipated. However recovery was not based on the traditional export trade of cotton, but on the international expansion of the railways, compounded by the demands of the Crimean War. While domestic railway construction continued at a reduced pace, investment in railways abroad, and particularly

in North America, provided an outlet for idle capital and stimulated an unprecedented boom in world trade, based, as far as
Britain was concerned, on the growth in exports of coal, iron, machinery and railway equipment and on the growth in imports of
food and raw materials. The railways in turn opened up new areas
as markets for manufactured goods and as sources of supply of food
and raw materials, stimulating the growth of shipbuilding and an
export boom that sustained the traditional export industries and
that opened up new opportunities. Although railway products provided a relatively small proportion of the increases in production
and trade, there is no doubt that the railways played the pivotal
role in breaking through the barriers of overproduction that had
regularly halted the traditional export industries in their tracks by
opening up export markets, the growth of which closely followed
the construction of railways. The growth of international trade
and investment stimulated the growth of British shipping and of
the financial institutions that provided the credit, finance, insurance and means of payment that increasingly made London the
financial centre of the world.

The boom in the early 1850s, associated with foreign railway
investment and the Crimean War, eventually broke in Europe in
1856 and in America in 1857, where bank failures spread rapidly to
Britain and led to a run on the Bank of England, which required
the suspension of the Bank Act to allow the reserves of the Issue
Department to support the Banking Department. The revival of
trade and investment at the end of the 1850s initiated the recovery. Although the American Civil War initially created financial
difficulties, and led to an acute shortage of cotton, the financial
problems were soon overcome and with the fall in interest rates
a new speculative investment boom was underway. This time the
crash, in 1866, could not be blamed on the unsound practices of foreign bankers, for it was one of the greatest of the London discount
houses, Overend, Gurney & Co, that failed. The Bank of England
again survived the subsequent run by the skin of its teeth, thanks
to the now traditional Treasury Letter offering indemnity against
breaking the Bank Act. Although the willingness of the Bank to
lend freely prevented the crisis from bringing down the banking
system, high rates of interest delayed recovery and created difficulties for commerce and industry, and particularly for shipbuilding,
before recovery eventually got underway with the greatest of all

the Victorian booms that lasted from 1869 to 1873.

The mid-Victorian boom was attributed by the bourgeoisie to the liberalisation of trade within a framework of sound money and finance. Growing prosperity in industry and agriculture seemed to extend to all classes of the population and appeared as the perfect vindication of bourgeois faith in the simple truths of political economy and in the virtues of thrift, frugality and self-improvement. However the liberalisation of trade played a relatively minor role in the boom. It was not the freeing of market forces that had stimulated the boom, but the massive investment in the railways. Moreover the surge of railway investment was not stimulated by the pressure of market forces, but by the successive waves of speculative mania that led to the construction of railways with little regard to any demand for improved methods of transport.

Railway promotions were stimulated by the prospect of speculative gains for the promoters, and were eagerly subscribed to by investors. In the 1840s domestic railway shares were only partly paid up, offering the prospect of substantial gains for a small investment, while foreign railway promotions were normally guaranteed by governments. In either case there was little need for the promoter or the investor to ask too much about the future profitability of the undertaking. Moreover domestic railway companies were incorporated by Parliamentary Acts, while the majority of foreign promotions were sponsored by national or local governments, so that political (and, particularly in the case of Indian railways, military) considerations played a more important part than economic factors in determining the pace and location of railway construction as every town sought to secure its place on the railway map, while there was considerable scope for fraud and corruption - the railways booms had more to do with the hidden backhander than with the hidden hand of the market. The result was that far more railways were projected than were ever built, and far more railways were built than could ever be justified economically. The successive waves of speculative mania were consequently followed by successive crashes as railway projects failed to realise the anticipated profits and as foreign governments found themselves unable or unwilling to honour their guarantees.

The cyclical fluctuations in railway investment, as speculative mania gave way to default and crash, communicated themselves to other branches of trade and industry and reverberated through the financial system on an increasingly international scale. Moreover such cyclical patterns of overinvestment and crisis were not confined to railway construction, but arose independently in other branches of production and in the building industry, whether on the basis of expected increases in demand, the introduction of new technology, or the cheapness of finance. Although there was a marked cyclical pattern overall, the impact of periods of depression and recovery on different sectors and different countries was uneven.

The cyclical pattern of growth did not lead to any questioning of the principles of political economy. Although each crash led to widespread bankruptcies, excess capacity, and unemployment, the physical investments largely remained in place, while the losses were borne by merchants and financiers. Excessive railway investment led to bankrupcty for railway companies and losses for investors, but the railways remained, reducing transport costs even if they could only be operated profitably by writing off the initial fixed investment. Excessive investment in mining and in the iron and shipbuilding industries created bankruptcy, excess capacity and unemployment in those industries, but it also created cheap coal, iron and ships to reduce the costs of industries using those resources. Thus each crash was rapidly followed by a revival in which prosperity reached new heights.

The cyclical pattern of growth was still seen as being essentially financial in origin, arising from human failings that underlay the persistence of unsound banking practices and were expressed in psychological waves of optimism and pessimism that continued to fuel speculation and over-investment in periods of boom. The remedy was therefore seen to lie in the development of ever more sophisticated methods of controlling the expansion of credit, although every extension of control simply led credit expansion to find new channels as soon as the prospects of profit re-emerged in the boom. The experience of the crisis of 1847 led the Bank of England to pursue more conservative banking policies, but this did not prevent the new joint-stock banks feeding chains of speculative credit in the 1850s and 1860s as they competed for ever more dubious business. The bank amalgamations from the 1870s reduced competition for domestic business, and so led to the adoption of more conservative banking policies by the joint-stock banks in their domestic lending. However this did not prevent the banks from feeding speculative ventures overseas.

For the bourgeoisie the blemishes on the face of capitalism in the mid-Victorian boom were its birthmarks, that would fade with maturity. The persistence of poverty was a residue of the mentality of feudal dependence that continued to afflict the working class, cyclical fluctuations were a residue of the speculative impulses of antediluvian forms of capitalism, wars and insurrections the result of the old autocracies' attempt to hang onto their power. However these birthmarks were not fading, but were becoming cancerous growths as they assumed new forms. Poverty was no longer the poverty of displaced petty producers, but the pauperism of the working class. Successive crises grew increasingly severe, and were less the result of financial indiscretions than of the emergence of overproduction on an increasing scale. Class struggle was less directed against the privilege and corruption of the old order, and more directed at capital and its state. Wars were less geopolitical conflicts and becoming more an extension of capitalist competition. Unless these forces could be contained the prospect was of the growing polarisation of society, intensifying crises, sharpening class struggles and more destructive wars. For Marx these tendencies were inherent in the capitalist mode of production, and would lead inevitably to its demise.

Chapter 4

Money, Credit and the Overaccumulation of Capital

The limits of liberalism and the critique of money

As students Marx and Engels were active in the movement that sought the revolutionary overthrow of the Prussian autocracy to establish a liberal democratic state. However their observations of the conditions of the working class in Germany, France and England, and their contact with the emerging working class movement, soon convinced them of the limits of constitutional reform, which had everything to do with the attempt of the bourgeoisie to free itself from political subordination, and nothing to do with the 'social question'. Whereas the bourgeoisie was oppressed by the power of the state, the mass of the population was oppressed by the power of money. The liberal state, far from freeing the mass of the population from such oppression, sought only to perfect the rule of money by freeing it from all political restraint. Thus Marx and Engels turned from the critique of the autocratic state to the critique of the power of money, from the critique of political philosophy to the critique of political economy.

Marx's critique of money lay at the heart of his writings of 1843–4. For Adam Smith money was a neutral mediator, a technical instrument subordinate to the needs of individuals as means of exchange. However for Marx money did not mediate the relationships between individuals who mutually recognised their need for one another, and so their social character, in the act of exchange. 'The essence of money is ... that the *mediating activity* or movement, the *human*, social act by which man's products mutually complement one another, is *estranged* from man and becomes the attribute of money, a *material thing outside man*'.[1] This estrangement of the social character of the human individual in the form of money leads to an inversion of the relationship between means and ends described by Smith. Money ceases to be the means and becomes the end of exchange, while human needs are not recognised as the end, but become merely the means to the acquisition of money. Thus money becomes an independent social power, which appears in its most developed form as capital.

When Marx returned to his economic studies in an attempt to understand the crisis of 1857 his starting point was again the critique of money. Marx's initial concern in the *Grundrisse* was to challenge the currency reformers who believed that the crisis was the result of the restrictive monetary policies of the banking system. For Marx, by contrast, monetary disturbances were the result of more deep-seated causes, expressing in a monetary form the contradictions inherent in the capitalist mode of production. Although it was the latter that preoccupied Marx in *Capital*, the critique of money remained at the heart of his critique of political economy and of the limits of liberalism. However Marx never completed the project sketched out in the *Grundrisse* to offer a developed theory of money, crisis and the state on the basis of the theory of *Capital*, although the elements of such a theory are scattered throughout his writings. The following two chapters do not pretend to fill this gap, but only to draw on Marx's inspiration to provide a theoretical framework within which to discuss the relationship between the contradictory tendencies of capital accumulation and the historical development of the capitalist state form.

---

[1] Karl Marx and Friedrich Engels, *Collected Works*, vol. 3, Lawrence and Wishart, London, 1975, p. 56.

Money and exchange in petty production.

For Marx, as for Smith, money emerged in response to the barriers to exchange inherent in the system of barter. However for Marx this was not a rational evolutionary development, but was a profoundly contradictory process.

The essential problem in a system of barter is that you may not be able to find somebody who wants your commodity who is willing and able to supply you with a commodity that you want in return. There are two aspects to this problem, that Smith conflated.

On the one hand, there is the problem of exchange relationships being multilateral. The shoemaker wants some meat, the butcher wants some bread, and the baker wants some shoes. This is the problem that Smith identified as giving rise to money. However it is a problem that is easily resolved, and its resolution does not require the use of money. The butcher merely takes the shoes and exchanges them for bread. The shoes serve as means of exchange as far as the butcher is concerned, but any commodity can serve as a means of exchange, provided that it is in sufficiently general use for its price in terms of other commodities to be known and relatively stable. Some commodities may be better suited to the role than others, but there is no reason why one particular commodity should be isolated and identified as money. Indeed it is more rational to use a variety of commodities as means of exchange, to provide some security against the depreciation of any one form, and historically this was the case until a relatively late stage in the development of money.

On the other hand, there is the much more serious problem that is inherent in the anarchic and unplanned character of commodity production, that there may be nobody who wants the shoemaker's shoes at all. This is the real barrier inherent in the system of barter, and the identification of one commodity as the money commodity does not dissolve it, for if there is no demand for shoes, the shoemaker will be unable to sell shoes to get the money to buy the meat, so the butcher will be no better off than he or she would have been if he or she had taken the shoes in the first place. Thus the introduction of money does not dissolve the barriers inherent in barter, it merely generalises them, developing and generalising the contradictory foundations of the exchange of commodities.

In the 'early and rude' state of society the foundation of property is the appropriation of nature through labour in production. Commodities are exchanged as the products of labour on the basis of the formal equality of the producers. However in the exchange of commodities this formal equality is translated into a substantive inequality.

If 'the sole aim of production is consumption', the amount of labour-time expended will be determined by the consumption needs of the household, defined according to the social norms of consumption. These norms will be constrained by the average level of productivity, and they may not be uniform if they express hierarchical social relations. Similarly the allocation of labour and the means of consumption within the household will be determined by social criteria, historically within a patriarchal framework. With these qualifications in mind, inequality will appear in the form of different amounts of labour-time expended by different households.

Within a particular branch of production those households who produce more efficiently will have to perform less labour to enjoy the normal standard of living than those less fortunate, less skilled or less diligent. On the other hand, in the relations between different branches of production there is no necessary relationship between effort and reward. In the system of commodity production labour is expended in the production of a commodity without knowledge of, or regard for, the need for the product, and there is no reason why the rise and fall of prices should so smoothly regulate the movement of labour between branches of production that 'the quantity of every commodity brought to market naturally suits itself to the effective demand'.[2]

Households in branches where too much has been produced will find that they cannot meet their consumption needs, while those in branches where too little has been produced to meet the effective demand for the product will enjoy an abundance of commodities. However the former cannot simply move to the latter branches of production, for the skills of a particular trade can take a lifetime to acquire, while money is needed to to buy the means of production required to set up in a new one. Thus the unfortunate can only respond to their poverty by working harder, in order to produce

---

[2] Smith, *Wealth of Nations*, vol. I, p. 50.

more, while the fortunate are able to reduce their labour-time, and so produce less. Far from adjusting supply to demand and equalising the fortunes of different households, such rational responses will intensify the inequality of the producers. Eventually the pauperised will be unable to renew their means of production, and will be left destitute. The more fortunate, meanwhile, may have built up a reserve of money, with which they can buy means of production and the labour-power of others with which to accumulate yet more money, which thus becomes capital.

The translation of the formal equality of the producers into their substantive inequality leads to the destruction of petty commodity production and its transformation into capitalist production, in which the 'sole aim of production' is no longer consumption, but the accumulation of money. In this transformation money comes to serve not as the means of exchange, but as the independent form of value, appropriated by capital as the basis of its social power. Inequality is no longer the contingent result, but the self-reproducing foundation of the mode of production.

The contradictory character of commodity exchange does not provide a sufficient explanation for the rise of capitalism, but rather explains why petty commodity production is never observed in its pure form. Where petty production is not directly regulated in accordance with social need, as through the Indian caste system, but involves the exchange of products as commodities, it is associated with customary and collective forms of regulation of prices, methods of production, the hours of labour, and the mutual obligations of households that limit the regulative role of money and hold the destructive tendencies inherent in petty commodity production in check. Capitalism could only emerge out of petty commodity production if it could break down the barriers of the customary regulation of the guilds and the 'moral economy' of the village. Thus capitalism initially confronted petty commodity production from outside, in the form of merchants' capital.

Commercial capitalism and the development of money

The historical basis for the emergence of the earliest forms of capital, as merchants' and money-dealing capital, was the appropriation of a surplus product in the form of rent. The appropriation of a surplus gave rise to a demand for luxury goods and for the instruments of war that soon come to be supplied through trade. This trade in the surplus product provided the basis for the first development of the world market on which specialised merchants could make large profits. It was only with the development of commercial capital that money appeared in its fully developed form.

The commercial capitalist needs money not as the mere instrument of exchange, but as the means of purchasing commodities for subsequent sale, in order to increase the sum of money in his possession. For the commercial capitalist the function of money as means of exchange is therefore subordinated to its function as the independent form of value, the universal equivalence of money expressing the universal subordination of commodities to money as capital. Money no longer serves as the transitory expression of the value of other commodities, other commodities function as the transitory embodiment of the value whose abstract and universal form is money. Thus it is only with the rise of commercial capital that money achieves its developed and adequate form as the independent expression of value, and comes to be fixed in one particular commodity that serves as universal equivalent. Henceforth all other forms of money lose their independent existence and become tokens of the one true money. This was the essential truth captured in the mercantilist conception of money.

The history of money is not the history of reason depicted by the economists, it is no more and no less than the history of capitalism. Commercial capital developed the primitive forms of money that emerged from petty commodity production, fixed on one commodity to serve as world money and then overcame the barriers of commodity money to create token and then credit money. Underlying the history of money is the contradiction between the functions of money as the means of exchange and as the substance of value. The rational side of money, which political economy delighted in, is its function in the circulation of commodities as use-values. The irrational side of money, which political economy ignored, is its function as the independent form of value, through which the circulation of commodities is subordinated to the social power of money as capital.

As means of exchange money must be constantly thrown into circulation, but as the independent form of value money can stand outside circulation in an idle hoard. This contradiction is resolved in the circulation of capital, for the capitalist can only accumulate money by throwing money into circulation in order to buy commodities whose sale will realise a profit. However the contradiction between the two functions of money reappears as soon as commercial capital comes up against barriers to its profitable employment, for the capitalist will then withdraw his money from circulation. Such a withdrawal on a large scale will lead to a decline in the price of commodities. Falling prices will increase the speculative demand for money, until the shortage of money as means of circulation leads to a collapse of exchange, the resumption of barter, and the inability of the money commodity to serve as money. This paradoxical polarisation of a massive accumulation of monetary wealth, on the one hand, and the collapse of the production and exchange of commodities, on the other, is no mere theoretical possibility, but is the form of regularly recurring capitalist crises.

In order to meet the fluctuating demands of trade the capitalist had to hold a certain quantity of the money commodity in an idle hoard, reducing the capital available for more productive employment. Capitalists sought to overcome this barrier by developing substitutes for money. Merchants' and money capital developed instruments of credit that could serve as means of exchange very early. The bill of exchange, the deposit certificate, the banker's draft and the bank note removed the need for the money commodity to serve as means of exchange between capitalists, the money commodity being required only to provide security for the capitalist's credit by providing an ultimate reserve of money as the means of payment. As the instruments of commercial and bank credit became negotiable they began to replace money in its role as means of payment, and even to take their place alongside the money commodity in the reserve of money as store of value. Thus the stock of the money commodity came to be concentrated in the vaults of the banks. The development of credit money did not simply economise on the stock of the money commodity, it gave money a new form, marking the subordination of exchange to the social power of capital. While the reserve of the money commodity is money serving as capital, credit money is not simply a symbol of the money commodity, it is capital serving as money. To function as money it is not sufficient for credit money to serve as means of exchange, it is necessary that exchange should be the means of increasing the money capital of which credit money is the token.

The banking system concentrated and socialised the money power of capital. Capitalists were no longer restricted in their enterprise by the money capital they could acquire in exchange for commodities, but could draw on the capital at the disposal of the capitalist class as a whole. Monied capitalists could detach themselves altogether from the vulgar world of commerce. With the development of the banking and financial system money appeared to lose the encumbrances of its attachment to the real world of commodities, to stand in all its purity as the independent form of value.

The ability of capital to overcome the contradiction inherent in the money form by detaching itself altogether from the world of commodities was an illusion. The credit system only dissolved the particular relation between the individual capital and the circulation of commodities in order to generalise it. Capital as a whole, concentrated and socialised in the financial system, confronted the world of commodities as a whole. While the opportunities facing the individual capitalist appeared unrestricted by the need to undertake profitable commercial enterprises, the expansion of capital would be no more than an accumulation of paper claims unless social capital could increase its power of command over commodities by appropriating an enlarged sum of value. Thus the expansion of credit could only be sustained to the extent that the capital created was employed productively.

The early attempts to generate prosperity, at least for the bankers, by issuing credit freely soon foundered as they came up against the barrier of the real world of commodities. Landowners and the state had borrowed in anticipation of repaying from increased revenues, commercial capitalists in anticipation of increased commercial profit. If revenues did not increase, or such profits were not realised on a sufficient scale, debtors would default. As the banks' losses mounted their creditors lost confidence and sought to redeem their notes or withdraw their deposits in cash, leading to a run on the bank. When the bank failed the prosperity it had generated proved illusory as the unwinding of the chain of credit brought down all those who had shared the dream of freeing themselves from the world of the commodity. Although such chastening experiences revealed to bankers the virtues of prudence, in each successive boom banks would still succumb to temptation and overextend their credit, only to fail in the ensuing crash.

While capitalists early enjoyed the privileges of token and credit money, they fought long and hard to deny such an advantage to the state. Although the state enjoyed a monopoly of coinage, any attempt by the state to break the link between the nominal value of the coin and its metallic content was fiercely resisted, denounced as 'debasement', although the soundness of the currency did not depend on its metallic content but on the stability of its value.

While the over-issue of debased coin could prove inflationary, and so socially and politically extremely disruptive, the credit-creating powers of the bankers were no less likely to prove inflationary than those of the state. The difference was that the state, unlike private bankers, could evade the consequences of over-issue by forcing the circulation of an unsound currency by declaring it legal tender in the payment of taxes and the settlement of contracts. Thus the real issue was not so much that of the metallic content of the currency as of the power that currency issue put into the hands of the state. The state could hardly be relied on to exercise restraint when the power of issue gave the crown the means of financing wars, paying off debts and buying allies, without reference to Parliament. Thus the monetary issues fought out from the seventeenth to the nineteenth centuries were by no means technical issues of the management of the currency, they were fundamentally class and political issues of the social power of capital and of the relation between capital and the state.

It was only after the bourgeois revolutions that the state permanently acquired the power of issuing paper currency, but that power was circumscribed by the requirement to guarantee the convertibility of token money into the money commodity on demand, and by the constitutional independence of the central bank. The convertibility of the currency secured the subordination of the power of the state to the power of money by securing the subordination of the domestic currency to gold and silver as world money.

Commercial capital and the rise of capitalism

The expansion of credit can only be sustained to the extent that borrowers are able to increase their revenues sufficiently to service their debts. In the period of commercial capitalism the possibilities of expanding the sum of value appropriated by capital, that could validate the expansion of credit, were limited by the limited penetration of capital into production and the slow growth of population, and the restricted development of the productive forces. Capital attempted to overcome these barriers by using the power of commercial monopoly and the lever of credit to tap the revenues of the state and the landowners. However such sources were limited, so the development of credit money in the period of commercial capitalism soon came up against the barriers of circulation, precipitating financial crises that checked its advance and confirmed its fetishistic attachment to the money commodity. The development of stable deposit and note-issuing banks had to await the penetration of capital into production.

The growth of their indebtedness to commercial capital provoked a deepening fiscal crisis for the state and financial crisis for the landowners. It was this dual crisis that underlay the conflicts within the dominant classes that marked the transition from feudalism to capitalism. The expropriation of the lands and revenues of the church could provide temporary relief, providing the space within which commercial capital could expand without directly confronting the state and the landed class, but at the cost of provoking a political confrontation between church and state which escalated into religious wars. As pressure mounted, a direct class confrontation between capital and the old order was further postponed as landowners forced up rents, the state increased taxation, and capitalists were persuaded to extend further credit. The system of mercantilism provided a means of stabilising class relations on a national basis, as foreign trade provided the means for the increased appropriation of value at the expense of foreign ruling classes. However this merely extended the contradiction on a world scale as nation states sought to resolve the domestic crisis by waging commercial and territorial wars, which imposed a further drain on the public purse and a further extension of state indebtedness. Commercial and military success provided a basis for the maintenance of an uneasy class collaboration. Nevertheless conflicts came to a head as landowners renounced their debts and resisted the forced sale of their lands to their capitalist creditors, and as the state resolved its fiscal crisis by challenging the power of money through the inflationary debasement of the coinage, by

extending taxes that fell directly or indirectly on capital, and by
forced loans or the direct confiscation of capitalist property.

The longer the confrontation had been postponed, the weaker
were the forces ranged on the side of the old order. The basis of
state power had been steadily eroded. The sale of crown lands and
the farming of taxes had made the state increasingly dependent
on capital to finance its expenditure. Popular resentment at the
burden of taxation undermined the authority of the state and provided popular support for the forces of the bourgeoisie. The power
of the landowners had also been eroded as the attempt to increase
rents and abandon old obligations fostered popular resistance, and
as bankruptcy forced them to sell their estates to their capitalist
creditors. In the Protestant countries the attack on the church had
removed a bastion of the authority of the old ruling class.

The triumph of the power of money over the political power of
the old order was first sealed in the seventeenth century constitutional settlements in England and the Netherlands. However the
final victory of capital could not be complete until it had brought
the whole of society under its command, and in particular taken
command of production in order to expand the mass of surplus
value that alone could validate the expansion of the money power
of capital. Thus the full development of money presupposed the
development of the capitalist mode of production.

The contradictions of political economy

Adam Smith presented the development of capitalism out of petty
commodity production as a quasi-natural process, a development
of the division of labour as stock accumulates in the hands of some
individuals, while others become wage labourers. Smith regarded
this development as being inherent in the differential moral, intellectual and physical capacities of different individuals. The frugal,
skilled and industrious accumulate stock beyond that required to
meet their own productive needs. The indolent and indigent, on
the other hand, dissipate their stock in immediate consumption.
The accumulation of stock in the hands of the former meritori-
ous individuals provides them with the means to give employment
to the latter improvident ones. The capitalist is merely reaping
the rewards of his own virtue. Because Smith abstracted from the

social form of commodity production he was unable to see that the development of the substantive inequality that underlies the capitalist mode of production is already inherent in the monetary regulation of commodity production, kept in check only by communal restraint and customary regulation. It was the subordination of petty production to the power of money in the era of commercial capitalism that swept away these constraints and underlay the emergence of a new form of social production.

For Smith there was no essential difference between the worker who sells labour to another in the form of a completed product, and the worker who sells the same labour directly to the capitalist, who thereby acquires title to the product. The wage labourer earns less, but only because the petty producer is also able to enjoy the profits of his or her stock. Because the wage labourer provides only one of the elements of production 'the whole produce of labour does not belong to the labourer. He must in most cases share it with the owner of the stock which [sic] employs him'.[3]

The basis of property in the capitalist mode of production, like that of petty production, is still appropriation through labour, the only difference being that the labourer sells not the product of his or her labour but the labour itself. However this gives rise to the famous contradiction that Marx identified at the heart of political economy, for labour now has two values. On the one hand is the wage, that corresponds to 'the produce of labour' which 'constitutes the natural recompense or wages of labour'.[4] On the other hand is the value of the product of labour, the 'real measure' of whose exchangeable value is labour.[5] However if both the wage and the value of the product correspond to the produce of labour the existence of profit (and rent) is inconceivable. This contradiction can be resolved in one of two ways, both of which solutions are found in Smith.

One solution is to abandon the idea that labour is the 'real price of everything', and so the real measure of exchangeable value, in favour of the idea that value is determined as the sum of the independent contributions of land, labour and capital to production, measured by their revenues (wages, rent and profit). However the idea that revenues correspond to the productive contributions of

---

[3] Smith, *Wealth of Nations*, vol. I, p. 43.
[4] ibid., vol. I, p. 57.
[5] ibid., vol. I, p. 27

the elements of production is based on a fundamental confusion between the physical process of production and the social form of production as the production of value. In any mode of production goods are produced by labour, using appropriate tools, machines, raw materials and land, but it makes no sense to ask what are the independent contributions to the product made by these indissociable elements of production. It is only when the means of production and subsistence are appropriated as private property and concentrated in the hands of a particular class that any such attribution becomes possible, but the basis on which 'productive contributions' are evaluated has nothing whatever to do with the relative importance of the various elements of production, but is based solely on the formation of revenues within particular historically developed social relations of production.

The alternative solution is to retain the idea that labour is the source of value, but to abandon the idea that the wage corresponds to the product of labour. Examination of the social regulation of the purchase and sale of labour makes it clear that there is no immediate relationship between the wage and the product of labour. The wage is determined, as Smith argued, by the supply and demand for labour, and the 'natural price' of labour, like that of any other commodity, is determined by its normal cost of production. The normal cost of production of labour is the labour required to produce the means necessary to sustain life. Profit and rent then correspond to the difference between the labour required to produce the necessary means of subsistence and the labour that is embodied in the final commodity. Far from corresponding to the independent productive contributions of stock and land, profit and rent on this analysis constitute forms of surplus labour that arise because labour as a commodity receives less than the full value of its product. This was the approach adopted by Ricardo.

The Ricardian approach had uncongenial ideological connotations, particularly when taken up by the Ricardian socialists, but it also comes up against a fundamental theoretical difficulty. If we ignore rent, which plays no part in determining the value of commodities, it implies that profit is proportional to the amount of labour employed. However it is clear that in a developed capitalist society the circulation of capital through the credit system ensures that profit is proportional not to the amount of labour employed, but to the size of the capital. There were therefore theoretical, as well as ideological, reasons for economists rejecting the Ricardian theory in favour of the theory of independent revenue sources.

The errors at the heart of these two approaches are complementary to one another, as each abstracts from the social form of capitalist production, the one to look only at the relations that appear in circulation, the other to look only at the relations that appear in production. Ricardo correctly adopted the view that the wage is an advance of capital, but he persisted in the belief that the exchange of commodities in the capitalist mode of production was regulated by the labour-time necessary for their production, a belief that cannot be reconciled with the tendency to the equalisation of the rate of profit. What Ricardo failed to realise was that the change in the social form of production also entailed a change in the form of circulation. In the capitalist mode of production the product is no longer exchanged as the product of labour, but as the product of capital. To understand the capitalist mode of production it is essential to understand the implications of the transformation in the social form of production that is implied in the transition from petty commodity production.

The social form of capitalist production

The capitalist mode of production does not abolish the active role of labour in the physical process of production. Within the limits of the existing technology the amount that can be produced depends on the amount of labour that is expended in the process of production. The harder the labourer works, and the longer the working day, the more will be produced. Moreover the subordination of production to the capitalist thirst for profit does not dispense with the need to regulate the reproduction of the capitalist mode of production in order to assure an appropriate allocation of social labour among the various branches of production. However the regulation of the allocation of social labour does not take place directly, through the exchange of commodities as the products of labour, but indirectly, through the exchange of commodities as the products of capital.

In selling his commodity the capitalist does not seek recompense for the labour expended in its production, he seeks to enlarge his capital. The measure of his success is the relation between the increase in his capital, and the original capital laid out, expressed in his rate of profit. Thus the social regulation of the allocation of labour is achieved not through the movement of labour in response to differences in the remuneration of the labour expended, but through the movement of capital in response to differences in the rate of profit. In the early stages of capitalist development this is a haphazard affair, but with the development of the credit system and, later, the joint stock company and the stock exchange, the average rate of profit finds a tangible expression in the rate of interest and the yield on stocks which appears to the capitalist as an external constraint in the form of the 'cost' of capital.

Once we have regard to the social form of capitalist production the basis of the Ricardian contradiction becomes clear. The determination of the value of the commodity as the product of labour relates to the production of commodities, expressing the limits to production imposed by the labour expended. The determination of the price of commodities and the formation of revenues relates to the specific social form through which the expenditure of social labour is regulated in the capitalist mode of production. The Ricardian contradiction expresses the contradiction between the production of commodities as the products of labour and the circulation of commodities as the products of capital, in which the capitalist buys not the product of labour, but the worker's labour-*power*, the capacity to labour for capital. This is not simply a logical contradiction. It is the constitutive contradiction of the capitalist mode of production, the final development of the contradiction inherent in the money form, as capital subordinates not only the circulation of use-values, but also the expenditure of social labour to the reproduction of the money power of capital.

The precondition of the capitalist mode of production is the separation of the labourer from the means of production and subsistence achieved by the dissolution of petty commodity production and of feudal relations of dependence, and the concentration of the power of money in the hands of capital achieved in the accumulation of commercial capital and the development of the credit system. In the capitalist mode of production the contradiction between the formal equality and substantive inequality of exchange is no longer the fortuitous result of the function of money as means of exchange, but the foundation of the subordination of labour to money as a social power. However the workers do not simply accept their subordination to capital. Capital is only able to secure and reproduce the subordination of labour through a pervasive, diffuse, and sometimes intense struggle in which capitalists attempt to force wages below the subsistence minimum, extend the working day, intensify labour and, to add insult to injury, foist adulterated products on their impoverished customers.

The drive to force down wages, intensify labour and expand sales is not a matter merely of the subjective motivation of the capitalist, but bears down on the capitalist with the objective force of competition, particularly when the development of the financial system means that the capitalist has to realise not simply his own capital, but also that of his creditors. Competition forces every capitalist to seek out means of reducing costs or accelerating the turnover of capital, the better to withstand immediate or anticipated competitive pressure. Thus the individual capitalist is no less subject to the power of money than is the worker.

Within the existing organisation of production and circulation the only means of reducing costs is by extending the working day, intensifying labour and reducing wages. However there are limits to the ability of the capitalist to achieve savings by such means, limits set by the competition of capitalists for scarce categories of labour-power, by the physical capacities of the workers, and by the determination of workers to defend the normatively defined terms and conditions of labour. In the face of such constraints the capitalist can only reduce costs by transforming the methods of production and circulation, primarily by revolutionising methods of production to economise in the use of labour, enabling him to produce a larger mass of commodities for a given outlay of capital.

The transformation of the methods of production is not an alternative to the intensification of exploitation. The 'progressive' capitalist may gild the chains that bind 'his' workers by paying higher wages as an incentive to keep up with the pace of 'his' machines, but the increased mass of commodities that he throws onto the market increases the pressure of competition. This compels less productive capitalists to intensify labour, extend the working day and force down wages in the attempt to survive, throws the workers unfortunate enough to work for the most incompetent employers onto the scrap heap, and lays waste to pre-capitalist forms of production, destroying not only units of production, but the entire fabric of society.

However much suffering it causes, it is the constant tendency to revolutionise the forces of production and to increase the productive powers of labour that is the driving force of, and historical justification for, capitalist production. This tendency is imposed on individual capitalists by the pressure of the market. But the pressure of the market is not imposed by the pressure of demand for the products of capital. On the contrary, competitive pressure to revolutionise the forces of production intensifies all the more as the increasing mass of commodities thrown on to the market comes into contradiction with the restricted consumption power of the mass of the population. As capitalists economise on living labour and force down wages in order to reduce their costs of production they increase the volume of commodities produced, while further restricting the effective demand for the product, so intensifying the pressure of competition. The more successful are capitalists in overcoming the barriers to the increased production of surplus value, the more certain is it that they will confront barriers to its realisation through the sale of the commodities produced. When the reproduction of capital becomes a barrier to the further development of the social powers of labour, capitalism loses the last remnants of its claim to a progressive historical role.

Capitalist competition and the overaccumulation of capital

The dynamics of capitalist production can be clearly identified. Against Smith's eminently rational claim that 'the purpose of all production is consumption', capital is subject to a different injunction: 'Accumulate, accumulate! That is Moses and the prophets!'[6] The historical tendency of the capitalist mode of production, its law of motion, is determined by the insatiable thirst of capital for surplus value, and the incessant accumulation of capital. This tendency drives the capitalist to intensify labour and constantly to revolutionise the methods of production. The result of this tendency is a constant increase in the mass of commodities produced. However these commodities have not been produced as use values, in accordance with the consumption needs of society. They

---

[6] Karl Marx, *Capital*, Lawrence and Wishart, London, 1961, vol. I, p. 595.

have been produced as values, as the embodiment of an expanded capital. The capitalist throws them into circulation not to convert them into other use values, but to convert them back into the money form of capital. Nevertheless, if this capital is to be realised in the form of money, the commodities have to prove themselves as use-values by finding a consumer. Consumption appears to the capitalist, therefore, not as the sole end of production, but as a barrier to the realisation of his capital.

The tendency to the overaccumulation of capital is not simply a matter of the misjudgement of the future development of the market, as capitalists respond to temporary shortages by overexpanding supply, although such misjudgements can certainly be a source of instability (which capitalists try to reduce by improved commercial intelligence and the formation of trade associations and cartels). More fundamentally it is the result of the constant tendency for capital to revolutionise the methods of production. If the capitalist is successful in developing a new method of production he will face the prospect of earning a surplus profit. In introducing the new method of production the capitalist will not restrict his ambition to the limits of the market, since his reduced costs of production will enable him to reduce his selling price and still earn a surplus profit.

Overproduction appears in the first instance as an accumulation of unsold stocks in the hands of capitalists. However capitalists will not willingly reduce their selling prices, for this will mean that they will fail to realise the anticipated profit, or even face the prospect of a loss. So long as the capitalist can maintain his selling price he will continue to show a paper profit, even if his capital is tied up in unsold stocks. As soon as the price of his commodity falls he will have to revalue his stocks, his paper profit will fall and may turn to a paper loss, his capital will be devalued, and his credit-worthiness undermined. Thus the first response of capitalists to the emergence of overproduction will be to maintain their selling prices and expand their credit to continue production, while they dispose of their unsold stocks by aggressive marketing. The pressure of competition that results from the overaccumulation of capital determines the tendency for capital to develop new needs and to expand the market on a world scale.

If the market is not sufficiently expanded and prices start to fall, the less efficient capitalists and petty producers will come under more intense pressure. However the fall in prices will still not lead to the immediate contraction of production to the limits of the market. Petty producers will respond to the decline in their incomes by working harder, mobilising the entire labour at the disposal of the household, and so will increase production, until the fall in price is such that farmers are forced to consume their seed corn and domestic manufacturers can no longer renew their means of production. Capitalists cannot immediately withdraw their capital in the face of a decline in the rate of profit and invest it in another branch of production since the bulk of that capital is tied up in stocks, fixed capital and work in progress, all of which will have been devalued by the fall in the rate of profit. The less efficient capitalists will continue to produce so long as they can cover their current costs, and will try to reduce costs by cutting wages, extending the working day and intensifying labour in the hope of weathering the storm, until they have exhausted their capital and are driven into liquidation. Better placed capitalists may seek to reduce their costs by introducing the new methods of production in their turn, further contributing to the escalating overproduction of commodities. The most advanced capitalists, if they are still able to earn above the average rate of profit, may increase their investment, intensify labour and extend the working day in the hope of capitalising on their good fortune before events take an unfavourable turn. However the very success of capitalists in improving the conditions for the production of surplus value by forcing down wages, intensifying labour, and introducing new methods of production merely intensifies the tendency to the overproduction of commodities and so the pressure of competition.

The tendency to the overaccumulation of capital implies that accumulation can never take the form of the smooth adjustment to the market depicted by the economists, but must take the form alternatively of chronic stagnation or violent cyclical fluctuations. If methods of production are only improved slowly surplus profits will be small, while backward petty producers and capitalists will be able to remain in production. Accumulation will proceed slowly and chronic overproduction may persist for some time.

If the new method of production represents a substantial advance on the old the surplus profit available will be greater, and so the accumulation of capital will be more rapid. The scale of overproduction will be all the greater the larger the size of the new

units of production and the longer it takes for increased investment
to result in an increase in the mass of commodities produced. Once
the increased product comes onto the market the fall of prices may
be so great as to eliminate the profits of even the most advanced
producers, leading to a generalised crisis in which capitalists accumulate debt, while they try to restore profits by increasing the rate
of exploitation, while petty producers struggle to survive. As the
crisis persists, debt mounts, and credit begins to dry up, capitalists
will be forced to unload their stocks to maintain cash flow, driving
prices down further. Petty producers will be eliminated, rising unemployment enables capitalists to force down wages and intensify
labour, while the more exposed capitalists will go bankrupt.

In the crisis it will not necessarily be the least efficient producers who are faced with bankruptcy. The conservative capitalist,
using antiquated equipment, but carrying a very small burden of
debt, reducing stocks by producing to order, and relying on cash
transactions will be better able to weather the storm, or achieve a
smooth liquidation, than the more enterprising, who has high fixed
costs and a large burden of debt. However, if the more advanced
capitalist is still able to cover his current costs, the devaluation
of his capital through bankruptcy will make it possible to restore
profitability. Thus the devaluation or liquidation of capital may
not be accompanied by the liquidation of the productive enterprise. If its indebtedness was primarily to the banks the latter may
take over ownership in settlement of its debt. If the enterprise was
financed by the issue of bonds it might be taken over by its bond-
holders. If it was financed by the issue of shares its capital will be
more smoothly devalued by the fall in its share price, although the
decline may precipitate a takeover by other capitalist enterprises.
Thus the crisis leads not only to a restructuring of production but
also of the property relations within the capitalist class. The centralisation and socialisation of the ownership of capital leads to its
progressive divorce from the management of the enterprise, so that
capital increasingly appears not in the person of the capitalist but
in the form of the abstract and impersonal power of money.

The destruction of productive capacity and the devaluation of
capital in the crisis eventually prepares the conditions for renewed
accumulation. The destruction of stocks and of productive capacity
will have reduced the extent of overproduction, expanding the market for the more advanced producers who survive, allowing prices

to recover, while reducing costs by relieving the pressure on the supply of raw materials and expanding the reserve army of labour far beyond the needs of the more advanced producers, who will be better able to hold down wages and intensify labour to restore profitability. The devaluation of capital will have reduced the size of the capital, allowing the rate of profit on the remaining capital to rise. The restructuring of capitalist production and property relations through the crisis will have prepared the way for renewed accumulation so that the cycle can begin afresh.

The tendency to overaccumulation appears in the form of the overproduction of commodities in relation to the limited extent of the market. However overproduction is not simply a symptom of disequilibrium, a feature of particular branches of production matched by shortages elsewhere. The tendency to overaccumulation is the essential form of accumulation common to all branches of production, although the uneven development of the various branches means that its impact appears unevenly.

Nor is overproduction simply the obverse of underconsumption, to be alleviated by expanding demand. The expansion of demand would relieve the pressure of the market, but only to stimulate renewed overaccumulation. Overaccumulation is not a pathology of the market, it is the necessary form of the accumulation of capital, the result of the uneven development of capital as each seeks to gain and 'capitalise' a competitive advantage.

Rapid accumulation, stagnation or decline in one branch of production transmits itself to other branches through its impact on the demand for means of production and subsistence and on the stability and confidence of the financial system. The development of new methods of production does not proceed evenly through time or across all branches of production. If there are few major advances in the dominant branches of production the pace of accumulation will be sluggish, the emergence of overproduction acting as a constant drag on accumulation and the growth of the market. On the other hand, the introduction of a revolutionary method of production in important branches of production may initiate a period of rapid accumulation, which will communicate itself to other branches of production. Once the new methods of production have been generalised in a particular branch of production even the more advanced capitalists will come under increasing competitive pressure as the overaccumulation of capital confronts the limit of the market, threatening to bring prosperity to a halt. However in the meantime a new spur to accumulation may be provided by the further development of the forces of production. The subordination of the development of science and technology to capital provides the conditions under which constant innovation becomes possible, creating the illusion that capital can overcome all natural and social barriers to its expansion.

The unevenness of accumulation within and between branches of production is accompanied by a geographical unevenness in the momentum of accumulation and the forms of the class struggle. The rapid accumulation of capital in new methods of production takes place in particular geographical centres where the new methods are first introduced, that may be remote from the older regions of production which bear the brunt of the depressive impact of the destruction of backward producers. While the former regions enjoy rapid accumulation and widespread prosperity, the latter suffer the generalised destruction of precapitalist modes of production and their associated social forms, the devaluation of capital, intensified class struggle and the massive dispossession and redundancy of labour.

The geographical unevenness of accumulation constitutes a barrier to the sustained accumulation of capital, for the rapid growth in the demand for labour-power and for the means of production and subsistence in the centres of accumulation is geographically distant from the productive resources freed by the destruction of archaic forms of production. While capital in the centres of accumulation comes up against shortages of labour-power and the means of production and subsistence, productive capacity in the remote regions is destroyed and labour-power lies idle in abundance. As the competitive position of capital in the metropolitan centres of accumulation is undermined by rising costs, capital may attempt to overcome this barrier by extending the new methods of production to the more remote regions, where they will enjoy the advantage of lower costs, or will seek to develop the older producing regions as sources of supply of scarce means of production and subsistence, and may seek to mobilise the displaced labour power through the migration of labour to the geographical centres of accumulation. Thus capital seeks to overcome the geographical unevenness of accumulation through the international movement not only of commodities, but also of labour-power and capital.

Money, credit and the overaccumulation of capital

The barriers to accumulation inherent in the contradictory form of capitalist production do not appear immediately to the individual capitalist. The capitalist mobilises his money power to buy labour-power and means of production, which he sets to work to produce a mass of commodities. As far as the individual capitalist is concerned this mass of commodities embodies his expanded capital, and all that remains is to find buyers for his commodities, who will pay a price sufficient to realise this expanded capital in the money form, with which he can renew production. Thus the barriers to accumulation confront the individual capitalist in the form of the limited supply of money, whether in the hands of his customers to purchase his commodities, or in his own hands to renew accumulation.

If accumulation were confined within the limits of the money in the hands of individual capitalists it would be constantly interrupted. The capitalist facing profitable prospects would have to wait until he had accumulated sufficient money to purchase the requisite labour-power and means of production. The capitalist facing less favourable prospects would have to sell at an immediate loss and curtail production. Credit provides the means to overcome these barriers. Moreover credit does not simply redistribute the sum of money available to serve as capital among the capitalist class. The credit-creating powers of the banks enable them to create additional capital, to free accumulation from the barrier of the limited supply of money.

In the boom credit appears to have the magical power of suspending altogether the barriers to the accumulation of capital, providing finance for new ventures, and sustaining unprofitable capitalists and impoverished petty producers through periods of difficulty. The only limit to accumulation appears to be the availability of credit. As the boom gathers momentum the ready availability of credit, and the negotiability of credit money, reduces the demand for cash, so that the banks are able to reduce their cash ratios and continue to feed the boom by expanding credit. As capital overcomes the barriers to accumulation debts are regularly repaid, a mood of optimism prevails and credit becomes cheap and freely available.

In suspending the barriers to accumulation, the expansion of credit gives free reign to the tendency to the overaccumulation of capital. At first the overproduction of commodities in a particular branch of production can be absorbed by the expansion of credit and by the liquidation of petty producers and smaller capitalists, who have limited access to credit and whose failure puts little pressure on the financial system. However the expansion of credit will stimulate the continued overaccumulation of capital, further inflating the demand for credit. Meanwhile the growth of credit increases the pressure of demand in other branches of production, raising prices and profits and stimulating new investment which further increases the pressure of demand, without yielding an immediate increase in supply. Rising prices will put further pressure on the profits of the capitalists in the overexpanded branches of production, which increases the demand for credit, the expansion of which fuels further inflation. Rising prices may sustain accumulation by eroding wages, inflating the paper profits of hard-pressed capitals, and devaluing money capital to the benefit of productive capital. However, if the barriers to accumulation are not overcome, the uneven development of the various branches of production will increase, the pressure on weaker capitalists will grow, and inflation will accelerate.

As the pressure of competition mounts investment plans will be shelved, unsold stocks will pile up, the more cautious capitalists will cut back their production and reduce their liabilities, while the more exposed will find themselves unable to repay their debts as their capital is exhausted, and bankruptcies and defaults will mount.

The contraction of the demand for credit from productive capitalists will reduce the growth of apparently profitable loans with which the banks can offset their growing losses. If the boom has reached an advanced stage this need not immediately precipitate a crisis, for the optimistic mood in financial markets will mean that banks will continue to extend credit to finance losses, in the increasingly vain hope that this will enable them to recover their investment, while cutbacks in the demand for credit to finance productive activity will lead to a frantic search for new outlets for profitable lending, stimulating speculative investments in commodities, property or on the stock exchange and financing public expenditure and private consumption which may sustain the boom by inflating demand, but only by stimulating the further overaccumulation of capital.

Eventually the boom must break. Inflation will progressively devalue credit money, and so undermine its ability to serve as capital. Domestic holders of money will seek to convert their notes and bank deposits into the money commodity. A deteriorating balance of trade will lead to a growing foreign drain and the depreciation of the currency to a contraction of international credit. Defaults will lead banks to expand their cash reserves. The rising demand for the money commodity will put growing pressure on the financial system, and force a contraction of credit. The event that precipitates the crash may be remote from the underlying cause of the crisis, and may be apparently insignificant. Whatever triggers the crash, it will gain momentum as the contraction of credit precipitates defaults that spread through the financial system. In the crisis the overaccumulation of capital suddenly appears in the form of a mass of worthless debt and an enormous overproduction of commodities.

The crisis is marked by the contraction of credit and a massive increase in the demand for cash. The contraction of trade means that productive capitalists have an increasing need for cash to meet their obligations as they fall due. Speculators who have traded on credit need cash when the prices of shares, property and commodities, against which they have secured their credit, fall. Banks fail when a run on the bank finds it with small cash reserves and supposedly liquid assets that cannot find a buyer, destroying the capital of the bank and the deposits of its customers. In the crisis the instruments of credit, that had seemed such perfect substitutes for money, suddenly lose their money character. The demand for a secure store of value leads to escalating interest rates, while the acute shortage of money may even lead to a resumption of barter and the use of primitive forms of commodity money. Meanwhile rising interest rates undermine the profitability of even the most secure industrial capitals, forcing them to intensify labour and drive down wages in the attempt to restore profitability, and driving the more exposed into bankruptcy. The interruption of the accumulation of productive capital reduces the demand for the means of subsistence and, particularly, the means of production, the widespread emergence of overproduction leading to the further devaluation of capital, the destruction of yet more productive capacity, and the laying off of more workers. The chain of bankruptcy and failure spreads throughout the system in a destructive spiral.

The contraction of production and exchange, the liquidation of unsound ventures and the collapse of investment eventually leads to a contraction in the demand for credit so that interest rates fall. Although the depressed state of the domestic market continues to depress the prospects for profitable investment, rising unemployment may enable capitalists to increase the rate of exploitation so as to restore profitability and increase international competitiveness, providing expanding outlets on world markets, while the further development of the forces of production may stimulate renewed domestic investment. The recovery of exports and investment will increase the demand for means of production and subsistence. As surplus capacity is absorbed profits will rise sharply, stimulating a generalised renewal of accumulation, and initiating a renewed cycle.

Overaccumulation crises and the development of state money

The cycle of boom and slump appears to be a monetary phenomenon. The boom has been stimulated by the expansion of credit, the crash provoked by the collapse of credit in the wake of bank failures. In the early stages of capitalist development accumulation was indeed regularly brought to a halt by financial crises, which did not bear any necessary relation to the prospects for accumulation. As we saw in the last chapter, each successive crisis led to new developments in the financial system, which made it more robust, but only at the risk of stimulating the ever greater overaccumulation of capital, and ever more severe financial crises. The pattern of financial development in Britain was reproduced in all the other metropolitan centres of accumulation, although the detailed arrangements differed according to the historical and political context in which they were introduced.

In the initial phase of development of the credit system accumulation was frequently disrupted at an early stage by the failure of local banks. Although this was often put down to unsound banking practices, it was primarily a result of the geographical unevenness of accumulation which led to imbalances in the inter-regional flows of commodities and of capital, which resulted in an inflow of money into some regions and an outflow from others. Banks in some regions accumulated ample reserves of the money commodity, while banks elsewhere found themselves under increasing pressure. This barrier was gradually overcome by the centralisation of the banking system, that ensured that regional imbalances were cleared by the return flow of bank deposits to the financial centre, although the increased integration of the financial system meant that when a crisis did strike it would reverberate through the whole system.

The centralisation of the banking system underlay the development of central banking. Central banks originally owed their position to their role as bankers to the government, a position they were able to exploit to centralise the power of money in their hands. As the central bank concentrated the reserves of the money commodity in its vaults, its deposits and notes took the place of the money commodity in the cash reserves of the banking system. The central bank could then increase the cash reserves of the banking system by increasing the note issue, through the normal banking practice of discounting commercial and government bills. This centralisation of the reserves of the money commodity greatly increased the power of the banking system to stimulate accumulation by the expansion of credit. However it also increased the danger that the over-expansion of credit would culminate in a devastating crisis.

The limit to the expansion of credit by the banking system as a whole was now set by the discount policy of the central bank. The central bank, like any other banker, was limited in its note issue by the need to maintain reserves of the money commodity to honour the claims of its creditors. It was also constantly tempted, like any other banker, to reduce its reserves to a minimum, to which temptation was added the pressure from the government to provide credit freely to sustain accumulation and augment the government's revenues.

In a crisis the over-expansion of credit appeared first as a drain on the cash reserves of the commercial bankers, who sought to augment their reserves by discounting bills with the central bank. However this transferred the pressure to the central bank, as it could only increase its discounts by reducing its own reserve ratio. If confidence in the ability of the central bank to meet demands for cash payment was undermined the entire financial system was threatened with collapse, as the notes of the central bank lost their ability to function as money in the reserves of the banking system. On the other hand, if the bank sought to protect its reserves by raising the discount rate and contracting credit, it threatened to curb accumulation and precipitate a financial crash.

The state could not countenance the collapse of the financial system in a crisis, and so would press the central bank to discount freely to sustain the commercial banks, and to bail out its bankrupt friends. If necessary the threat to the reserves of the central bank could be checked by freeing the bank from its legal obligations to its creditors by suspending the convertibility of its notes. The continued domestic circulation of its notes as means of exchange could be maintained, despite their inconvertibility into the money commodity, by the forced circulation of the currency by virtue of its status as legal tender, its convertibility into commodities being guaranteed by its acceptability in payment of taxation. Thus the domestic currency came to be backed ultimately not by the reserves of the money commodity but by the revenues of the state and by the domestic convertibility of the currency into commodities. On this basis even an inconvertible currency was able to function as the cash base of the banking system.

While the government could force the domestic circulation of the currency, it had no such powers over its international circulation. The central bank therefore had less latitude to accommodate a foreign drain on its reserves than it had in the case of a domestic drain. While it might be forced to respond to a foreign drain by suspending convertibility, suspension would undermine the ability of the currency to substitute for world money in the international circulation of capital, so that international transactions would be confined within the limits of the domestic supply of world money, until confidence in the stability of the international value of the currency was restored by the achievement of a surplus in the balance of international payments. The global character of the accumulation of capital meant that the management of the domestic currency could not ignore the fundamental importance of maintaining the stability of the international value of the currency in order to permit the integration of the domestic accumulation of capital into the accumulation of capital on a world scale.

Once the central bank secured the legal privileges associated with the enforced circulation of its notes as legal tender, its notes assumed the status of the national currency, to which the note issue of private banks was subordinated. Thus the formation of central banking was closely associated with the financial and monetary integration of accumulation on a national basis, and with the consolidation of the fiscal and monetary unity and authority of the nation state.

From the hidden hand to monetary policy

The centralisation and integration of the domestic banking system was achieved in the course of successive financial crises through which the central bank was able to exploit its privileged position to concentrate the power of money in its own hands. As the power of the central bank increased so did its responsibilities. The over-expansion of credit in the boom and its excessive contraction in the crash could no longer be so easily blamed on the irresponsibility of private bankers. Thus the persistence of the cyclical form of overaccumulation and crisis focussed attention on the monetary policies of the central bank.

In the wake of a crisis two contrasting views confronted one another. Political economy articulated a perspective shared in principle, if not in practice, by cosmopolitan capitalists, for whom the cycle was caused by the excessive expansion of credit in the boom, that sustained unprofitable producers, stimulated unsound investments, drove up domestic prices, and undermined international competitiveness. The accumulation of unsold stocks as the boom reached its final stages was the result of overproduction stimulated by the over-expansion of credit, reinforced by the diversion of capital from productive employment into the speculative accumulation of commodities in the face of rising prices. The drain on the reserves of the central bank imposed an entirely appropriate deflationary policy that purged the excesses of the boom, liquidating unsound investments and restoring the stability of the currency by forcing domestic prices back to their normal level, and so preparing the way for renewed accumulation.

Currency reformers, and later social credit, populist and social democratic parties, expressed the view of the weaker productive capitalists and petty producers, oriented to the domestic market, and of the workers who faced lower wages, intensified exploitation and redundancy as a result of their employers' difficulties. From this perspective the boom was not the result of the over-expansion of credit, for even at the height of the boom the weaker producers were under fierce competitive pressure, and many fell by the way-side because they could not secure credit. The boom was rather marked by the bankers' diverting credit from productive employment to finance the lavish consumption, foreign investments and speculation of their rich and powerful friends, which stimulated the foreign drain, as luxury imports poured in and capital flowed abroad, and stoked domestic inflation as speculators engrossed supplies of essential commodities. The crisis was provoked as the bankers contracted credit to exploit their monopoly of the money commodity in the hour of need, sacrificing the productive activity that is the source of the employment and prosperity of the mass of the population to their own selfish greed.

For both political economy and the currency reformers the crisis revealed the need to curb the power of the bankers. However for political economy the need was to subordinate the power of the bankers to the integrity of the currency. The inflationary expansion of credit was the result of the government's profligacy and its pandering to popular inflationism. The need was to subordinate the power of the state to the power of money by restricting the ability of the central bank to expand credit beyond the limit of the bank's reserves of the money commodity. For the currency reformers, by contrast, the need was to subordinate the credit-creating powers of the bankers to the needs of production. In the United States populists saw in bimetallism a way of reducing the power of the banks and their political friends, but elsewhere currency reformers sought to break the power of the banks by abandoning the fetishistic attachment to the money commodity in order to bring the provision of credit under collective control, whether through cooperation or nationalisation, to provide easy credit for productive investment while restraining its speculative expansion.

The crucial issue that divided political economy from the currency reformers was that of the relation between the power of the state and the power of money. For the currency reformers the creation of state money made it possible to subordinate the anonymous power of the money commodity to the political power of the state, bringing accumulation under conscious control through the pursuit of a discretionary monetary policy, freed from the restriction of the limited supply of the money commodity. For political economy, on the other hand, the subordination of the power of the state to the power of money and secured by the restriction of the central bank's power of issue, was the only barrier to the inflationism that was the source of periodic crises.

These two perspectives express conflicting class viewpoints that were fought out, and continue to be fought out, in political conflicts around the regulation of accumulation. More fundamentally they express the two sides of the contradiction inherent in the money form between the function of money as means of exchange, coordinating production and consumption, and the function of money as capital, subordinating the circulation of commodities to the reproduction of capital. The expansion of credit frees accumulation from the limits of its capitalist form, the contraction of credit brings accumulation back within those limits. However the expansion and contraction of credit is not simply a matter of the whim of bankers, but expresses the contradiction between the tendency for capital to develop the productive forces without limit, and the need to confine production within the limits of the expanded reproduction of capital. The currency reformers took political economy seriously in insisting that monetary policy should be determined by the need to ensure a sufficient supply of the means of exchange to guarantee a market for the product, failing to understand that the social form of capitalist production demands that the function of money as means of exchange be subordinated to its function as capital, and so to the preservation of its power as the independent form of value. Political economy's attachment to commodity money was irrational, but the irrationality lay not with political economy but with capitalism.

The currency reformers were correct in stressing the role of credit expansion in sustaining accumulation. An overly restrictive credit regime, which confined accumulation within the limits of the market, would deny capital the means and opportunity to overcome the barriers to accumulation by improving the methods of production, opening up new sources of supply and developing new markets. While capital is able to overcome those barriers, and so to validate the expansion of credit by expanding it as capital, the expansion is entirely justified. Although the currency reformers denied that their schemes were inflationary, inflation may prove a powerful stimulus to accumulation, to the extent that it inflates profits at the expense of wages and devalues money capital to the benefit of productive capital. However the currency reformers were in error in believing that the expansion of credit could in itself remove the barriers to accumulation. If capital failed to overcome those barriers the expansion of credit would stimulate the increasing overaccumulation of capital, the surplus product being absorbed by the expansion of credit, and paper profits being sustained by rising prices, until the inevitable crash.

The conservative principles of political economy, embodied in the 1844 Bank Act, and generalised with the international adoption of the gold standard, appeared to define an extraordinarily restrictive credit regime, which minimised the discretion of the monetary authorities by confining the note issue strictly to the limits of the reserves of the money commodity, augmented by a small fiduciary issue. What the Currency School failed to understand, and the bankers were careful to conceal from the politicians, was that the Bank Act still gave the banking system considerable scope for expanding credit. Moreover the willingness of the Bank of England to act as lender of last resort meant that sound bills were a near-perfect substitute for cash, so that the credit-creating powers of the banks were increasingly limited not by their cash reserves, but by the supply of liquid assets, over which neither the government nor the central bank had much control before the First World War, since they were primarily commercial bills. Thus the gold standard regime provided the framework within which the central bank could pursue a discretionary monetary policy, while the monetary theory of the Currency School enabled it to disclaim all responsibility for policies supposedly dictated by the specie-flow mechanism.

Although the gold standard mechanism did not dictate the monetary policy to be pursued by the central bank, it did define the limits of discretion in confining monetary policy within limits defined by the need to maintain the free convertibility of the domestic currency into gold at a fixed exchange rate. This fundamental principle did not represent an irrational subordination of the credit needs of domestic production to the bankers' fetishistic attachment to a sound currency, as its critics charged. The maintenance of a sound currency was fundamental not only to the international bankers and merchants, whose interests it immediately served, nor only to the exporting capitalists who sought to maintain their international markets, but also to the sustained accumulation of domestic productive capital as a whole.

The conflict between political economy and the currency reformers expressed the immediate conflict of interests between capitalists producing for world markets and those producing for the
domestic market. However behind this apparent conflict, these different capitalists shared a common interest in the sustained accumulation of capital as a whole, which alone maintained the growth
of the domestic market. Capital in the more dynamic branches
of production could only overcome the barriers thrown up by the
overaccumulation of capital by seeking sources of supply of scarce
means of production and subsistence, and outlets for surplus money
and commodity capital, on a world scale. The maintenance of a
sound currency was the key to overcoming the domestic barriers to
accumulation because it allowed the domestic currency to serve as
a substitute for world money, and so as the basis of international
credit that could finance trade imbalances and permit the export of
surplus capital, whose domestic employment would otherwise press
further on the rate of profit.

While the gold standard subordinated monetary policy to the
maintenance of a sound currency, it did not determine the appropriate policy to achieve that end. In the event of a foreign drain it
required the bank to raise interest rates to attract foreign capital
and to contract domestic credit so as to relieve pressure on the
reserves. However the principle of monetary policy was to avoid
the need for such a contraction by preventing the over-expansion
of credit that resulted in the drain. The problem is that the over-
expansion of credit cannot be identified as such in advance of the
crisis.

It is of the essence of credit that it is extended in the anticipation of an uncertain outcome. There are no clear signs that credited
has been over-extended. Defaults may merely reflect the unsound
judgement of the lender, rather than the over-expansion of credit
as a whole. The emergence of inflation is not necessarily a sign
that credit is over-extended, for inflation may be merely temporary,
to be checked once new investments have expanded production to
meet increased demand. The development of international credit
makes it possible to finance an imbalance of international trade, in
the expectation that domestic supplies can be increased and new
export markets opened up. In the course of the boom the expansion of credit appears to be entirely appropriate as the payment

of interest and repayment of debts indicates the profitability of the undertakings it has financed, while imbalances in international trade are matched by the return flow of investment and international credit. The call is not for less credit, but for more, to free accumulation from the barrier of the limited domestic and international market. As the barriers to accumulation re-emerge in the form of pressure on profits, a deteriorating balance of international trade and the accumulation of unsold stocks these appear at first as merely temporary setbacks, accommodated by the further growth of domestic and international credit, and if the barriers are overcome this judgement is validated.

The forced circulation of the domestic currency effectively frees the expansion of credit from domestic constraints. However the international credit system has no central authority than can force the circulation of a world currency and so extend international credit without limit. The ultimate barrier to sustained accumulation thus appears in the limited availability of international credit. It is correspondingly a foreign drain on the reserves that is the first definitive indicator of the over-expansion of credit. However by the time the drain appears it can only be countered by the contraction of credit and raising of interest rates by the central bank. Deflationary pressures then drive apparently sound projects into liquidation, threatening an increasing chain of bankruptcies. The over-extension of credit appears in the failure of unsound ventures in the crash, but the unsoundness of these ventures is itself largely the result of the deflationary policies that have precipitated the crash. As the Whig, George Tierney, remarked in the midst of the recriminations following the crisis of 1825-6:

'Overtrading did they call it? What was the meaning of the word? It was, when a man did not succeed he was nicknamed an overtrader: it reminded him of the distich about treason -

"Treason does never prosper - what's the reason?
Why, when it prospers, 'tis no longer treason."

So when success followed the speculator, then he became the sagacious and adventurous British merchant'.[7]

The development of state money and of the credit system enables the state to regulate the pace of accumulation by regulating the expansion of credit. However the state cannot overcome the

---

[7]Hansard, n.s. 14, 1826, pp. 550–1, quoted Barry Gordon, *Economic Doctrine and Tory Liberalism*, Macmillan, London, 1979, p. 48

contradictory form of accumulation, it can merely reinforce one or the other pole of the contradiction. A conservative policy limits the growth of the domestic market and confines accumulation within the limits of the valorisation of capital. If the dynamic capitals are able to overcome the barrier of the limited domestic market by opening up the world market as an outlet for their surplus product, a conservative policy can provide the basis for sustained domestic accumulation. However, if capital is not so successful, the pressure of overproduction on profits will act as a drag on accumulation, leading to a fall in investment, rising unemployment, falling public revenues, sharpening class struggle, and growing pressure on the government to adopt expansionary policies to expand the market. An expansionary policy can stimulate the accumulation of capital by suspending the discipline of the market. However, if capital does not overcome the barriers to accumulation, the overaccumulation of capital will culminate in a crisis that is all the more devastating the greater the extent of the overaccumulation of capital that credit has encouraged.

The subordination of state money to world money did not overcome the crisis-ridden tendencies of accumulation, but rather led to increasingly violent cycles. In each crisis the subordination of the state and civil society to the power of money became not only a matter of scholarly debate, but also of intense struggle as demands arose for the state to intervene to curb the destructive power of money. However before we can understand the response of the state to such demands we have to look more closely at the question of the form and the class character of the capitalist state, that defines the limits and possibilities of such intervention.

Chapter 5

The Form of the Capitalist State

Capital and the state

In *The Communist Manifesto* Marx and Engels described 'the executive of the modern State' as 'but a committee for managing the common affairs of the whole bourgeoisie'.[1] However we have already seen in our account of the rise of the capitalist state in the nineteenth century that the industrial bourgeoisie played very little part in the formation of state policy. The political revolutions and constitutional reforms of the late eighteenth and the first half of the nineteenth century, in Europe as in Britain, broadened the base of political representation, allowing the big merchants and financiers in particular to play a more active political role, but the industrial bourgeoisie remained largely outside the political apparatus, representing its diverse interests through such organisations as the Manchester Chamber of Commerce, that petitioned Parliament and sought to influence public opinion but that had little direct influence over the executive.[2] The centralisation of the state,

---

[1] Karl Marx and Friedrich Engels, *Collected Works*, vol. 6, Lawrence and Wishart, London, 1976, p. 486.

[2] It is important not to ignore the political influence of capitalists. See Ralph Miliband, *The State in Capitalist Society*, Weidenfeld and Nicolson, London, 1979, and Kees van der Pijl, op. cit. However it is the politicians who establish the consensus among their paymasters, on the basis of their

and the progressive separation of public from private power, put political power increasingly into the hands of a stratum of professional politicians and civil servants of increasingly diverse class origins. Although politicians became answerable to their parties, the electoral base of political parties rarely has a well-defined class character, nor can their political programmes be reduced to the interests of the classes or strata they supposedly represent. The most cursory examination of the historical evidence seems to disprove Marx and Engels' characterisation of the capitalist state.

In their political writings Marx and Engels were well aware of the disjunction between the industrial bourgeoisie and the state. In their writings on the revolutions of 1848 the industrial bourgeoisie is one of the least significant political actors. In discussing particular state policies they frequently note that the state is in the hands of the aristocracy of land and finance, that uses its political power to secure its own narrow interests. The Bank Acts for Marx were an expression of the power of the 'big money-lenders and usurers', restricting credit in times of difficulty to force up interest rates and to give them 'a fabulous power not only to decimate the industrial capitalists periodically, but also to interfere in actual production in the most dangerous manner - and this crew know nothing of production and have nothing at all to do with it'.[3] Similarly the Factory Acts were carried, against the vehement opposition of the manufacturers, by landed Tories in revenge for the repeal of the Corn Laws, which the industrial bourgeoisie had only been able to secure by mobilising popular opinion against the state.

The apparent contradiction between the claim that the state serves the interests of capital and the empirical observation of the institutional autonomy of the state has led many to reject or abandon the Marxist theory of the state. However the problem is not simply a problem for Marxists. It is as much a problem for liberal political theorists, who equally have to explain how the institutional autonomy of the state is reconciled with the need for the state to secure the economic and social reproduction of capitalist society. According to Whig interpretations of history this reconciliation is achieved through the wisdom and far-sightedness of statesmen, but this kind of idealist solution is no more adequate than

own political concerns. It is the capitalist form of the state that underlies the political influence of capitalists, rather than vice versa.

[3] Karl Marx, *Capital*, vol. 3, Penguin, Harmondsworth, 1981, pp. 678–9.

the reductionism of crude Marxist conceptions of the state, for it cannot explain how the statesman can rise above immediate political pressures, any more than can the crude Marxist theory explain how the general interest of capital prevails despite such particular pressures.

It is clear that the state cannot be immediately related to the general interest, whether of capital or of society as a whole, as that interest is expressed through the formal and informal representation of particular interests, not least because the political representation of interests is structured by the constitutional form of the state. However this is not merely a contingent failure that derives from the particular constitutional form of the state. It derives from the fact that the general interest is essentially an abstract concept. Thus the theoretical problem of the relationship between the state and the general interest is essentially the problem of specifying the relationship between the general interest and particular interests.

The key to the paradoxical character of the capitalist state is the distinction between particular capitals and capital-in-general. Capital-in-general represents the total social capital that is available to mobilise labour-power in the production of surplus value. However capital-in-general only exists in the form of particular capitals, and the relationships between these particular capitals are essentially contradictory. When we consider the capitalist system of production from the physical point of view, as the production and exchange of use-values, the particular capitals are interdependent, their interdependence expressed through Smith's concept of the division of labour. On the other hand, in the capitalist form of production the production and exchange of use-values are not determined by the planned coordination of production, but by the circulation of commodities as values. The interdependence of capitals appears only in the circulation of commodities. However this interdependence does not appear immediately in the particular relations of purchase and sale into which the individual capitalist enters, for each particular relation is one of a conflict of interests. The producer of shoes cannot function as a capitalist without the producer of leather. However shoe producers do not relate to leather producers as a whole. A particular shoe producer buys shoes from a particular leather producer. In this immediate relationship the producer of shoes only has an interest in buying leather as cheaply as possible. The result of shoe producers successfully forcing down the price of leather might well be the destruction of the leather industry, and consequently of the shoe producers in their turn. Thus the interests of particular capitalists do not merely conflict with one another, but are essentially contradictory. If the capitalist were free to pursue his immediate interest, he would undermine the conditions of his own reproduction as a capitalist.

The role of the market is precisely to mediate the contradiction between the individual interests of particular capitals and their interest as parts of social capital. The individual interest of a particular capitalist is expressed in his attempt to realise an increased capital by selling the mass of commodities that his workers have produced for as high a price as possible. However these commodities have been produced without any regard for the social need for them as use-values within the accumulation of capital as a whole. The market evaluates the contributions of particular capitals in accordance with their contribution to the reproduction of the total social capital, devaluing overproduced commodities and revaluing those in short supply. Thus the general interest of capital appears to each individual capitalist as a barrier to the realisation of his individual capital expressed in the competition of other capitals. The contradictory character of the interests of capital appears in the interest of each individual capitalist in the subordination of all capitalists but himself to the rule of the market. The *hypocrisy* of capital is not a moral failing of the individual capitalist, it arises directly out of the social form of capitalist production.

Each individual capitalist seeks, by one means or another, to overcome the barrier of the market. However the reproduction of capital as a whole depends on the subordination of all individual capitals to the discipline of the market. Thus the interest of capital-in-general appears not as the sum of the interests of the individual capitals that are its component parts, but as an external force that stands opposed to the interests of all particular capitals and that confronts them as a barrier, in the form of competition in the market. 'The division of labour implies the contradiction between the interest of the separate individual ... and the communal interest of all individuals who have intercourse with one another'.[4] It is this opposition between the interests of particular capitals and the general interest of capital that underlies the separation of the state

[4] Karl Marx and Friedrich Engels, *The German Ideology*, Lawrence and Wishart, London, 1964, p. 44.

from civil society.

The authority of the market cannot be maintained merely by the tacit agreement of individual capitals. Unless the authority of the market is imposed on all particular capitals they will individually and severally seek to overcome the barrier of the market by suppressing competition, by fraud and, *in extremis*, by force. Thus the authority of the market can only be maintained by an external power that can meet force by force. 'Out of this very contradiction between the interest of the individual and that of the community the latter takes an independent form as the *State*, divorced from the real interests of individual and community.' The state, like the market, appears as an external power to which all individual interests are compelled to submit. 'Just because individuals seek *only* their particular interest, which for them does not coincide with their communal interest, ... the latter will be imposed on them as an interest "alien" to them, and "independent" of them, as in its turn a particular, peculiar, "general" interest .... On the other hand, too, the *practical* struggle of these particular interests, which constantly *really* run counter to the communal and illusory communal interests, makes *practical* intervention and control necessary through the illusory "general" interest in the form of the State. The social power ... appears to these individuals ... not as their own united power, but as an alien force existing outside them, of the origin and goal of which they are ignorant, which they thus cannot control, which on the contrary passes through a peculiar series of phases and stages independent of the will and the action of man, nay even being the prime governor of these'.[5]

The state secures the general interest of capital in the first instance not by overriding the rule of the market, but by enforcing the rule of the money and the law, which are the alienated forms through which the rule of the market is imposed not only on the working class, but also on all particular capitals. However the rule of the market does not resolve the contradiction between the individual and the social interests of particular capitals, but gives rise to periodic crises which call for the substantive intervention of the state. Nevertheless, although such intervention must favour some interests against others, if the substantive intervention of the state is to conform with its social form the state must seek to secure the

---

[5] ibid, pp. 45–6.

'illusory communal interests' against all particular interests. The class character of the state does not lie in its expressing the interests of capitalists, but in the duality of money and the state as the complementary forms of existence of capital-in-general. In this respect Marx was merely following Smith, for whom all proposals from capitalists should be viewed with suspicion, for capitalists are not to be trusted in matters of public policy. 'The proposal of any new law or regulation of commerce which comes from this order ought always to be listened to with great precaution ... It comes from an order of men whose interest is never exactly the same with that of the public, who have generally an interest to deceive and even to oppress the public'.[6] Not only are such proposals frequently against the interests of the public, and of capital as a whole, they are often likely to be against the ultimate interests of their proponents, who can only see the immediate results of their schemes. As Huskisson noted in the Parliamentary debates on trade liberalisation in 1824 'I am quite aware I shall be told, that the trade is the best judge of their own particular interests ... but I ... deny, as a general proposition, that any branch of trade is necessarily the best judge of the peculiar interests which are connected with their calling'.[7]

The capitalist character of the state was determined, for Marx, not by the subordination of the state to interests that arise in civil society, but by the radical separation of the state from civil society and the formal character of state power that is the essential characteristic of the capitalist state form. Thus Marx did not disagree with Smith's analysis of the capitalist state, but only with his identification of the 'illusory' common interest represented by the state and the market with the 'real interests of individual and community'. In the first volume of *Theories of Surplus Value* Marx echoed the famous phrase in *The Communist Manifesto*, noting that, for Adam Smith, 'State, church, etc. are only justified in so far as they are committees to superintend or administer the common interests of the productive bourgeoisie'.[8]

---

[6] Smith, *Wealth of Nations*, vol. I, p. 232.

[7] *Hansard*, n.s. 10, 1824, 811, quoted Gordon, op. cit., pp. 17–18.

[8] Karl Marx, *Theories of Surplus Value*, Part 1, Lawrence and Wishart, London, n.d., p. 291.

Civil society and the state

In his earliest writings on the state Marx contrasted the separation
of the state from civil society characteristic of modern society with
their integration in the Middle Ages. He argued that in feudal society there was no distinction between the state and civil society
because civil society was itself organised into corporate bodies (estates, corporations, guilds etc.) that came together in the state.
Political organisation was therefore coextensive with the organisation of civil society.

The development of the modern state was marked by the radical separation of the state from civil society. In modern society the
corporate bodies of the middle ages have given way to contractual
relationships between property owners, and property has increasingly assumed the form of money. The condition for the rise of the
modern state is the dissolution of all corporate forms of property,
and of all natural, communal and personal attachments as property assumes the exclusive form of money, the relations between
property owners being regulated by the circulation of commodities
as values subject to the rule of money and the law. Thus the revolution that gave rise to the modern state, most dramatically in
the French Revolution, was not only a political but more fundamentally a social revolution. The separation of the state from civil
society depended on the dissolution of the political element of civil
society, its corporate forms of organisation. 'The *establishment of
the political state* and the dissolution of civil society into independent *individuals* — whose relations with one another depend on
law ... — is accomplished by *one and the same act*'.[9]

The individuals who comprise civil society are by no means
the asocial monads of natural law theory. Their individuality is
constituted by the dissolution of all the communal and personal
affiliations associated with previous forms of property, as property
assumes the abstract and impersonal form of money, and money
becomes the mediating term in the relationships between individuals.

The capitalist state no longer serves as the supreme temporal
power, integrating the diverse corporate interests of civil society.
The state is increasingly separated from all particular interests,
serving to formalise and to enforce the property rights and money

---

[9]Marx and Engels, *Collected Works*, vol. 3, p. 167.

form on which modern society rests. Moreover the separation of
the state from civil society means that it no longer bestows property rights, as it did in the middle ages, it merely gives juridical
form to the property rights created in civil society, enforcing those
rights through the legal forms of the person, property and contract
and of money as legal tender. 'The true basis of private property,
possession, is a *fact*, an *inexplicable fact, not a right*',[10] a fact that
lies outside the state, in civil society.

The formal separation of the capitalist state from civil society
sets limits to its powers. The state merely gives form to social
relations whose substance is determined in civil society, which the
state regards 'as the *basis of its existence*, as a *precondition* not requiring further substantiation, and therefore as its *natural basis*'.[11]
It is civil society that is the precondition and limit of the modern
state, so that the state 'has to confine itself to a *formal* and *negative* activity, for where civil life and its labour begin, there the
power of the administration ends'.[12]

The separation of the state from civil society in no way implies the 'neutrality' or the 'autonomy' of the state. The essential
feature of the liberal form of the state is the formal and abstract
character of state power most adequately embodied in the rule of
law and of money. With the development of capitalism property
becomes its own foundation and money its only measure. The formal freedom and equality of the citizen before the law is merely
the other side of the formal freedom and equality of the individual in the face of money. The state secures the reproduction of
civil society by enforcing the rule of money and the law, which are
at the same time its own presupposition. Thus the liberal form
of the state secures the mutual subordination of civil society and
the state to the anonymous rule of money and the law. The 'independence' of the judiciary and of the Central Bank is the most
adequate institutional form of the alienated power of money and
the law, expressing the complementarity of civil society and the
state and providing the constitutional guarantee of the integrity
of its form. The formal and abstract character of the law is the
complement of the abstract form of property as money. As we have
seen, however, the equality of commodity owners confronting one

---

[10]ibid, p. 110.
[11]ibid, p. 167.
[12]ibid, p. 198.

another in the market is precisely the form through which their substantive inequality is reinforced and reproduced. It is on the basis of the formal equality of exchange that property is accumulated in the form of capital at one pole of society, while propertylessness is reproduced at the other.

The liberal form of the state is the appropriate form to secure the political power of the bourgeoisie because their social power is embodied in the abstract form of money. 'The middle classes being powerful by money only, cannot acquire political power but by making money the only qualification for the legislative capacity of an individual. They must merge all feudalistic privileges, all political monopolies of past ages, in the one great privilege and monopoly of *money*. The political dominion of the middle classes is, therefore, of an essentially *liberal* appearance'.[13]

The separation of the state from civil society, and the formal and abstract character of state power, is the means by which the bourgeoisie secures its dominion over both civil society and the state. However the substance of state power, as the power of a particular class, contradicts its form, as expression of the general interest. It is this contradiction that the statesman has constantly to resolve.

The abstract character of state power, that expresses its separation from all particular interests, is the basis on which the liberal state represents itself ideologically as the embodiment of the general interest of society and as the neutral arbiter of all particularistic claims. The universalistic claims of the liberal state are not based on particular theories of government, nor on an accounting of interests, but are the very identity of the state, embodied in the constitution, and expressed in the concentration of military and political power in its hands.

Against the universalistic claims of the liberal state all other corporate bodies that arise to represent the interests of particular sections of society appear merely as the representatives of particular interests. The contradiction at the heart of the liberal form of the capitalist state is practically resolved as the statesman resolves conflicts of interest within the constitution. However if particular interests pursue their aims outside the constitution they challenge both the authority and the legitimacy of the state. Faced with

---

[13] Marx and Engels, *Collected Works*, vol. 6, p. 28.

such a challenge the state has to maintain its authority, if necessary by the use of brute force, repressing competing powers in the name of the general interest embodied in the constitution. The *tyranny* of the bourgeois state is not a deformation of its liberal form, but is inherent in its need to assert its claim to neutrality and to universality.

Liberal political theory and political economy were the ideological forms in which the identification of the domination of capital with the general interest of society was expressed theoretically. However the theoretical, no less than the political, expression of the general interest of capital can only be represented in opposition to all particular capitalist interests. This was why these ideologies were formulated by thinkers who, whatever their individual class origins, could appear as disinterested intellectuals. The problems that these ideologies addressed did not flow directly from the interests of particular capitalists, or even of the capitalist class as a whole. They were the problems of the constitution, of the legal, administrative and financial forms, and of the policies of the capitalist state. Political economy was adopted as the ideology of the state because it gave coherence to a programme which resolved the political problems faced by statesmen in a period in which the development of capitalism had established the separation of civil society from the state, and had correspondingly undermined the mercantilist forms of political regulation, leading to a crisis in both the politics and the ideology of the state. Political economy legitimated the abandonment of policies that the state no longer had the authority or resources to enforce, and so the disengagement of the state from political struggles that threatened to engulf it. Once adopted it then guided the statesmen in the construction of a form of the state adequate to the capitalist mode of production.

The theory of political economy identified the general interest of society with the security of property and the anonymous rule of law and of money. This rule was imposed on society by the state, through its responsibility for the rule of law and the regulation of the currency. Within this framework the interests of all particular capitalists would then be reconciled with the interests of society as a whole by the rule of the market. The major constitutional problem was to ensure that the state was in turn subordinated to the rule of law and of money, and conducted its duties expeditiously and efficiently. These concerns determined the appropriate form of the state and lay behind the reform of the constitution, of the forms of administration, of public finance and of the fiscal and monetary policies of the state. The system of parliamentary representation, with a property franchise, provided a check on the temptation of the state to violate the rights of property and to impose an excessive burden of taxation. The independence of the administration from direct, and ideally indirect, parliamentary supervision ensured that politics would not interfere with the task of government. However the key to the substantive subordination of the state to capital lay not in the system of representation, but in the separation of the state from civil society that underlay the dependence of the state on the reproduction of capitalist social relations.

Capital and the development of the capitalist state form

The class character of the capitalist state is not a matter of the subordination of the state to the power of a particular class, but is inherent in the very form of capitalist state power. The historical process through which the capitalist state emerged was not, therefore, simply a matter of the transfer of power from one class to another, but more fundamentally represented a change in the form of the state, underlying which was a change in the social relations of production.

Although the development of the capitalist state form was associated with more or less violent revolutionary uprisings, these political developments were secondary, as Marx indicated, to the underlying social revolution that dissolved the corporate institutions, on which the power of the old regimes was based, as it dissolved civil society into independent individuals whose relationships were based on law and on money. While the origins of the modern state lay in the beginnings of commodity circulation and the appropriation of the means of production as private property, its full development presupposed the generalisation of commodity relations with the generalisation of wage labour.

The early capitalist class did not seek access to state power for its own sake. Those who aspired to social position and public office could acquire an estate, by purchase or by marriage, but most merely wanted to go about their business without impediment, subject only to the impartial rule of law and of money. Thus the revolutionary aspirations of the bourgeoisie were essentially negative, resisting the subordination of the power of the state to vested interests which appeared to the bourgeoisie as corruption, privilege and the abuse of the fiscal and monetary authority of the state. The bourgeoisie sought not the subordination of the state to one vested interest in place of another, although every particular interest sought to enlist the support of the state in its favour, but the subordination of the state itself to the rule of money and the law. The bourgeoisie could unite in its struggle to free civil society from the burden of the state, but when it came to substantive policy issues the bourgeoisie was by no means united, for the relations between capitals are relations of competition and conflict. It is precisely because there is no basis on which the capitalist class can achieve a spontaneous unity to express a coherent and consistent class interest that its economic and political unity has to imposed on it by the external forces of money and the state.[14]

Where privilege, corruption and public profligacy presented a barrier to the advance of the bourgeoisie it might capitalise on popular distress and popular resentment against the burden of the state to mobilise politically outside the constitution, demanding the democratic representation of property as the means of checking the partisan abuse of state power. However the revolutionary ardour of the bourgeoisie was strongly tempered by the fear of popular radicalism, particularly after the experience of the French Revolution. The bourgeoisie, like political economy, was more interested in good government, and if good government could be secured without the potential for divisions, turmoil and unrest associated with elections, all the better. Thus the reconstitution of the administrative, legal, fiscal, monetary and financial apparatuses of the state was much more significant for the bourgeoisie than the more dramatic changes in the system of political representation.

The reconstitution of the state was ultimately determined not by the political triumph of the bourgeoisie but by the transformation of the social relations of production. It was the social revolution that undermined the foundations of the power of the landed

---

[14] Colin Leys, 'Thatcherism and British Manufacturing', *New Left Review*, 151, 1985, is typical of many in regarding the absence of such a spontaneous unity as being a peculiar feature of British capital, rather than the normal condition of the capitalist class.

aristocracy and of the precapitalist state, and that provided a new framework for political integration on the basis of the national and international integration of the circulation of commodities and of money. The political struggles to which this social transformation gave rise could not be ignored by the state, but they confronted the state as constraints, not as determinants of its development. Thus it was not the political strength of the bourgeoisie that was decisive in the rise of the capitalist state, but the crisis of the state form. The political crisis required even those autocratic states in which the old aristocracy retained a monopoly of political power to develop new forms of revenue and authority, based on the new forms of social relations embodied in the rule of money.

This explains the apparent paradox that the outcome of the revolutionary movements was often a strengthening of the direct hold of the old aristocracy over the state apparatus, as they sought to preserve the vestiges of their social power and to compensate for its erosion by clinging to the state apparatus to preserve a social position whose foundations in civil society had been undermined. The condition under which such a constitutional compromise was possible was precisely the consolidation of the capitalist state form, marked by the subordination of state and society alike to the rule of law and of money, within the framework of an apparently archaic constitution. The residual powers of the landowning class depended increasingly on the persistence of precapitalist social relations and forms of authority in the countryside, the protection of agriculture preserving not only the power of the aristocracy, but also the subordination of the mass of the rural population. It was only with the generalisation of capitalist social relations of production that the transformation of the state form was complete. The political triumph of the bourgeoisie was not the initiator of this transformation, but was its culmination.

Although the bourgeoisie had contested the tyranny of the absolutist state, its democratic enthusiasm was limited, for the democratic constitution was a means of imposing a negative check on the state, a framework within which to exercise the power of money, not a means of exercising the power of the state. The working class had more radical objectives in seeking admission to the franchise. The attempts of the state to subordinate the working class to the money power of capital appeared to the working class in the first instance as a subversion of the disinterested rule of the state by the power of property, leading the working class to confront legality with the demand for justice, the rule of money with the demand for the social and economic rights of labour, and to claim admission to the franchise as the means of securing recognition of its legitimate interests by subordinating the power of property to the power of the state.

So long as the state apparatus remained in the exclusive hands of the aristocracy of land and finance its constitutional stability was constantly threatened as democratic elements of the bourgeoisie and petit bourgeoisie allied themselves with the working class demand for democratic rights. Political stability depended on the development of a constitutional form adequate to the universalistic claims of the liberal state. The foundations of such a development were laid with the political assimilation of the bourgeoisie to the nation state. which was achieved in Europe through the French Revolution, the Napoleonic Reforms, and the British Reform Bill, culminating in the constitutional settlements that followed the wave of revolution and counter-revolution of 1848, and in the colonies through the wars of independence, extending from the American Revolution, through the Latin American Revolutions of the nineteenth century, to the anti-colonial movements that followed the Second World War. Its completion depended on the extension of the franchise to the working class. However the extension of the franchise depended on the ability of the state to confine the political aspirations of the working class within the constitutional limits of the liberal state form.

The limits of the liberal state form

The struggle for the vote was the last stage in the struggle of the bourgeoisie for emancipation from the autocratic state. However it was only the first stage in the struggle of the working class for its emancipation from property. The working class sought to use its organised strength and its constitutional rights as the means of asserting its social claims. The struggle of the working class was a struggle for *social* democracy, but its struggle focused inevitably on the state.

For political economy the adequacy of the liberal state form was ensured by the adequacy of money and the law as the means of reconciling the particular interests of capital with the general interest of society through the rule of the market. However political economy failed to grasp the contradictory form of capitalist production that appears in the tendency to the overaccumulation of capital. The overaccumulation of capital appears in the constant pressure of competition through which capitalists are forced to hold down wages, intensify labour and replace living labour by machines, through which pre-capitalist social forms are destroyed, backward capitals displaced, and workers discarded, and which leads to the eruption of ever more violent crises through which production is confined within the limits of its capitalist form. The struggle of the working class brought to the fore the contradiction at the heart of the capitalist state between its class character and its universalistic claims.

The underlying contradiction of the capitalist mode of production does not appear immediately as such. It appears to individual capitals as profits are squeezed between the pressure of competition and the resistance of the working class. Capitalists seek to overcome the barrier of competition by the socialisation of production and the restructuring of capitalist property relations. The concentration and centralisation of capital led to the development of the limited liability company, in which capital is divorced from the person of the capitalist and becomes an independent social power; to the emergence of the giant corporation, within which production is not regulated by the market, but by forms of bureaucratic management and financial regulation; and to the centralisation of the banking system, through which the ownership of capital is socialised, and the accumulation of capital freed from the limits of the market. However the socialisation of capitalist production and of capitalist property still takes place within the social relations of capitalist production, and the development of social production remains subordinate to the expanded reproduction of capital. Far from dissolving the contradictions of the capitalist mode of production, the socialisation of production within the capitalist mode of production concentrates the autocratic power of capital and intensifies the crisis tendencies of capital accumulation.

The concentration of capital fosters the development of trades unionism as it brings workers together in larger units. Trades unions overcome the divisions between workers imposed by the rule of money and the individualism of the law to mobilise the collective strength of the working class to resist capitalist attempts to force down wages and intensify labour in the face of increased competition, and to take advantage of favourable conditions to raise the wages of sections of the working class. Although trades unionism provides a basis on which workers can develop their subjective and organisational unity and formulate their democratic aspirations, the continued subordination of civil society to the rule of money and the law limits the ability of the working class to realise its aspirations through trades unionism, and reinforces divisions within the working class. In such circumstances the only social power that appears able to constitute the unity of society and to realise the democratic aspirations of the working class by bringing social production under democratic control is the state. As Marx noted, so long as the state appears to be the only institutionalised form of human social power, it continues to express, 'within the limits of its form as a particular kind of state, all social struggles'.[15]

The socialisation of production defines the objective conditions for the transcendence of the capitalist mode of production. The collective organisation of the working class provides the social force whose democratic aspirations can only be realised by abolishing the contradictory form of capitalist production. However the creation of a democratic form of social production can only be achieved by overcoming the alienated forms of capitalist economic and political domination. The emancipation of the working class can only be achieved through a social and political revolution that will overcome the separation of the state from civil society, to create a new form of society in which 'man' recognises and organises his own powers 'as *social* forces, and consequently no longer separates social power from himself in the shape of *political* power'.[16]

The response of the state to the working class challenge is not determined simply by the political character of the regime, but is inscribed in the contradictory character of the liberal form of the state. The state responds to the aspirations of the working class 'within the limits of its form as a particular kind of state'. The attempt of the working class to assert its democratic claims on the basis of its collective strength appears to the state not as a means of transcending the limits of its form, but as a challenge to its legal power and constitutional authority. The reproduction of the

---

[15] Marx and Engels, *Collected Works*, vol. 3, p. 143.
[16] ibid, p. 168.

state requires that it respond to such a challenge not by abdicating its power but by reasserting its authority. However the state cannot simply resort to repression, without opening up the contradiction between the class character and the universalistic form of the state, and risking a revolutionary confrontation in which the state confronts the working class as the organised power of capital. The state has to resolve this contradiction by responding to the substantive aspirations of the working class, while attempting to confine the workers' pursuit of those aspirations within the limits of the constitution, through a judicious combination of concession and repression that aims above all to separate the workers' pursuit of their material aspirations from their assertion of their democratic claims by separating the industrial struggles of the working class, on the basis of its collective strength, from its political struggles, on the basis of the constitutional forms provided for it, thereby undermining the emerging unity of the working class and subordinating it to the substantive power of capital, on the one hand, and securing the purely formal character of democracy, on the other.

The separation of the state from civil society, and the subordination of social production to the reproduction of capital, immediately implies that the ability of the state to respond to the material aspirations of the working class is confined, directly or indirectly, within the limits of capital, for the reproduction of the capitalist state ultimately presupposes the reproduction of capital, and the state eventually confronts barriers to the expanded reproduction of capital as barriers to its own reproduction. Thus the state sponsored the development of new social institutions through which it could respond to the material aspirations of the working class while reinforcing the social reproduction of the working class in its subordination to the money power of capital and the constitutional authority of the state.

The working class and the state

The development of capitalism involved the transition from the patriarchal relations of dependence of pre-capitalist society to the monetary relations of subordination characteristic of the capitalist mode of production. However the working class constantly resisted its subordination to the power of money. In the early stages

of capitalist development such resistance took the form of sporadic outbursts of civil disorder, which could escalate into localised
insurrection in periods of acute distress. Although such unrest
might put the limited resources of the state under serious pressure, it could normally be contained by the provision of poor relief,
the protection of hard-pressed branches of production, particularly
agriculture, and by military and police repression.

The growth of an organised working class movement presented
a more permanent challenge to the state. On the one hand, the
collective organisation of the working class undermined the residual ties of authoritarian paternalism. On the other hand, it proved
a more pervasive and insidious threat to the power of capital and
the authority of the state. Capital responded to the challenge by
developing new forms of hierarchical organisation of the labour
process, which offered higher pay and status to the better organised skilled workers, by developing incentive payment systems, that
tied pay more closely to the profitability of the enterprise, and by
accommodating trades unions within new systems of 'industrial
relations'. However such an accommodation was a double-edged
weapon. While it enabled the better-placed employers to stabilise
their labour relations, it also enabled the trades unions to consolidate their organisation, to provide a base from which to resist attempts by employers to erode their gains when the pressure of overaccumulation put profitability at risk, and to build a wider class
unity to pursue not only the sectional aims of particular groups of
workers, but the democratic aspirations of the working class as a
whole.

While the state could meet the challenge of civil disorder with
a combination of repression and relief, it had to respond to the
political challenge of the organised working class by making more
fundamental concessions through which it could accommodate the
working class within the constitution. These concessions involved
the rigorous separation of the legitimate exercise of the collective
strength of the working class within the industrial sphere, on the
one hand, from its pursuit of its democratic social aspirations in
the political sphere, on the other. The former concern led the state
to recognise the legal rights of trades unions and to sponsor the
generalisation of 'industrial relations', which provided a constitutional channel through which the working class could pursue its
unavoidably class-based trades union aspirations, while reinforcing

sectional divisions and reproducing the subordination of the working class to the wage form. The latter concern led the state to develop institutions through which it could respond to the wider material aspirations of the working class, within the limits of the liberal state form, through the socialisation of the reproduction of the working class, the reinforcement of family dependence, and the more active involvement of the state in the regulation of the wage relation. 'Social reform' involved the development of a system of 'social administration' which categorised and fragmented the working class in the attempt to confine it within the limits of the forms of the wage and the family, while providing education, housing, health and welfare benefits.

Industrial relations and social administration responded to the material aspirations of the working class, but the price the working class paid for such material concessions was the more rigorous and systematic subordination of its social reproduction to the demands of capital, and the fragmentation of working class unity through sectional trades unionism and the differentiated forms of social administration. The working class could not turn its back on these institutions, for they were the only means through which individual workers could secure their physical and social reproduction. Nevertheless the working class constantly sought to transcend these forms. Workers individually and collectively resisted the intrusive, degrading, humiliating and often overtly repressive administration of social reform, and demanded the more liberal and generous dispensation of relief. They refused to confine their aspirations within the limits of capital imposed through the system of industrial relations. Women resisted their subordination within the form of the family, struggling not only against men, who were the immediate source of their oppression, but also against the state, whose social policies played an increasing role in reproducing and reinforcing that subordination. Through such industrial and social struggles the working class constantly sought to break through the attempts of capital and the state to confine its aspirations within the limits of the systems of industrial relations and social administration, overcoming the divisions imposed on the working class by such forms, to develop an emerging political unity. Thus the generalisation of industrial relations and the development of a system of social administration did not contain the class struggle, but gave it new dimensions and new forms.

The political agitation of the working class resulted from the inability of capital and the state to meet its social aspirations through the alienated forms of the wage and social welfare. So long as the state restricted the franchise workers would continue to pursue their social aspirations by mobilising politically on the basis of their collective strength, and so would present a permanent threat to the constitutional stability of the state, which could only be met by generalised repression, undermining the legitimacy of the state by bringing to the fore the contradiction between its class character and its democratic claims, and threatening to escalate into a revolutionary confrontation.

The extension of the franchise did not in itself threaten the power of capital, for the power of capital was not embodied in its privileged access to state power, but in the liberal form of the state. However the extension of the franchise would provide constitutional channels through which the working class could consolidate the power of trades unions by an extension of their legal rights, improve their conditions by protective and minimum wage legislation, and secure more generous welfare provision, without regard to the profitability of capital or the financial resources at the disposal of the state. The fear of the bourgeoisie was that such working class aspirations would be fuelled by populist politicians, who would seek election on the basis of grandiose promises, which could only be fulfilled by raising taxation or through the inflationary expansion of credit. It was the fear of such populist inflationism (articulated by the currency reformers in Britain, by the Proudhonists in France, and, to more effect, by agrarian populism in the United States), as much as of the direct challenge to the sanctity of property, that lay behind the caution with which even the most democratic of liberals approached the question of the franchise.

The foundations for the political stabilisation of the liberal state form on the basis of the admission of the working class to the franchise were laid by the accommodation of the trades unions to the wage form within the emerging system of industrial relations, the accommodation of the working class within the system of social administration through the sufficiently generous provision of relief, and the political incorporation of the various fractions of the petty bourgeoisie as a counterweight to the electoral strength of the working class.

The material conditions for the accommodation of the working class in the more advanced centres of accumulation were laid by the growth of productivity associated with the generalisation of more advanced methods of production in the second half of the nineteenth century, particularly in agriculture and transport, that reconciled rising real wages with the profitability of capital, relieved the pressure on the system of poor relief by absorbing the surplus population, and that expanded the financial resources at the disposal of the state.

The political counterweight to the working class was provided by the old middle class of petty producers and the new middle class of professional, scientific and administrative workers. In mainland Britain the political weight of petty producers had been much reduced by the extinction of the peasantry and the destruction of the dominant branches of domestic industry. Elsewhere the incorporation of the petty producers, threatened with extinction by capitalist competition, was achieved by the gradual transition from pre-capitalist forms of paternalistic dependence to modern forms of political patronage on the basis of the selective protection of the affected branches of production, particularly agriculture, from the full force of competition. The cost paid by capital for such concessions was that they tended to inflate wages by inflating the price of the means of subsistence, while they also bolstered the political privileges of backward landed and commercial capitalists by protecting the sources of their revenues and the basis of their social power, but this was a small price to pay for securing the stabilisation of the liberal state form.

The generalisation of capitalist production destroyed the old middle class, but at the same time the concentration and centralisation of capital, the separation of mental from manual labour, the growth of private and public bureaucracies, and the expansion of social administration provided the basis for the rapid growth of a new middle class which owed its position not so much to its ownership of its requisite means of production, as to its educational and professional qualifications and expertise. Its privileged income and status derived in part from its position of authority within bureaucratic hierarchies, but it preserved its privileges by restricting access to the appropriate educational and professional institutions through which it bestowed qualifications on itself, in the name not of sectional trades unionism, but of intellectual and professional standards which it alone was competent to adjudicate.

The increasing routinisation of bureaucratic tasks, the development of a division of intellectual labour, and the expansion of public education threatened to erode the privileges of the professional middle class. Its ability to resist such an erosion by maintaining restricted access to advanced education, and by securing legal endorsement for professional qualifications, was determined in part by the fact that the state apparatus and the education system was itself staffed by elements of that class, but was primarily determined by its significance as a social and political counterweight to the advance of the working class.

The progressive extension of the franchise assimilated the working class to the constitution by providing a form through which workers could pursue their aspirations not as workers but as individual citizens. The individuality of workers as citizens was defined by their differentiated interests as particular categories of worker, as consumers, as taxpayers, as consumers of public services and as recipients of welfare benefits. Thus the extension of the franchise provided the form through which the state could foster the political recomposition of the working class on the basis of such differentiated interests, within the context of the political unity not of the class but of the nation. The democratic franchise correspondingly legitimated the repression of attempts of workers to pursue their aims outside the legal and constitutional framework of the liberal state form by all the means at the disposal of the state. Thus the extension of the franchise completed the development of the institutional forms through which the working class was assimilated to the wage relation and the liberal state form, institutionalising the dual strategy of repression and concession in the constitutional form of the liberal democratic state. It is essentially these institutions, whose developed forms were systematically rationalised in the 'welfare state', that have defined the continuing relationship between the state and the working class.

Although the class struggle has developed through the institutional forms of industrial relations, social administration and electoral representation, it has never been confined within those forms. The political stabilisation of the liberal state form can only ever be provisional, for the crisis-ridden tendency of capital accumulation constantly creates new barriers to the attempts of workers to secure their physical and social reproduction and to realise their democratic aspirations, and imposes new limits on the ability of the capital and the state to respond to the workers' aspirations within the institutional forms through which they seek to accommodate the working class to the reproduction of capitalist domination. Thus the class struggle constantly overflows the institutional forms provided for it. The development of the capitalist state form is correspondingly not determined by the unfolding of historical laws, nor by the functional adaptation of the state to the 'needs' of capital, but by the development of the class struggle, which is not simply a struggle for state power, nor a struggle between the organised working class and the power of the state, but a struggle over the form of the state, conducted in and against the differentiated institutional forms of capitalist domination.

The institutional forms of industrial relations, social administration and the democratic franchise were the means by which the state sought to decompose the emerging organisational unity of the working class in order to recompose the working class politically. However these forms did nothing to counter the underlying cause of the class struggle that lies in the contradictory form of capitalist production. While the sustained accumulation of capital increased the mass of surplus value which enabled capital to meet demands for rising real wages, and which provided rising revenues to finance the growth of public expenditure, the state could respond to the demands of the working class within the limits of its form. However, as the overaccumulation of capital led to the devaluation of capital, intensified industrial conflict, the destruction of productive capacity, the redundancy of labour and the pauperisation of a growing mass of the population, the demands made on the state increased, while the resources at its disposal contracted. The political forms of industrial relations and social administration institutionalised working class expectations of stable wages and a minimum level of subsistence, while electoral representation provided the means by which the working class could impose such expectations on the state. The stability of the state was therefore increasingly dependent on its ability to ameliorate the impact of the overaccumulation of capital by intervening more actively in the regulation of accumulation. Such intervention was not simply an 'economic', but also a deeply political matter, as the state sought to respond to the economic and political impact of overaccumulation to secure its economic, political and ideological reproduction,

within the limits of its contradictory form as a class state but also
as a national state.

Overaccumulation, class struggle and the nation state

The tendency to overaccumulation is a global phenomenon, as capital tries to overcome the barrier of the limited domestic market
by seeking out markets on a global scale. However the capitalist
state is constituted on a national basis. The concern of the state is
not with the global accumulation of capital, but with securing the
accumulation of domestic productive capital at a pace sufficient to
absorb the surplus population, provide stable or rising wages, and
growing public revenues.[17] With the rise of social reform and the
extension of the franchise the state became increasingly concerned
with the issue of 'national efficiency', which involved the creation
of a healthy, educated and enterprising labour force, the development of systems of industrial finance, the fiscal encouragement of
investment, the promotion of scientific research, and a range of infrastructural investments. However the intervention of the nation
state in promoting the accumulation of domestic productive capital only reinforced the tendencies to the global overaccumulation of
capital, while it gave the resulting class and competitive struggles
an increasingly political form.

The pressure of overaccumulation appears in the form of pressure on profits, intensified industrial conflict, pressure on the banks
and financial markets, and rising unemployment, initially in particular branches of production, but as the crisis grows the pressure
extends to all branches of production. As trades unions come into
conflict with the repressive power of the courts and the police,

---

[17] The concept of domestic productive capital, which refers to the geographical location of productive labour, is quite different from that of the 'national
capital', which is usually used to refer to the portion of global capital in national ownership. The nationality of ownership is itself an ambiguous concept.
The term might refer to the very different concepts of the nationality or domicile of individual owners, or to the nationality or domicile of corporate bodies.
This ambiguity in itself should be sufficient to indicate the error of attempting to use the concept of 'national capital' to explain the relationship between
capital and the state, an approach that suppresses the *contradictory* character
of the relation between global capital and the nation state.

and the unemployed come into conflict with the repressive forms of poor relief, the class struggle takes on a directly political form and threatens to overflow the constitutional channels provided for it. At the same time the scope for material concessions is narrowed as profits are squeezed and as the state faces a fiscal crisis, as revenues fall while expenditure rises; a financial crisis, as the state has difficulty funding its debt on hard-pressed financial markets; and a monetary crisis, in the face of speculation against the currency and a drain on the reserves.

The orthodox response in the face of such a crisis was for the state to pursue deflationary monetary policies to restore financial and monetary stability and to confine accumulation within the limits of the market. This was the course advocated by political economy, and generally adopted in Europe in the middle decades of the nineteenth century, when crises tended to be short and sharp, and recovery relatively rapid, while working class resistance tended to be localised and sporadic. However exclusive reliance on such a deflationary response became politically untenable in the more severe global crises of overaccumulation after 1870, and as the organisational and institutional basis of working class resistance, in and against the state, became more developed. Thus the state had to develop new forms of intervention in the attempt to reduce the domestic impact of the crisis. However the possibilities of intervention available to the state were constrained by the economic pressures to which it was subject and by the political struggles to which such intervention might give rise.

The obvious alternative to deflationary policies was for the state to adopt expansionary monetary and fiscal policies in response to the clamour for relief. The state can relieve the domestic impact of the crisis at a stroke by using its monetary powers to stimulate the expansion of credit. Credit expansion eases the pressure on the banks and financial markets, enabling the state to meet its financial needs and cover its spending, and relieving the pressure on capitals. However, unless capitals take advantage of such an expansionary environment to transform methods of production to improve their international competitive position, the expansion of credit will stimulate inflation, and lead to a deterioration in the balance of trade. Inflation threatens to provoke domestic industrial and political conflict, as it erodes wages and devalues rentier capital, and to provoke speculation against the currency. The limits to the ability of the state to resolve the crisis by such expansionary means appear in the form of the political conflicts unleashed by escalating inflation, on the one hand, and the financial pressures of a deteriorating external position, on the other.

Although inflationism presented a grave threat to property, and to the financial and political stability of the state, its immediate benefits made it very attractive to opportunistic politicians, an attraction that was considerably increased with the extension of the franchise and the beginnings of social reform. It was this fear that had led to the general adoption of the gold standard and the doctrine of the balanced budget as constitutional guarantees by the leading capitalist powers in the last quarter of the nineteenth century.

The principles of the balanced budget and the gold standard meant that the limit to expansionary policies was set at the national level by the gold reserves, and globally by the supply of gold. The possibility of overcoming these limits appeared to lie in the possibility of overcoming the barrier of the limited supply and commodity form of world money. This possibility was expressed in the nineteenth century by bimetallism, which proposed to add silver to gold as a form of world money. However the association of bimetallism with popular inflationism, and the reluctance of the world's financial centres to see their monopoly of gold undermined, kept bimetallism in check. The rise of sterling as a world currency, based on its guaranteed convertibility into gold that was underpinned by the financial strength of the City of London, provided a more flexible basis for the growth of world liquidity and the internationalisation of money capital, while keeping control of the world monetary system in 'responsible hands'. The internationalisation of credit money with the rise of the gold-exchange standard made it possible to ease domestic and international political tensions by sustaining the increasingly inflationary world boom that led up to the First World War.

The stability of the currency, the constitutional principles of the gold standard and the balanced budget, and political opposition to inflationism limited the scope for expansionary solutions to the crisis. However the state could relieve the domestic impact of a global crisis by intervening directly to relieve domestic productive capital from the pressure of foreign competition by protective tariffs, industrial subsidies and imperialism. However such mercantilist policies would relieve the pressure by favouring particular capitals at the expense of others at home and abroad, and so threaten to politicise domestic and international competition, the latter inviting foreign retaliation which could easily escalate into diplomatic, political and military confrontation. Thus the attempt to resolve the contradiction between the class character and democratic form of the state, in the face of an intensification of the domestic class struggle, by mobilising the power of the state in support of domestic productive capital at the expense of foreign competitors, merely opens up the contradiction between the global character of accumulation and the national form of the state.

Despite the dangers of provoking retaliation, protectionism and imperialism could immediately ease the domestic impact of a global overaccumulation crisis, foster the nationalist identification of the working class with the state, and create the space within which capital and the state could make the concessions required to recompose the working class politically. In the face of a growing political challenge from the working class, within and outside the constitution, the appeal of such a strategy to politicians, and to capitalists facing extinction, could prove irresistible. Once adopted, however, such policies tended to acquire their own momentum. Nationalist and imperialist sentiments, once unleashed, were powerful ideological forces, and militarism promised enormous profits for the relevant branches of production, to say nothing of its attraction to the military. Thus the rise of protectionism and imperialism from the late 1870s, and again in the 1930s, created the tensions that culminated in the First and Second World Wars.

Protectionism not only threatens to unleash the forces of nationalism and militarism, it also disrupts the integration of domestic accumulation by disrupting the relationship between the various branches of production. Thus protectionism has generally been associated with the increasingly direct intervention of the state in the regulation of accumulation. Such direct intervention, to replace the market by the state-sponsored rationalisation and monopolisation of production, and the coordinated planning of production and investment, is the most obvious means of overcoming the tendency to overaccumulation since it gets to the root of the problem, freeing the development of social production from the limits of its capitalist form. However direct intervention also raises the question of the form of the state.

The direct involvement of the state in production oversteps the boundaries between the state and civil society, integrating the power of capital and the power of the state, as the state exercises its power in support of particular capitals, raising the questions of the neutrality of the state and the democratic accountability of capital, and setting precedents for future intervention. The integration of capital and the state threatens to integrate the social and political struggles of the working class, as trades unionism brings workers directly into conflict with the state, while the political advance of the working class holds out the possibility of its bringing social production under democratic control. The possibility of direct intervention, and the forms that such intervention takes, is therefore constrained by the balance of class forces and by the latitude available for capital and the state to make concessions to the working class sufficient to contain the class struggle within the capitalist state form.

Where overaccumulation arises in branches of production protected from foreign competition it tends to take the form of chronic and persistent surplus capacity, which can be eliminated by the monopolisation and rationalisation of production, while the freedom to control prices enables such monopolies to make substantive concessions to the workers in order to contain the class struggle. This was generally the course adopted at an early stage in the development of gas, water and electricity supply, the posts and the telegraph, and in the domestic transport system. Economists provided the theory of 'public services' and 'public utilities' that could explain the exceptional character of such industries and so serve as an ideological barrier to using them as a precedent for the generalisation of public ownership. Overaccumulation in domestic agriculture was similarly combated by price support schemes or by cooperative marketing arrangements, reinforced by subsidies or tariff protection.

Political considerations have meant that state-sponsored monopolisation has usually been associated with public regulation, or public ownership, to prevent particular capitals from exercising their monopoly powers against other capitals, and with a degree of responsiveness and accountability of management not only to the political priorities of the state, but also to the aspirations of the workforce for stable employment and improved working conditions, if not always for reasonable wages, particularly if public employment was tacitly used as a means of absorbing the surplus population and as an instrument of political patronage. The state has attempted to reconcile its direct intervention in production with its liberal form by distancing such intervention from the political sphere, reproducing the separation of the state from civil society within the state apparatus, typically in the form of the public corporation and of the tripartite representation of the interests of trades unions, capitalists and the state on consultative and regulatory bodies.

Where overaccumulation arises in branches of production that face foreign competition in domestic or world markets, competitive pressure imposes more severe constraints on the intervention of the state in the rationalisation of production, in particular reducing the scope for concessions to the working class to accommodate the workforce to the intensification of labour and the displacement of living labour by machines required to strengthen international competitiveness. Where the branches of production in question command the world market surplus profits can provide the scope for such concessions. However in the face of growing competitive pressure the contradictions of state intervention come to the fore as the industrial struggle is increasingly politicised, threatening not only the class character but also the liberal form of the capitalist state. It is such political fears, as much as concern for the interests of capitalists, that have made politicians reluctant to intervene directly in production. Where such intervention is already established the state has tended to respond to the political pressures created by a crisis of overaccumulation alternatively by withdrawing from the sphere of production by 'privatising' public monopolies and submitting them to the tender mercies of the market, or by relieving the pressure of competition by adopting mercantilist policies, at the cost of raising taxation and domestic prices and increasing international tensions. Thus the direct intervention of the state in production has reinforced tendencies to economic nationalism, protectionism and imperialism.

The forms of intervention of the state in the regulation of accumulation have not been determined simply by the needs of capital, nor by the need to subordinate capital to the growth of production, but by the attempt of the state to resolve the contradiction between the tendency for capital to expand the forces of production without limit and its need to confine the growth of production within the limits of its capitalist form. This contradiction does not appear to the state immediately, but is mediated politically, appearing in the attempt of the state to overcome the contradiction inherent in its form, as both a class and a national state.

Before the First World War the direct intervention of the state in production was largely confined to the public utilities, although parts of the German coal and steel industries were in public ownership, despite capitalist pressure to privatise the industries. With the outbreak of war the capitalist form of production presented an increasing barrier to the war effort. However the state regulation of international trade in wartime protected capital from foreign competition, while popular nationalism secured the political integration of the working class, and the demands of the military provided unlimited outlets for the products of capital, creating conditions under which the state could take direct control over capitalist production without immediately politicising the class struggle. However resistance to the war grew and increasingly assumed a class character, particularly in the autocratic European states, the interventionist apparatus providing a basis on which the social and political struggles of the working class were fused in the struggle for state power. Although only the Russian Revolution survived the counter-revolutionary offensive, revolutionary and insurrectionary movements, based on the strength of the organised working class, spread throughout the capitalist world. The immediate revolutionary threat was met with repression, while the state accommodated the immediate aspirations of the working class with inflationism, which generated new conflicts in its turn.

The political conflicts unleashed by the wartime intervention in production and post-war inflation reinforced the orthodox commitment to monetary stability embodied in the gold standard, and to the rule of the market in the regulation of accumulation. However the lesson drawn by both capital and the state from the experience was of the urgent need to remove the barriers to the global accumulation of capital, the disruption of which had intensified both class and national conflict. These barriers had appeared most dramatically in the monetary crises that had forced national governments to adopt deflationary policies or to resort to protection in order to defend the currency, which then reverberated through the world in a deflationary or a protectionist spiral. These barriers could be removed by rebuilding the international monetary system that would provide the international liquidity required to finance imbalances of international payments and so permit national governments to dismantle the apparatus of wartime intervention and sustain accumulation by expansionary policies within the framework of the restored gold standard. The construction of the gold-exchange standard was therefore the cornerstone of the attempt to reconstitute the liberal state form in the aftermath of war and revolution.

The gold-exchange standard indeed led to an enormous growth in international liquidity. However the expansion of credit stimulated the renewed overaccumulation of capital and an increasingly inflationary boom, that culminated in the crash of 1929. Meanwhile the gold-exchange standard had not overcome the contradiction between the global character of accumulation and the national form of the state. Despite the growth of international credit, national currencies still came under pressure in the face of a drain on the reserves and speculation against the currency, while an overstrong currency threatened to generate inflationary pressures. Rather than allow free reign to the destabilising forces of the specie-flow mechanism, national governments were tempted to manipulate exchange rates and interest rates and to sterilise reserves in pursuit of national policy aims, weakening the gold-exchange standard, which finally collapsed in 1931.

The collapse of the international financial system reinforced the recession that had followed the 1929 crash. The contraction of credit led to a deflationary spiral that plunged the world into acute depression and led to a resurgence of protectionism and militarism, which culminated in the Second World War.

The Second World War merely reinforced the lessons of the First, and the priorities of post-war reconstruction were very similar. The inter-war failure of liberalisation was attributed to the failure to address the political issue of nationalism and imperialism, to the failure sufficiently to liberalise trade, and above all to the weakness of the gold-exchange standard. The reconstruction of the international monetary system on a more secure foundation was seen from an early stage in the war as the key to post-war reconstruction. The immediate post-war political challenge of the working class was accommodated variously by inflationism and by political concessions, but the political and economic priority was to reconstruct a liberal world order in which the growth of international

credit would allow national governments to pursue expansionary
policies by accommodating imbalances of international payments.
Sustained accumulation would in turn permit the liberalisation of
trade, that would undermine economic nationalism, and the rising
wages, high levels of employment, and improved standards of welfare provision that would secure the political incorporation of the
working class. The prime architect of the reconstructed international monetary system was Keynes. The expansionary strategies
that the system permitted became known as 'Keynesian', and the
institutional form of the liberal state associated with such strategies was commonly referred to as the 'Keynesian Welfare State'.
It remained to be seen whether Keynes's plans would at last allow
capital to overcome the tendencies to overaccumulation and allow
the state to overcome the limits of its class character and its national form, or whether Keynesianism would prove to be merely a
recipe for global inflationism, as the expansion of credit stimulated
the increasingly inflationary overaccumulation of capital on a world
scale.

Economics, politics and the ideology of the state

The increasing intervention of the state in civil society raised not
only political, but also ideological questions. The legitimacy of the
liberal democratic state depends only in the last instance on its
formal claims to a monopoly of political authority and legitimate
violence. Its everyday legitimacy rests on the more solid basis of its
substantive claim to exercise its powers in the general interest. The
class character of the state means that such claims are necessarily
ideological, but the ideology of the state is a powerful political force
in confining politics within the limits of the constitution. Moreover
the ideology of the state gives coherence to the diverse policies and
institutions through which the state accommodates the pressures
to which it is subject. The ideology of the state consequently has
its own momentum. Once adopted, a particular ideology serves in
its turn as a constraint on the activities of the state as the latter seeks to secure not only its material and political, but also its
ideological reproduction. As we have seen in the case of mercantilism, the state may cling to the dominant ideology long past the

point at which the balance of social and political forces that it articulates has dissolved, testing it to destruction and beyond. As the economic and political pressures on the state mount, and an outmoded ideology becomes a barrier to the reproduction of the state, the political crisis of the state gives rise to an ideological crisis, at which point the state seeks out a new ideology to articulate and legitimate policies and institutions dictated by new social and political circumstances.

Political economy had legitimated a regime of laissez faire. This by no means implied the passivity of the state, but rather the subordination of all particular interests to the anonymous rule of money and the law. Such subordination required the systematic rationalisation of the state apparatus and the centralisation of political power rigorously to enforce the rule of money and the law. In practice political expediency dictated the increasingly extensive intervention of the state in substantive matters. However political economy could accommodate such interventions ideologically as exceptions to its that were necessary not because of the failures of money and the law, but because of human ignorance and moral weakness that subverted their operation.

Political economy had established its ideological dominance in Britain by the middle of the nineteenth century, as liberalism bore fruit in the mid-Victorian boom. Elsewhere the truths of political economy continued to face resistance from romantic conservatism, that sought to preserve pre-capitalist patriarchal relations; populist inflationism, that defended petty producers from the money power of capital; positivistic socialism, that saw the state enforcing the rule not of money and the law but of science and technology; and nationalistic protectionism, that saw the nation state as a mercantilist weapon in pursuit of national prosperity. The continued social power of the landed class, the strength of the petty bourgeoisie, and the persistence of mercantilist industrial and commercial policies in the face of the global penetration of British capital were the social and political forces behind such ideologies. However the rapid generalisation of capitalist production, associated particularly with the expansion of the railways, brought liberalism to the fore from the 1840s, although nowhere did it establish a dominance to match that achieved in Britain.

By the 1870s political economy had been reduced to a set of dogmas that had little bearing on the substantive political issues of the day. While the doctrines of the gold standard and the balanced budget were hardly challenged, the rise of social reform and the recognition of trades unionism undermined political economy's analytical foundations, while protectionism in Europe undermined the dogma of free trade. The extension of the franchise, the beginnings of social reform, and the rise of protectionism and imperialism called for new ideologies to articulate and legitimate the competing interventionist strategies at the disposal of the state, the new ideologies often drawing on older traditions. However the growing challenge of socialism made it imperative, both politically and ideologically, that the state set limits to such intervention. These limits were articulated ideologically by the new economics that emerged from the marginalist revolution.

Marginalist economics rejected the dogmatism of political economy, but it did not overturn the latter's theoretical foundations, and reinforced the orthodox commitment to the principles of the gold standard and the balanced budget. The fate of the new economics was therefore intimately associated with the fate of the attempt to overcome the contradictory tendencies of accumulation by the liberalisation of the international trade and monetary systems after the First World War. The crash of 1929, and the ensuing depression, undermined this liberal strategy, and led to the rise of corporatist alternatives, in the form of the state capitalism of fascism and the state socialism of communism, which presented not only a political, but also an ideological challenge to liberalism. The liberal response to this challenge was Keynesianism, which proposed to overcome the limits of orthodoxy by abandoning its most cherished principles. The gold standard would be replaced by a managed system of international money and credit, and the balanced budget by discretionary fiscal policy, the new Keynesian principles reconciling the sustained accumulation of domestic productive capital with the sustained accumulation of capital on a global scale on the basis of rising mass consumption and the growth of international credit.

Although the state has developed in different countries on the basis of historically different class structures and different political and ideological traditions, its historical development has increasingly been dominated by the uneven impact of the tendency to the overaccumulation and uneven development of capital on a world scale. In the following chapters I intend to trace in more detail the development of the capitalist state form, culminating in an examination of the political and ideological crisis of the Keynesian welfare state, by concentrating on the British example. However the aim is to draw out the issues of general comparative and theoretical significance by abstracting from the contingent elements in the British experience that derive from idiosyncratic elements of British historical traditions and class configurations, the personalities of particular politicians, or the contingency of political privilege and political influence. Such factors are important for a full explanation of the strategies adopted by the British state, but are a distraction from the purpose of the present study which is concerned above all by the constraints imposed on such strategies by the contradictory form of capital accumulation and the contradictory form of the liberal state.

Chapter 6

Class Struggle and the State: the Limits of Social Reform

Capital, the state and the reproduction of the working class

The subordination of society to the unfettered rule of money and the law undermined the reproduction of the working class, individually and collectively. While the expansion of capitalist enterprise created new opportunities, and liberated the worker from the restraint of archaic social forms, the constant tendency to dispense with living labour by revolutionising the means of production created an ever growing surplus population as petty producers were destroyed and redundant workers displaced. The individual form of the wage undermined the family and the household as the primary institutions of social reproduction. The destruction of precapitalist social forms removed social barriers to the growth of population, and destroyed the institutions through which the old, the disabled and the infirm could make a productive contribution and secure their means of subsistence. The destruction of traditional crafts and skills undermined the guilds and trades unions through which a section of the working class could retain an element of control

155

of the conditions of its labour and maintain a living wage. The inevitable result of the advance of capital was the pauperisation and demoralisation of a growing mass of the population on a world scale.

The working class did not reconcile itself to its fate without an intense and pervasive struggle. In the early stages of capitalist development this struggle primarily took the form of a defence of the old corporate, co-operative and paternalistic social institutions threatened with dissolution by the advancing power of capital. As these institutions were destroyed, and the reproduction of the working class was increasingly subordinated to the wage form, this struggle took on the dual form of a struggle of the wage labourers with the capitalists over the wage and the conditions of labour, which led to the growth of trades unions as the working class sought to mobilise its collective power, and the demand of the pauperised for work or relief, a demand that came to be directed primarily at the state. These two aspects of the struggle were distinct, and so a potential source of division within the working class as trades unions sought to overcome the barrier of competition from the surplus population, but they were also closely related, and so provided a basis for solidarity, for the division of the working class between the employed and the pauperised is neither rigid nor static. Poverty defines the condition of the vast majority of the employed working class, as the wage is insufficient to secure the physical and social reproduction of the household. Pauperism is a threat that hangs over the entire working class, as its prospective fate in the event of redundancy, injury, infirmity or old age. The desperation of poverty undermines the solidarity of the working class, enabling the capitalist to force down the wages and intensify the labour of the employed.

Capital enjoys a contradictory relation to the reproduction of the working class. As the accumulation of capital pauperises and demoralises the working class it undermines the foundations of the production and realisation of surplus value. This contradiction appears in the interests of every individual capital in paying as low a wage and employing as few workers as possible, while all other capitals pay high wages and provide plentiful employment to sustain a growing market. Similarly every capital has an interest in minimising the provision of public relief, which ultimately constitutes a drain on surplus value and weakens the disciplining force of the reserve army of labour, while at the same time having an interest in the reproduction of the reserve army as a body of potential wage labourers and, particularly for capitalists producing means of consumption, as an outlet for their surplus products. If the reserve army is growing fast, and accumulation does not confront the barrier of the limited consumption of the mass of the domestic population, the former interest will predominate. If the appropriate qualities of labour-power are becoming scarce and capital seeks to expand the domestic market, the latter interest may come to the fore. However in the last analysis it is not the immediate interests of capital, but the social and political challenge of the working class, that is the decisive factor.

Although the reproduction of capital presupposes the reproduction of the working class, the state did not intervene to regulate working class reproduction at the behest of capitalists, but in response to working class political pressure. However the state could only respond to such pressures within the limits of its form. The immediate task of the state was to relieve distress in order to contain disorder. However the state could not meet the aspirations of the working class for an adequate level of subsistence, for the state did not have the resources to meet such a demand, nor did it have the power to guarantee employment. The central thrust of social reform was not to alleviate the condition of the working class directly, but to develop an increasingly complex and differentiated system of social administration that would ensure that the working class could provide for its own needs, through wage labour, social insurance, and family dependence, supplemented by a punitive and highly selective system of poor relief. Thus the state responded to the challenge of the working class not by subordinating social production to social need, but by developing an increasingly elaborate network of bureaucratic apparatuses to regulate the physical and social reproduction of the working class as a class of wage labourers for capital. Social reform undoubtedly improved the condition of the working class, and to that extent represented a material advance. However social reform also involved the growth of a centralised and bureaucratic system of social administration, increasingly insulated from democratic control, through which the state sought, against determined and persistent working class resistance, to enforce the systematic subordination of the working class to the wage form and of women to family dependence.

Pauperism and the state

The erosion of the personal relations of feudal authority had led to
the Elizabethan Poor Law, which lay at the heart of a complex web
of protective legislation that gave legal sanction and fiscal authority
to the detailed regulation of the reproduction of the working class
by the local gentry, who, in their capacity as Justices of the Peace,
could regulate the terms and conditions of labour and the prices of
essential commodities, subsidise wages, provide relief and maintain
order by administering the criminal law and calling on the military.
The Old Poor Law was based on pre-capitalist forms of labour, in
which few were wholly dependent on the wage, most of the population struggling to survive on a combination of subsistence production, wage labour and petty commodity production, within social
relations that retained strong communal and patriarchal elements.
The generalisation of capitalist production destroyed the social and
economic foundations of these transitional forms of production. As
the social relations of authority and dependence were eroded, and
the mass of the population was forced into reliance on an inadequate wage, the forms of regulation associated with the Old Poor
Law broke down under the pressure of the escalating cost of relief
and popular resistance.

Despite the faith of political economy in the moralising and
disciplining force of the wage form, the state could not simply dismantle the apparatus of relief, repression and moral regulation of
the Old Poor Law. It rather had to reform the system of regulation
to make it more adequate to the wage form. The New Poor Law
lay the foundations for the subsequent development of the 'social'
administration of the working class by the state. The principal
features of this reform were the replacement of a discretionary and
comprehensive system of regulation, based on the social relations
of the local community, by a uniform and differentiated system
of regulation, based on administrative and legal relations. Thus
the Justices were by-passed by the establishment of locally elected
Guardians, supervised by a central Board, while the scope of the
Poor Law was narrowed as the powers to regulate the terms and
conditions of labour, to subsidise wages and to control prices were
finally abolished, the Guardians responsibilities being confined to
the relief, disciplining and moral education of the destitute. Meanwhile the Justices retained their responsibility for the criminal law

and the militia were gradually replaced by the development of a specialised and permanent police force. The New Poor Law and the police provided the disciplinary reinforcement for the wage form, and the revival of religion and the spread of education provided a moralising force, but the abolition of outdoor relief removed the responsibility of the Poor Law for the subsistence and direct regulation of the waged and of the petty commodity producers.

The removal of the waged from the purview of the Poor Law was not determined only by the desire to reduce the costs of relief, but also had an important political dimension, for the comprehensive form of the Old Poor Law had played a major part in uniting and politicising popular grievances as the pauperised, the petty producers and the wage labourers confronted the undifferentiated authority of the Justices. The functional differentiation of the repressive and regulatory apparatus of the state undermined this unity by fragmenting the grievances of the mass of the population, making possible differentiated political responses that served to reproduce and exaggerate divisions within the working class. The withdrawal of the state from direct responsibility for the regulation of the wage relation was particularly important since it detached the state from direct involvement in the immediate struggles of wage labourers. The repeal of the Combination Acts were an important anticipation of the reform of the Poor Law in this respect, although trades unions were still subject to the full force of the civil and criminal law, which brought effective trades unionism into direct confrontation with the state.

The reform of the Poor Law presupposed the generalisation of wage labour and the adequacy of the wage to secure the reproduction of the employed and their dependents. Until these conditions were realised the Poor Law remained under severe pressure, and the implementation of the reform met fierce resistance. The generalisation of wage labour was largely achieved by the massive destruction of petty production in the depression of the 1840s and the expansion of wage labour in the mid-Victorian boom. On the other hand, the pressure of surplus population enabled employers to hold down wages so that the bulk of wage labourers could barely support themselves, let alone the wives and children whom male labourers were required by law to maintain. Many men abandoned their families to the Poor Law, while they went in search of work. Pressure of poverty undermined wider kinship and community re-

lations, the sick, the elderly, the infirm or the destitute being taken
into the workhouse under the Poor Law, while forcing women and
children to work long hours for meagre wages to maintain the immediate family, and all workers to accept dangerous and unhealthy
working conditions, leading to further demands on the Poor Law
from the sick, the injured and the exhausted. Thus the demands
on the Poor Law were not reduced by reform, they continued to
escalate.

The Guardians responsed to these pressures by developing an
increasingly differentiated system of administration, that sought to
deal with the different moral issues raised by the various forms of
poverty, and to prevent the moral contamination of one form of
dereliction by another. Thus the workhouse separated the insane,
the elderly, the young, the infirm and the able-bodied and spawned
a series of differentiated institutions. The Guardians attempted to
prevent the poor from falling back entirely on the Poor Law by
continuing to dispense outdoor relief, their efforts increasingly supplemented by private charity. Meanwhile pressure mounted from
the Poor Law authorities, from humanitarians and from the trades
unions for public health measures to reduce the incidence of disease; for legislation to restrict child and female labour, which it
was hoped would strengthen the family and working class morality
and help to raise male wages; and factory inspection to reduce the
incidence of industrial injuries. The efforts of evangelism and education to strengthen the family were in vain while male wages were
too low to support the family, and this led to a more favourable
view of trades unions, the generalisation of which, it was hoped,
would secure greater uniformity of wages and working conditions,
improving the lot of the most exploited workers at the expense of
the better paid.

It was not until the brutal defeat of Chartism and the social
peace and growing prosperity of the mid-Victorian boom that the
implementation of the New Poor Law and the subordination of
the working class to the wage form was more or less complete
in England. While the Poor Law administration categorised, in-
spected, educated, disciplined and degraded those who fell within
its clutches, the working class made every effort to avoid the humiliation of official pauperism. Trades unions and friendly societies
provided benefits to members in the event of sickness, unemployment or old age, although only the best paid workers could afford

to cover themselves for the full range of benefits, the less fortunate falling back on private charity rather than public relief. Nevertheless the hope that the moralising and disciplining effect of the New Poor Law would be sufficient to eliminate poverty was far from being realised.

Political reform and social administration

By the 1860s industrial growth had provided employment opportunities for impoverished agricultural labourers and displaced domestic producers, but it had not in general led to rising wages. Mass and persistent pauperism, mainly in the rural districts, that had been the main form of poverty in the first half of the century, gave way in mainland Britain to urban pauperism, that affected not only the old, demoralised or infirm who lacked the skills and physical capacities required for industrial employment, but also extended, particularly in London, to large numbers of unskilled, casual and sweated labourers, leading to a rapid increase in the cost of the Poor Law, despite the enormous growth of private charity. The problem was not simply that of cost, but of the fear that the liberal dispensation of relief was reinforcing the demoralisation of the poor, undermining the rule of law and the subordination of the working class to the wage form.

The problem of pauperism continued to be seen by the ruling class primarily as a moral problem. The 'residuum' was seen as a pool of degraded humanity, breeding criminality, prostitution, disease, and degeneration that could threaten the moral and physical health of the population as a whole as demoralisation spread to the employed working class, a fear that grew with renewed working class political agitation from the 1860s. However it was not poverty that caused the moral degradation of the residuum, but rather its moral failings that were the cause of its poverty, moral failings that had been encouraged by the indiscriminate dispensation of charity that had replaced outdoor relief. The solution to the problem was therefore to strengthen the stick of the Poor Law, while bringing the carrot of private charity under closer control, to ensure that provision was made not as a right but only for deserving cases, and as a means of encouraging the development of self-reliance. This was the basis on which the Charity Organisation Society was established in 1869 and later the basis on which charitable housing was provided, the provision of relief and subsidised housing being accompanied by the systematic organisation of charitable visiting and rent collection as instruments of moral education and reinforcement of the family form.

The resurgence of working class political agitation from the 1860s raised the question not only of the regulation of the poor, but also of the employed working class. Although the state had expected the repeal of the Combination Acts to separate trades unionism from political agitation, such an expectation was naive, for while trades union activity was subject to the civil law of contract and the criminal law of conspiracy effective trades unionism inevitably brought not only individual workers, but the trades unions themselves into conflict with the law. Moreover the peculiar form of the wage relation meant that the law of contract was extremely one-sided. Although the law defined the wage bargain as a freely entered contract, the peculiar character of the commodity labour-power meant that the terms of the contract could not be precisely codified in law. As far as the trades unions were concerned the employer had a duty to pay customary wage rates and to recognise established job demarcations, apprenticeship regulations and manning levels. However, even if the trade union was able to secure the agreement of the employer to recognise the established rights of the trade, there was no way of giving this agreement the force of law. Under the Master and Servant laws the wage contract was an individual bargain in which the worker submitted himself to the direction of the capitalist. There was nothing to stop the capitalist from employing labour below trades union rates and from importing blacklegs in the event of a strike. Should trades unionists try to enforce their rights by imposing solidarity they stood liable to meet the full force of the civil and criminal law. Thus trades union activity brought the organised working class increasingly into conflict with a class law, and behind that law with the state.

These issues came to a head as employers sought to attack the rights of skilled workers from the 1850s. As the unions came up against the force of the law they began to agitate for the reform of the franchise, as the means of securing their rights through legal reform. The reform agitation grew increasingly militant, as the urban poor combined with the organised working class and the urban petty bourgeoisie. However the demands of the organised working class were more limited than had been the demands of Chartism, while the state was better equipped to accommodate them than it had been twenty years earlier. Thus the state responded not with intensified repression but with reform, attempting to divide the skilled working class, that was undoubtedly beginning to enjoy the fruits of capitalist prosperity, from the class as a whole, and to confine working class activity to constitutional channels by separating the unavoidably class-based demands of trades unionism from the political aspirations of the working class.

The reform of 1867 extended the franchise to the men of the skilled working class and urban petty bourgeoisie. The trades union legislation that followed did not codify trades union rights, but it did provide limited legal immunities that made it possible for trades unions to organise, to strike, and to picket peacefully, although not to enforce their solidarity, without confronting the law.

Like the 1832 Reform Bill, that of 1867 had little immediate impact on the class composition of the House of Commons or the alignment of political forces. The franchise still embraced less than 15 per cent of the population over the age of 20 (although it was further extended to cover nearly 30 per cent in 1884), providing little scope for independent labour representation. Moreover, as with the bourgeoisie following the 1832 reform, once the organised working class had achieved its constitutional ambitions and secured some recognition of its trades unions rights, the main political issues of the day were not class issues, nor did the trades unions' immediate concerns dictate a class perspective.

The working class was admitted to the constitution not on the basis of class, but of citizenship. Once the wages issue was settled the trades unions had as strong an interest as their employers in the prosperity of their particular branch of production, in minimising the burden of taxation, in maintaining price stability, in conquering world markets and in securing cheap supplies of imported food and raw materials. While some unions favoured protective legislation and social insurance, others saw such paternalistic measures as a threat to trades unionism by undermining their collective defence of working conditions and collective provision for adversity. The framework within which these sectional differences were resolved was not that of the unity of the class, but the unity of the nation, expressed in the common interest of all workers in growing prosperity and expanding employment opportunities, if necessary at the expense of the workers of other nations, which gave a political foundation to those chauvinistic and nationalist sentiments that the bourgeoisie had long tried to foster ideologically.

The immediate significance of the extension of the franchise was that it strengthened the power of the national government, rather than that of the working class, enabling it to pursue the task of centralising and rationalising the system of public administration, although its efforts met with determined resistance, at first from local vested interests, and later from democratically elected local bodies. The 1867 Reform Bill was followed by a wave of reforming legislation, most notably the 1870 Education Act and the Public Health and Housing Acts of 1875. These reforms were not seen so much as a means of ameliorating the condition of the working class, as of encouraging the working class to help itself, reflecting a belief that grew steadily over the last decades of the century that environmental conditions were as much a cause as a consequence of pauperism, so that the improvement of sanitation and of housing was as much a moralising force as were education and charitable provision.

The initial wave of legislation was concerned to rationalise existing provision, which had largely been a matter for local initiative, rather than marking a new departure. The proliferation of local bodies, the ineffectiveness of judicial supervision of public administration and the marked disparity of performance between different local authorities increased the pressure on central government to play a more active role in initiating social reform and in directing its administration, while the extension of the franchise both increased the electoral pressure on the government to act, and provided it with the means to undermine resistance from local vested interests whose intransigence threatened to provoke deepening class conflict. On the other hand, the reform of government finances in the 1860s provided the regular systems of accounting and financial control that enabled the government to mobilise its resources more effectively, while the reform of the civil service provided it with the means of developing systems of bureaucratic regulation. Thus the extension of the franchise provided the political basis on which the state could eliminate the power of local vested interests and rationalise the system of social administration within the framework of the capitalist state form.

The proliferation of local administrative bodies was ended with the establishment of multi-purpose elected local authorities that took over their duties. This development provided local government bodies that had the administrative and financial resources to undertake more ambitious programmes and that were much more responsive to political pressure for social reform. Thus the development of such authorities was soon followed by the rapid growth of expenditure on education and public health and the municipalisation of gas, water and electricity from the late nineteenth century, followed by the growth in expenditure on public assistance and, to a limited extent, housing at the beginning of the twentieth century. This expansion was far greater than could be financed by local resources. The development of specific exchequer grants to local authorities, starting with education, progressively reduced the dependence of local authorities on rate revenues, and simultaneously brought them under increasing central government control.

The crisis of 1873 and the Great Depression

The sustained accumulation of the mid-Victorian boom enabled the state to contain the class struggle by a judicious combination of repression and legal and administrative reform, while making few substantive concessions to the aspirations of the working class. Periods of depression were brief, as crises were soon followed by fairly rapid, if uneven, recovery, so that mass unrest did not escalate to the stage of class confrontation, nor precipitate a serious political crisis. Thus the Reform agitation could be safely accommodated by the limited extension of the franchise and the demands of the trades unions by the grant of limited immunities. However this situation was not to last for much longer, for the form of accumulation on a world scale through which Britain had prospered reached its limits in the world crisis of overaccumulation of 1873.

In the first half of the nineteenth century the overaccumulation of capital in manufacturing had been reconciled with the limited consumption power of the mass of the population and the technological backwardness of agriculture primarily by the destruction of petty commodity producers and the extension of the margin of cultivation on a world scale. The overproduction of manufactured goods led to falling prices, but falling prices stimulated continuing improvements in productivity that sustained profits, while rising prices of raw materials stimulated the search for new sources of supply.

The possibilities for sustaining accumulation on this basis soon confronted the barrier of the costs of transport. As overaccumulation in manufacturing came up against the barrier of the market in the 1840s the depression was communicated world-wide. Profits were squeezed, petty producers swept aside and class conflict intensified, culminating in the Revolutions of 1848. However the barrier of the limited market was overcome by the massive investment in the means of transport, and above all railways, which lifted the world economy out of the depression and carried it forward into the mid-Victorian boom.

The mid-Victorian boom was dominated by railway investment. Productivity in manufacturing grew only slowly, but accumulation was sustained by the massive reduction in transport costs that opened up new sources of food and raw materials, despite the continued technological backwardness of agriculture, and expanded the market for manufacturing, despite the limited consumption power of the mass of the population.

Accumulation did not proceed smoothly, but only through the mechanism of overaccumulation and crisis. Until the 1840s crises were not usually a sign that accumulation had reached its limits, but were merely temporary setbacks, often exaggerated by the weaknesses of a financial system in which the expansion of bank credit was virtually uncontrolled, and which was vulnerable to collapse in the face of relatively small financial shocks, caused by harvest failures or the temporary closure of markets or by speculative collapses. In the crises it was primarily petty producers and commercial and financial capitalists who failed, while productive capitalists, who carried little debt, largely survived. Accumulation would then be resumed once the financial system had stabilised and credit again became available.

By the 1850s the international financial system had become more sophisticated and rather more robust. The City of London had become the world's financial centre, financing much of the world's trade and investment flows and providing the ultimate source of liquidity for the world banking system. Thus the Bank of England provided the funds that sustained accumulation on a world scale. However railway promotions, with their opportunities for fraud, stimulated overaccumulation on an unprecedented scale, and crises were typically precipitated by the failure of railway promotions. Nevertheless the devaluation of railway investments left the railways in place, the reduction in transport costs stimulating renewed accumulation, which was driven forward by a further wave of railway construction and promotion.

The crisis of 1873 revealed the limits of this form of accumulation. The penetration of the more populous regions of the world by the railways was more or less complete. The extent of fraudulent and speculative promotions revealed by the crisis, the proliferation of unprofitable railways, and the more conservative lending policies of the banks that survived the crash, meant that there was no basis for a new promotional boom in the wake of the crisis. On the other hand, the domestic sources of recovery were still restricted by the limited consumption power of the mass of the population. Even though falling food prices led to rising living standards, the bulk of working class incomes was devoted to food, clothing and housing, providing a stimulus to the development of agriculture, construction and public utilities, but little direct demand for the products of factory industry beyond the traditional textile industry. Thus the renewed accumulation of capital on the basis of the revolutionising of the forces of production constantly came up against the barrier of the limited market. Having overcome the external natural and social barriers to accumulation with the extension of the railways and the elimination of petty production, the further development of the forces of production came up against the barrier of the capitalist social relations of production, leading to intensified competition between capitalists. Intensified competition in turn stimulated the further development of the forces of production and the further overaccumulation of capital, leading to growing pressure on profits, the devaluation of capital and the destruction of productive capacity. From 1873 the barrier to the accumulation of capital had become capital itself.

The crisis of 1873, which broke with the collapse of a railway investment boom in Central Europe and the United States, soon spread world-wide. The immediate impact of the crisis in Britain was not as dramatic as had been that of previous crises. For the first time the Bank of England was able to weather an international financial crisis without major bank failures and without having to suspend the Bank Act. However the impact of the crisis overseas was more severe. The emergence of massive overproduction, particularly in coal, iron, steel and textiles, in the wake of the crisis of 1873 threatened to destroy newly developing industries, particularly in Germany and the United States, where capitalists carried the high fixed costs of recent investment, much of which had been financed by borrowing, and enjoyed only limited access to world markets. The reduction in the demand for food and raw materials, together with the increased supply as newly opened territories came into production, extended the crisis to agriculture, prices being supported in the middle of the decade only by a series of bad European harvests.

Although the British financial system had survived the crisis, its depressive impact on Britain's markets was soon felt in intensified competition which pressed hard on profits. However the British commercial and manufacturing system was well-adapted to absorbing such shocks. British manufacturers carried little debt, had a large home market and diversified foreign markets at their command, access to those markets being secured by British commercial and financial supremacy. Capitalist agriculture was already well developed in England, though not in Ireland, and the main victims were landowners who faced falling rents, while farmers were able to diversify into the production of meat and vegetables.

In the US and Continental Europe the destruction of capacity and the restructuring of capital in the crisis provided the basis for domestic recovery, but in Britain much less capacity was liquidated, while the relative stagnation of world trade and investment removed the traditional bases of recovery, so that the period from 1873 to 1896 came to be known as the Great Depression.

Depression, industrial relations and social insurance

Although the depression was not as severe in Britain as elsewhere, it was more persistent. British manufacturers responded to the depression in their well-tried ways, cutting back production levels and accepting lower prices and profits, without incurring the costs of developing and applying new methods of production and without significant changes in business organisation, in the expectation that commercial capitalists would soon open up new markets. However the failure of new markets to materialise meant that the brief spurts of recovery were soon checked until new forces could emerge to stimulate the renewal of accumulation on a world scale. When the world boom began to gather pace, unevenly at first, from the end of the century, Britain was dragged along with it, although productivity continued to stagnate, domestic industrial profits were by no means spectacular, and rising food prices steadily eroded real wages.

The period was not one of uniform depression, but of brief periods of recovery that were checked as accumulation came up against the barrier of the limited market, and of considerable unevenness in the fate of the various branches of production. Prices, profits and unemployment rose and fell, but within a trend of generally falling prices, low profits and relatively high unemployment. This was the context in which the class struggle developed in and against the constitutional framework provided by the trades union and electoral reforms.

Trades unionism had tended to follow the course of the cycle, with unions thriving in the boom and being weakened or destroyed as the employers sought to reduce wages in the depression. However the long boom had provided a favourable context for the growth and consolidation of skilled trades unions, although fluctuations in the fortunes of their employers still provoked sharp conflicts and many setbacks. At first the Great Depression was no different from previous periods of difficulty, as employers sought to force down wages. However the persistence of price instability within a falling trend meant that such disputes proved very costly, both to the trades unions and the employers, while competitive wage cutting intensified conflicts with the unions and competition among employers. The fall in food prices from the end of the 1870s provided the context within which trades unions were prepared to negotiate wage cuts for their members as the price of industrial peace. There was therefore a rapid development of mechanisms for negotiation, conciliation and arbitration from the 1880s that provided constitutional channels for the regulation of 'industrial relations', allowing for the adjustment of wages without costly strikes.

The state shared the interest of trades unions and employers in the institutionalisation of the wage relation within a stable indus-

trial relations framework which established the uniformity and stability of wages, with disputes being resolved by negotiation, rather
than through strike action which brought the trades unions inevitably into confrontation with the state. Thus the state played
an increasingly active role from the middle of the 1890s in encouraging the growth of industrial relations and in sponsoring negotiation
and arbitration when industrial relations broke down.

Persistent depression and the limitations of sectional trades
unionism encouraged the growth of socialism in the 1880s, the socialists playing a leading role in the unemployed agitation in the
depression of the middle of the decade and the spectacular growth
of the 'new unionism' of the less skilled workers at the end of the
decade. Although unskilled unionism was largely destroyed in the
subsequent slump, the unemployed agitation aroused considerable
anxiety on the part of the state and focussed attention on the
'problem' of the unemployed. The political fear, realised in unruly
demonstrations in London in 1886 and 1887, was that the trades
unions and the unemployed would join forces with the pauperised
residuum to present a serious threat to public order, which the socialists could convert into a threat to the constitution. This fear
was expressed in a concern that the employed working class would
be morally contaminated by contact with the residuum if it fell
back on the Poor Law. This concern led to the provision of relief
for the cyclically unemployed outside the Poor Law, and later underlay the development of social insurance, distinct from the Poor
Law, to deal with the problems of cyclical unemployment, sickness
and old age.

As the locus of working class agitation shifted from London to
the industrial districts the immediate political threat of the urban poor waned. On the other hand, the humiliation of the Poor
Law and the degradation of the workhouse threatened the whole
working class in periods of sickness, unemployment and old age,
providing a basis for class unity and a recruiting ground for socialism. The hope that the employed would be able to support
themselves in adversity by taking out private or cooperative insurance was unrealistic when low pay was widespread, bouts of cyclical
unemployment more frequent, and wages falling from the turn of
the century. This led to a new approach to the problem of poverty
on the part of the state. On the one hand, the problem of chronic
pauperism was distinguished from that of the residuum, poverty

being seen primarily as a problem of low pay and casual labour. In an attempt to deal with the problem, and relieve the Poor Law, the state established Trade Boards, to regulate industrial relations in industries where trades unionism was undeveloped, and inserted fair wage clauses in public contracts. On the other hand, the state established a compulsory state-administered scheme of sickness and unemployment insurance, financed by employers, workers and the state, and introduced old age pensions, which freed growing numbers of workers from the harshness of the Poor Law.

The limits of social reform

The reform of trades union and industrial legislation, the growth of public expenditure on health, education and housing, the provision of social insurance and the alleviation of the harshness of the Poor Law, all represented limited concessions to the aspirations of the working class, expressed both through the electoral system and through extra-parliamentary agitation. Although such reforms did not necessarily conflict with the interests of capital, the important point is that they reflected an increasingly explicit recognition that capital, through the rule of money and the law, could not secure the physical, moral and social reproduction of the working class, which had therefore to be secured through collective provision. However the socialisation of the reproduction of the working class through social administration, social insurance and the system of industrial relations was circumscribed by the continued subordination of the individual worker to the wage form and of women within the family form. This meant that the working class had no unqualified right to subsistence. Such a right could only be earned by hard labour and regular insurance contributions, or by female dependence. But the working class had no right to work either. Thus a growing proportion of the population was disqualified from a right to subsistence not because they were unwilling to make a productive contribution to society, but because capital could not provide them with the opportunity to make such a contribution within the wage form. Denied the right to work, the worker had to submit to degrading inspection and supervision to qualify for support, proving eligibility on the grounds of sickness, insanity, old age or disability. Women and children could only secure subsistence if they could prove that there was no man who could be compelled to support them. Able-bodied men could only secure subsistence by submitting their willingness to work to the 'workhouse test'. The low paid were disqualified from relief by the principle of 'less eligibility'.

The limits of social reform were not simply a reflection of the political power of capital, but more fundamentally reflected the limits of the capitalist state form. The state had no power to grant a right to work, nor the resources to provide large-scale employment or indiscriminate relief. Even the limited scale of provision imposed a heavy burden of taxation by contemporary standards, the financing of the Edwardian social insurance system provoking a constitutional crisis. The only way the state could hope to relieve poverty was by encouraging the absorption of the poor into wage labour and seeking to eliminate casual and sweated labour. Thus the essential thrust of social reform from the 1870s was not to relieve want through more generous public provision but rather to develop forms of regulation that would increase the ability and obligation of workers to make provision for their own subsistence needs on the basis of the wage form, a possibility that became more realistic with the general rise in wages during the Great Depression. The development of trades unionism and collective bargaining, and later Wages Boards, minimum wage legislation, and increased levels of benefit for the unemployed, provided a means of securing a living wage for those in work. The strengthening of the family through moral and religious exhortation, through legal and administrative regulation, through the provision of housing, welfare services and medical inspection, strengthened the obligation on able-bodied adults to support their family members. The extension of public education sought to provide the working class with the social, moral and technical skills required for wage labour. The working class was encouraged, and later compelled, to make provision for the cyclical problems of unemployment, sickness and old age through insurance. The functional differentiation of the Poor Law focussed its punitive thrust on the able-bodied poor. Thus the state responded to the struggle of the working class to secure its individual and social reproduction by developing a system of social reform in which the working class was the object of an increasingly complex web of regulation, inspection and supervision that sought to reconcile the physical reproduction of the worker with the subordination of the working class to the perceived needs of capital.

The working class enjoyed a contradictory relation to the apparatus of social reform. On the one hand, the apparatus of social reform improved the ability of the working class family to reproduce itself, at least at a minimal level of subsistence, and even to improve its condition. On the other hand, the apparatus only provided support on the basis of the subordination of the worker to the power of capital, through the wage form, and the state, through the form of social administration. The working class did not accept that accidents of birth or fortune should condemn the worker to subordination to the power of capital or to the agencies of the state. While the working class accepted the wage, poor relief, sickness or unemployment benefit, it did not accept the price it was asked to pay for its meagre subsistence. However generous the scale of public provision, and however high the wage, the working class constantly resented and resisted the forms through which it secured its subsistence, challenging and confronting the power of capital and the state and the alienated forms of public provision.

Working class resistance appeared spontaneously in workers' everyday relations with capital and the state. Trades unionism provided the working class with a basis on which to develop its collective strength, the vote with a basis on which to pursue the struggle for the democratisation of public administration, and socialism an ideology within which to formulate its collective aspirations. The state could not countenance the attempt of the working class to challenge its constitutional authority by mobilising this collective strength in support of its aspirations, but sought to confine working class struggles within the constitutional framework provided for it through a dual strategy of repression and concession.

The constitutional framework of working class representation was embodied in the dual forms of industrial relations and parliamentary representation. The expression of working class aspirations through the fragmented forms of industrial relations and electoral politics confined those aspirations within the dual forms of capital's power, the state and the wage relation, and concessions to the working class were made primarily to contain its struggles within those channels, reaffirming its continued subordination to capital. However the wage form and the state form equally set limits to the ability of capital and the state to respond to the aspirations of the working class by providing higher wages, employment and welfare benefits. When the aspirations of the working class threatened to press beyond those limits the working class struggle could no longer be confined within the constitutional forms provided for it.

Industrial relations provided an appropriate framework for the trades unions to express working class aspirations within the wage form. Parliamentary representation provided an appropriate channel for trades unions to seek the reform of the law and for Fabian socialists to pursue their demands for radical social reform. However constitutional trades unionism and constitutional politics were unable to secure stable wages, guaranteed employment, adequate housing, education and welfare benefits, and above all were unable to challenge the everyday subordination of the working class to the economic and political power of capital. Such organisational and political forms did not appear very promising to the rank and file movement that took root in the boom immediately preceeding the First World War, which was increasingly attracted to the class politics of direct action socialism that sought workers' control on the basis of industrial unionism. While the former could be accommodated by the state, the latter was fiercely resisted in the name not of the power of capital, but of the defence of the constitution. However the confrontation with the state was postponed by the outbreak of war, when the state mobilised its last and most powerful weapon, national chauvinism.

The limits of social reform were set by the limits of the liberal state form. Social reform could attempt to reconcile the reproduction of the working class with its subordination to the wage form, but it could not provide jobs for the unemployed, nor adequate wages for those in work. The rise of social reform was accompanied by a growing concern of the state with the issues of national prosperity, rising wages and the growth of employment. This concern was partly in response to growing political pressures, but also in response to the financial pressures arising from the costs of social reform and poor relief.

The barriers to sustained accumulation no longer appeared as the physical barriers of limited productive capacity, nor as the natural barriers of transport difficulties, nor as the social barrier of the resistance of the working class. The barrier to accumulation was now capital itself, a barrier that appeared in the growing pressure of

international competition, which was the result of the overaccumulation of capital on a world scale. The attempt of the nation state
to secure the sustained accumulation of domestic productive capital
in the face of such competition brought to the fore the contradiction between the global character of accumulation and the national
form of the state as the intervention of nation states politicised the
competitive struggle, presented new barriers to accumulation, and
eventually degenerated into inter-imperialist war.

Chapter 7

Overaccumulation and the Limits of the Nation State

The national form of the capitalist state

The state consolidated the power of capital on a national basis. The national form of the capitalist state was in part a legacy of the national form of the pre-existing state. On the other hand, the national form of the capitalist state was not simply a contingent historical residue. The social revolution that undermined the basis of the earlier form of the state also undermined the basis on which the national character of its sovereignty was established, while providing new foundations on which to establish national unity.

The unity of the precapitalist state was essentially an expression of the political unity of the class on whose social power the authority of the state ultimately rested. The rise of commodity and capitalist production gradually dissolved the personal and corporate foundations of this power, to submit society to the homogeneous and abstract rule of money. National unity could no longer be constituted on the basis of the unification of fragmented and localised powers. The unity of the nation was now defined by the uniform rule of the emerging social power of money.

The reconstitution of the nation state was centred on the creation of an integrated national economy regulated by a uniform currency. Such a development concerned not only the monetary system, for the rule of money required the dissolution of all social, political and even natural barriers to its power. Thus it involved the unification and rationalisation of the legal system, the subordination of administration to legal regulation, the removal of all legal and fiscal barriers to the free mobility of labour, capital and commodities, and the development of a national transport system. In securing the uniform rule of the national currency and the national legal system these developments simultaneously defined the national sovereignty of the state against all particularistic powers within its boundaries, on the one hand, and against the sovereignty of other nation states beyond its boundaries, on the other.

The geographical unevenness of the accumulation of capital and of the destruction of precapitalist social forms meant that the attempt to reconstitute the nation state on the basis of capital met with concerted resistance, particularly in localities in which the development of capitalist social relations was less advanced. Such resistance might be ruthlessly repressed, but where constitutional channels for local resistance were available it could appear as a struggle within the apparatus of the state between the central government and local or provincial authorities.

In Britain the resistance of local authorities to the imposition of the authority of the central government was fierce. The Act of Union, and the suppression of the risings of 1715 and 1745, integrated Scotland into the national state, although it kept its own legal and banking system, while even the most ruthless repression could not subordinate Ireland to the British state. In the United States the federal system of government and the democratic constitution provided much more scope for resistance to national economic integration and political unification. Conflict between the Eastern financial and commercial centres, the Western States, and Southern export interests underlay the uneven development and marked instability of the US banking system, which intensified commercial and financial fluctuations in the Atlantic trade that had world-wide repercussions throughout the nineteenth century. The issues of tariffs, the currency, land settlement and railway building were central to the struggle for States' rights against the integrationist aspirations of the Federal government, culminating in the secession of the Southern States and the Civil War in the wake of the crisis of 1857. The victory of the North laid the foundations for national political unification on the basis of the domestic integration of accumulation through the free mobility of commodities, labour and capital and the extension of the frontier, protected behind high external tariff barriers that kept up domestic prices and so sustained petty producers while providing large profits for big capital. However conflict over the currency issue persisted even after the reintroduction of central banking and the adoption of the gold standard. The populist alliance of small farmers and silver producers pressed vigorously for bimetallism and easy credit until it was decisively defeated in the election of 1896.

In the United States the Federal government eventually asserted its authority over the States. Elsewhere, however, local resistance was more successful, particularly where cultural factors gave such resistance a national form, leading eventually to the fragmentation of the Austrian and Imperial Russian Empires and to the partial independence of Ireland and, more recently, to the successful anti-colonial movements for national independence. On the other hand, cultural factors could also give ideological form to movements for national integration, as in the case of Germany, where Prussia broke down the barriers between previously independent states, whether by mutual agreement or by force.

The state constituted the power of capital on a national basis, breaking down internal political barriers to the rule of law and of money. However capital was from its birth a global power which sought to overcome the barriers of national frontiers and local currencies to command labour and open up markets on a world scale. Thus the struggle to break down political barriers to the rule of capital had both national and international dimensions. While the nation state was a means of securing the rule of capital at the national level, on a global scale it presented a barrier to capital's ambitions.

The international system of nation states

The attempt of capital to break down the political barriers to accumulation on a world scale focussed on the same issues of the currency and the freedom of trade that dominated the struggle to break down internal political barriers. Thus the question of the national integration of the state could not be divorced from that of the integration of the international state system. The centralisation of the national financial system secured the uniform rule of money in the domestic economy, but the parallel formation of state money carried with it the danger that the state would respond to fiscal and political pressures by overexpanding the currency, the subsequent inflation undermining the international circulation of commodities and capital, devaluing capital and disrupting accumulation. The state might similarly respond to such pressures by imposing tariffs and restricting the free international movement of commodities, capital and labour-power, threatening a return to the short-sighted policies of mercantilism and commercial wars. For political economy the principles of free trade, the balanced budget and the gold standard were the means by which the contradiction between the national form of the state and the international character of capital accumulation were to be reconciled as domestic accumulation was subordinated to the accumulation of capital on a world scale, and the nation state subordinated to the power of world money. However it was not sufficient for political economy to demonstrate the wisdom of such liberal policies. They could only prevail through often intense political struggles.

The advocacy of free trade and the gold standard by political economy was not merely an ideological cloak for the interests of British capital, as the protectionist theorists of the 'national economy' charged, but rather expressed the cosmopolitanism of advanced capitals on a world scale, who sought free access to the world market as a source of cheap means of production and subsistence and an outlet for their products. Free trade was correspondingly resisted most vigorously by weaker capitals, supported by the workers who depended on them, and petty producers who sought protection from the ravages of competition. These issues were fought out in the first instance at the level of the nation state, and there was no guarantee that the interests of cosmopolitan capital would prevail. The state was not only subject to popular and partisan political pressures, but fiscal and monetary considerations could also make the state reluctant to adopt free trade and the gold standard. Governments were reluctant to abandon much-needed sources of revenue and feared the immediate impact of liberalisation on the balance of international payments. These considerations, in addition to the landowners' defence of the Corn Laws, delayed the introduction of free trade in Britain into the 1840s.

The complementary accumulation of manufacturing capital in Britain and agricultural and mining capital in the rest of the world provided the basis for the rise of an international freemasonry of capital in the nineteenth century. Domestic resistance to trade liberalisation and monetary conservatism was ameliorated to the extent that backward agricultural capital in Britain and manufacturing capital elsewhere enjoyed a degree of protection variously from residual tariff barriers, protective legislation, high transport costs, low wages, cheap raw materials or specialisation. Moreover the primary victims in crises of overaccumulation were merchants and bankers, who had speculated injudiciously, and petty producers and the working class, whose resistance was usually met with repression (although the democratic constitution in the United States gave petty producers a constitutional basis for resistance and so presented a barrier to both the national and the international integration of US capital).

The issues of free trade and the gold standard expressed divisions within the capitalist class that cut across national frontiers. Thus the relations between nation states within the international system of capitalist states did not express the relations between competing national capitals, although individual capitalists were only too happy to enlist the state's support in their global adventures, but rather the contradictory relation between the protectionist tendencies of weaker capitalists and petty producers and the cosmopolitanism of advanced capitals. Correspondingly the issues of free trade and the gold standard were not fought out only at a national, but also at an international level. Trade liberalisation and the development of an appropriate international legal and monetary framework was primarily achieved by international negotiation, and was supported by the global power and influence of British capital and the British state.

London was the world centre for the international circulation of commodities and money. Local merchants depended on their British connections for access to the world markets that provided outlets for exports of primary products and sources of manufactured goods, industrial raw materials and means of production. Local bankers depended on their British connections for access to

London's bullion and financial markets to secure their cash reserves by buying gold or by borrowing. National governments similarly relied on British financial markets to secure loans to finance increasing expenditure or to stabilise their currencies. The British state was able to exploit this commercial and financial power to cajole foreign governments into adopting appropriate commercial and financial policies. Thus London provided the loans necessary to stabilise European currencies in the wake of the Napoleonic Wars. The revolutions of 1848 similarly provided Britain with opportunities to exert pressure for trade liberalisation and monetary stabilisation on the basis of its provision of political, diplomatic and financial support for the counter-revolutions.

Where the balance of domestic political forces could not be tipped by international negotiation Britain played the primary role in using its diplomatic and military power to further trade liberalisation and currency stabilisation on a world scale. In the name of free trade Britain fought the Napoleonic Wars, backed the national liberal revolutions in Latin America, destroyed the monopoly of its own East India and Levant Companies, opened up China in the Opium Wars, checked Russian expansionism in the Crimea, and unsuccessfully supported the secessionists in the American Civil War. The British navy enforced the security of property on the high seas and in the peripheral regions.

The development of the political struggles over the national unification and international integration of the state was dominated by the rhythm of accumulation on a world scale. While sustained accumulation on a world scale strengthened the forces of cosmopolitanism, the struggle tended to intensify in the wake of crises of overaccumulation, in which advanced capitals sought to expand the market, while weaker capitals, sections of the working class, and petty producers sought protection and relief. Thus the crisis of 1847 precipitated the unsuccessful European revolutions of 1848, which had both a class and a national character, while the crisis of 1857 precipitated both the European movements towards national unification and the Southern secession in the United States. It was the mid-Victorian boom that ultimately provided the favourable circumstances for the liberalisation of trade and the construction of an international legal and monetary system. The growth of the international financial system centred on London relieved national governments of the pressure on public finances and their currencies that were the immediate result of liberalisation, while the growth of world trade strengthened the position of cosmopolitan capitals and, in the agricultural exporting countries, the landed class, giving them the upper hand in the renewed class conflicts following the crisis of 1857, with the significant exception of the more democratic United States, so that by 1870 the Cobdenite dream of a world order of peace and prosperity based on free trade seemed close to realisation, the Franco-Prussian War appearing as the last gasp of an old order. The dream was shattered by the political tensions opened up by the crisis of 1873.

The 1873 crisis, the nation state and the rise of imperialism

The crisis of 1873 had a devastating impact in continental Europe and, to a lesser extent, the United States. Petty producers were destroyed, banks collapsed, unemployment rose and industrial struggles intensified. In Germany in particular new industries were threatened with destruction as international competition intensified, leading to demands for protection, that were at first unheeded by the state. The first reaction to the crisis in Germany and the United States was defensive. Capitalists sought to limit the impact of competition by forming monopolies and cartels and through vertical integration, such 'rationalisation' usually being sponsored by credit banks in Germany and investment banks in the US, the financiers being concerned to protect their investment. However such measures had only limited impact on the ability of capitalists to control the market so long as they continued to be vulnerable to foreign competition. In the US the victory of the North in the Civil War had already confirmed the retention of protection, and indeed the crisis precipitated a limited liberalisation of trade in the attempt to reduce the cost of essential imports, but in Europe agitation for protection intensified through the 1870s amid accusations of British dumping. Although the monopolisation of capital and the growing integration of financial and manufacturing capital considerably increased the political weight of the latter, their agitation continued to be ineffective until the emergence of agricultural overproduction on a world scale towards the end of the decade led agriculture, and the politically dominant landowners, to join the call for protection.

Even when the major branches of production all called for protection the demand was not necessarily a basis for political unity. Agricultural and manufacturing capitalists might each favour protection of their own branch of production, while virulently opposing that of the other. The protection of agriculture raised food prices, and so the wages paid by manufacturers, while manufacturing protection risked retaliation and a loss of agricultural export markets. The decisive factor in the introduction of protection was not so much the interests of capital as the crisis of the state to which the crisis of accumulation gave rise.

Increased international competition and the destabilisation of the balance of trade disrupted international political alliances based on complementary trading relations. The deterioration in the balance of trade as the crisis deepened put increasing pressure on the bullion reserves, threatening the state with a monetary crisis. The decline in trade eroded the revenues of the state, threatening a fiscal crisis. The contraction of the international financial system meant that the state could not cover its balance of payments or budget deficits by foreign borrowing. The orthodox remedy for such a crisis was to raise interest rates, contract credit, raise taxes and cut expenditure in order to stabilise the currency and the financial system and force down prices to restore international competitiveness while liquidating unsound investments. However deflation merely intensified the depression. The protests of weaker capitalists at such a deflation were stilled as soon as they were liquidated as capitalists. Redundant workers, on the other hand, were not liquidated but joined the ranks of the unemployed, providing fertile ground for socialist agitation, while distressed urban and rural petty producers were drawn into the populist assault on the subordination of the state to the power of the bankers and landowners. When the depression extended to agriculture these forces threatened to combine to present a political challenge to the state and to the ruling class. The crisis was most acute in Germany, where pressure on the rural population threatened the breakdown of the patriarchal social structure, already undermined by the rapid development of capitalist agriculture on the estates of the landed aristocracy. Thus in Germany the call of the landowners for protection was closely connected with the resurgence of a conservative desire to restore social order by restoring patriarchal social relations in the countryside. It was this political threat that was the decisive factor in the turn to protectionism in Europe.

Although protection only relieved some capitalists at the expense of others, and raised new barriers to the accumulation of capital on a world scale, for the nation state it resolved the political crisis in one fell swoop. It not only promised to limit the rise in unemployment and ease the pressure on peasants and petty producers, but it also provided a means of checking the drain on the reserves by reducing imports, while tariffs provided a much needed source of revenue, relieving the pressure to adopt deflationary policies. Moreover the nationalistic ideology within which calls for protection were couched had the added appeal of providing a framework for the ideological identification of the working class with the state. Thus in Germany the introduction of protection was closely associated with the ruthless suppression of the Social Democratic Party and the beginnings of social reform. By the late 1870s the appeal of protectionism in Continental Europe had become irresistible, even at the risk of provoking retaliation and tariff wars that would increase international tension and intensify the spiral of decline. Although protection did provoke retaliation, and increased international tension, as it led to a restructuring of international political relations on the basis of a restructuring of trading relationships, its escalation was contained because Britain remained committed to free trade.

In Britain protection was irrelevant to productive capitalists as they were not immediately threatened by foreign competition in the home market. Independent petty production in agriculture and manufacture had been virtually destroyed, the Irish peasantry being appeased by land reform and contained by repression. The working class was strongly committed to free trade, which provided employment in the export trades and increasingly cheap food. Although recovery in Germany and the United States led to growing British imports of manufactured goods from the late 1880s these were primarily complementary rather than competitive, comprising new products such as chemicals, electrical equipment, scientific instruments and advanced machine tools. Thus Britain remained committed to free trade in its domestic markets.

While British productive capital was not threatened in its domestic markets, and could do little about the barriers to trade in protected markets, it was crucially dependent on its position in neutral markets. The depression created serious difficulties for commercial capitalists in such markets. Indigenous suppliers resisted the attempts of merchants to pass on the decline in world prices, while increased competition from third parties threatened a loss of markets and a loss of influence. In response to this threat established commercial interests sought to enlist the support of the metropolitan state in consolidating their political position by annexation of the territory. Strategic considerations, linked to the growing political tensions associated with increased competition on a world scale, and a belief that the colonies might provide outlets for the surplus population, persuaded the metropolitan state to bow to the pressure. While the US made it clear that no British expansionism in the Americas would be tolerated, Britain dominated the scramble for colonies in Africa and Asia that ensued.

Imperialism was all the more enthusiastically pursued as its ideological and political benefits became clear, securing the identification of the working class with the state in its imperialist adventures. Imperialism promised to open up the wealth of continents to provide markets that would secure jobs for the working class, and supplies of cheap food that would raise working class living standards to undreamt of heights. The expansion of gold mining in South Africa, secured by the brutal war against the native population and the established Boer settlers, provided the most appropriate symbolic expression of these fantasies. Although some sections of the working class identified with the victims of imperialism, the majority were caught up in the jingoistic fever of imperialism. However the fostering of chauvinistic and imperialist sentiment was a double-edged weapon. While imperialism provided a powerful basis on which to secure the political reconciliation of the working class to the rule of capital, the international conflicts that it aroused threatened the liberal world order on which the accumulation of capital on a world scale depended. However the tensions associated with the imperialist scramble for colonies were reduced by the Berlin Conference, and by Britain's and Germany's commitment to free trade in their colonies, so that the partition of the world was achieved without the imperialist powers coming to blows, violence being directed entirely against the indigenous colonial populations.

By the time protection was introduced it was largely irrelevant as a barrier to trade in manufactures since the German and US producers who had survived the crash, or been reconstructed on the basis of takeovers and mergers, could withstand any competitive threat. Similarly in France manufacturers had responded to increased competition by judicious specialisation. In agriculture protection was much more significant, bolstering the power of the declining landed class and preserving the peasantry as a political counterweight to the working class.

The primary significance of protection in manufacture was the stimulus it gave to the monopolisation and restructuring of manufacturing capital in Germany and the United States. Tariffs raised prices in domestic markets, boosting profits and so stimulating the renewed overaccumulation of capital. However monopolies and cartels were able to prevent domestic competition from driving down prices, the surplus product being sold cheaply abroad, enabling the more advanced producers to sustain accumulation by penetrating world markets. The large enterprise provided the basis for the development and application of advanced technology, particularly in Germany which had a well-established system of technical and scientific education, and of modern methods of business organisation, particularly in the United States. In these large enterprises management replaced the market as the means of coordinating production and distribution in order to reap the advantages of large scale and continuous production. The close relation with financial capital provided the capital resources required to finance such enterprises, in the absence of developed capital markets, and considerably increased the political weight of big capital against that of the landowners in Germany, and the populist petty bourgeoisie in the United States. The technical, managerial and financial advantages of such large scale enterprises provided a further stimulus to horizontal and vertical integration, which began to extend beyond the national borders to embrace foreign sources of supply and foreign markets. Thus protection enabled monopoly capital in Germany and the US to prepare for its assault on the world market.

Protectionism did not mark a retreat from the world market, but rather enabled the state to stabilise the currency and regulate the balance of trade without recourse to sharply deflationary policies that undermined the domestic authority of the state and the ruling class. Thus protectionism was closely associated with the formal adoption of the gold standard, that implied a commitment to pursuing conservative monetary policies to maintain international competitiveness, and with imperialism, that sought to open up world markets. In Germany protectionism was already becoming a barrier to accumulation in the late 1880s as it raised industrial costs and restricted access to neighbouring markets in the East. With the fall of Bismark the new Liberal government initiated a series of mutual tariff reductions, notably with Russia.

Recovery, first in Germany and then in the United States, stimulated the renewal of accumulation on a world scale on the basis of the introduction of new products and new technologies. The growing demand for food and raw materials towards the end of the century provided the stimulus to open up new sources of supply with the further extension of the railways at the end of the century, particularly in Australia, Africa and Latin America, and the expansion of steam shipping, expanding the demand for the products of heavy industry and the world market for manufactured goods. The complementarity of trade reduced the significance of tariff barriers, while Britain's open market provided an outlet for the products of new industries and new technologies. Despite rising imports of manufactured goods Britain's balance of payments remained strong. The less sophisticated markets of the primary producing countries, stimulated by buoyant export demand and substantial overseas investment, provided an outlet for Britain's traditional manufactures, although competitiveness could only be maintained by holding down wages in the face of rising prices in the decade before the war. The iron, steel, coal, heavy engineering and shipbuilding industries were sustained by the demands of the railways and shipping. The growth of world trade provided booming profits for the City of London, which continued to dominate international finance, shipping and insurance. Thus buoyant export demand enabled Britain to keep its domestic market open to the technologically more sophisticated products of its industrial competitors, so sustaining their demand for the products of the primary producers who purchased traditional British products in their turn.

Britain's international financial and commercial strength enabled the City of London to continue to play its role as the coordinating centre of the international freemasonry of capital. The adoption of the gold standard stabilised the international integration of the world monetary system, with the leading financial centres handling domestic and regional clearances, while the City of London integrated and regulated the system as a whole by providing the financial centre for the multilateral clearing of international payments. London provided short-term credit and long-term investment that sustained accumulation on a world scale by financing substantial payments imbalances. Although the fixed exchange rates and free convertibility of currencies associated with the gold standard restrained national governments from pursuing inflationary domestic monetary and budgetary policies, the specie-flow mechanism did not correct imbalances by inducing changes in relative price levels, as the economists continued to believe, but by inducing movements of short-term capital in response to changes in relative interest rates. Domestic policies were determined primarily by domestic economic and political objectives, rather than by the foreign balance. While the gold standard served to accommodate payments imbalances, it did not provide any adequate mechanism for rectifying such imbalances. Where chronic imbalances arose, particularly in the peripheral regions, governments did not permit the foreign drain to precipitate massive deflation, political destabilisation and economic collapse, but introduced protective tariffs, devalued their currencies or went off gold altogether.

The Bank of England administered the gold standard on the basis of remarkably small reserves, and so was very vulnerable to a run on the reserves if foreign bankers chose to present large sums of sterling for payment, or raised their interest rates to draw funds from London. Thus the stability of the system, and London's dominance within it, depended on the tacit cooperation of the major competing financial centres and the responsiveness of the Bank of England to foreign pressures. This provided a check on any temptation the Bank of England may have been under to allow national interests to dictate its international monetary policies. Nevertheless the ability of the Bank of England to act as the central banker to the international monetary system depended on its avoiding a conflict between its domestic and its international responsibilities. In general the consistency of these responsibilities was underpinned by the continued dependence of domestic accumulation on its integration into the sustained accumulation of capital on a world scale. However Britain no longer dominated accumulation on a world scale, so the requirements of domestic and international monetary policy no longer coincided as closely as they had half a century earlier. In practice conflict was avoided as the Bank dissociated its domestic from its international responsibilities by developing policy instruments that enabled it to defend the reserves by regulating international capital movements, while having as small an impact as possible on the domestic financial system. The result was that the Bank of England pursued an active monetary policy in relation to its foreign objectives, independently of domestic considerations.

Although the reappearance of inflation from the mid-1890s led to proposals that the Bank should be more active in securing domestic price stability, it continued to pursue a largely passive and accommodating policy in relation to domestic financial demands. The regulation of domestic accumulation was primarily in the hands of the commercial banks, who maintained their own ample reserves and had little reason to call on the Bank of England, tendencies to the speculative overexpansion of credit being checked not by the Bank of England, but by the conservative lending policies of the monopolistic joint-stock banks.

Overaccumulation and imperialist war

By the 1890s the restabilisation of the liberal world order seemed to be complete. Falling food prices, the franchise, industrial relations, imperialism and social reform appeared to be on the way to banishing poverty and class struggle in the metropolitan centres. The strength of London as the centre of the international financial system made it possible for accumulation to be sustained without the appearance of a major international crisis, despite marked cyclical fluctuations. Although militarism and international tensions remained, the flow of productive, financial and commodity capital across national frontiers was growing at an increasing rate, sustaining a strengthening world boom and raising hopes that the cosmopolitanism of capital would overcome the barriers of the national state form. However, as the overaccumulation of capital began to come up once more against the barrier of the limited market, increased competition intensified domestic class struggles and renewed international tensions. The boom was sustained by massive international flows of investment and credit and by rapidly increasing military expenditure, only checked by a brief slump in 1908. However by 1913 there were clear signs that the boom was about to break. Only the outbreak of war, which led to massive increases in military expenditure and the more active intervention of the state in the regulation of production, staved off the inevitable crisis.

Although Germany was most active in provoking hostilities, the international tensions that erupted in war were underlain by the same contradiction between the accumulation of capital on a world scale and the national form of the state that had underlain the rise of protectionism and imperialism from the 1870s, a contradiction that re-emerged as soon as the pressure of overaccumulation increased international competition. On the one hand, the nation state presented a barrier to the accumulation of capital on a world scale. On the other hand, the liberalisation of international trade and finance threatened the political and constitutional stability of the nation state, on the basis of which the political power of capital was constituted, as the pressure of international competition intensified industrial conflict, destroyed jobs, and liquidated urban and rural petty producers. The confrontation of the imperialist powers was not simply a political expression of the competition between distinct national capitals, which was more a result than a cause of imperialism, but rather of the contradiction inherent in the national form of the capitalist state as it sought to preserve its financial and political stability in the face of the global crisis of overaccumulation.

As in the 1870s the contradictions unleashed by increasing international competition from the 1890s were most acute in those countries in which the domestic development of capitalist social relations of production was most uneven, above all in Central and Eastern Europe. In Germany the revival of liberalism in the early 1890s proved to be only a brief interlude as the domestic and international tensions unleashed led to a renewal of a militaristic imperialism. An alliance of conservative landowners and big capital used selective tariffs as a weapon in an imperialistic commercial policy aimed primarily at Russia, where a similar alliance reacted with similar policies. However the conflict assumed larger proportions primarily because of Germany's fear of British intentions.

Accumulation on a world scale was sustained by an international financial system based on the strength of sterling, and by the British commitment to free trade that guaranteed access to the British market for manufactured exports and to Britain's colonies as sources of supply of essential food and raw materials. However Britain was only able to perform this role for as long as Britain was able to sustain domestic accumulation on the basis of free trade and the gold standard. Doubts about the long-term viability of Britain's commitment to free trade were increasingly raised with the growing pressure of competition from its technologically more advanced competitors.

Although there had been calls for protection in Britain in the 1880s, the issue was first vigorously pressed by Joseph Chamberlain's Tariff Reform League between 1903 and 1906, that proposed a programme of protection, imperial preference and social reform. While there was widespread agreement on the need for social reform to contain class conflict and to deal with the problem of 'race degeneration', that was seen as a major cause of the loss of competitiveness, and on the importance of the empire, the issue of protection was much more contentious. Pressure for protection and imperial preference came most strongly from the iron and steel industry, which faced severe competition from the more advanced producers in Belgium, Germany and the United States, and from the metal manufacturers of the Midlands, who faced growing competition in Canadian and Australian markets. Protection also had the attraction that tariff revenues would pay for social reform. However, shipbuilding and engineering benefited from cheap imports of iron and steel, while textiles would face large cost increases if tariffs were imposed on imported raw materials. Above all the working class, and most employers, remained strongly committed to free trade that provided cheap imported food. The result was that the Conservatives, committed to Chamberlain's programme, were trounced in the 1906 election, and social reform was paid for by increases in direct taxation.

Despite the defeat of protectionism in the 1906 election, the Tariff Reform League, and the associated rise of anti-German sentiment, reinforced German fears of British intentions. If Britain were to abandon free trade its navy, its colonial empire and its financial strength gave it powerful weapons to use in defence of its national interests with which it could devastate the economies of its competitors. Germany was particularly vulnerable, with difficult access to world trade routes, no significant colonial empire, and growing reliance on the world market. Thus Germany's revival of the imperialist strategy from the late 1890s had precipitated the forging of international alliances and an arms race in which British determination to maintain overwhelming naval superiority

vied with German determination to acquire the means to secure
its trade routes against any British opposition. Paradoxically the
arms race played a major role in postponing the economic crisis,
that might well have realised German fears, by providing an outlet
for the products of those heavy industries in which the strongest
tendencies to overproduction had already begun to appear. However by 1914, as the world boom was showing clear signs that it
was about to break, the growth of militarism, domestic class conflict and international tension had reached such a pitch that the
outbreak of war had become inevitable.

Chapter 8

War, Revolution and Depression: The Limits of Liberalism

The impact of war

Protectionism, imperialism and social reform led to a substantial growth in the administrative and military apparatus of the state, and were associated with a centralisation and bureaucratisation of state power, but they did not mark a fundamental break with the liberal form of the state. However the priorities of war dictated that social production be brought under political control to secure its subordination to the war effort, while the need to secure the active collaboration of the working class in the imperialist war meant that the state had to be more responsive to working class economic, social and political aspirations. However the growing integration of the power of capital and the power of the state, and the political advance of the working class, threw into question both the class character and the liberal form of the state.

The outbreak of war did not immediately lead to the development of new forms of economic regulation. The war was expected to be short, and the belief was that governments could secure the necessary manpower and military supplies by relying on the market, financing expenditure by the traditional wartime expedient of borrowing. However, while military expenditure absorbed the overproduction that had emerged in the later stages of the pre-war boom, it soon became clear that capital could not respond adequately to the signals of the price mechanism. Increased government demand led to shortages of supply and price increases, while military recruitment led to manpower shortages. Inflation and profiteering led to growing working class unrest, while labour shortages strengthened the hand of the trades unions. The wartime priority accorded to the development of the forces of production suspended the resistance of capital to the direct intervention of the state in the regulation of production, in exchange for guaranteed profits. Direct controls were imposed on production, strategic industries were requisitioned and wages and the allocation and use of labour brought under increasingly rigorous and comprehensive control. The need to increase production and to develop substitutes for scarce imports led to government intervention to rationalise production units, introduce new methods of production and new forms of work organisation, and sponsor scientific and industrial research.

War-time expenditure was financed by government borrowing, but much of this borrowing was financed in turn by credit expansion that increased inflationary pressures, a further twist being added by increased levels of indirect taxation. Inflation was contained to a limited extent by increases in direct taxation and by price controls, but it was only when working class resistance to profiteering and the erosion of real wages threatened to get out of hand that systematic price controls, food rationing and increases in taxation reduced inflationary pressures.

The limited resources of the state meant that the apparatus of planning and control gave capitalists unprecedented opportunities to reverse the working class gains of the previous decades. However the closer association between capital and the state undermined the claim of the state to be directing the war effort in the national interest. On the other hand, the need to secure the willing body of recruits and conscripts to provide an energetic labour force at home and cannon fodder for the front made it imperative that the working class be persuaded not merely to acquiesce passively in the war effort, but to identify itself with the war aims of the state. The war split the nominally internationalist European working class parties, the majority factions identifying more or less enthusiastically with the war effort. The trades union leadership was accommodated to the restrictions on trades union rights and the concession of hard-won advances by promises of regulated wages, secure employment and a post-war restoration of the status quo. The collaboration of the working class leadership in the war effort was sealed by its admission to the corridors of power, the political leadership participating in government, the trades union leadership being represented on consultative and administrative bodies, in the hope that it would be able to secure its political advance permanently after the war, socialists seeing the apparatus of wartime control as a stage in the inevitable advance towards socialism.

The participation of the working class leadership in government brought few immediate advantages to the rank and file. On the whole the organised working class initially accepted the erosion of real wages as a contribution to the war effort. However the contrast between low wage rates, compensated only by long hours of overtime, and widespread profiteering by employers, shopkeepers and landlords, led to growing resentment. The haphazard development of payments systems, restrictions on the mobility of labour, the abolition of trades union rights and the extensive dilution of skilled labour eroded differentials, while the collaboration of the trades union leadership in government closed off the normal channels through which the affected workers could express their grievances. Growing resentment, particularly among skilled male workers, found its outlet in the development of rank and file organisation that crossed union and plant boundaries, and was strongly influenced by syndicalist ideas of direct action socialism and workers' control, finding its political expression in the socialist parties that had opposed the war.

These tendencies were manifested to a greater or lesser degree in all the contending powers. In Britain the Clyde rent strike of 1915 led to the Rent Restriction Act, while the Clyde revolt of 1916 and the more widespread engineering strike of 1917 secured closer control of the price and supply of food; the institutionalisation of national wage determination, with significant wage increases; concessions on dilution and labour mobility; the extension of unemployment insurance; the development of progressive taxation, including company taxation; and promises of a new Jerusalem to be built after the war. These measures served to defuse rank and file protest until military successes rekindled patriotic enthusiasm and optimisitic expectations of the new world to be built.

In Russia the autocratic state was less well-placed to represent itself as the embodiment of the national spirit and found itself increasingly isolated as the working class parties cemented an alliance between the rank and file workers, the peasantry and disaffected soldiers. The revolution of February 1917, that installed a liberal democratic government, did nothing to eliminate military and administrative corruption, nor to halt the deterioration in the economic and military position, and was followed by the Bolshevik victory in the October Revolution.

In Germany the working class movement was sharply divided. Economic breakdown and military failure towards the end of the war strengthened the revolutionary movement. However the Social Democratic Party saw the massive bureaucratisation and nationalisation of industry in the later stages of the war as the basis of a post-war regime of state socialism, and so was strongly committed to maintaining the authority of the state. Thus the Social Democratic Party participated enthusiastically in the suppression of the German Revolution, so sealing the fate of the revolutionary uprisings in the rest of Central Europe.

The post-war reconstruction of liberalism

The war had seen fundamental changes in the form of the state, involving the extensive socialisation of production, a pervasive system of controls, and a strengthening of working class political representation. The fundamental issue in the immediate post-war period was that of the form of the state, and of the relationship between the power of capital, the power of the state and the power of the organised working class.

Working class parties had entered government in the expectation of participating in the construction of a 'New Social Order', as the 1918 Labour Party Manifesto described it. Labour's programme retained a commitment to free trade, the gold standard and the balanced budget, but anticipated a considerable increase in the scope of government economic intervention. This programme built on the work of the Ministry of Reconstruction, that had drawn up elaborate plans to cope with the problems of the transition to peace, using the newly developed systems of control and administration to maintain a stable and growing peacetime economy. In Germany the Social Democrats had even more ambitious plans to use their control of the state apparatus to build a regime of state socialism. On the left, on the other hand, revolutionary syndicalism and direct action socialism was given a stronger political dimension by the example of the Russian Revolution and sought to achieve socialism not through the state but through the development of revolutionary industrial unionism and shop floor organisation. The revolutionary left anticipated the replacement of the capitalist state by a corporate form of democratic administration built on workers' councils or guilds representing consumers and producers.

The bourgeoisie, on the other hand, saw the war as no more than a brief interruption of its triumphal progress, the causes of the war lying not in the contradictions of capital accumulation, but in the militarism and intransigence of the European autocracies, while the interventionist apparatus, which was the basis of socialist ambitions, was seen as a wartime expedient whose retention in peacetime risked a resurgence of nationalism, militarism, and revolution. The primary aim of the bourgeoisie was to reconstruct the pre-war world, restoring the liberal state form within a liberal world order based on free trade and the gold standard. However the first priority was to check the aspirations of the working class. The context within which the struggle was fought out was that of a world restocking boom, that unleashed the pent up inflation of the wartime years before its collapse in 1921 was followed by severe recession.

In Germany the Social Democratic government faced an insuperable financial problem. The government was unable to introduce significant increases in taxation, for fear of alienating its working class supporters, or to renounce interest payments on the massive wartime debt, for fear of alienating the middle class on a proportion of whose votes it had come to depend, while it faced the heavy costs of welfare expenditure and food subsidies to quell working class unrest, in addition to the costs of economic reconstruction and reparations payments. The result was a soaring budget deficit that could only be financed by monetary expansion, stimulating hyper-inflation and an eventual relapse into barter. The effect of inflation was to reduce real wages, only partially compensated by food handouts and welfare benefits, and to devalue debts, dispossessing the frugal and patriotic middle class at the expense of speculators, farmers and big industrial capital, discrediting the Social Democratic government in the eyes of its middle and working class supporters, who turned to the more radical parties of the left and right. The grandiose dreams of Social Democracy collapsed as the government found itself presiding over a massive concentration of wealth in the hands of capital, and relying on the military to preserve the authority of the state by suppressing working class resistance and the Nazi putsch, preparing the way for political, economic and financial reconstruction on the basis not of the power of the working class, but that of capital.

In Britain the legacy of the war was a contradictory one. The state had made considerable progress in the domestication of the industrial and political organisations of the working class. The bulk of the Labour leadership had participated enthusiastically in the war, and the Party had committed itself to constitutional politics. Trades union leaders had collaborated in the development of systems of negotiation and arbitration and of national agreements which established a stable industrial relations framework, in which the unions played the ambivalent role of representing their members' interests in negotiations, but subsequently imposing an agreed settlement on any recalcitrant elements of their own membership. On the other hand, the increased power and status of the trades unions saw a massive increase in trades union membership over the war years, while the collaborative zeal of some of the leadership stimulated the growth of an increasingly militant and organised shop stewards' movement. These developments were reflected politically in the closer attachment of the trade union leadership to pursuing their political ends through the Labour Party (that was reconstituted in 1918), on the one hand, and in the further growth of direct action socialism, with its roots in the shop stewards' movement, on the other.

The fear of the state was not of an organised working class as such, for it had played a major role in legitimating that organisation, but of a working class that challenged the power of the state by pursuing its political aims outside the constitution, on the basis of its own collective strength. Thus the problem was not simply that of the increased strength and assertiveness of the organised working class, but was more fundamentally that of the forms of working class struggle and the form of the state. The political task was a familiar one, to secure the radical separation of trades union from political activity, ensuring that the mobilisation of the collective strength of the working class was confined to the pursuit of sectional industrial interests, while workers pursued their democratic aspirations as citizens, through the constitutional channel of the ballot box. The development of the machinery of industrial relations and the 1918 extension of the franchise provided a constitutional framework within which the working class could pursue its legitimate trades union and political aims.

The political problem was that of confining working class aspirations within this framework. The direct intervention of the state in production meant that industrial struggles against the employers immediately developed into political struggles against the state, and to demands that state power should be used to bring social production under democratic control. The political stabilisation of the state therefore depended not simply on the defeat of the militant sections of the working class, but also on restructuring class relations on the basis of the separation of civil society and the state, the restoration of the rule of money and the market, and the reconstitution of the liberal state form.

The growing militancy of the rank and file movement in the strategic industries had led the government to make considerable concessions in the later stages of the war. The end of the war brought new political dangers as troops returned from the front and workers and employers confronted one another as each sought to build on their wartime gains. The immediate fear was of wage-cutting as demobilised troops flooded the labour market, and this fear lay behind the government's reluctance to curb the inflationary boom. In late 1918 legislation was introduced, prohibiting wage cuts for a period of six months, and establishing further Trade Boards, Joint Industrial Councils and an Industrial Court.

1919 saw a wave of 'political' strikes involving the miners, the railway workers and even the police, directed as much at the government as at the employers. The immediate response of the government was conciliatory, although a further miners' strike in 1920 was accompanied by intensive military preparations on the part of the government and the introduction of the draconian Emergency Powers Act, which was brought into play in the 1921 lock-out and the 1926 General Strike.

A conciliatory approach to the trades unions was accompanied by plans for the extension of the Edwardian social reforms. Unemployment insurance was made almost universal, and non-contributory benefits were made available to keep those who had exhausted their entitlement out of the clutches of the Poor Law. Old Age Pensions were doubled and substantial subsidies offered to local authorities to expand education and housing.

The ending of the boom, with a rapid rise in unemployment and a collapse in prices, fundamentally altered the balance of power. The rapid dismantling of wartime controls over production, wages and the allocation of labour freed the employers, particularly in engineering, to move onto the offensive and to abrogate wartime agreements. However the sharpest political confrontations were threatened in the mines and on the railways, which were still effectively in public ownership. The obvious solution to the structural problems of these industries, which were both plagued by inadequate investment, excess capacity and too many small and fiercely competitive enterprises, was nationalisation, and this was both the demand of the working class and, in the case of the mines, the recommendation of the Sankey Commission of 1919. The alternative, proposed by the owners, was to return the industries to private ownership with generous subsidies and, preferably, monopoly powers.

There was nothing inherently socialist in the proposal for nationalisation. Public ownership had long been established as the form through which the state limited the ability of particular capitals to exploit monopoly powers. It was a remedy that had already been well tested as a means of restructuring capital and rationalising supply in the bus and tram, gas, water and electricity industries, where the duplication of facilities as a result of competition had led to chronic excess capacity, and abroad the public ownership of mines and railways was common.

Despite the eminent political and economic rationality of public ownership, the government returned the mines and railways to their former owners, reorganising the railways in the Act of 1921 that gave the owners monopoly powers with a guaranteed rate of return on their capital, while institutionalising collective bargaining and establishing a National Wages Board. The reason for this move was not simply the resistance of employers to the encroachment of the state, but more the anticipation on the part of the government of the fierce class struggles that the attempt to force down wages and rationalise production was bound to unleash, struggles that would inevitably be politicised if the government was directly involved as one party to the dispute. The restoration of the mines and railways to private ownership was therefore essential if the state was to restructure class relations and confine the class struggle within the constitutional limits of the liberal state form.[1]

The restoration of private ownership in the mines was immediately followed by a bitter strike in which the miners were soundly defeated. The defeat of the engineers in 1922 completed the rout of the most militant sections of the working class. The passing of the political threat, and the need to make economies to achieve a balanced budget, also led to substantial cuts in the programme of social reform, particularly in the areas most costly to the Exchequer of education and housing, although the housing cuts were soon reversed amid a deepening housing crisis.

With the fall of the minority 1924 Labour government the stage was set for the final defeat of the rank and file movement, the opportunity for which was provided by the struggle in the mines as the employers responded to the 1925 slump by seeking further wage cuts and an extension of the working day. The government stalled for time while it built up its defences, and then drew the TUC into the General Strike of 1926, presenting the trades union leadership with the stark alternative of putting itself at the head of a revolutionary movement, whose mass base had already been undermined, or committing itself to the constitutional path.

The collapse of the general strike sealed a victory that had already been won by the failure of direct action socialism to extend far beyond its industrial base in the rank and file movement, a base that had already been shattered in the strikes of 1921-2, and by the disengagement of the state from direct intervention in production, which had largely deprived syndicalism of its political significance. It finally destroyed the hopes of the direct action socialists that the

---

[1] It was an awareness of this contradiction that later underlay the persistent ambivalence of the Labour Party and trades union leadership over the issue of nationalisation, that was supposedly the lynchpin of their socialism. The contradiction was resolved later in the 1920s with the adoption of the public corporation as the appropriate institutional form for the nationalised industry, a form to which the Labour Party became firmly attached, and in the continuation of the practice pioneered in wartime of including trades unionists on the various commissions, committees, boards and councils that played a part in the formulation and implementation of industrial policies.

working class could achieve workers' control simply on the basis of workers' power, and confirmed the trades union leadership in the futility of using political pressure to secure trades union demands. The syndicalists were absorbed into the Labour and Communist Parties, while the trades union leadership sought to distance itself from politics. The 1927 Trade Disputes and Trades Union Act was primarily directed at the political role of the trades unions and at the extension of strike activity beyond the immediate employer, reinforcing the tendency for local negotiation to replace national bargaining, and for politics to be confined to constitutional channels, through the Labour Party and representations to government. Although the trades unions used their political weight inside the Labour Party, they were wary of forging too close a link with the Labour Party since they hoped to negotiate with whichever government happened to be in power. Thus the trades unions sought to establish a direct relationship with the state bureaucracy, a relationship the state was willing to accept so long as it was on a consultative basis and did not imply the trades unions using their collective strength to secure political ends.

While continued depression and the defeat of the general strike reduced the strength of the trades unions in the staple industries, the growth of new industries producing for the home market provided a basis for a more conciliatory approach to industrial relations, the trades unions developing a positive enthusiasm for cooperation with the employers in 'rationalisation' schemes, that involved increasing investment to secure the stability and security of incomes and employment. Although the employers in the new industries did not share the unions' enthusiasm for co-operation, they did favour stable industrial relations to maintain the continuity of production, which was particularly important if they were to cover their high fixed costs. The unions in the staple industries meanwhile looked to the government for solutions to the problems of overcapacity and persistent unemployment.

Although minority Labour governments took power in 1924 and 1929, and some Labour local authorities pursued energetic programmes to expand public education and housing and to ameliorate the harshness of the Poor Law, the highpoint of working class advance had already been reached in 1921. Despite the growth of trades unionism and the extension of the franchise the working class remained the object and not the subject of state power. While working class militancy was seen as a serious political threat significant social reforms could be wrested from the state, but once the constitutional threat had passed the government's enthusiasm for reform waned. The day-to-day struggle of workers to exist brought them into conflict with employers, landlords and the state, but the reconstitution of the liberal state form, the defeat of direct action socialism, and the retreat of the Labour Party and the TUC in the wake of the General Strike meant that the struggles emerging from such everyday conflicts tended to be isolated and fragmented. The working class had been very effectively brought back within the limits of the liberal state form.

The reconstruction of the liberal world order

The wartime apparatus of intervention was not only politically objectionable to the bourgeoisie, but was also inappropriate to the economic problems raised by post-war reconstruction. The wartime apparatus had been directed at the maximisation of production and its subordination to the war effort, the valorisation of capital being guaranteed by the state. This apparatus remained appropriate in the immediate post-war boom, when the explosion of pent-up demand offered apparently unlimited opportunities, but with the collapse of the boom, on top of the sharp contraction of government contracts, capital was left to its own devices. The barrier to accumulation was no longer limited productive capacity and the limited supply of labour, but the limited market that appeared primarily in the form of overproduction in the staple industries. The foundation of this barrier was the overaccumulation of capital on a world scale that was a legacy of the pre-war boom. The war had reinforced overaccumulation in the basic industries, and had also reinforced the uneven sectoral and geographical development of the forces of production on a world scale. The demands of war and the immediate post war restocking boom had concealed the excess capacity, but overproduction on a world scale soon brought the boom to a shuddering halt.

The problem appeared not to be one of overproduction so much as of limited access to world markets. The revival of international trade was restricted by the suspension of the institutions of international money and credit, that had made it possible to overcome the barrier of the market by reconciling sustained accumulation with payments imbalances, and by the proliferation of protective tariffs. Against the demand of the working class to bring capital under democratic control, the immediate priority of the bourgeoisie was the reconstruction of the international monetary system, based on the gold standard, and the liberalisation of trade.

The restoration of the gold standard had a political as well as an economic rationale. On the one hand, the gold standard was seen as the key to the reconstruction of the international political system, checking economic nationalism by subordinating the nation state to the supranational authority of gold. Thus the reconstruction of the gold standard was one of the first tasks undertaken under the aegis of the new League of Nations. On the other hand, the gold standard was seen as the key to domestic political stability in providing the only check on the temptation of governments to respond to popular pressure by resorting to the inflationary financing of social expenditure.

Keynes, the foremost critic of the gold standard, expressed a common view in regarding inflation and price instability as the greatest threats to the survival of capitalism. Not only does inflation undermine rational capitalist calculation, and generate cyclical fluctuations, but it also breeds popular unrest, as shown most menacingly in Russia and Germany. As Keynes noted, 'To convert the businessman into the profiteer is to strike a blow at capitalism, because it destroys the psychological equilibrium which permits the perpetuance of unequal rewards. The economic doctrine of normal profits, vaguely apprehended by everyone, is a necessary condition for the justification of capitalism'.[2] The crucial issue for Keynes was whether the gold standard would achieve such stability.

Keynes was one of the first economists to wake up to the fact that the gold standard did not work through the specie-flow mechanism, but was rather a system of managed currencies, although he believed that this was a relatively recent development. Keynes's objection to the restoration of the gold standard was based on his fear that the enormous gold reserves of the United States would give free reign to domestic inflationism, which would then be communicated throughout the world because of the financial power

---

[2] John Maynard Keynes, *Tract on Monetary Reform*, [1923], The Collected Writings of John Maynard Keynes, vol IV., Macmillan, London, 1971, p.24.

of the US. For Keynes both political and economic considerations dictated a monetary policy that was directed at domestic price stability rather than the stability of the exchange rate.

Although most economists and bankers felt that exchange rate stability was the essential foundation of a stable international monetary system, Keynes was by no means alone in recognising the superiority in principle of a managed currency. Nevertheless in practice Keynes's proposals were regarded as politically naïve, for the removal of the discipline of the gold standard merely extended the inflationary latitude enjoyed by US politicians to all governments. Inflationism should therefore be combatted within the gold standard regime by agreement between central banks. The flexibility of exchange rates carried the additional threat of governments' using currency manipulation as a nationalistic weapon, as they had used tariffs before the war, leading to competitive devaluations and persistent economic and political instability.

Underlying the conflict between the two positions was the familiar contradiction that the capitalist state has to resolve of reconciling domestic economic and political stability with the accumulation of capital on a world scale. Faced with the choice Keynes opted for the former. However Keynes was almost alone in the early 1920s in believing that there was a conflict between the two objectives. Thus there was almost universal agreement that a return to gold was the essential foundation of both accumulation on a world scale and domestic order and prosperity.

The reconstruction of the gold standard was no simple task, for it implied the subordination of the nation state once more to the power of world money, while the parity at which gold was restored defined the terms on which domestic capitals were integrated into the accumulation of capital on a world scale. Thus the reconstruction of the gold standard could only be achieved through a coordinated international effort, and preferably one that was conducted by central bankers, with as little reference to politicians, who would be subject to narrow nationalistic pressures, as possible.

The leading role in this task of reconstruction was played by Montagu Norman, Governor of the Bank of England, in close collaboration with Benjamin Strong, head of the New York Federal Reserve Bank. Although Norman and Strong certainly sought to strengthen the position of London and New York as international financial centres, and so aroused the antagonism of Paris, there was no alternative to rebuilding the gold standard around the London–New York axis, based on an alliance between the financial strength of New York and the expertise and institutional strength of London.

The war had seen a transformation in the trading and financial position of the United States, with New York emerging as the world's strongest financial centre. However New York was not in a position to take over London's role as centre of the international financial system. On the one hand, the New York banking system simply had not developed the institutions and wealth of experience in handling complex international transactions that London had built up over a century. On the other hand, the US economy was far less dependent on world markets than was the British, while strong populist currents continued to resist the exercise of the power of the banks. Thus there was a potential conflict between the international responsibilities of New York in the regulation of the financial system and the vulnerability of the banks to political and economic pressure to regulate the financial system in accordance with domestic political objectives.

Britain had been able to resolve the dilemma before the war because its commercial and financial strength, and the sophistication of its financial institutions, enabled the Bank of England to pursue domestic and international financial policies more or less independently of one another. Although Britain's commercial and financial position had been weakened by the war, the underlying weaknesses were not immediately apparent. While it had lost many of its traditional markets to domestic producers or foreign competitors, the balance of payments had been maintained by an improvement in the terms of trade and the virtual cessation of long-term foreign investment, while buoyant exports in the immediate post-war boom held out some prospect of revival. While it had had to borrow heavily from the US to protect its reserves in the later stages of the war, these liabilities were more or less matched by the substantial loans Britain had extended to its allies. While Britain's gold reserves were only a quarter the size of the Americans', they were very respectable by historical standards. Thus Britain seemed as well equipped to manage the gold standard as it had been before the war, provided that it could secure a degree of co-operation from the US authorities, particularly in making US gold available in case sterling came under pressure. Moreover the City of London was reluctant to abandon its leading role, which brought substantial profits to London bankers, shippers and insurers, and considerable invisible earnings to cover the deficit on Britain's trade.

The first task facing the European governments' attempt to restore the gold standard was to bring domestic inflation under control in order to establish stable price levels against which to fix the parity of the participating currencies. The immediate problem was the enormous burden of war debt, the servicing and repayment of which imposed considerable pressure on state finances. This created a problem for monetary control because of the forms of financing that had been adopted during the war, which had inflated domestic price levels and left an enormous overhang of liquidity. Governments could only bring inflation under control if they could reduce their budget deficits and mop up the excess liquidity. However such policies implied increases in taxation, cuts in public expenditure and a tight monetary policy, the deflationary impact of which would only fuel the sharp class struggles of the immediate post-war period. Thus inflation was allowed to persist through the immediate post-war boom, and the reconstruction of the gold standard postponed until the balance of class forces had shifted decisively in favour of capital.

Norman and Strong played the leading role in the stabilisation of the European currencies, often working through the new League of Nations which channeled stabilisation funds, much of which was provided by private banks. The most dramatic success was in Germany, where hyperinflation had destroyed the currency, but laid the foundations for a solution by devaluing the government's debt. The stabilisation of the currency in 1923 was followed by the Dawes plan, that provided a large US loan to meet the immediate difficulties and that rescheduled reparations payments. The restoration of stability provided the basis for the return to gold in 1924 and stimulated a dramatic German recovery, which attracted a large inflow of US capital to cover the subsequent flow of reparations payments.

France presented greater difficulties. The government had expected its problems to be solved by German reparations and so continued to run a large budget deficit, while inflation was accommodated by the effective devaluation of the franc. However British and American speculation against the franc, and then the Dawes plan, undermined this strategy and justifiably aroused French suspicions that Britain was trying to rebuild Germany as a counter-weight to France. Thus France rejected Norman's overtures and maintained an undervalued franc to build up its reserves so as to establish its independence, strengthening the competitiveness of French exporters into the bargain. The undervalued franc was stabilised from 1926, although France did not officially return to the gold standard until 1928. In the meantime France's attempt to go its own way was an important factor in the weakening of the gold standard.

In Britain there was little support for the Labour Party's proposal to deal with the problem of financial stabilisation by means of a capital levy to reduce the government debt, even though debt service and repayment meant heavy increases in taxation to produce the required budget surplus. There was also very little support for Keynes's proposal of devaluation, to accommodate the wartime inflation. Both devaluation and a capital levy were regarded as morally and politically unacceptable, a violation of the rights of property and a renunciation of the government's contractual obligations, which would set a precedent that was inconsistent with London's international financial role.

The return to gold closely followed the pattern of events of the return to convertibility a century earlier, although the issue this time was far less contentious. The price to be paid for a return to free convertibility at the existing parity was recognised to be a bout of deflation, to bring the British price level back into line with that of the US. However the political consequences of a sharp deflation at the end of the war were unacceptable, so the government formally went off gold in 1919, to buy the time in which to restore domestic monetary control by mopping up the surplus liquidity in the banking system. The deflationary impact of its budget surplus and tight monetary policy was just beginning to bite when the boom broke, so that the restoration of convertibility was postponed, pending the stabilisation of the other European currencies and in the hope that US inflation would remove the need to apply the last deflationary twist. In the event speculation against the return to convertibility pushed up the pound so that restoration in 1925 went remarkably smoothly. Although the overvalued pound added to the difficulties of the staple industries, and prompted speculation against sterling, it kept down the costs of imported food and raw materials and so boosted the newer industries, producing primarily for the domestic market, in the hesitant recovery.

The first years of the restored gold standard gave no indication of what was to come. The Bank of England was able to manage the gold standard and defend the reserves with very few changes in Bank Rate, relying on the gold devices, foreign exchange operations and co-operation among central banks, so insulating the domestic economy from its international operations, although it did have to maintain relatively high interest rates. The League of Nations sponsored attempts to break down the high tariffs and import controls that had been imposed in the war and immediate post-war period, which checked the growth of protectionism. World trade expanded rapidly and Europe played the leading role in the world boom from 1925. It appeared that the restoration of the liberal regime was bearing more fruit than even its most optimistic adherents could have dreamed a few years before. Yet liberal self-confidence was about to be shattered.

The problem of the staple industries

Although the restoration of financial stability and the growth of world trade pulled the British economy out of the post-war slump, Britain did not participate fully in the world boom of the late 1920s. The main problem was that of the staple industries, in which global overproduction was most marked and in which British productivity lagged behind that of its competitors.

The depression in the staple industries was at first generally believed to be merely a cyclical phenomenon, the normal purgative reaction to the inflationary post-war boom. However the growth of world trade as the European economies recovered from war and their currencies were stabilised did not lead to a reopening of markets for the staple industries, but an intensification of competition as the capacity that had been expanded during the war and the post-war reconstruction boom sought outlets on the world market. Coal faced competition from more efficient European producers which intensified sharply in 1925. Iron and steel continued to face protective tariffs in foreign markets and increased competition at home. Shipbuilding was faced by enormous overcapacity at home and competition from abroad. Textiles were progressively squeezed between the more efficient producers of the advanced countries and the low-wage producers of the periphery.

The employers saw the problem as one of high interest rates and high wages at home, an overvalued pound and protective tariffs abroad. However they did not favour devaluation to relieve the financial pressures, because they feared that devaluation would increase wage and raw material costs and inhibit the flow of foreign investment that was expected to stimulate exports. Thus they saw wage cuts as the key to increased competitiveness and were increasingly attracted to protection and imperialism, summed up in the movement for 'Empire Free Trade', as the means of expanding markets. However these panaceas evaded the fundamental problem, which was that of the low productivity that was the result of low investment, outdated production methods, a fragmented industrial structure and incompetent management.

Concern about the impact of foreign competition lay behind the 'rationalisation' movement that gathered momentum from 1924. Rationalisation, following the German example, involved the concentration and centralisation of capital to facilitate the achievement of continuous and integrated production, the application of modern scientific and managerial principles, and monopolistic control of markets, in order to plan capacity as much as to control prices.

The rationalisation movement progressed rapidly in the new industries, which built on war-time advances by adopting more sophisticated methods of production, including the assembly line and continuous process production, within large corporations which protected their markets through monopolies and cartels. However the fragmented ownership of capital in the staple industries, which were marked by severe competition, meant that the institutional and financial basis for expensive rationalisation programmes was lacking. Mergers and amalgamations in the staple industries were primarily defensive and limited in scope, involving financial integration but little managerial or technical rationalisation. Trade associations restricted themselves to price fixing, and many collapsed in the slump of 1920–21. The banks had only limited and fragmented exposure to industry and so had little interest in sponsoring rationalisation, protecting their investments by nursing unprofitable enterprises along. Thus the limited rationalisation of the staple industries, far from stimulating productivity increases and the elimination of excess capacity, merely served to make the problem worse by sustaining excess capacity and supporting unprofitable enterprises.

The obvious alternative was for the state to take the initiative in sponsoring more radical rationalisation. The Labour Party had long endorsed monopolisation under public control as an inevitable stage on the way to nationalisation. Opinion in the Conservative Party moved in favour of monopolisation as an alternative to na-tionalisation as it became clear that competitive pressure was not leading to rationalisation and the elimination of uncompetitive pro-ducers. As the Balfour Committee noted in 1929, 'There can be no doubt that the operation of free competition is a very slow and costly method [of eliminating excess capacity] ... The tenacity of business working at a loss is sometimes extraordinary'.[3] Although the Liberals were slower to abandon their faith in the market, by the end of the decade they recognised the inefficiency of compe-tition, the Liberal Industrial Inquiry of 1929 even proposing that incorporated trade associations should have the legal powers to enforce their rules throughout the appropriate trade or industry.

Despite the growing strength of interventionist opinion in all political parties, effective measures were constantly resisted by the owners, who continued to hang on in the hope that the growth of world markets, or the introduction of 'Empire Free Trade' would prove their salvation. The government was equally reluctant to take the initiative. This inactivity was not simply the result of ig-norance or bloody-mindedness. On the one hand, the government was reluctant to intervene for fear of setting precedents that would lead capitalists to outbid each other in their pleas for support. For this reason every effort was made to keep industrial policy out of the hands of Parliament. On the other hand, the restructuring of the staple industries could only be solved by the massive destruc-tion of outdated capacity, heavy investment in the most modern methods of production, and the sacking of large numbers of work-ers in a context of high regional unemployment. The unemployed themselves did not constitute a serious political threat, but the process of restructuring would inevitably lead to a renewal of the struggles of the early 1920s. The government and employers were equally concerned to avoid such a prospect, and so allowed the sta-ple industries to stagnate. Meanwhile the unemployed were accom-

---

[3] Quoted in Mike Best and Jane Humphries, 'The City and Industrial De-cline', in Bernard Elbaum and William Lazonick, eds, *The Decline of the British Economy*, Clarendon, Oxford, 1986, p. 231.

modated by the increasingly liberal dispensation of relief. However the crash of 1929 and the ensuing world depression brought the issues to a head once more.

The 1929 crash and the collapse of the gold standard

The depression of the 1930s was inaugurated by the stock exchange crash in New York in 1929. The financial crisis had its roots in the overaccumulation of US capital over the previous decade. Accumulation was sustained by low interest rates and easy credit even as the stock market boom assumed an increasingly speculative dimension. As the boom gathered momentum the Federal Reserve Banks lost control of the market altogether and money poured into New York to feed the boom. The boom persisted through 1929, despite the piling up of unsold stocks, particularly in the new automobile and consumer durable industries, the cutting back of production and the rise in unemployment. The inevitable collapse of the bubble precipitated widespread bankruptcies that turned recession into severe depression.

The gold standard survived the 1929 crash. However the subsequent depression revealed the fragility of its foundations. The post-war gold standard was much more vulnerable than its predecessor. The internationalisation of money capital meant that there was far more short-term capital flowing around the system in search of speculative gains, competition between London and Paris undermined attempts to pursue a coordinated interest rate policy, and the higher degree of integration of domestic and international financial markets made the domestic economy more sensitive to interest rate changes so that international monetary policies were constrained by domestic considerations. While high unemployment and the cost of debt service made the British government reluctant to allow interest rates to rise to strengthen the pound, the French government was reluctant to allow them to fall, in its determination to maintain a strong franc. Strong kept down New York rates to relieve the pressure on London, feeding the speculative boom, until, with the death of Strong and then the crash, domestic considerations dictated high US interest rates in the attempt to stabilise the domestic banking system and strengthen the dollar.

Britain was the weak link in the system, holding only small reserves of gold against which to set a large volume of net short-term foreign debt and foreign holdings of sterling, the position being covered only by long-term foreign assets, many of which were of dubious status. Although France and the United States held large reserves, they were reluctant to free their reserves for fear of undermining their currencies. Thus the system suffered from an acute shortage of liquidity in relation to the demands being made of it.

The crash undermined confidence in the stability of the gold standard, weakening the ability of domestic currencies to serve as substitutes for world money in its function as store of value and so leading to a sharp contraction in liquidity, intensified by gold hoarding on the part of France and the US. The weakening of confidence further increased speculative movements of 'hot money'. The collapse of long-term foreign investment undermined the balance of payments of the capital importers, and the collapse of exports to the US undermined that of the primary exporters. The shortage of liquidity forced a contraction of world trade in response to the US depression as governments reacted to payments imbalances by imposing deflationary policies and protective tariffs to defend their reserves. Primary producers were especially hard hit as the decline in US imports sent primary product prices, that had already been weakening as overproduction emerged before the crash, spiralling downwards. The pressure was then transmitted to London as primary producers drew on their sterling balances and reduced their imports from Britain. The pressure on the international financial system was further intensified by the new isolationism of the US Federal Reserve system, compounded by its inability to perform the domestic central banking role of lender of last resort, which led it repeatedly to tighten credit and so to turn panics into banking crises.

By 1931 the British balance of payments had moved into deficit, the empire countries had run down their sterling deposits, and London faced a steady drain to Paris and Berlin, the reserves only being defended at the expense of high interest rates. A renewed financial crisis in Central Europe led to heavy calls on London for accommodation and precipitated a crisis in confidence and flight of hot money that could only be countered, without suspending convertibility, by punitive interest rates or by raising loans abroad.

Meanwhile the rising cost of unemployment relief and falling revenues as insurance contributions fell threatened a budget deficit. The May Committee's Report finally shattered the confidence of domestic and international financial markets by forecasting a substantial budget deficit and proposing widespread cuts in public expenditure, and particularly in unemployment benefit. It was made clear to the Labour government that foreign loans would only be forthcoming if the May Report's proposals were adopted. The Labour government split, the bulk of the leadership joining the Conservatives in implementing the cuts, but a renewed drain finally forced Britain off gold, allowing the Bank of England to stabilise an undervalued pound and accumulate reserves.

The speculation that forced Britain off gold delivered the death blow to the gold standard. Thirty two countries followed Britain off gold in 1932, anxious not to suffer a competitive disadvantage in the face of British devaluation. The British withdrawal from the gold standard focussed speculative attention on the next link in the chain, the United States. The United States initially responded to speculative pressure with monetary contraction. However monetary stringency forced the government to reverse an expansionary fiscal policy, which halted the US recovery in its tracks, provoking renewed populist agitation against the bankers.

In a last ditch attempt to stabilise the system a World Economic Conference was called in London in 1933. However the United States devalued the dollar on the eve of the Conference, and refused to commit itself to the stabilisation of the dollar for fear of the domestic political consequences. Britain, now free from deflationary pressure and with the position of the City of London preserved as the centre of a network of lesser currencies tied to sterling, similarly refused to resume its global role, and firmly resisted proposals for a co-operative solution based on the coordinated reflation of the leading national economies for fear of its inflationary consequences. The result was that France was left at the head of a gold block with Belgium, Swizerland and the Netherlands, which sustained the gold standard until it finally collapsed in 1936.

The failure of the World Economic Conference did not lead to the collapse of the world economy. The failure of the Conference was in part due to the success that had already been achieved in securing international co-operation on a more limited basis, as bilateral and multilateral agreements led to the formation of currency blocks and preferential tariff treatment between trading partners, centred on the dominant powers.

In the case of Britain the substantial devaluation of 1931 relieved the immediate speculative pressures and enabled the Bank of England to build up large gold and foreign currency reserves with which to defend the exchange rate of the currency. This freed domestic monetary policy from immediate international constraints, and allowed a substantial fall in interest rates which limited the inflow of speculative funds. However the stabilisation of the currency in the longer term depended on strengthening the balance of international payments, so that devaluation was immediately followed by the imposition of protective tariffs and the strengthening of controls on foreign lending. The danger of a tariff war with the countries of the Empire was averted by the introduction of the system of imperial preference, to which further countries were added through bilateral agreements. Financial stability within this framework of limited multilateral trade was strengthened by tying the currencies of the countries of the 'Sterling Area' directly to the pound.

Similar arrangements led to the formation of the dollar area, covering the Americas; the Central and South East European exchange control area dominated by Germany; the yen area in the Far East; and the gold bloc in Western Europe. International capital flows, apart from capital flight, were largely confined within these currency blocs, within which some progress was made in reciprocal trade liberalisation. Finally, some stability in the international monetary system was re-established, following the devaluation of the dollar and subsequent pressure on the franc, by the Tripartite Agreement by which the French, British and US authorities agreed to intervene to maintain fixed exchange rates between the three major currency areas. Thus some degree of multilateral trade and finance was salvaged from the maelstrom.

Money and credit in the crisis of overaccumulation

At first sight the crisis and ensuing depression appeared to be a monetary phenomenon, a classic example of the pursuit of unsound banking practices as the Federal Reserve had stimulated a massive speculative boom through over-expansionary monetary policies, which forced the authorities to adopt severely restrictive policies in the ensuing crash. However we have seen that the tendency to overaccumulation is not the result of unsound banking practices, but is inherent in the form of capitalist accumulation.

The boom of the 1920s was dominated by the development of the new consumer durables sector in the United States. The growth of this sector had been made possible by nineteenth century technological developments, but the market was initially very limited. However the bureaucratisation of both government and capitalist enterprise, associated with the development of public and private monopolies and the growing administrative functions of the state, was creating a growing middle class, the upper echelons of which enjoyed comfortable incomes. The same tendencies to monopolisation created the large scale enterprise that was able to reduce the costs of production by reaping the economies of standardisation and mass production. Although the middle class market was by no means a mass market, the sheer size of the United States made the market large enough to permit the development of these new branches of production. On the basis of the buoyant home market US manufacturers were able to export to European markets, that were individually too small to sustain such industries. The growing export surplus of the United States provided the means for US capital to move abroad in search of profitable outlets, the inflow of US investment being the driving force underlying the European boom of the second half of the decade, in which the foundations of the new industries were laid in Europe, alongside the established branches of production that flourished, except in Britain, in the boom.

However the basis of this boom was narrow, for the market for the new consumer products remained limited almost entirely to the middle class. The new industries, crying out for labour, paid relatively good wages. Piece rates and bonus schemes, designed to maintain the continuity and increase the pace of production, enabled some to boost their wages further. But although many industrial workers earned high enough wages to afford more diversified food, clothing and adequate housing, and to buy simple manufactures such as bicycles and sewing machines, few could afford the more expensive cars and consumer durables, even when the offer of 'easy payment' lured them into debt. Moreover the basis of the world boom was extremely fragile, resting as it did on the continued flow of US capital to Europe to finance Europe's trade deficit with the US.

As US investment extended the US boom to Europe, rising European imports intensified the boom in the US. As the mood of optimism spread to Wall Street the boom entered its speculative phase and capital flooded back from Europe, putting the international financial system under severe pressure, which it was nevertheless able to withstand. However as the increased capacity created in the boom came into production, it came up against the barrier of the limited market. While productive capitalists were able to finance growing stocks and trading losses on credit, the speculative boom on Wall Street could persist. But once the chain of credit began to break down, the bubble had to burst.

The gold standard had been remarkably successful in sustaining the boom despite the acute geographical and sectoral unevenness of accumulation, the severity of the crash being testimony to the extent to which international capital movements and the co-operation between New York and London had been able to accommodate the pressures. The international financial system offered a means of suspending the barriers to accumulation by providing credit, but it did not provide any means of overcoming those barriers. Moreover, while accumulation could be sustained on the basis of the expansion of credit, bankers were under considerable political pressure to maintain low interest rates and easy credit to avoid checking the boom, and New York kept interest rates down to support London, and so maintain the gold standard. While in retrospect it is clear that credit was overextended, at the time the bankers were only sharing the optimistic mood of the capitalist class as a whole. Had the barrier of the limited market and the uneven development of accumulation been overcome, the bankers would have been applauded for their wisdom and their faith.

It was ultimately the failure of capital to overcome these barriers that progressively increased the pressure on the international financial system. The collapse of the financial system, first in the US and then on a world scale, led to a massive contraction of credit that brought accumulation back within the limits of the market. But the bankers were not responsible for the extent of the crash. Once the chain of credit had broken down the priority was to restore the stability of the monetary system, as the essential precondition for the resumption of accumulation and the renewed expansion of credit. Bankers may have been unduly cautious in the depression, as they may have been unduly liberal in the boom, but again their caution was bred of the pessimism they shared with the whole of the capitalist class.

The weaknesses of the gold standard appeared to lie in the shortage of international liquidity that arose from the limited supplies and uneven distribution of the world's gold reserves and the increasingly multilateral and decentralised network of international payments. However the system was very successful in its short life in supplementing supplies of gold with supplies of convertible currency, so that there was far more international liquidity available than there had been before the war, both in public and in private hands. The underlying problem was not the shortage of liquidity, but the extent of the geographical and sectoral unevenness of accumulation that the financial system was called upon to accommodate. Acute trade imbalances were covered by international capital movements as the surplus capital created by the expansion of credit sought profitable outlets around the world. However the reliance on such movements meant that the system would inevitably come under pressure, however much liquidity was available, as the crisis of overaccumulation struck and capital was diverted into increasingly speculative ventures. The crisis was only warded off by the continued expansion of credit, which fuelled inflation and speculation on a world scale as capital failed to overcome the barriers to accumulation. Once the crisis broke, financial reconstruction could only proceed once the basis of sound credit had been restored by bringing accumulation back within the limits of the market.

The expansion of credit in the boom had intensified the global overaccumulation and uneven development of capital. With the massive contraction of domestic and international credit in the crash stability could only be restored by the familiar means of the devaluation of capital and the destruction of productive capacity on an enormous scale. As in previous crises, however, the nation state could not simply stand aside and permit the sacrifice of domestic production and employment on the altar of gold.

The crisis initially appeared to the nation state in the form of a drain on the reserves and a weakening of the currency. However the adoption of deflationary policies to check speculation against the currency and to restore the balance of international payments led to the contraction of domestic production and employment; a budget deficit as tax revenues fell while expenditure, particularly on unemployment relief, rose; and growing political unrest. The attempt to meet the budget deficit by borrowing would stimulate the domestic economy, but at the risk of provoking further speculation against the currency. On the other hand, cuts in public expenditure and increased taxation would intensify the depression and sharpen the class struggle.

The suspension of gold convertibility, devaluation of the currency and introduction of protective tariffs provided the means by which the nation state could relieve the pressure on the currency by contracting imports and stemming the flight of capital, and so reduce the immediate domestic impact of the crisis. However the adoption of such policies on a world scale led to a further contraction of international credit and decline in world trade which only intensified the depression. Thus domestic stabilisation policies could only succeed if complemented by the reconstruction of the system of international trade and payments.

In the wake of the crisis of 1873 Britain's commitment to free trade and the strength of sterling had confined protectionism within limits and had permitted the recovery of accumulation on a world scale on the basis of a substantial growth of international credit. However the global character of the crisis of the 1930s meant that no national government could afford to make the sacrifices, or take the political risks, of further restraining domestic accumulation to make its currency sufficiently strong to serve as the basis for the reconstruction of the international monetary system. The only way in which the reconstruction of international trade and finance could succeed was through bilateral negotiations on the basis of complementary trading and investment patterns, reinforced by the state's regulation of the international movement of commodities, money and capital within discrete financial blocks. Where such complementarity could not be achieved by mutual agreement between nation states it was achieved by the exercise of the financial, commercial, political and ultimately military power of the dominant nation states, creating the international tensions between the blocks that culminated in war.

With the collapse of the gold standard and the use of protection and exchange controls to maintain the balance of payments, domestic monetary policies were freed from international constraint.

However policies of cheap money were not sufficient to secure recovery. While world trade remained severely depressed excess capacity persisted in the staple industries, and the growth of new industries was limited by the relative stagnation of the domestic market. The failure of the market to achieve the appropriate restructuring of capital and the failure of easy monetary policies to secure renewed accumulation raised the question of more active state intervention in the regulation of accumulation, and threw increasing doubt on the liberal orthodoxies. In Germany the Nazis destroyed the organised strength of the working class and constructed a corporate state which dissolved the distinction between the money power of capital and its political power as it fused civil society and the state to install a totalitarian state capitalism. In the Soviet Union the crisis consolidated the grip of Stalin and confirmed the move towards a totalitarian state socialism. Meanwhile the liberal bourgeoisie sought a middle way between the two extremes. Liberalism rose to the challenge with the 'Keynesian Revolution'.

Chapter 9

Economists and the State: The Keynesian Revolution

The marginalist revolution in economics

The Keynesian Revolution has been popularly depicted, following Keynes's own presentation, as a political revolution underpinned by an intellectual revolution, as a revolutionary theory won over a state dominated by classical ignorance. However this characterisation ignores the diversity of pre-Keynesian economists' views, overestimates the originality of Keynes, and exaggerates both the political influence of economists and the extent of the political changes that took place. The Keynesian Revolution was not so much a scientific or a political as an ideological revolution.

Economists had long since abandoned the naïve faith of political economy in the virtues of a strict regime of laissez faire. Nevertheless a faith in the beneficence of the rule of money and the market remained the foundation of economic ideology, as an ideal to be aspired to if not as an accurate depiction of reality. The conceptual apparatus of economics was constructed on the basis of an abstract model of the market, so that the limits of market regulation also marked the limits of the economists' competence. Keynes, for all his insights, was not able to advance beyond this framework.

Ever since the austere dogmatism of Ricardo political economy had conceded an increasing role to the state under the rubric of Smith's 'public works and public institutions', and measures to counter fraud and the abuse of power. The principles of free trade, the Bank Act and the balanced budget had ceased to be politically contentious in the optimism of the mid-Victorian boom and became pillars of the constitution that no longer required the analytical support of political economy. By the 1860s political economy was most closely associated with the dogmatic adherence to the Malthusian theory of population and the wages-fund doctrine, which established the inability of either trades unionism or social reform to relieve the condition of the working class, and to the doctrine of free trade. It was the pressure for reform in the 1860s that finally broke political economy, whose last analytical defence was breached with Mill's recognition of the collapse of the wages-fund doctrine in 1869.[1]

Political economy was not immediately replaced by a new economic theory. The principles of the gold standard, the balanced budget, and government frugality were by now embedded in the constitutional theory of the state. Economic instability was seen as deriving from external circumstances: foreign politics, harvest failures, the financial irresponsibility of foreigners, and overtrading stimulated by psychological waves of optimism, to be countered by responsible monetary policies whose implementation was a technical matter for the bankers. The control of public finances, including the financial aspects of social reform, were essentially matters for actuaries and accountants, not for economists. Wages, industrial relations, unemployment and even tariff protection were seen primarily as social and political, rather than economic, issues. The main questions that called for economic analysis were those raised by a concern with the distributional impact of taxation, on the one hand, and the problems of pricing raised by the regulation of natural monopolies and public utilities, on the other. It was particularly in relation to these issues that the new marginalist methods of economic analysis were first developed. Not surprisingly marginalist economics did not immediately take the world by storm!

Demands for increasing state intervention from the 1860s were not expressed in a new economic theory, but in new conceptions

---

[1] I have discussed the decline of classical political economy and the marginalist revolution more fully in *Marx, Marginalism and Modern Sociology*, op. cit.

of the state, that drew heavily on older traditions, resurrecting the view of the state as the embodiment of a moral and political community, charged with securing the welfare of all its citizens. Far from the market defining the limits of the state, the state had to define the limits of the market. With the decline of political economy the field was left open for moralists, utopians, statisticians, eugenicists, historians, theologians, positivists, comparatists, sociologists, institutionalists, Fabians and socialists to propose measures of social reform and political regulation, supporting their proposals with statistical and survey investigations, comparative and historical examples, and moral and religious principles, while politicians evaluated such proposals in terms of political expediency, within the limits of the constitutional principles of money and finance, rather than on the basis of any analytical theory.

The proliferation of demands for political intervention and social reform were checked only by the doctrine of the balanced budget and the principle of public frugality. Although public expenditure did not grow as a proportion of the national income in Britain, until the pre-war wave of rearmament and social reform increased the proportion by a third, it rose steadily in absolute terms, and socialists and social reformers were pressing for an increasingly pervasive role for the state. The collapse of political economy meant that there was no coherent basis on which to conceptualise the limits to state intervention, and in particular to draw the line between social reform and socialism. This was the ideological space that marginalist economics came to fill as the growing socialist challenge towards the end of the century demanded that the defence of the market should be set on a more rigorous foundation.

The technical details of the marginalist revolution need not detain us since they are well-known. The marginalist revolution offered a technique that made it possible to provide a much more rigorous analysis of the market, and so to establish the conditions under which the market would achieve the optimal equilibrium that political economy had simply presumed. But although the marginalists introduced powerful new methods, they offered remarkably few new ideas. They started, as had Smith, from the model of a simple barter economy, and then told the same story of the inconvenience of barter, the emergence of money as the rational instrument of exchange, and of capital as some form of 'stock' that brought together labour, land and means of production. Money

remained neutral, the rate of interest equated savings and investment, free trade was beneficial to all parties and Say's law still
ruled the best of all possible worlds.

The main innovation of the marginalist revolution was the introduction of a new concept of value, and correspondingly a different conception of the role of the market. Political economy had
confined economics to the study of exchange values, ultimately determined by the cost of production. The role of money and the
market was to coordinate the division of labour. The justification
of the system lay in its efficient co-ordination of production and
in its dynamism that enhanced the wealth of the nation as profits
were reinvested.

The Great Depression was a period conspicuously lacking in dynamism and the efficient co-ordination of production. On the other
hand, it was a period in which rising real wages and the growth of
the middle class led to rising mass consumption and an increasing
diversity of consumption goods available. The idea of consumer
choice, that would have been laughable to most of the population
in the middle of the century, was acquiring a new reality. It was
this idea that the marginalist revolution brought to the centre of
the stage. For marginalists the role of the market was not to coordinate the system of production, but to subordinate the allocation of
productive resources to the desires of consumers. The economy was
no longer seen as a self-sustaining system of production, but rather
as a network of exchange relations between individual economic
agents, each starting with an initial set of resources. The market
reconciled not the market price to the natural price, but supply to
demand. Equilibrium was not defined by the equalisation of the
rate of profit, but by the equalisation of marginal utility, at which
point it was impossible to increase the welfare of one individual
without reducing that of another. The central task of marginalist economics was to establish the conditions for the uniqueness,
stability and optimality of this equilibrium.

Instead of merely presuming that free competition would lead
to the best of all possible worlds, the marginalists sought to establish precisely the conditions under which such a result would arise.
They were therefore more aware than had been their predecessors
of the simplifying assumptions on which their model rested, and
indeed it turned out that the assumptions required to achieve the
desired results were extraordinarily restrictive. The gap between

model and reality was both the scientific weakness and the ideological strength of marginalist economics, that has sustained it to this day.

It is clear that the assumptions of the model, as of any abstract theory, are grossly unrealistic. This would not matter if it were possible to identify the divergences between the model and reality. However in this case such an identification is impossible. The underlying assumptions concern a host of unobservable parameters: the changing tastes and preferences of millions of individuals, the degree of complementarity and substitutability of commodities and of productive resources, and the knowledge and expectations of present and future prices and costs. There is no way of knowing whether a particular market, or the system as a whole, is competitive, or whether it is in equilibrium, or whether the existing allocation of resources is efficient. There is no way of knowing whether excessive profits are a result of monopoly powers, of chronic disequilibrium, or a premium for added risk. There is no way of knowing whether changes represent a movement towards or away from equilibrium or reflect changing parameters. Thus marginalist economics provides an ideological framework of inexhaustible potential precisely because it has no empirical content.

This lack of an empirical foundation was recognised most clearly by the Austrians, who were by far the most theoretically sophisticated of the marginalists. The Austrians came to regard empiricism as the first step on the road to socialism, in fostering the illusion that if economists could understand the world they might be able to change it. They therefore insisted that economics is an a priori and not an empirical discipline, the laws of economics resting on such indubitable psychological truths as Smith's assertion that 'the purpose of all production is consumption'. This later led Hayek and von Mises to the conclusion that any violation of the freedom of the market is affront to human reason and an offence against human nature.

Although economists sought to answer the pressing questions of the day on the basis of their theories, the weight of academic opinion largely reflected the weight of political opinion in the class from which the academics were drawn, because their theories gave the economists no better basis for judgement than their own political prejudices. While their theoretical explanations were vacuous, the impact of their few empirical studies was minimal, partly because of the limited scope and reliability of statistical sources, and partly because it was difficult to find any clear-cut relationships to set against the accumulated wisdom of capitalists, bankers, politicians and civil servants. Thus economists were wheeled out to produce congenial platitudes that echoed the politicians, whether it be about the excessive power of the trades unions or of the employers, the need to curb monopolies or restrict competition, the need for tariffs or the virtues of free trade, the dangers of excessive taxation or the need to increase government subsidies, the virtues of the market or the need for government regulation. While the bankers, politicians and civil servants thought they knew the answers, academic economists had very little political influence, and were almost uniformly regarded with contempt when they ventured independent views. Nevertheless economists continued to serve an important ideological role as 'experts', who gave the stamp of scientific authority to the political prejudices of their paymasters, and who defined the boundaries of political reality in subordinating political discretion to the yardstick of money.

The economists and the depression of the 1920s

Pre-Keynesian economists were not so naïve as they are often depicted. They could hardly deny the possibility of persistent unemployment when it was such a conspicuous feature of the capitalist economy. However they did not believe that unemployment reflected any shortcoming of the market or of monetary regulation, let alone of the capitalist mode of production, but rather of human and institutional failures that impeded the proper operation of economic forces. It was not that the market failed society, but that society failed to live up to the standards of the market.

Although market forces ensured a permanent tendency to a full employment equilibrium, market forces took time to operate. Unequal rates of profit and unequal wages provided the incentive for capital and workers to move between branches of production and between occupations, but if they failed to respond then low profits and low wages would persist. When unprofitable enterprises were eventually liquidated workers would be unemployed. However new employment opportunities would open up as capital sought more profitable outlets. If unemployment persisted it could only be because workers were not prepared to seek out such opportunities, or because they demanded a level of wages that was too high to be consistent with the profitability of investment.

In the crisis of the early 1920s persistent unemployment was widely blamed on the excessive power of the trades unions, which were able to resist the requisite wage reductions. However by the middle of the 1920s the defeat of militant trades unionism and the close association of long-term unemployment with the problem of the staple industries was undermining the more punitive attitudes to unemployment as it was increasingly recognised, even by economists, that workers faced real barriers in seeking work, while wage cuts had done little to improve the prospects of the staple industries. Moreover the experience of the fierce class struggles to which wage cuts and the more rigorous application of the Poor Law gave rise ruled these out as realistic solutions to the problem of unemployment. Thus the more liberal remedies concentrated on the development of labour exchanges, industrial retraining and relocation allowances as the remedy for persistent unemployment, with the rigour of the Poor Law being reserved for a separate category, the 'work-shy'. The rationalisation movement analogously focused on barriers to the mobility of capital in response to market incentives.

Although the remedy for long-term unemployment still lay in the hands of the worker, in the short-term the problem was exacerbated by the cyclical fluctuations in economic activity to which the capitalist economy was prone, cyclical fluctuations for which the worker could hardly be held responsible. The problem of cyclical unemployment was addressed through the theory of the 'trade cycle'. Marshall, following Mill and Bagehot, had seen the source of the trade cycle in the waves of optimism and pessimism that spread through the capitalist class, a wave of optimism stimulating expansion that culminated in an inflationary boom. Monetary theories, going back to Thornton, saw the cycle as the result of divergences between the rate of interest and the rate of profit. Hawtrey saw such divergences as being inherent in credit money, and mainly affecting stocks and working capital. Hayek saw them as being the result of discretionary monetary policies, and mainly affecting fixed investment. For all these theories the remedy for cyclical fluctuations was an appropriate monetary policy, although they differed as to what that policy should be.

These various monetary theories of the cycle underlay the main contending explanations for the persistence of unemployment in the depression of the 1920s. The most orthodox economists at LSE saw the depth of the depression as merely the counterpart to the monetary laxity that had underlain the excesses of the preceding boom. For Hawtrey the problem was the discouragement of investment by the excessive interest rates required to defend gold. Pigou saw the essential problem as the inflexibility of wages and the immobility of labour that prevented the adjustment mechanism of the market from restoring full unemployment, although he rejected wage cuts as the solution.

Robertson offered the most heretical diagnosis, seeing the depression as the result not of the monetary policies of the government, the rigidity of the market, or the intransigence of the working class, but in terms of a theory of overinvestment.[2] For Robertson low investment resulted from a drying up of investment opportunities and the depressed expectations of entrepreneurs, so he proposed public works to stimulate demand and boost investment. Keynes originally was close to Hawtrey and Pigou, but soon came round to Robertson's views, rejecting wage cuts as undesirable and politically impractical, and seeing the problem as one of the mobilisation of savings and the allocation of investment, although he was far from theorising his analysis.

Keynes's remedy, which was eventually adopted by the Liberal Party, was increased public investment, primarily in roads and electricity supply, to be financed by the mobilisation of 'idle balances' and the repatriation of investment that had flowed abroad in the absence of profitable opportunities at home. The expansionary impact of such policies would then create a more favourable environment for the restructuring of the economy by providing new opportunities for labour and capital displaced from the declining industries. The Labour Party, like the Liberals, was strongly influenced by Hobson's underconsumptionist theory, but placed more emphasis on raising wages and increasing welfare benefits than on public investment. However neither the Liberals nor the Labour

---

[2] Such theories were much more common in Central Europe, drawing on Marxist theories of overaccumulation and the investment cycle, and tending to lead to corporatist proposals for planned investment within the framework alternatively of state capitalism or state socialism.

Party were able to reconcile their palliatives with their continued commitment to the doctrine of sound finance. It was not at all clear why increased public investment or private consumption would be any less inflationary than an increase in private investment stimulated by a more relaxed monetary policy, and so it was not at all clear how such proposals differed from old-fashioned inflationism, nor why they should be more appropriate than traditional forms of monetary stimulation. Faced with such widespread disagreement and theoretical confusion amongst the economists, it is not surprising that the politicians, bankers and civil servants felt fully justified in sticking to the well-trodden paths of fiscal and monetary orthodoxy, while they sought to reduce market rigidities and expand world markets.

Although a few economists felt that Britain's problems had been intensified by high interest rates and an overvalued pound, there was no significant pressure to leave the gold standard or to abandon the principle of the balanced budget. The problem was not seen as Britain's commitment to the gold standard so much as the barriers presented to the staple industries by the failure to complete the liberalisation of the world economy by breaking down tariff barriers. The doctrine of the balanced budget, like the gold standard, secured almost universal support as a check on the profligacy of governments and guarantee against inflation. The experience of the recent political effects of inflation at home, and even more menacingly in Central Europe, meant that this was no irrational fear. Whether or not budget deficits would have provoked inflation, the government's fear simply reflected that of capitalists, the burden of debt management making the government very vulnerable to a weakening in the confidence of financial markets if a budget deficit aroused inflationary fears. Thus the emergence of deficits in the late 1920s was carefully concealed from the public and financial markets, and the May Committee's projection of a deficit in 1931 brought down the Labour government.

The state and the depression of the 1930s

The onset of depression in 1929 brought the problems of unemployment and the depressed industries to the fore once more. The main thrust of the Labour government's thinking was influenced by the rationalisation movement, with its emphasis on the inability of competition to secure the necessary restructuring of capital, and so the need for government and the banks to take the lead in sponsoring rationalisation to eliminate excess capacity, introduce advanced methods of production and increase investment on the basis of cooperation between employers and unions. The Coal Mines Act of 1930 sought to impose a cartel on the coal industry, with limited success, but the main thrust was to seek bank sponsorship of rationalisation. The Bankers Industrial Development Co, established in 1930 under the Bank of England, sponsored limited reconstruction schemes in shipbuilding and textiles, but on the whole the banks were more concerned to use rationalisation to reduce their exposure to industry rather than to throw good money after bad. Moreover the onset of depression meant that the emphasis of rationalisation schemes was increasingly less on expansionary investment and more on the elimination of excess capacity and reduction of costs that only created further unemployment. Thus rationalisation began to be considered in the broader framework of the problem of unemployment. The government, in search of new ideas, established the Macmillan Committee on Finance and Industry and the Economic Advisory Council which involved economists, trades unionists and employers.

The Economic Advisory Council provided a forum for economists to offer their advice, but since the economists could hardly agree on the time of day the Council proved ineffective. The recommendations of the Macmillan Committee, published just before the 1931 crisis, were largely ignored. Keynes's proposals for deficit-financed public investment received little support. With the fall of the Labour government the day belonged not to Keynes, but to the traditional Tory remedies of sound finance, protective tariffs and the Empire, while more radical measures were being proposed by the advocates of rationalisation and planning.

The collapse of the gold standard, far from undermining orthodoxy, gave it a new lease of life. Protective tariffs, devaluation and the suspension of convertibility enabled the Bank of England to build up large reserves with which to stabilise an undervalued pound, freeing budgetary policy from the constraints imposed by the gold standard. Interest rates fell sharply, relieving the pressure on the budget. 'Cheap money' became the cornerstone of monetary policy for the next two decades, low interest rates being maintained not only to keep out speculative 'hot money' and relieve the debt burden, but also in the hope of stimulating investment, although the main contribution in the 1930s was probably to the domestic construction boom rather than to industrial investment.

Cheap money meant that the authorities could no longer use the traditional instrument of the interest rate as the means of controlling the supply of money and credit, relying instead on the direct control of the supply of cash to the banks, which gave the Bank of England leverage over the lending policies of the banks. However it also meant that the burden of checking inflationary pressures fell more heavily on the budget, so that the continued fear of inflation meant that a liberal monetary policy was counterbalanced by a rigid fiscal conservatism.

Protection and financial stabilisation was accompanied by some increase in the direct intervention of the state in the domestic economy. However intervention sought not to replace the market by administrative controls but to reinforce the stimulus of the market with appropriate institutional and fiscal encouragement. The historic Tory commitment to protectionism and imperial preference was combined with the development of an industrial policy that sought to restructure domestic industry and employment. Domestic agriculture was encouraged by the establishment of Marketing Boards that stabilised prices and provided subsidies. The state sponsored further rationalisation schemes and the imposition of cartels in coal, iron and steel, textiles and shipbuilding and brought road transport under close regulation to eliminate the destructive, and dangerous, tendencies of unfettered competition, while competition in retail trade was reduced through the extension of retail price maintenance. The Special Areas Acts provided subsidies to firms setting up in the depressed areas. The provision of relief was rationalised and made gradually less punitive in response to working class pressure.

The radical alternative to Tory orthodoxy was provided by the corporatist heirs of the rationalisation movement. For the advocates of rationalisation the failure of capitalism had been identified as a failure of the competitive market to regulate accumulation, the persistence of excess capacity and of intense competition preventing the introduction of more advanced methods of production. In the 1920s the emphasis had been on the role of the banks in imposing rationalisation. However the limited involvement of the banks in industrial finance, and the failure of trade associations and cartels to enforce their rules on individual members, led the proponents of rationalisation in an increasingly corporatist direction, within which the state would play a more active role in sponsoring the formation of cartels, that would have the administrative resources and legal powers to enforce their rules on the industry as a whole. Moreover the onset of depression led the advocates of rationalisation to move beyond schemes to deal with the problems of individual industries to consider rationalisation within the broader framework of economic planning.

In the 1920s the rationalisation movement had primarily addressed the 'microeconomic' problems of industrial restructuring, without seriously questioning the primary role of money and the market in 'macroeconomic' regulation. The presumption was that rationalisation would make industry more responsive to market pressures and establish a favourable environment for the spontaneous recovery of trade and investment. Proposals for a degree of economic planning had centred on the redirection of investment, particularly towards domestic industry, whether through Mosley's Economic Council, the Liberal *Yellow Book*'s National Investment Board or the Macmillan Committee's proposals for a closer relation between banking and industry.

With the onset of depression the problem became wider, concerning not only the direction but also the scale of investment. However financial constraints still largely excluded consideration of expansionary public expenditure as a solution to the latter problem. Thus proposals for state intervention sought to encourage private investment by extending the corporatist principles of rationalisation from particular industries to the economy as a whole. Mosley soon came to draw on the example of Mussolini's Italy to propose a full-blown corporate state in which each industry would be organised on corporate lines, the various corporations coming together in a National Council for Corporations. Such ideas, without the fascist politics, also made considerable headway amongst radical Conservatives. The example of the Soviet Union provided a similar inspiration to many on the Left.

Corporatism raised major political questions. In bringing capital directly under the control of the state, corporatism replaced regulation by the market with regulation by political bodies, in accordance with their own political priorities. Thus the question of who was to control the corporatist apparatus assumed major importance. Neither capitalists nor the working class were deceived by the illusions of the liberal corporatists that corporatism could be based on a political partnership, as an extension of the well-established mechanisms of joint consultation, for they knew, with Marx, that the community of the state is an 'illusory community'. Any attempt to go beyond joint consultation to give a tangible reality to that community could only lead to political polarisation as the class struggle took on the immediate form of a struggle for state power. The capitalist fear that the corporatist state might hand power over capital to the working class or to populist politicians was matched by the working class fear of the unification and consolidation of the power of capital in the hands of the state. Thus, while corporatist solutions to the crisis were eminently rational, they were politically completely unrealistic in a country in which, unlike Germany, Italy and the Soviet Union, the political class struggle had not been fought through to a decisive result, and were increasingly unattractive as it became clear that corporatist economic strategies could not be detached from a corporatist politics that implied the destruction of the liberal state.

The Labour Party, increasingly dominated by the TUC, was' deeply suspicious of any corporatist developments. This was partly for political reasons, but also because the centre of gravity of the TUC remained the staple industries, whose recovery depended not on domestic expansion but on increased international competitiveness and a growing world market. Despite its long-standing commitment to nationalisation as the solution to the problems of particular industries, the Labour Party had little interest in corporatist planning, nationalisation being seen primarily as a means of expanding investment and employment by increasing efficiency, rather than as an instrument of planning, let alone an instrument of workers' control. Similarly proposals for central planning did not go far beyond vague suggestions of the state direction of investment, supplemented later in the 1930s by a commitment to a strong policy of regional subsidies. The proposal of the Left for the nationalisation of the banks won a brief victory in the wake of the 1931 debacle, but was immediately reversed. The key to recovery was seen to lie in international efforts to secure financial reconstruction and a revival of world trade, rather than in central

planning directed at confining production within the limits of the
domestic market. Unemployment was to be combatted by the traditional methods of early retirement, a raising of the school leaving
age, a shorter working week and improved welfare benefits. The
Labour Party's programme offered no serious alternative, amount-
ing to little more than Toryism with a human face.

Disillusionment with corporatism, and lack of faith in orthodoxy, led to the search for a *Middle Way*, the title of Harold
Macmillan's influential book of 1938. Such a middle way would be
based on class collaboration, not class conflict, within the framework of the liberal state form, relying primarily on the legal, fiscal
and monetary powers of the state, rather than on corporatist state
direction. Practical examples were provided by the relative success
of the populist New Deal in the USA and the programme of deficit-
financed public works in Sweden. The theoretical foundations for
the middle way were provided by Keynes.

The Keynesian Revolution

During the 1920s Keynes had been a heretic, opposing the return
to the gold standard and proposing public works, but he had been
no revolutionary. The roots of the Keynesian Revolution lay in
Keynes's struggle to resolve the theoretical issues raised by the
attempt to reconcile the proposed programme of public works with
the principle of the balanced budget.

The primary argument against deficit finance in the 1920s had
been that a loss of confidence would drive capital abroad, so that
any increase in public investment would be more than compensated
by the decline in private domestic investment. Initially Keynes
merely reversed this claim to argue that psychological factors disrupted the allocation of investment, leading to excessive foreign
investment and the holding of 'idle balances', and so should be
countered by restricting foreign investment and mobilising the idle
balances. However this was hardly more satisfactory than the Treasury view that it opposed in lacking any theory that could explain
the factors determining savings and investment. In order to put
his arguments on a more secure theoretical foundation Keynes was
led to a reexamination of the foundations of monetary theory.

The first fruit of Keynes's labours, *A Treatise on Money*, was peculiarly indigestible, but nevertheless contained some fundamental insights. Keynes's critique of economic orthodoxy focused on its weakest point, its conception of money. Whereas orthodox economists had accepted without question Smith's proposition that the function of money is to serve as a means of exchange, the *Treatise* began with a direct challenge to the classical position, arguing that true money only appears with the development of what Keynes called 'money-of-account'. He insisted that the 'money' that appears in the classical parable is not really money, for the form of exchange is still essentially one of barter. What he meant by this was that it is only when things come regularly to have their value expressed in terms of money that we see the development of a monetary system, for it is only then that exchange has a systematic significance and things acquire relatively stable values. Thus the classical parable is merely a story about the private and accidental barter relationships that are entered into in a society in which exchange is not yet a regular feature of economic life. It has nothing to do with the development of money as a systematic, and so social, institution.

The critical development is that values come to be expressed in the form of money, which is an ideal relationship independent of any particular exchange or of the existence of any particular money commodity. The designation of a particular thing to embody money-of-account is then a secondary consideration, but it involves a conventional designation, rather than being a 'natural' development, as Smith and his successors argued. Thus Keynes argued that in all developed economies money is state-money. His conclusion was that if the essence of money is its role as money-of-account, it has a very minor role to play as the means of exchange, a role much reduced by the development of the credit system.

Keynes's redefinition of the nature of money has quite fundamental implications, for if the development of money presupposes the development of a regular system of exchange money can no longer be seen as a spontaneously-evolved rational instrument, but rather, as Marx saw it, as the means of articulation of a particular system of social relationships. However Keynes did not follow through this implication, primarily because his insistence on the character of money as state-money meant that he saw money as only a symbol of value, and not as the independent form of value, so reproducing the classical dichotomy of the real and the mone-

tary systems. Thus Keynes did not address the contradictory form
of money as capital, passing instead to the investigation of the various forms of money created by the state and the banking system,
and then to the role of the rate of interest in coordinating savings
and investment, remaining firmly within the classical theoretical
framework, as developed by Fisher, Hawtrey and Wicksell.

Keynes did not develop the policy implications of his analysis in
the *Treatise*, but did so in his evidence to the Macmillan Committee. Although the Committee was impressed by his eloquence, the
majority did not endorse his call for loan-financed public works.
Nor did the *Treatise* itself have any greater impact. Indeed by
the time of publication Keynes had moved on from the *Treatise* to
develop the arguments that would make up his *General Theory*.

The central idea of the *General Theory* was that the role of
money derives from the existence of ignorance and uncertainty from
which the classical system abstracted. Once ignorance and uncertainty are invoked money ceases to be a passive lubricant and comes
to play a more active role in the operation of the system. Moreover, ignorance and uncertainty break the link, that is fundamental
to the classical system, between monetary and 'real' magnitudes.
For the classical system monetary prices are simply the symbolic
representation of real relationships, so that in making decisions on
the basis of monetary magnitudes economic agents are simultaneously making decisions about real magnitudes. But if economic
agents are uncertain of present and future market conditions, they
are uncertain of present and future prices. This means that in all
monetary transactions they are uncertain of the purchasing power
of the money that they acquire as a result of such transactions.
Thus, for example, Keynes argued that the wage bargain is made
in monetary terms, but changes in the money wage do not necessarily correspond to changes in the real wage. The result is that
the classical mechanism by which a full employment equilibrium
is reached, according to which a decline in real wages restores the
profitability of investment sufficiently to achieve full employment,
may not work, even if workers freely accept a fall in money wages.
If prices fall pari passu with wages, a fall in money wages will not
translate into a fall in real wages.

For Keynes the dislocation between the real and the monetary
systems was not an expression of the contradictory form of money
as capital. It was merely a matter of ignorance and uncertainty

that disrupted the operation of the market in the co-ordination of economic decisions over time. Thus Keynes did not break fundamentally with the classical dichotomy, and again passed on directly to the exploration of the particular implications of his insight for the theory of money and interest.

While the demand for money as means of payment and means of exchange is limited, the introduction of ignorance and uncertainty makes it clear that it is quite rational to hold money, in preference to interest-bearing assets, for speculative reasons. The speculative demand for money will depend on the rate of interest and on expectations as to its future course. If rates are expected to rise, holders of existing financial assets will realise a capital loss as their price depreciates. Those expecting a significant rise in the rate of interest will therefore choose to hold money, while those expecting a fall will seek to reduce their money holdings. The rate of interest serves to achieve an equilibrium between the demand for and supply of the stock of money, and this mechanism far outweighs the interaction of the supply and demand for loanable funds as a whole that played a central role in the classical theory, and that provided the means by which savings and investment were equilibrated at full employment.

While the rate of interest is determined in the money market, savings are brought into equilibrium with the volume of investment planned at a given rate of interest by fluctuations in income, a cutback in investment leading to a fall in incomes until equilibrium between saving and investment plans is established, and vice versa. Since the market rate of interest is determined by the expectations of investors, there is no reason to believe that the market rate of interest will correspond to that which will draw forth the volume of investment corresponding to full employment savings. The monetary authorities may be able to intervene in financial markets to alter the rate of interest, selling bonds to drive up the rate of interest, or buying bonds to drive it down. However very large changes in the supply of money may be necessary to change interest rates in the face of contrary market expectations. Moreover in a depression, while prices are expected to continue to fall, the nominal rate of interest required to achieve a recovery may even be negative. Finally, large changes in the money market might adversely affect the confidence of entrepreneurs, and so dissuade them from investing. For all these reasons it may prove impossible for monetary policy to achieve a recovery from depression. On the other hand, a relatively painless route to recovery is offered by loan-financed public investment, increased government spending generating the income that, through increased tax revenue and savings, will provide the resources to finance the increase in expenditure and that will justify the expansion of the money supply required to fund the initial deficit.

The main opposition to Keynes came from LSE, and was led by Hayek and Robbins. Hayek had developed his own theory of the market as an information network, the relationship between monetary and real variables being maintained by a rigid adherence to the classical conception of money. For Hayek the condition for prices to carry information about real variables was simply that the money supply should remain constant, ignorance and uncertainty being dispelled by the constant search of entrepreneurs for new opportunities. Thus Hayek sharply criticised Keynes for ignoring the operation of the price system in his preoccupation with spurious 'macroeconomic aggregates' and his reliance on the irrational psychological force of 'expectations'. This led Keynes to ignore the possibility that had been at the heart of the theorising of the 1920s, that persistent unemployment was not the result of a deficiency of overall demand, but of structural dislocation that was a result of the disruption of the market mechanism by monetary instability. It was unstable monetary policies that bred uncertainty and so broke the link between monetary and real variables. Uncertainty reinforced the barriers to the achievement of equilibrium that arose from the heterogeneity of the capital stock, the immobility of labour, monopoly power, trades unions, and misguided state intervention. The Keynesian remedy of deficit financing would merely intensify the problem by leading to the further inflationary disruption of the price mechanism, unless it was accompanied by the kinds of planning envisaged by the corporatists to contain inflationary pressures and oversee the direction of investment and labour to the appropriate branches of production. For Hayek this implied that Keynesian fiscal laxity was merely the first step on *The Road to Serfdom*, the title of his wartime manifesto.

Although Hayek's own theory was touchingly naïve, his criticisms of Keynes were by no means misplaced. Keynes had indeed failed to develop the implications of his criticisms of economic orthodoxy. His criticism of the classical theory of money was not matched by any criticism of the classical theory of the market. Indeed his belief that public investment could expand incomes and employment without leading to inflation implied a faith in the market mechanism that far exceeded that of his adversaries, for it implied that all branches of production could respond immediately to an increase in demand by increasing production, so that any price increases would be at worst temporary. The rigidities of the market, which prevented such a smooth reallocation of resources, had lain at the heart of the orthodox objections to loan-financed public works. Keynes did not rebuff these criticisms, he merely ignored them. Similarly Keynes's neglect of the market, in which capitalists' expectations are put to the test, meant that he treated the ignorance and uncertainty inherent in the anarchy of the capitalist mode of production as a purely subjective phenomenon, expressed in the irrational psychological impulses of entrepreneurs, so that his disagreement with the 'Treasury view' over the implications of deficit financing merely came down to a different assessment of its impact on speculators' confidence.

Hayek was correct in seeing the limits of Keynesianism as being inherent in its 'macroeconomic' formulation. Keynes ignored the social form of capitalist production in abstracting from the existence of independent capitals, so that the relation between the production and realisation of surplus value was treated simply as a matter of the relation between aggregate demand and total supply. As soon as competition between capitals is admitted it becomes clear that individual capitals confront the market not as a limit, but as a barrier to be overcome by transforming methods of production and opening up new markets. However Hayek's naïvety lay in his belief that the overaccumulation and uneven development of capital was merely a result of the overexpansion of credit. Within the capitalist mode of production the tendency to overproduction is neither the result of the failure of the market to ensure that demand keeps pace with the growth of supply, nor of the failure of the monetary authorities to confine production within the limits of the market. It is competition between capitals that gives rise to the tendency for the transformation of methods of production to take the form of overaccumulation and crisis, so that accumulation constantly runs ahead of the growth of the market. The more rapid growth of the market, far from restraining the tendency to overaccumulation, gives it free reign. Thus Hayek was correct in

his diagnosis of Keynesianism as inflationary, but naïve in his belief
that the contradictions of accumulation could be simply removed
by competition within a restrictive monetary regime.

The criticisms of the Hayekians went largely unheard. Hayek's
own interpretation of the depression, and his insistence that the
road to recovery was the stabilisation of the gold standard and the
liberalisation of trade, was discredited by the irreversible collapse
of the gold standard and the wave of protectionism from 1931.
Keynes, on the other hand, offered both economists and politicians
some hope of salvation in mapping out a middle way between the
corporatism of the left and the right. Keynesian policies would
salvage all the benefits of regulation by money and the market,
while avoiding the costs that were becoming politically increasingly
unacceptable. The only revolution that Keynes proposed was to
accord the state more discretion in its fiscal and monetary policies.
This was a small price to pay, provided only that the state had
sound guidance: 'Dangerous acts can be done safely in a community
which thinks and feels rightly, which would be the way to hell if
they were executed by those who think and feel wrongly'.[3]

The limitations of Keynes's *General Theory*, which undermined
its revolutionary potential, proved its greatest strength by guaranteeing its ready acceptability. Although LSE held out, Keynesianism swept through the younger economists at Oxford and
Cambridge, and soon crossed the Atlantic. While some drew more
radical implications from Keynes's theory, it was soon reintegrated
into the mainstream of classical economics on the basis of the orthodox theory of the market process. The 'neoclassical synthesis'
neutralised Keynes's critique of the classical conception of money
by adding the speculative motive as an additional component in
the demand for money as a reserve of the means of exchange, and
so reduced his theory of money to a part of the theory of 'portfolio
selection'. Keynes's analysis of the limitations of monetary policy
was reduced to a special case of the classical theory, dependent for
its results on the assumption of inelastic expectations. His criticism
of the classical analysis of the deflationary mechanism, on the basis of his argument that lack of homogeneity of real and monetary
variables meant that a fall in money wages would not necessarily
lead to a fall in real wages, was reduced to the old assumption of

---

[3] Quoted Roy Harrod, *The Life of John Maynard Keynes*, Macmillan, London, 1951, pp. 436–7.

wage rigidities. Thus the Keynesian Revolution was reduced to the argument that market rigidities and the role of expectations meant that fiscal policy had a role to play alongside monetary policy in the stabilisation of accumulation.

This reduction was not merely the result of the conservatism of economists, unable to recognise the revolutionary potential of Keynes's thought, or of Keynes's own confusions. Despite the critical force of Keynes's arguments, his critique was based on the disruptive power of exogenous expectations, which for Keynes were essentially subjective and irrational. No rigorous economic theory could be constructed on such an arbitrary basis. Thus the very survival of economics as a pseudo-scientific discipline depended on purging this irrational element by making expectations endogenous. However the assumptions about expectations on which the neoclassical synthesis was based were equally arbitrary. When the ideological limitations of Keynesianism appeared in the 1970s the arbitrariness of its underlying assumptions became transparent, opening the door to Friedman's monetarism, the revival of Austrianism, and rational expectations theory, each of which ultimately rested on different, but equally arbitrary, assumptions about the formation of expectations.

The political impact of Keynesianism

While Keynes's ideas soon became the cornerstone of a new economic orthodoxy, they had little immediate political impact. By the time *The General Theory* was published the recovery was well under way. Protection had helped agriculture and the iron and steel industry, while low interest rates had given a boost to construction. Protection and imperial preference also provided a framework within which the new consumer durable industries could become established, although their growth was still restricted by the limited size of the middle class market. The move of new industries to the Midlands and Southeast, made possible by earlier investment in electricity supply, and rising wages for those in work, gave a substantial boost to the demand for housing. The contraction of world trade meant that coal, textiles, shipbuilding and parts of engineering continued to be severely depressed, and regional unemployment extremely high, while new investment, outside housing and construction, and industrial profits remained low. However unemployment did not pose a serious political threat; the trades unions were cowed by unemployment in the declining industries, and had not yet become established in the new industries; the Liberal Party was in terminal decline; the Labour Party had not emerged from its crisis with any alternative programme; while the radical Left and Right showed no signs of building on their small bases. The government had little reason to doubt the wisdom of its policies, and certainly had no intention of undermining its success by adopting potentially destabilising Keynesian policies.

Keynes's ideas made some headway in the established political parties. Harold Macmillan, on the radical wing of the Conservative Party, enthusiastically adopted Keynes's ideas as an alternative to the corporatism that he had previously advocated. Many of the younger Keynesian economists sought a political platform in the Liberal and, increasingly, the Labour Parties. However their influence in the latter should not be exaggerated. Many of the older generation in the Labour Party continued to pin their political hopes on the collapse of capitalism, and saw Keynesianism merely as a means of postponing the fateful day. The 'bankers' ramp' of 1931 persuaded the Left of the need to nationalise the banking system. Keynesian policies merely accommodated the anti-social inclinations of the bankers, rather than challenging their power. The underconsumptionist strand in the Labour Party was Hobsonian, rather than Keynesian, seeing the deficiency of demand as a result of the inequality of income, an inequality that might be reduced but that could not be eradicated under capitalism. The syndicalist and guild socialist strands saw the deficiencies of capitalism as inherent in the anarchy of the market, depression being the result of the failure of the market to secure the structural integration of accumulation, the remedy being planning and nationalisation under workers' control. These strands were closer to Robbins, a one-time guild socialist, and Hayek than to Keynes, while rejecting Hayek's fatalistic view of the slump in believing that the productive capacity expanded during the boom did not have to be liquidated, but could provide the basis for a recovery sustained by the planning of investment.

Keynes's work probably had a greater immediate impact on civil servants than on politicians. The attraction of Keynesianism to the latter was that it at last offered a coherent theory on which to base the formation of budgetary policy, replacing the rule of thumb of the doctrine of the balanced budget.

When government expenditure had been a small proportion of the national product, its budgetary policies were significant for their monetary rather than their fiscal implications. The doctrine of the balanced budget expressed the government's desire to maintain its freedom of manoeuvre. Borrowing made the government dependent for its revenues on the state of the financial market, while restricting its ability to pursue an independent monetary policy. The dangers of an unbalanced budget in these respects had been amply revealed by the two periods in which the government had relied on borrowing, the Napoleonic and First World Wars. However the growth of government expenditure meant that its budgetary decisions had an increasing impact on the pressure of demand. While the government remained on the gold standard the monetary constraint had to remain paramount. Once the government had left the gold standard and stabilised the currency, the doctrine of the balanced budget had lost its rationale and appeared merely as an archaic dogma. Keynes provided the theory that could set budgetary policy on a more rigorous foundation in these new circumstances. However it was not until the public finances came under renewed pressure with the strains of wartime expenditure that the Keynesians were able to come out of the closet.

Chapter 10

Post-War Reconstruction and The Keynesian Welfare State

Wartime planning and the budget

The policy of the British government in the Second World War drew on the lessons of the First. There was an immediate realisation that the demands of war would impose severe economic and political pressures that could only be accommodated by establishing a rigorous system of controls and by enlisting the support of the working class for the war effort. The circumstances were much more propitious than they had been 25 years before. Administrative and consultative apparatuses had already been developed to implement the limited interventionist measures of the 1930s. The working class had been brought within the constitution, pursuing its trades union aspirations through an institutionalised system of industrial relations, and its political aspirations through the Labour Party. The radical elements in the Labour Party, that briefly came to the fore after 1931, had been defeated. The Communist Party was isolated as a result of the Stalin-Hitler pact. Popular anti-fascism provided a powerful ideological basis for working class commitment to an imperialist war.

The main economic constraints faced by the planners were the availability of labour and shipping space, and it was the allocation of these resources that provided the basis of the planning system, which worked primarily through a licensing system rather than direct control. The growing deficit on the balance of trade was met by foreign borrowing and the massive liquidation of British overseas investments, the deficit with the United States being covered by lend-lease. Food subsidies and price and rent controls, soon supplemented by rationing, were enlisted to combat inflation.

The Labour Party was brought into the coalition government in May 1940, and Labour given key Ministries. There were limited welfare improvements, mainly aimed at the old and at children, and there was a considerable expansion in the health service, which was for the first time set on a national footing. On the other hand the raising of the school leaving age was abandoned, the housing programme came to a halt, and the long overdue reform of the system of social insurance was postponed. The principal wartime concessions were, not surprisingly, to the trades unions. Trades unionists were brought into the apparatus of production planning from shop-floor to ministerial level. Existing negotiating machinery was frozen, and a National Arbitration Tribunal established to resolve outstanding disputes. The introduction of fair wage clauses, statutory wage determination and restrictions on labour mobility and the right of dismissal led to a fall in civilian wage rates, more than compensated by increased overtime, a compression of wage differentials, and a considerable growth in the membership of trades unions. As in the First War the main concessions were admission to the corridors of power and the promise of new world to be built.

The main threat to the war effort, both political and economic, was inflation, and this raised the question of public finance. The lesson initially drawn from the First War was the need to contain inflationary pressure by minimising borrowing and to keep down the burden of debt by maintaining low interest rates. However the balance between taxation and borrowing was determined in an entirely ad hoc way. Immediately after the outbreak of war Keynes pointed out the inflationary consequences of excessive borrowing, although his proposals for sharp increases in taxation met with a hostile response. However continued inflation, the failure of a small

War Loan in March 1940, and the realisation, following the fall of France, that the war would be long and hard fought led to Keynes being brought into the Treasury with the change of government.

The 1941 Kingsley Wood budget was the first Keynesian budget. However it was not Keynesian in the sense of using fiscal policy to regulate the market economy, for the economy was regulated by the pervasive system of controls. It was Keynesian in the more limited sense of applying Keynesian principles of public finance to the formulation of the budget. The budget was accompanied by the first White Paper on National Income and Expenditure, which integrated the accounts of the public and private sector to estimate the 'inflationary gap' that had to be covered by increases in taxation. The adoption of Keynesian budgetary principles led to an influx of economists and statisticians into the Treasury not to take over the role of economic planning, but to develop a more sophisticated system of national accounting on the basis of which to determine budgetary policy.

The system of controls and financial planning was largely successful in containing inflationary pressure. The liquidation of foreign assets and foreign borrowing enabled Britain to maintain the flow of essential supplies. The absorption of the Labour and trades union leadership into the state apparatus secured their enthusiastic participation in the war effort. The extension of such assimilation to the shop-floor level ensured that the energy of the shop stewards organisation was largely directed towards, rather than against, the war effort. Although there was some industrial unrest, particularly in the mines, there were no signs of the potentially revolutionary outbursts that had threatened the fabric of the state during the First World War.

Planning for post-war reconstruction

The question of post-war reconstruction was addressed at an early stage in the war. In general there was a remarkable degree of political consensus over the framework for post-war reconstruction. There were three inter-related priorities underlying the reconstruction plans. Firstly, to secure the foundations for the sustained growth of income and employment by opening up export markets and rebuilding the international monetary system. Secondly, to secure the foundations for the growth of national efficiency, the better to withstand the expected onslaught of foreign, primarily US, competition, particularly through the promotion of investment, education and scientific research. Thirdly, to secure the foundations for political stability by developing a comprehensive system of social security. Political differences were more a matter of emphasis than of principle. The Labour Party, despite its commitment to an extension of nationalisation and planning, remained wedded to the view that capitalism was best run by capitalists, while the trades unions were committed to retaining their autonomy. The primary emphasis of Labour's plans, therefore, was not on the socialisation of production but on the reform and extension of the welfare system as a means of alleviating poverty, improving national efficiency, and staving off recession by boosting consumption. The framework for post-war planning was laid out in a series of White Papers published in 1944, covering Social Insurance, Health, and Employment, and in the 1944 Education Act, each of which expressed a broad political consensus.

The system of social insurance had long been due for reform, having developed in an ad hoc way in response to conflicting pressures. In the inter-war period various schemes had been introduced to keep the unemployed out of the clutches of the Poor Law, which had become gradually less punitive in response to working class pressure before it was finally abolished in 1937, but despite endless Commissions and revisions the insurance system remained incoherent, administratively inefficient, and actuarially unsound. Provision appeared arbitrary and unfair, which, with its punitive elements, provoked considerable popular hostility. The basis for reform was the 1942 Beveridge Report, which laid down six principles. First, it should be comprehensive, including health care and the provision of family allowances, the latter long opposed by the TUC as a subsidy to low wages. Second, it should have a unified administration. Third, contributions and benefits should be clearly laid down, according to the contributory classes: wage earners, the self employed, housewives, others of working age, the young and the old. Fourth, the payment of adequate benefits. Fifth, the payment of flat-rate benefits according only to family size. Sixth, flat-rate contributions, of which 50 per cent would be paid by the state, 30 per cent by the insured and 20 per cent by employers. Although this would imply an increase in cost of about two-thirds, if unemployment could be controlled, the initial cost of the proposals was kept down by deferring the payment of the full old-age pension. The comprehensive coverage of the system, and the regressive forms of taxation and contributions that would finance it, meant that the scheme would have little redistributive impact.

The Beveridge scheme rationalised and generalised existing provision. Although its greater coverage and the anticipated higher rates of benefit increased the cost of the system, it did not alter the fundamental principles of social administration. Health care and old age pensions were provided universally, but the Beveridge scheme was still an insurance scheme, rights being earned by insurance contributions or family dependence, so the scheme was still based on, and reinforced, the subordination of the worker to the wage form and the subordination of women to the family form. Unemployment benefit was intended, in association with the network of labour exchanges, to facilitate the restructuring of capital by lubricating the labour market, not to provide a guaranteed right to subsistence. Thus the National Assistance Board would provide for those unable to earn a minimum subsistence through wage labour, insurance contributions or female dependence, while a modified workhouse test continued to be applied to the able-bodied poor in the form of a means test and a judgement of willingness to work.

The Treasury was strongly opposed to Beveridge's scheme, primarily on grounds of cost. The Treasury was not sufficiently Keynesian to share Beveridge's belief that its contribution to the maintenance of demand would prevent the post-war slump which many feared, so that it would effectively pay for itself, while the 'socialisation of consumption' would offer a liberal alternative to the socialisation of production. However the Report was met with widespread popular enthusiasm, many employers at least tacitly supporting a scheme which they hoped would improve national efficiency and secure social peace at relatively small cost to themselves, and Churchill reversed his initial opposition and came to regard acceptance of Beveridge's scheme as crucial to maintaining working class morale. Thus the 1944 White Papers on Health and Social Insurance largely accepted Beveridge's proposals, although they reduced the scale of benefits. The 1944 Education Act similarly extended free secondary education to all, largely on the grounds of national efficiency.

The viability of a comprehensive system of social insurance, with the associated safety net of a reformed Poor Law, depended on the achievement of a reasonably high level of employment to preserve the financial soundness of the scheme. Beveridge's original plan was actuarially based on the assumption of a rate of unemployment no higher than 10 per cent on the inter-war definition. The maintenance of a high and stable level of employment was accepted as a political priority in the 1944 Employment White Paper, although this commitment was severely circumscribed, the achievement of full employment depending on the international reconstruction of export markets, the achievement of competitiveness, wage and price stability and labour mobility. Although contra-cyclical public works were envisaged as a stabilisation measure, the White Paper rejected deficit financing in favour of a budget balanced over the cycle. Keynes himself shared the view of the committee that the post-war priority was the expansion of exports, and from 1941 threw himself into the task of rebuilding the international monetary system, which culminated in the establishment of the International Monetary Fund and the International Bank for Reconstruction and Development at Bretton Woods in 1944. Parallel negotiations to secure the post-war liberalisation of trade culminated in the General Agreement on Tariffs and Trade in 1947, while the political framework for international reconstruction was to be provided by the United Nations and associated agencies, some of which had survived from the days of the League of Nations.

Planning for a new international order

The collapse of the international economic order had led to two devastating world wars. The reconstruction of the international economic order was the first priority of the Western allies when the anticipated victory came. However such a reconstruction was not simply an economic but also a deeply political question. The German attempt to build the thousand year Reich on the basis of its political and military dominance was matched by the attempt of the US to achieve the liberal millenium on the basis of its economic dominance. Neither project was politically realistic. While military defeat put paid to the former, the contradiction between the nationalist and internationalist aspirations of the US state undermined the latter. The barrier of the national state form could only be overcome by constructing a new international order.

The US did not share Britain's view of the war as exclusively an anti-fascist war. For the US the war had arisen as a struggle between declining political imperialisms. International reconstruction required the dismantling of both the German and the British Empires, and the subordination of nation states to the power of world money, which in the immediate post-war context meant the dollar. However Britain was not going to let go of its imperialist 'obligations' easily. Britain constantly resisted US attempts to open the world market to US capital by breaking down the barriers of protectionism and discrimination, arguing that such a scheme could only lead to a post-war resurgence of nationalism, corporatism and socialism as national governments sought to stabilise their position in the face of the American onslaught. Keynes initially proposed a scheme of international reconstruction based on the extension of the benefits of the Sterling Area and Imperial preference to Europe, a liberal version of the New Economic Order that the Germans were proposing for Europe. Such a scheme could hardly be expected to appeal to the Americans. The Atlantic Charter of 1941 extracted a paper commitment from Britain to collaborate in the construction of a multilateral order as the Americans made lend-lease conditional on the post-war dismantling of 'discrimination', in exchange for which the US committed itself to domestic expansionism.

The first priority was international monetary reconstruction. The IMF was designed to overcome the limitations of the gold standard by expanding international liquidity on the basis of the stabilisation of exchange rates and the pooling of reserves. In the immediate post-war period it was clear that the IMF would primarily serve as a source of dollars to the rest of the world. Although the free flow of dollars through the IMF would remove the barriers to accumulation in the US by removing the barriers to the accumulation of capital on a world scale, it also implied that the power of the dollar would be placed in the hands of an international agency in which the power of the US would be wielded by the US Treasury.

Although Roosevelt was sympathetic to such an international New Deal, which would be expected to benefit the US working class, the political implications were unacceptable to Congress, on populist and nationalistic grounds. However, despite some isolationist sentiment, the issue was not so much one of nationalism versus internationalism, for there was a widespread determination to overcome the nationalism that had destroyed the pre-war economic order and ended in war, while the US urgently needed access to world markets to mobilise its surplus capital and avoid a post-war recession. The issue was rather the form of internationalism, and in particular the relationship between the international economic and the international political order, which had domestic implications for the relation between the power of money and the power of the state. For Morgenthau and his colleagues in the US Treasury the international economic order should be subject to political regulation within a framework of international political co-operation, based on the democratisation of the occupied powers and building on the wartime alliance, including the Soviet Union. On the other hand the Eastern bankers vigorously pressed the Key Currency strategy of international reconstruction on the basis of the Wall Street–London axis, with sterling restored, subordinate to the dollar, by a large reconstruction loan within a multilateralist economic order dominated by the global power of the dollar. This perspective was shared by those in the State Department who saw the basis for international political reconstruction not in a political internationalism, but in a US-dominated Atlantic Alliance. Although the US Treasury was politically isolated, it retained considerable influence until Roosevelt's death and it was not until 1947–8 that liberal Atlanticism finally triumphed over progressive internationalism with the adoption of the Marshall Plan, the formation of NATO and the confrontation with the Soviet Union over Berlin.

The anticipated financial role of sterling and political role of Britain meant that the Atlanticist position was not unacceptable to the City of London or to the British government. However Britain had no intention of accepting political subordination to the US or economic subordination to the dollar. Thus the British strategy that evolved was one of exploiting the contradictions in the US position to rebuild a role for an independent British imperialism on the basis of the Empire and the Sterling Area, with a view to constructing an Atlantic Alliance of equal partnership.

The Atlanticist perspective prevailed in the compromise reached in the IMF negotiations. The US insisted on limiting the quota contributions to be made to the Fund, and similarly limited the resources available for long-term lending to the World Bank. The limitation on the resources available to the Fund was compensated by the obligation imposed on surplus and deficit countries alike to rectify persistent payment imbalances, an obligation that had been negated under the gold standard by the sterilisation of gold reserves by the surplus countries, and that was to be honoured more in the breach than in the observance under the IMF regime. The 'scarce currency clause', added at British insistence, which permitted retaliatory measures against countries in persistent surplus, was a weak substitute for Keynes's proposal to impose an escalating scale of penalty charges on surplus countries. Apart from this clause the articles of the Fund prohibited discrimination and envisaged a gradual return to full convertibility. Exchange rate variations were permitted only to correct a 'fundamental disequilibrium'.

The limited resources available to the IMF meant that it would only be able to finance small payments deficits. Although some controls on capital movements were permitted, the commitment to free convertibility, fixed exchange rates and non-discrimination implied that the financing of persistent imbalances could only be provided bilaterally, outside the IMF framework, the only source of such finance in the post-war world being the US. Thus, while it expanded international liquidity, the IMF did not overcome the limitations of the gold standard, and the international economic system was once more vulnerable to the vagaries of US policy, while the new power of the dollar gave the US a potential stranglehold on the reconstruction of the international economic and political system.

The reconstruction of Anglo-American imperialism

The framework for post-war economic reconstruction had already been laid down before the 1945 election by the international agreements which committed Britain to the reconstruction of the liberal world order based on trade and monetary liberalisation. The domestic commitments to full employment and to the construction of a comprehensive welfare system were backed by no such international guarantees. Although popular enthusiasm ensured a landslide Labour victory in 1945, its promises would be worth no more than had been those of Lloyd George in 1918 if it could not prove itself more successful in the task of economic reconstruction.

While Britain's international agreements specifically endorsed the right of the government to pursue domestic social and political policies of its own choosing, the commitment to trade and monetary liberalisation implied the dismantling of the apparatus of wartime control, while the need to secure dollar loans to finance reconstruction gave the US enormous political leverage. Although there were elements in the US who sought, in the emerging Cold War atmosphere, to use this leverage to block the dangerously socialist plans of the Labour government, the application of such pressure could hardly coexist with the commitment to democracy that was the ideological basis on which the war had been fought and on which the resistance to the communist threat was founded. Meanwhile the Labour government showed no inclination to renege on its international obligations by extending the system of wartime controls to put into practice its long-standing commitment to socialist planning, a strategy that would have met not only with concerted US opposition, but also with obstruction from the civil service and capital alike. Nevertheless such a strategy might prove unavoidable if reconstruction on the basis of Britain's international commitments failed, a danger that ensured that the Labour government retained the grudging support of those domestic and foreign forces that had severe reservations about its welfare policies.

The liquidation of British overseas investments, the sudden termination of lend-lease at the end of the war, the accumulated sterling balances and the heavy import demands of reconstruction meant that the economic priority was to build up exports by recovering old markets and conquering new ones. The scale of the task was enormous, for many markets had been lost in the course of the war, while the anticipated deficit called for an increase to at least 175 per cent of the pre-war level of exports, with a large increase in dollar exports to finance the demands of Britain and the Sterling Area for US imports. The need to expand exports had two dimensions. On the one hand, the physical need to expand production in export and import-substituting industries. This priority dominated domestic economic planning and preoccupied Labour Ministers. On the other hand, the need to strengthen the balance of international payments in order to reduce the dependence of sterling on the dollar and lay the foundations for the reconstruction of British imperialism within the framework of an equal partnership in the Atlantic Alliance. The latter task was clearly of interest to the City of London, but it was also of wider concern, for unless the international standing of sterling could be restored, so that sterling could serve as the means of international payment, trade and production would continue to be restricted by the availability of gold and dollars. This priority dominated the reconstruction of British international economic and political relationships, the economic aspects of which were effected primarily by civil servants and bankers,[1] with little reference to Ministers who neither understood nor had much interest in what they were doing, while the political aspects were dominated by the development of Anglo-US military co-operation. Nevertheless the Labour government had no reservations about a strategy which gave free vent to its virulent anti-Communism and its historical commitment to British imperialism, tempered only by its identification with the cause of Indian nationalism and a concern for the development of the colonies that was motivated more by the need for dollar-saving and dollar-earning than any concern for the destitution of the colonial populations.

The first priority of the new government was to secure a large US loan. However the United States government was not prepared to provide a loan that would simply shore up British imperialism, or create the space within which the government could give free reign to any socialist aspirations, and so demanded that the multilateralist provisions of Bretton Woods should be honoured by the dismantling of discriminatory trading practices and the restoration of the full convertibility of sterling within one year of granting the loan, a demand that the Labour Left resisted, but that Britain had no choice but to accept, at least on paper, even though Britain's adverse trading and financial position made such a prospect quite unrealistic.

Although Britain accepted the terms of the US loan, it had no intention of putting those terms into effect. The result was that, alongside the paper commitment to multilateralism, the British government immediately sought to secure its position by negotiating bilateral agreements with its trading and monetary partners, a strategy anticipated in Keynes's original plan of 1941 that envisaged extending Imperial Preference and the Sterling Area to Europe. Although convertibility was restored as agreed in 1947, the drain on the reserves meant that it had to be suspended almost

---

[1] Peter Burnham, *The British State and Capital Accumulation, 1945–51*, PhD thesis, University of Warwick, 1987.

immediately, and Britain did virtually nothing to implement the non-discrimination terms of its solemn agreements with the US.

The failure of British convertibility in 1947 sealed the fate of the Key Currency strategy as Britain threatened to go its own way in extending the Sterling Area through bilateral negotiations, rather than dismantling it on the basis of dollar convertibility. The underlying problem facing the US was that its multilateralist ambitions could never be reconciled with its attempt to use the power of the dollar as a political weapon. The issue came to a head with a looming political crisis in Europe which urgently demanded direct military, political and economic action, opening the way to an alternative internationalist strategy based on the direct intervention of the US in the economic and political reconstruction of Europe.

Marshall Aid and the rebuilding of Europe

By 1947 it was clear that the US policy of retribution against the defeated powers was undermining the attempt to establish political stability by exporting the US model of trades unionism and the principles of the New Deal as bulwarks of democracy, and was merely playing into the Russians' hands by shifting the balance of class forces in favour of the working class in the occupied countries. The failure to solve the problem of the dollar shortage was similarly playing into the hands of the Left in Western Europe by undermining the attempt at monetary stabilisation and economic reconstruction, while the attempt to work through Britain was being thwarted by Britain's own imperialist ambitions. The British withdrawal from Greece, in order to concentrate its military forces on maintaining the Empire, finally made it clear that the fate of Europe was in the hands of the US.

The basis of the new strategy of rebuilding Western Europe, centred on Germany, as a bulwark against communism, was the integration of Western Europe into an Atlantic economy in which economic interdependence would provide a firm basis for the Atlanticist political alliance. This could not be done by using the dollar to subordinate Western Europe to narrow US interests, but only by an internationalist programme of economic and political reconstruction.

The starting point was the German currency reform, vigorously opposed by the Soviet Union, which precipitated the division of Germany as joint allied control broke down, and culminated in the Berlin blockade. The solution to the problem of the dollar gap was Marshall Aid, a free gift of $13 billion to finance reconstruction and currency stabilisation, which had the added merit of staving off the looming US recession by expanding US exports. The programme had the longer-term cosmopolitan objective of stimulating a flow of US private investment to Europe, to secure the integration of Europe into an Atlantic economy and to raise European productivity levels to overcome the uneven development of the forces of production that was the primary barrier to the recovery of accumulation on a world scale. However Marshall Aid was far more than an economic programme. It was the lynchpin of a strategy to secure the social and political reconstruction of Europe on the American model, by providing the expansionary economic environment in which to foster collaborative industrial relations and American mass production methods, while launching a political offensive against the Left in the trades unions and sponsoring right-wing political regimes.[2]

Unlike the Dawes plan Marshall Aid envisaged the reconstruction of Europe on a regional rather than a national basis, hoping to ensure that Marshall Aid did not allow the latitude to national governments which had permitted the inter-war resurgence of German and British imperialism and that now threatened to drive Europe into the hands of Communism. Thus Marshall Aid was aimed primarily at fostering the integration of the Western European economy, and its insulation from that of the East, making a mockery of the claim that Marshall was offered to the Soviet Union on an equal basis. European integration would similarly undercut the British system of Imperial Preference.

The proponents of an international New Deal based on the wartime alliance found themselves in full retreat, denounced as agents of international communism. The Soviet Union was successfully isolated in the United Nations, while new international organisations were established to give political form to the new internationalism, notably NATO and the OEEC, through which

---

[2] Thus it would be more accurate to describe the post-war regime of accumulation as 'Marshallism', rather than 'Keynesianism' or 'Fordism', which strictly describe only elements of the strategy.

Marshall Aid was channeled. However the hope that European integration would undercut the British system of Imperial Preference and by-pass sterling was over-optimistic.

The weak link in the plan was the failure of the Marshall programme to solve the problem of the international monetary system. The hope that the problem of intra-European settlements could be solved by establishing the free convertibility of the European currencies was naive, for most European governments were not prepared to allow their neighbours free access to their reserves of scarce US dollars. This weakness in the programme left a gap which Britain could once more exploit to its own advantage, forging a temporary alliance with France, which had unhappy memories of the previous US attempt to rebuild Germany.

Britain was quite willing to participate in the co-ordination of policy in Western Europe, and was more than willing to accept dollar aid, provided that such participation did not compromise its wider imperialist role based on the Sterling Area, through which Britain secured privileged access to export markets and cheap food and raw materials. Britain took a lead in sponsoring trade liberalisation to open the European market to its exporters, but only to head off more radical proposals, while its domination of the OEEC ensured that the organisation was denied any supra-national powers, acting only as the coordinating agency for the independent policies of national governments. Britain similarly sought to subvert the US attempt to impose a multilateral payments system on Europe by resisting the US demand for the free transferability of Marshall dollars, intra-European settlements still being primarily on a bilateral basis.

The 1949 sterling crisis led to a re-evaluation of the British strategy, confirming Britain's commitment to the Empire. The crisis was partly precipitated by the impact of the US recession (from which Continental Europe was largely insulated) on the exports of the Sterling Area, drawing attention once more to the dependence of Britain on the dollar earnings of the Sterling Area. On the other hand, Western European trade was still predominantly intra-European, while the British share of such trade was declining and the payments arrangements associated with the Marshall Plan offered little prospect of Britain gaining from increased European dollar earnings. The result was to confirm Britain's long-term strategy of establishing a relationship with the dollar on the basis of the strength of the Sterling Area, the culmination of the strategy being the restoration of dollar convertibility. The sharp devaluation of the pound in 1949 and controls on dollar imports strengthened sterling, and Britain's bargaining position with the US, and laid the foundations on which this strategy could be pursued to fruition.

The strengthening of sterling also changed the British approach to what became the European Payments Union. The free transferability of reserves, combined with the need to maintain European restrictions on dollar convertibility, provided an opening for sterling to establish itself as the dominant European currency, provided only that Britain could establish a privileged status for sterling within the Union. However unilateral British devaluation and Britain's bilateral negotiations with the US aroused deep European suspicions. The US threat to establish the EPU without Britain persuaded the British government to join on the basis of guarantees that made EPU claims freely convertible into sterling, while limiting the convertibility of sterling into EPUs. Although sterling did benefit from participation in the EPU, the easing of the European dollar shortage meant that sterling was not able to establish its supremacy over the other European currencies, while growing intra-European trade and Britain's continued commitment to the Empire strengthened the basis for an European integration that would exclude Britain. Thus Britain remained aloof from the Schuman Plan to integrate the European coal and steel industries, and kept out of the ECSC set up to implement it, out of which the EEC eventually emerged.

Marshall Aid had still not solved the problem of the dollar gap, while the anticipated flow of US investment to Europe had not materialised. The EPU provided a framework within which intra-European trade could grow rapidly, but the shortage of dollars still held back US exports to Europe and so both the US leverage over European reconstruction and domestic accumulation in the US. The solution proposed by the State Department was rearmament, which was justified by the supposed threat of an imminent Soviet invasion of Western Europe and the emergence of the Chinese peril, and which was defended in pure Keynesian terms as a costless form of expenditure as the multiplier effect of increased expenditure increased the national product and so the means to pay for it. Increased US military expenditure in Europe would emphasise more forcefully than had the Marshall programme the dependence of European reconstruction on the US, while helping to fill the dollar gap both directly, and by increasing the confidence of US investors in the security of Western Europe. The Korean War provided the opportunity to implement this programme. At the same time enthusiastic participation in the war and the rearmament drive provided the Labour government with the opportunity to prove that it had established Britain's full independence and maturity as a world power that could stand shoulder to shoulder, etc......

Planning and the budget

Despite its rhetoric, and the rearguard action of the Left, the Labour government was committed from its inception to a strategy based not on planning but on the reconstruction of the liberal state form, within the framework of a resurgent British imperialism. The dollar loan and the growing strength of sterling provided a framework within which the government could address the problem of exports and import-saving, which was its immediate domestic priority. Although the strategy envisaged the dismantling of wartime controls, there was no question of doing so immediately, for fear of unleashing an inflationary boom and crash such as had followed the end of the First War. However the system of controls could hardly be called an apparatus of planning, for the government had no direct control over production. During the war the government could control the growth of the military industries because it was their only customer, but it had no such power over peace-time industry. Thus controls primarily took the negative form of the rationing of consumer goods and the licensing of investment, raw material supplies and imports, although agriculture and investment were encouraged by subsidies, grants and tax relief, which were initially used to direct industry to the development areas. Nationalisation primarily affected industries that were already in public ownership or under direct state control, although it was extended to the mines, railways, iron and steel and the health service, the main motive being the rationalisation of the industries in question rather than to assist overall planning, let alone to establish democratic control. Even a Central Economic Planning Staff was not established until 1947. In the absence of any administrative apparatus to oversee the comprehensive planning of reconstruction, positive measures were largely limited to exhortation through the Development Councils that had emerged from the wartime tripartite working parties for particular industries.

The main task of reconstruction was to rebuild the export and related capital goods industries, while damping down domestic and import demand through taxation, rationing, licensing, the subsidisation of agriculture and the restriction of house building. There was no problem in selling goods abroad, for the economic dislocation of Europe and the dollar shortage meant that the world market was wide open, although penetrating the US market was more difficult. Thus the export industries responded to the opportunities that confronted them to achieve a spectacular increase in production and exports. The most dramatic growth was in the new industries, led by motor vehicles, aviation and electronics, which had grown up in response to the more sophisticated demands of modern war, but even the traditional industries held their own.

Improvements in productivity, already well below US levels, were not so dramatic. Although overall manufacturing productivity increased considerably, much of the improvement was due to the scrapping of archaic plant. Some of the new industries achieved high levels of productivity, using up-to-date plant and modern management, but few even approached US standards. This was partly because the dollar shortage limited imports of the most advanced machinery, but was also because the success of manufacturers in increasing their exports in soft markets, where they faced little or no competition, removed any incentive to introduce the most advanced methods of production and management, or to dismantle the apparatus of shop-floor power that was a legacy of wartime collaboration. Indeed while production was the bottleneck employers were often only too glad to concede control over manning levels and job demarcations to the shop floor in exchange for industrial peace and increased production, particularly where management had little knowledge or understanding of the complexities of the production process.

The main threat to Labour's commitment to full employment continued to be the shortage of dollars to buy essential food and means of production. Although exports soared, the demand for imports also increased rapidly. The only way of preventing such a situation from weakening sterling and halting recovery was to retain strict controls on imports, a policy which proved successful to the extent that the government weathered successive sterling crises by tightening controls without having to resort to deflationary policies. Thus, apart from the 1947 fuel crisis, unemployment never rose as high as even the optimists' target of 3 per cent. By 1949 British exporters were beginning to face increasing competition in world markets as the European recovery got under way and the dollar shortage began to ease. The sterling crisis threatened to curb the recovery, but tightened controls cut dollar imports and the devaluation of sterling increased the competitiveness of British exports and ensured that the growth in both volume and value was maintained, although it also increased inflationary pressure.

While full employment was maintained by the success of the export drive and controls on imports the main fear of the government was not rising unemployment but inflation, with the memory of the post-World War I experience of an inflationary boom followed by a slump always in mind. Thus the government had no clear target for the level of unemployment until Gaitskell defined a target rate of 3 per cent in 1951, its budgetary policies being dictated by the strength of inflationary fears. The government maintained the wartime policy of cheap money, which ruled out the use of an active monetary policy to curb inflation, so the government continued to use the wartime expedients of controls and fiscal adjustments.

Although the commitment to full employment branded the government as Keynesian in the eyes of history, it was some time before even its budgetary policy was formulated according to Keynesian principles. With the death of Keynes the Treasury lost its only professional economist, while the Economic Section of the Cabinet had no departmental responsibility. Although the Cabinet included several economists, none of the leading members were fully fledged Keynesians until Gaitskell became Chancellor in the dying days of the Labour government. Thus Dalton's early budgets were formulated on the basis of the 'manpower gap', rather than the Keynesian 'inflationary gap', and according to the principle of balancing the budget over the cycle, rather than applying Keynesian budgetary principles, while inflation was primarily checked by direct controls and food subsidies. Nevertheless successive crises from 1947 forced the government to have greater regard to the inflationary pressures created by high levels of demand. Even when fiscal adjustments came to play a greater role in the control of inflation they tended to be ad hoc crisis measures, rather than being instruments of systematic Keynesian demand management.

The failure to adopt systematic Keynesian policies and the retention of controls reflected the pressures to which the various Chancellors were subject. The first priority was neither full employment nor price stability but the production drive. It was only when inflationary pressures threatened to undermine the production drive that the government acted to contain them, and in such circumstances price stability took priority over full employment. Thus Cripps sought to relieve inflationary pressure in 1948 by constraining the building industry, anticipating a 50 per cent increase in unemployment. The inflationary bias was reinforced by pressures to maintain government expenditure in support of the production drive and, towards the end of the government's term, to meet the escalating demands of the health service and rearmament, and by the fear that further increases in taxation would prove politically unacceptable and, by eroding savings, counterproductive. These pressures combined to make successive Chancellors reluctant to relieve inflationary pressure by budgetary means, preferring to make patriotic appeals to the public to save. The result was that the residual burden fell on direct controls.

Food subsidies, rationing and price controls kept the prices of essential goods in check, and shortages probably encouraged saving, but at the cost of increasing taxation, a growing black market and increasing the prices of uncontrolled goods, which threatened to divert supplies from export to the domestic market. The unpopularity of controls, with the government as much as with the public and the civil service, led to their dismantling as soon as the easing of the financial pressures made it possible to do so without undermining the external position, although they had to be tightened and reimposed in successive crises.

Consumer prices rose by around a quarter over the Labour government's first term, part of which can be explained by rising world prices, but which also reflected the very low level of unemployment. Labour shortages in the expanding sectors meant that employers willingly conceded higher wages. The continued growth of trades union membership, the strength of trades union organisation, the removal of some of the legal disabilities of trades unions, and the extension of the Wages Council system meant that workers elsewhere were well placed to press for increases in money wages to compensate for inflation. The danger was that if workers were successful in this the result would be an inflationary spiral.

Until 1948 the government relied on its support among the trades union leadership and patriotic exhortation to persuade the trades unions to restrain their wage demands, strikes being restrained by the retention of the wartime apparatus of compulsory arbitration. However as inflation persisted the government secured the formal agreement of the TUC to a policy of wage restraint in exchange for a freeze on rents and profits, wage increases to be justified only on the grounds of increased productivity or labour shortages in strategic sectors. Although the TUC added low wages and the maintenance of differentials as grounds for wage increases, which in theory undermined the policy, and abandoned its commitment to wage restraint in 1950, in practice the trades union leadership did contain pressure for wage increases, so that after 1946 real wage rates fell steadily. On the other hand, the collaboration of unions in wage restraint and the constraints on official strikes imposed by compulsory arbitration led to a further growth in the strength of unofficial shop-floor organisation and an increase in unofficial strikes.

The legacy of Labour

The successful reintegration of Britain into the world economy on the basis of the Empire and the Sterling Area laid the foundations for a dramatic recovery, permitting the maintenance of high levels of employment and the implementation of the government's welfare programme. The very low rate of unemployment and low rates of benefit, further eroded by inflation, kept the cost of the welfare programme down, although expenditure on the health service increased far more than had been anticipated. The universalism of the system, combined with the regressive impact of flat rate contributions and heavy indirect taxation, meant that it involved very limited redistribution of income, the cost of relieving primary poverty falling on the employed working class. Nevertheless full employment and a comprehensive system of health and social security transformed the condition of the working class by relieving it from the fear, if not of poverty, at least of starvation. Moreover low unemployment, the universalism of family allowances, and rates of benefit considerably below the lowest industrial wages made it possible to respond to working class aspirations by reducing the punitive elements of the old system without fear of eroding the discipline of the wage-form. Social security gradually lost its charitable connotations, and a minimum level of health, education and subsistence came to be seen as a right of all citizens, earned through the hardship of war and post-war austerity. On the other hand, this also implied that the system of relief had lost much of its power as a moralising and disciplining force. This did not mean that the state ceased to concern itself with such matters, but rather that the burden was shifted to different state agencies: education, the courts, the police, the system of industrial relations, and the rapid growth of 'social work', that had developed out of the Victorian and Edwardian institutions of charitable and public health visiting.

Although there was a substantial increase in the national income, the bulk of that increase was absorbed by the deterioration in the terms of trade (much of which was due to devaluation), the export and investment drive, and increased government spending, while population growth left little room for improved living standards. The fall in real wage rates was only compensated by increased overtime and the move into higher wage occupations, while salaries suffered a sharper fall. Although supplies of the essential means of subsistence increased, restrictions on house building had led to an enormous backlog of demand and an acute housing shortage. Rampant inflation was only kept in check by the restriction of trades union activity and a pervasive network of controls.

By 1950 the Labour government had largely completed the programme on which it had been elected. It had been remarkably successful in reconstructing British imperialism, and in consolidating and rationalising the form of the welfare state. However the price the working class had to pay for handing its leadership the levers of political power was its continued subordination to the alienated forms of the wage and the capitalist state. The Labour government had rationalised and extended the welfare system, but only at the cost of its increasing bureaucratisation. Health, education, social work, the nationalised industries and national insurance were all administered by professional civil servants, doctors, teachers, social workers, managers, actuaries and accountants within bureaucratic hierarchies regulated by a dense network of administrative, financial and legal regulation, financed increasingly by central government out of general taxation and insurance contributions. The repressive agencies of the National Assistance Board, the courts, the police and the military were even less subject to democratic pressure and democratic control. Even the trades unions were drawn into an uneasy alliance with the capitalist state, as they sought to reconcile their responsibility to their membership with the political imperative of the production drive, leading to a growing gap between the strategy of the leadership and the aspirations of their members expressed in the growing strength of rank and file organisation. However, far from building on shop floor trades unionism, and on rank and file organisations such as tenants associations, as the basis on which to create new forms of democratic participation which could confront the power of capital with the power of the organised working class, the government saw such autonomous challenges to the economic and political power of capital as challenges to its own authority.

Meanwhile the means of regulating the production and circulation of use-values in accordance with collective needs that had been established in war on the basis of military demand were progressively dismantled as the production drive was subordinated not to popular needs, but to the reconstruction of British imperialism and the confinement of the working class within the wage form as the basis on which to restore the domestic and international rule of money. The contradiction was resolved ideologically because the expansion of exports was undoubtedly necessary not only to secure the expanded reproduction of capital, but also to secure the essential food and means of production that could not be produced domestically, a physical constraint dramatically brought home by the 1947 fuel crisis and more mundanely symbolised by the ration book. Thus the ideological watchword of Labour's strategy was not Keynes but austerity, not consumption as the spur to production but production as the limit to consumption.

While the construction of the welfare state and the maintenance of full employment was a source of considerable popular support, the continuation of rationing and controls, the erosion of living standards by inflation, and the growing shortage of housing was a source of widespread dissatisfaction with the government's record. Nevertheless the stabilisation of the balance of payments, the moderation of inflation, and the 'bonfire of controls' made it appear that progress was being made on these fronts, until the government ran into a new crisis precipitated by the strains of rearmament and the Korean War boom.

The Korean War boom in the United States came on top of the pressures set up by the European reconstruction boom, leading to a massive increase in import prices and sharp deterioration in the balance of payments. The deterioration in the balance of payments and the inflationary pressure of rearmament at home led to increases in taxation, direct controls on credit, cuts in public expenditure, the reimposition of controls on consumption and investment, and an attempt to impose wage restraint that was rejected by the TUC, all of which appeared to reverse the gains of the previous years, while divisions within the government made it clear that it had lost its way. Although Labour secured a majority of the popular vote in the 1951 election, with the highest vote it has ever recorded, the Conservatives secured a majority of seats and formed a new government.

The Conservatives came to power on a programme that aimed to contain class conflict by responding to the economic aspirations of the working class, promising to maintain the welfare state, to remove the restrictions on collective bargaining and considerably to expand the housing programme, and committing the government to maintaining full employment as its first priority. Thus it proposed not to reverse Labour's project, but to complete it by dismantling the apparatus of control that successive crises had forced Labour to maintain. However it was not immediately clear how the commitment to full employment could be reconciled with the Conservative's commitment to the orthodox principles of sound money and prudent government as the means of securing price stability, since the programme immediately implied increases in money wages and in public expenditure that could only erode profits and lead to increased unemployment, unless they were accommodated by inflation. Thus the question immediately arose of whether the Conservative's primary commitment was to price stability or to full employment.

In fact the Conservative's priority was clear. Price stability was the only secure basis on which to manage the economy and to achieve high levels of employment in the long run. The commitment to full employment was not a commitment to make full employment the immediate policy objective, but an expression of faith in the ability of the market to achieve full employment on the basis of sound monetary and financial policies. The test of sound policy was the balance of payments, while monetary policy was seen as the most flexible and effective means of responding to fluctuations in the reserves, and the rapid restoration of sterling convertibility was seen as the best means of ensuring that appropriate policies were pursued. In short it seemed that the Conservatives intended to restore the well-worn principles of fiscal rectitude and the gold-exchange standard, pursuing an active monetary policy to maintain monetary stability, with Keynesian principles being relegated to their passive wartime role of ensuring the non-inflationary financing of public expenditure.

At first the government seemed to be set on this course. The policy of cheap money was abandoned as the government raised bank rate and imposed controls on consumer credit, reinforcing the recession that was already underway. However the circumstances that had brought about the fall of Labour had already passed. Import prices fell sharply, reinforcing the impact of the domestic recession in curbing inflationary pressures and relieving the balance of payments, so that the requirements of monetary and financial stability were no longer inconsistent with those of full employment, unemployment soon falling from the post-war peak of 2 per cent in 1952. By 1953 the government was able to reduce both income tax and bank rate in the first expansionary budget since the war, which added to the reflationary impact of the housing programme. The post-war boom was under way.

Although the boom permitted a sustained rise in wages and public expenditure, it was not driven forward by the growth of domestic demand, but by high rates of investment and the rapid growth of exports. The post-war boom was, from its inception, a world boom whose foundations had been laid in the period of reconstruction.

The foundations of the post-war boom

The post-war boom was initially based on the generalisation of 'Fordist' methods of mass production of consumer goods, and the associated steel, power and machine tool industries. The new forms of Fordist production had been pioneered in the United States in the 1920s, and first took root in Europe in the boom at the end of that decade, continuing to expand in the depression of the 1930s when, despite high unemployment, living standards of those in work rose as food prices fell. However the growth of these new industries continued to be restricted by the limited size of the market, while protectionist barriers confined them to the domestic market. The more sophisticated military demands of the Second World War led to an enormous expansion of the new industries, particularly vehicles, aviation and electronics. In the immediate post-war period the reconversion of these branches of military production to peacetime conditions was possible in Britain, despite the severe restrictions on civilian consumption, because the world market lay at Britain's feet, although their growth was limited by supplies of power, steel and labour.

Marshall Aid and the surge of US investment after the Korean War soon spread the latest methods of production to Continental Europe, with the state playing a central role in the development of the new industries, and of the machine tool, steel and power supply industries necessary to provide the appropriate means of production. In Japan the Dodge Plan had halted reparations payments, fostered the rapid monopolisation of capital and the close integration of financial and productive capital with the state, and checked the advance of the labour movement on the basis of a sharply deflationary package, paving the way for capital to take advantage of the stimulus provided by US military expenditure in the Korean War. Even in the United States the state was heavily involved in promoting the development of the military sector, which had extensive civilian spin-offs.

Britain spent the vast majority of its Marshall allocation on food, and British employers were very resistant to the attempt to spread American methods. This was partly because the fragmentation of production units meant that British manufacturers did not regard the market as being sufficiently large to justify mass production methods, and partly because they felt that attempts to introduce American 'time and motion' methods would undermine the existing system of industrial relations. For similar reasons manufacturers and unions alike were unsympathetic to attempts to attract new American investors to set up in Britain. Thus British industry lagged in the adoption of the most advanced production methods, and continued to be marked by a proliferation of producers, competition taking the form of a high degree of product

differentiation. This established a vicious circle in which the proliferation of end products presented a barrier to the standardisation
of parts and so the development of mass production techniques in
the component and machine tool industries, which in turn inhibited
the development of such techniques in the production of end products. The monopolisation of industry in Europe, the destruction
of trades unionism in the war, and the Marshall-inspired Americanisation of post-war European industrial relations meant that
European capitalists faced few such barriers to the adoption of the
new methods.

The Americanisation of European industry did not simply involve technical changes. It presupposed and encouraged monopolisation to reap the necessary economies of scale and to stabilise production and markets. It required appropriate systems of education
and industrial training, and financial systems that could channel
capital into industrial reconstruction. Moreover it required the intensification of labour to achieve the high levels of output required
to cover the heavy costs of fixed investment, and a corresponding
system of industrial relations that included plant-level bargaining
that could accommodate regular changes in production methods
and that could maintain continuity of production by avoiding industrial disputes. The workers were reconciled to such a system by
being paid relatively high wages. The co-operation of the workers
in the constant introduction of new methods of production was secured by the granting of regular wage increases, sometimes directly
linked to productivity or profits, while more or less generous unemployment insurance reduced working class resistance to industrial
restructuring.

High profits and booming markets meant that the effective barrier to accumulation in the reconstruction period was the supply
of means of production and subsistence, which appeared to national governments in the form of the dollar shortage. This barrier
was overcome by the coordinated state sponsorship of the development of the production of the means of production and subsistence,
by currency adjustments, direct controls of international flows of
capital and commodities, long-term investment and the development of the system of international money and credit. The success
of this international effort was the basis on which the planning
mechanisms of the immediate post-war period could be dismantled
and the liberalisation of trade and payments could proceed rapidly

through the 1950s.

Before the Second World War the growth of the new industries had been restricted by the limited extent of the market. The fear in the reconstruction period had been that the post-war reconstruction boom would soon come up against the same barrier, leading to a renewed slump. However the new system of industrial relations, pioneered in somewhat different forms in the US and Britain in the 1930s, established the relationship between the growth of production and the growth of wages that, the planners hoped, would overcome the barrier of the market. Increased working class consumption was supplemented by the rapid growth of the middle class, associated with the monopolisation of industry and the expansion of public administration. Consumer credit widened the market for automobiles, electrical goods and consumer durables. Large sections of the working class were thus drawn into the market for the new industries, the price they paid being a burden of housing and consumer debt that claimed a rising proportion of disposable income, and that inhibited workers from taking strike action, so contributing to the stabilisation of the system of industrial relations. A substantial increase in the rate of private saving, primarily to pay for pensions and house purchase, provided funds for the expansion of private house construction, through building societies, and to finance a substantial increase in the rate of productive investment, through pension funds and insurance companies, without a correspondingly large increase in the rate of profit.

Rapid accumulation in manufacturing was accompanied by the even more rapid development of capitalist agriculture on a world scale. The autarchic policies of the 1930s and 1940s had already led to considerable increases in agricultural productivity in Europe and to the development of the colonies as sources of food and raw materials, still largely on an extensive basis making use of plentiful supplies of cheap labour. The wartime development of vehicles and chemicals provided the means of production for the rapid development of capitalist agriculture in the metropolitan countries in the 1950s, spurred on by falling prices as agricultural overproduction flooded world markets, the impact of which was ameliorated by systematic state support for agricultural prices. The same low prices forced third world governments to expand their export agriculture in a desperate race to keep export earnings sufficient to meet essential import requirements. Similarly the opening up of

new reserves of minerals, coal and oil meant that supplies of fuel
and raw materials more than kept pace with the rapidly increasing
demand.

Welfare, wages and the working class

The foundations of the post-war boom were laid by pervasive state
intervention in the restructuring of the technical, social, monetary, financial and political framework of capitalist production.
Throughout the post-war boom the state was more or less actively
involved in fostering the accumulation of domestic productive capital by promoting national efficiency and international competitiveness by expanding public education, supporting scientific and
industrial research, channelling industrial finance, providing fiscal
incentives to investment, sponsoring monopolisation and industrial
rationalisation, and in removing barriers to accumulation by providing infrastructural investments, particularly in power, transport
and steel. Nevertheless the dismantling of the systems of production planning of the war and reconstruction period and the rapid
liberalisation of domestic and international markets meant that,
however extensive the intervention of the state, the driving force,
and ultimate limit, of accumulation was the profitability of productive investment. Thus more or less extensive public investment
was matched by the rapid liberalisation of the regulation of accumulation, and the subordination of both capital and the state to
the global rule of money, expressed in the constraint of profitability
on the capitalist enterprise, and in the monetary, fiscal and financial constraints imposed on the state by the need to maintain the
stability of the currency and to finance its expenditure within the
limits of the liberal state form.

The rapid accumulation of capital in the post-war boom imposed a heavy burden on the working class. Structural changes
required a high degree of labour mobility, uprooting workers and
destroying their communities. Technological changes demanded a
high degree of adaptability on the part of workers, and imposed a
progressive intensification of labour to meet competitive pressure
by putting expensive machinery to the fullest use. The working
class as a whole was reconciled to such pressures by the generalisation of the collaborative system of industrial relations on the basis

of a generalised expectation of a rising standard of living, and by the extension and rationalisation of the welfare apparatus, largely completing the socialisation of the reproduction of the working class through a combination of private and public social insurance, the extension of public housing, education and health care, and a more or less comprehensive system of social security. As Beveridge had anticipated, the socialisation of consumption was the liberal alternative to the socialisation of production as the means of securing the social and political integration of the working class into the capitalist order.

The development of the system of industrial relations, and the institutionalisation of an expectation of regular wage increases, did not occur spontaneously, but was actively encouraged by the state, building on the US example of the Roosevelt era, which was extended to Europe and Japan by the occupying powers as the centrepiece of the initial phase of reconstruction. Rising wages within a stable industrial relations framework were seen as the basis of the political stabilisation of the liberal state form, and simultaneously as the means of overcoming the barriers to accumulation presented by the limited mass market that had impeded recovery, and precipitated the crash, after the First World War. In Britain the institutionalisation of industrial relations in the new industries was extended in the war and post-war reconstruction period to all branches of production, initially as the means of reconciling the working class to austerity against the promise of better times ahead that arrived once the immediate barriers to accumulation were overcome.

Wage determination had little to do with the classical model of supply and demand. The rapid growth in employment eased the high degree of labour mobility required by the uneven development of the various branches of production, employment growing rapidly in the service sector, where productivity grew slowly, and in managerial, technical and administrative occupations, associated with the monopolisation of industry, the growth of public services, and the separation of mental and manual labour that marked the new methods of production, while manual employment in manufacturing industry grew little (or even fell) after the reconstruction period as new methods of production dispensed with living labour. Changing wage differentials played a minor role in allocating labour. Displaced rural workers, married women workers, and rising numbers of immigrants from the end of the 1950s, provided an ample supply of labour to match the growing demand in low-wage occupations, while the post-war expansion of the public education system provided a growing supply of white collar and technical workers. Thus occupational and industrial differentials were largely embedded in established, and fiercely defended, social norms. Differentials were remarkably stable considering the enormous structural changes in employment in the course of the boom.

Trades unionism was relevant primarily in the defence of wage differentials. The general level of real wages was not determined through pay bargaining but by the relationship between the rise in money wages and the rate of inflation. Although the pace was set by manufacturing industry, the expectation of rising wages soon became embodied in a steadily rising consumption norm that extended to all branches of employment, reinforced by the attempt of trades unions to maintain differentials. The expectation of regular pay increases stimulated a rise in trades union membership within an industrial relations framework with an emphasis on national bargaining to set the norm for the annual pay round, supplemented by company and plant bargaining to take account of local circumstances.

Reconstruction and the Korean War boom provided the inflationary environment in which such a system of wage determination could become established in the annual pay round, though which trades unions negotiated pay increases to maintain or increase real wages in the face of inflation. Continued inflation made it possible to accommodate rising real wages without requiring cuts in prices and in money wages, which had in the past been a potent source of industrial conflict, to accommodate the uneven development of the forces of production in various branches of production. Thus employers in slowly growing branches of production could respond to an increase in money wages that threatened to erode profits by raising their prices, while increased money wages and the expansion of credit to meet the rising costs of production expanded the domestic market so that capitalists were able to realise their expanded capital at the increased prices.

The post-war boom took off on the basis of relatively low wage rates, a legacy of the destruction or containment of the organised working class over the previous two decades; the stabilisation of currencies and of payments imbalances through exchange rate adjustments and direct controls in the reconstruction period; and, after the reconstruction and Korean War boom, falling prices of food and raw materials. In such favourable circumstances the early stages of the boom saw a further rise in the rate of profit in most of the metropolitan centres of accumulation.

Higher profits stimulated more rapid accumulation, while the rapid growth of employment increased the bargaining strength of the workers. The result was that during the 1950s the rate of increase of real wages became institutionalised in a rising consumption norm, that differed from one country to another, relating primarily to the rate of growth of productivity, the terms of international trade, and the normal rate of profit, while having little to do with the strength of the organised labour movement. Indeed the relationship was if anything the reverse, the most prosperous capitalists being able to defeat militant trades unionism and install collaborative industrial relations systems by offering relatively generous pay increases, while weaker capitals had less space in which to establish such accommodative labour relations.

Rapid accumulation, improving terms of trade and reductions in military expenditure provided metropolitan governments with the latitude within which they could respond to the social aspirations of the working class, and confine working class political activity within constitutional channels, by increasing welfare expenditure and raising public sector wages. Welfare benefits and the provision of public services tended to increase in line with the rate of growth of real wages, as rising incomes generated growing tax revenues. Working class expectations were constantly encouraged by national governments, which increasingly made rising wages and more generous welfare benefits and public services the basis of their appeal to the electorate and the measure of the success of their policies.

The considerable increase in public expenditure, financed primarily by direct taxation and insurance contributions, and the institutionalisation of the rising expectations of the working class through the system of industrial relations and electoral politics, meant that the fiscal, financial and political pressures on the state to ensure the sustained accumulation of capital were much stronger than they had been in the pre-war era. It was these pressures that were expressed in the Keynesian commitment to full employment.

The precise institutional forms of the 'Keynesian Welfare State', and particularly the relative weight given to its different elements, differed from one country to another, depending primarily on the political context in which they were introduced. There is not the space to explore such differences here. However it is striking that the political strength of the organised working class tended to be correlated positively with the extent of the socialisation of consumption and with state intervention focused on the regulation of labour, and negatively with the extent of the socialisation of production and with state intervention focused on the regulation of investment, which would tend to confirm the argument developed above that the strength of the organised working class restricts the direct intervention of the state in production by presenting a barrier to the attempt of the state to restructure production on the basis of capital. This would imply that Keynesian welfarism and corporatism are by no means complementary, as many have argued, but are divergent strategies, corresponding to a very different balance of class forces, Keynesianism offering precisely the 'middle way' between monetary orthodoxy and corporatism.[3]

The differences between the various national forms of institutionalised class collaboration appeared to be dissolving as the boom reached its height in the late 1960s. However they became extremely important in determining diverging patterns in the face of the breakdown of Keynesian integration, to such an extent that in retrospect doubts were raised as to whether there had ever been such a thing as the Keynesian Welfare State. Nevertheless what they all had in common was the increasingly systematic and pervasive involvement of the state, directly and indirectly, in the regulation of the reproduction of the working class through the wage, social insurance and social security, on the basis of a generalised expectation of rising wages, a guaranteed minimum subsistence, and a political commitment to full employment.

Keynesianism and the boom

Keynesianism offered a state ideology entirely appropriate to the conditions of the post-war boom. The commitment to full employment was not simply a concession to the aspirations of the work-

---

[3] See the suggestive article by Jonas Pontusson, 'Comparative Political Economy of Advanced Capitalist Societies: Sweden and France', *Kapitalistate*, 10/11, 1983.

ing class, but also expressed the actuarial constraints embodied in the welfare state, and contributed to the confidence of capitalists that accumulation would be sustained by expansionary policies. More fundamentally Keynesianism expressed the belief that rising wages and public expenditure would resolve the contradictions inherent in capital accumulation. On the one hand, the growth of the mass market would banish the problem of overproduction that had underlain crises, depressions and wars. On the other hand, rising wages, welfare benefits and public services would reconcile the working class to its subordination to the wage form while providing the healthy, educated and contented labour force required to sustain accumulation.

For Keynesians the state could overcome the cyclical alternation of inflation and unemployment through an active budgetary policy, ensuring that demand grew sufficiently rapidly to maintain full employment without spilling over into inflation, while an accommodating monetary policy ensured that investment would not be discouraged by high interest rates or a shortage of funds. Keynes had proposed that stabilisation policy should focus on investment through public works programmes in periods of unemployment. However such a form of regulation was not appropriate to the kind of fine-tuning envisaged by post-war Keynesians, since investment programmes had a long planning horizon. Moreover political considerations favoured tax reductions and increases in current expenditure as means of stimulating the economy, since these had an immediate and obvious impact on the electorate. On the other hand, similar considerations favoured the postponement or cancellation of public investment and restrictive monetary policy as the means of containing inflationary pressures.

Keynesians did not believe that there was any conflict between their objective of full employment and the orthodox objectives of price and monetary stability, primarily because of their exaggerated faith in the allocative efficiency of the market. Whereas classical economists had seen unemployment as a symptom of the misallocation of resources, to be remedied only by the restructuring of prices and production within a framework of sound money, Keynesians saw unemployment as a symptom of a deficiency of demand, to be remedied by an injection of spending. Classical economists saw Keynesian remedies as inflationary, as the expansion of demand to absorb unemployment in the overexpanded branches of production led to rising prices of products in short supply, inhibiting the restructuring of relative prices and production by sustaining backward producers, and undermining the regulatory role of the market, only serving to postpone and intensify the inevitable crisis. Keynesians, by contrast, saw classical remedies as deflationary, carrying the danger of a cumulative decline. The fear of a deflationary spiral, and the belief that a modest degree of inflation would ease microeconomic adjustments, gave Keynesianism a mild inflationary bias, but Keynesians were confident that demand-management policies would reconcile full employment with price stability.

Keynes himself had been well aware of the dangers of inflationism, although he was confident that sound governments would not succumb to the temptation. His greater fear was that international constraints would force a reversal of expansionary policies, as they led to a temporary surge in imports and diversion of exports to the home market, before domestic producers had an opportunity to respond to the stimulus of increasing demand. Thus the key to the pursuit of Keynesian domestic policies was the development of international monetary institutions which could finance the transitional imbalances of international payments that would arise as a result of the temporary misallocation of domestic resources. Keynes had played the leading role in the construction of such institutions, which sought to overcome the deficiencies of the inter-war gold standard, which supposedly lay in the shortage of liquidity and the rigidity of exchange rates, by expanding international liquidity and providing for exchange rate adjustments, policed by the IMF, to compensate for differential rates of domestic inflation. Thus the pursuit of domestic Keynesian policies depended in its turn on the ability of the international institutions to pursue Keynesian policies on a global scale.

The regulation of accumulation on a world scale

Rising wages and the growth of consumer credit provided a growing domestic market to absorb the product of manufacturing industry. Monopolistic pricing policies, initially reinforced by tariff barriers and the costs of transport, limited domestic price competition, so that competition was primarily on the basis of product specification and advertising, leading to a steady rise in unproductive advertising and research and development expenditure, while the devaluation of capital in the face of rapid technical change was anticipated in high rates of depreciation of capital goods. However accumulation was not confined within the limits of the market. If domestic accumulation was to be sustained advanced capitals had to overcome the barrier of the limited domestic market by expanding the market on a world scale. In the early stages of the post-war boom advanced capitals were able to use their high domestic profits as a launching pad from which to conquer world markets. However tariffs, exchange controls and transport costs at first presented barriers to the penetration of overseas markets. These barriers were overcome by the internationalisation of productive capital, as US companies sought out the cheap labour and booming markets of Europe, while European companies began to seek access to the most advanced technology available in the US. The growing international integration of accumulation underlay the liberalisation of international trade and payments through the 1950s, while the reduction of the costs of shipping and road transport further reduced the barriers to international trade.

The liberalisation of world trade was to some extent based on an international division of labour between the various branches of production, with, for example, Scandinavia, the Dominions and North America exporting temperate foodstuffs, the US advanced means of production, aircraft and military equipment, Germany automobiles, scientific equipment and machine tools, Italy consumer durables, Japan steel, ships and textiles and the third world agricultural products and minerals. Accumulation on a world scale based on such comparative advantages established a virtuous circle for the more advanced producers, the growing market and booming profits providing the stimulus to increased investment which further increased productivity and comparative advantage, while the corresponding overproduction of commodities put the weaker producers under increasing competitive pressure. Moreover, where a leading branch of domestic production could command the world market, the stimulus communicated itself to other branches of production, as a growing domestic market stimulated investment and the adoption of more advanced production methods, so that a technological lead established in a dominant branch of production was soon communicated to other branches. Thus the domestic integration of accumulation on the basis of a growing mass market considerably reduced the unevenness of development of the branches of production on a domestic scale. However the same forces increased the unevenness of development on a world scale, so that international trade acquired an increasingly competitive dimension, the unevenness appearing in growing trade imbalances once post-war controls were dismantled.

As the global overaccumulation of capital led to the uneven development of accumulation on a world scale imbalances in international payments were accommodated within the gold-exchange standard by the growth of international liquidity, fed by the British, and above all the US balance of payments deficits, on which a pyramid of international credit was built from the late 1950s. The growth of trade, and the growth of US overseas investment and military expenditure, eased the dollar shortage and permitted the restoration of the convertibility of the leading currencies. The internationalisation of money capital proceeded far more rapidly than did the growth of official reserves and IMF quotas. While the rapid increase in international liquidity made it possible to finance growing trade imbalances, and so sustain accumulation on a world scale, the internationalisation of money capital increased the risk of currency speculation. The stability of the international monetary system could only be secured by the parallel expansion of IMF and official reserves through gold-pooling, currency swaps, and the creation of international credit money, in the form of EPU units and later the IMF's Special Drawing Rights, and the mobilisation of reserves through central bank cooperation. Thus the management of world money was kept under a precarious international political control through the 1950s and 1960s.

International monetary institutions and the cooperating central banks did not have the power of the nation state over the circulation of the currency, and so did not have any direct control over the expansion of international credit that accommodated growing international payments imbalances. However they were able to use their power as lender of last resort to make balance of payments finance and stabilisation loans conditional on national governments' correcting payments imbalances by containing domestic inflation, and so provided some check on the unrestrained growth of international credit. To this extent the international monetary institutions constituted the nucleus of a world state by providing a framework

within which the power of world money could be imposed on recalcitrant national governments and their unstable currencies. Although the power of money was mobilised by foreign bankers, the
exercise of such power did not express the subordination of the
nation either to foreigners or to bankers, as their populist critics
claimed, but rather the subordination of domestic accumulation,
and the policies of national governments, to the accumulation of
capital on a world scale, expressed in the subordination of national
currencies to world money and in the commitment, expressed in
GATT and embodied in the Articles of the IMF, to repudiate discriminatory trading practices.

On the other hand, the power of the dollar limited the leverage of the international institutions and cooperating Central Banks
over the US authorities, who appeared able to run payments deficits
with impunity. The regulation of accumulation on a global scale
was thus constantly threatened by the US inflationism that had
worried Keynes in 1923 as the internationalisation of money capital,
fuelled by the growing US deficit, expanded international liquidity
and stimulated inflationary overaccumulation on a global scale. It
appeared that Keynesianism had provided the means of overcoming
the barriers to domestic expansionism only by producing a recipe
for global inflation.

The limits of liberal Keynesianism

The planning mechanisms of the reconstruction period, exchange
rate adjustments, and international capital flows had established
the conditions under which the international system of trade and
payments could be liberalised without payments imbalances immediately undermining the domestic commitment to full employment.
During the early 1950s the rapid growth of productivity, improving
terms of trade and reductions in military expenditure made it possible for capitalists to absorb money wage increases and the state
to absorb increases in expenditure, so that high levels of employment were consistent with price stability. In terms of economic
policy Keynesian objectives were broadly consistent with orthodox
objectives, so the theoretical basis of fiscal and monetary policy
had little practical significance.

Keynesian policies played little active role in promoting the boom. The main problem was inflation, rather than the threat of unemployment, as accumulation in the leading branches of production ran ahead of the supply of labour power and means of production. Governments increasingly determined their fiscal stance in accordance with the Keynesian principle of the 'inflationary gap', running surpluses to absorb inflationary pressure, rather than following the orthodox prescription of balancing the budget and relying exclusively on restrictive monetary policies to contain inflation. This was not simply because they had been converted to Keynesianism, but was also for technical reasons, monetary policy proving ineffective in the face of excess liquidity in the financial system and the booming profits of the corporate sector. Although Keynesianism was soon adopted as the legitimating ideology of the state, as governments took credit for the boom, the substantive issues that divided Keynesian from classical economists did not come to a head until the emergence of barriers to accumulation confronted governments with the dilemma of choosing between full employment and price stability.

It was not long before the overaccumulation of capital on a world scale came up against the barrier of the limited market, leading to growing competition which eroded the super-profits of the more advanced producers, and put the weaker capitals under increasing pressure. The institutionalisation of trades unionism within a system of industrial relations had accommodated the working class to its subordination to the wage form. However the system of industrial relations institutionalised the expectation of regular increases in wages, and provided constitutional channels through which the working class could seek to realise its aspirations, while low rates of unemployment strengthened the hand of the trades unions. Thus hard-pressed capitals could not force down wages and intensify labour unilaterally without facing costly and damaging strikes. The state similarly tended to hold back from encouraging aggressive employers for fear of the destabilising political impact of such class confrontations. In such circumstances the only means of sustaining profits in the face of growing competition and rising wages was by transforming methods of production.

The transformation of methods of production in the face of growing competition further intensified the global overaccumulation of capital, putting the weaker capitals under even greater competitive pressure. The displacement of labour by the more advanced producers, and the liquidation of weaker capitals, tended to increase unemployment. In such circumstances Keynesian objectives implied an expansionary response, reducing interest rates and increasing demand to boost employment, wages and profits by absorbing excess capacity and stimulating new investment.

Keynesians recognised that the immediate impact of expansionary policies would be to raise prices and to weaken the balance of payments. However expansionary policies provided a more favourable environment in which productive capitals could introduce more advanced methods of production, by expanding the domestic market to relieve the pressure on profits and providing the capital required to finance new investment. If capitalists responded to such incentives increased productivity would enable them to absorb the wage increases required to compensate for higher prices, so that inflationary pressure would be relieved, and would enable them to face the competitive challenge, relieving the pressure on the balance of payments. Thus price increases would be temporary, and transitional payments imbalances could be accommodated by international credit.

The limits of Keynesianism appeared when capitalists failed to respond appropriately to the opportunities presented to them. Expansionary policies did not in themselves provide any means of ensuring such a response. On the contrary, in relieving the pressure on backward capitals they reduced the pressure to achieve such a restructuring as inflation eased the pressure on profits by eroding real wages and by devaluing money capital to the benefit of productive capital, and as cheap credit relieved the pressure on liquidity. In such circumstances inflation threatened to become cumulative, as money wages rose to compensate for price increases, leading to a further deterioration in international competitiveness and a weakening balance of payments.

The impact of Keynesian policies depended on the response of capitalists. This response was not simply a matter of the subjective inclinations of capitalists, but primarily of the domestic conditions of accumulation in the context of the uneven development of capital on a world scale. The more advanced capitals were able to take advantage of profits inflated by expansionary domestic policies to increase their productive capacity by absorbing weaker capitals, investing in new plant, and adopting more advanced methods of production, high domestic profits facilitating the penetration of world markets and the payment of higher wages to reconcile the workforce to the intensification of labour and the restructuring of production and employment. On the other hand, weaker capitals had limited scope for expanding exports in the face of stiff foreign competition, and so had little incentive to expand capacity by investing in new plant, while low profits and a stagnant market made it difficult for even the more ambitious to secure industrial finance and provided little scope for paying higher wages. In such cases mergers and takeovers were designed more to consolidate a domestic monopoly than to pave the way for increased investment. The result was that Keynesian policies tended to intensify the overaccumulation and uneven development of capital by sustaining backward capitals while stimulating renewed accumulation on the part of the more advanced.

Keynesian policies were pursued at the level of the nation state. The ability of the nation state to pursue full employment policies was constrained by the relative competitive strength of domestic productive capital in the face of the overaccumulation of capital on a world scale. Where capital in the leading branches of production commanded world markets, Keynesian full employment policies could sustain a virtuous circle of rapid accumulation and rising living standards. Rising exports provided the means to pay for imports required to meet the growing demand for means of production and subsistence stimulated by the more rapid pace of accumulation. The rapid growth of productivity relieved inflationary pressure, while booming investment and exports provided jobs for workers displaced by the liquidation of backward capitals and the adoption of more advanced methods of production. Healthy profits and rising state revenues provided the means to pay higher wages, relatively generous redundancy payments and unemployment benefits, to expand employment in public services, and to develop ambitious training programmes, reducing trades union resistance to the intensification of labour and the restructuring of production and employment. However it was not Keynesian policies that sustained accumulation in such circumstances, but rather it was sustained accumulation that permitted the pursuit of Keynesian policies, the primary function of which was not to maintain full employment but to contain inflation.

In the less advanced centres of accumulation Keynesian expansionary policies maintained full employment by sustaining backward producers, at the cost of rising inflation and a deteriorating balance of payments. Rising inflation increased the pressure of foreign competition, which extended to the more advanced domestic capitals. The erosion of real wages by inflation stimulated higher wage demands, which met with growing resistance from employers. The devaluation of money capital and rentier incomes increased the political pressure on the government to contain inflation, while the deterioration in the balance of payments, reinforced by an outflow of surplus capital, precipitated speculation against the currency.

In the face of rising inflation and growing pressure on the balance of payments governments were forced to adopt deflationary policies to restore confidence in the stability of the currency. Deflation brought accumulation back within the limits of the market. Increased competition, higher interest rates and reduced capacity working increased the pressure on profitability, reduced the ability of capitalists to raise prices, and stiffened their resistance to demands for higher wages. However, while restrictive policies contained inflation, they led to rising unemployment, growing industrial conflict, and electoral dissatisfaction with rising levels of taxation and cuts in public expenditure, which made it increasingly difficult for governments to persist with such policies, particularly if an election was approaching. Thus deflationary policies would be reversed, and expansionary policies reintroduced under the banner of Keynes to combat unemployment and raise living standards by boosting demand. At first the absorption of surplus capacity and surplus labour could make it possible for wages, profits and public expenditure to rise together. However sooner or later inflation would rise, the balance of payments deteriorate, and the cycle would begin again.

The limits of Keynesianism appeared as the rapid growth of the world market, stimulated by the expansion of credit, gave free reign to the overaccumulation of capital. While Keynesianism increased the armoury of the government in regulating the pace of domestic accumulation, by adding fiscal to monetary instruments, it did not provide any alternative means to secure the restructuring of capital in the face of a crisis of overaccumulation than the classical deflationary mechanism. When it was put to the test Keynesian demand management proved to be nothing more than old-fashioned inflationism.

The limits of liberal Keynesianism did not appear to the state immediately as such, but in the form of the barriers of inflation and the balance of payments, which forced the government to reverse expansionist policies. Such barriers were no surprise to orthodox economists, for whom inflation was the necessary result of the Keynesian attempt to override the operation of the market under the rule of money, balance of payments crises having the entirely positive role of limiting Keynesian profligacy. Right-wing Keynesians continued to press for the subordination of macroeconomic regulation to the primary constraint of price stability, legitimating their arguments by developing the concept of "overfull" employment, in which trades unions were able to take advantage of labour shortages to raise money wages more rapidly than was justified by productivity increases, and various statistical exercises were carried out to establish the level of unemployment consistent with price stability.

However the issue was not a matter of economic analysis, but of political imperatives. Keynesianism was not simply an economic theory, it had become the ideological expression of institutionalised forms of regulation of capitalist reproduction, which embodied working class expectations of rising wages, increasing standards of public provision, and employment opportunities and which could not simply be discarded at will. Thus the failure of Keynesian policies did not immediately lead to the abandonment of Keynesianism, but to the extension of state intervention, within the liberal framework of the Keynesian Welfare State, as governments sought to remove the barriers to sustained accumulation, and to reconcile full employment, rising wages and price stability in the attempt to preserve the Keynesian framework of class collaboration.

On a global scale the barrier to sustained accumulation appeared as the limited supply of official reserves with which to support national currencies in the face of speculative movements of private capital. Keynesian remedies therefore centred on the expansion of such reserves and the development of new forms of official credit. Although the rapid internationalisation of capital gave all nation states an interest in sustaining accumulation on a world scale, such remedies had limited prospects of success because they merely increased the scope for global inflationism. Thus the growth of official funds continued to lag behind the internationalisation of money capital, and the primary source of balance of payments finance remained private capital markets, whose stabilisation depended increasingly on ad hoc cooperation between Central Banks. The resulting vulnerability of the weaker currencies to speculation focused interventionist attention more firmly on the problems of the international competitiveness of domestic productive capital. At the national level the problem appeared at first as that of the relation between wage increases and the growth of productivity.

Chapter 11

Keynesianism, Monetarism and the Crisis of the State

The brief triumph of Keynesianism

In Britain the conflict between the Keynesian objective of full employment and the orthodox objective of price stability appeared at a very early stage in the post-war boom. By 1955 unemployment had reached a post-war low of 1.1 per cent, but inflation was rising and the balance of payments deteriorating. The government tightened monetary policy in the attempt to check inflation, but neutralised the expected impact on employment by cutting income tax in the pre-election budget, thus putting to the test for the first time the Keynesian emphasis on expenditure against the orthodox emphasis on the money market as the primary means of regulation. In the event Keynes appeared to be vindicated, as a further tightening of monetary policy failed to check the boom, a sterling crisis being followed by increases in indirect taxation and cuts in public investment. However such restrictive measures did not lead to increases in unemployment. The world boom provided buoyant export demand, so that growth and employment levels were maintained alongside monetary stability. Bank rate adjustments proved sufficient to maintain the external balance by inducing compensatory capital flows. Controls on consumer credit and changes in public investment plans were the primary means of containing inflationary pressures.

Until 1957 the government pursued policies that were more or less equally acceptable to Keynesians and to the advocates of orthodoxy. However the persistence of inflation caused increasing concern. The feeling grew rapidly amongst economists and politicians alike that low levels of unemployment were enabling the trades unions to push for wage increases that employers were unable to resist, but the government was reluctant to force up unemployment for political reasons, and so attempted to reduce the pressure of wage increases on profits by direct intervention. However the TUC rejected the government's appeal for wage restraint in 1956. Attempts over the next two years by employers, with strong government encouragement, and the government itself to resist pay claims led to a wave of industrial disputes throughout the public and private sector, so that the government rapidly backed away from attempting to hold back wages by a frontal assault on the trades unions. However a run on the pound in the autumn of 1957, partly caused by suspicions that Britain would allow the pound to float to compensate for domestic inflation, brought the issue to a head.

Thorneycroft, who became Chancellor in January 1957, believed that the remedy for inflation was monetary restraint and established the Radcliffe Committee on the Working of the Monetary System, which he expected to vindicate his views, and provide an answer to the practical problem of bringing bank credit under effective control. While waiting for the Committee to report he established a Council on Prices, Productivity and Incomes, to explore the relation between wages and inflation. The Council reported in 1958 that wage increases were caused primarily by trades unions, who were able to exploit high levels of employment to exert their power, and consequently that a wage freeze was a desirable counter-inflationary policy, but that higher levels of unemployment might be required to achieve it. However the autumn crisis led Thorneycroft to anticipate both reports, based on his conviction that only sound monetary policies could contain inflation. If public expenditure and bank credit were not allowed to increase, attempts by employers to compensate for wage increases by raising prices would merely reduce demand and so employment. Thus the burden would be placed on the trades unions, who would have to choose between exorbitant wage demands and full employment. Thorneycroft accordingly increased the bank rate to 7 per cent, which had an immediate impact on confidence and relieved the pressure on the pound, although it did not restrict the growth of the money supply. However when he attempted to stabilise public expenditure to regain control of the money supply the Prime Minister, Harold Macmillan, overruled him and Thorneycroft, along with his Junior Ministers, resigned. Macmillan had been an early convert to Keynesianism, but more importantly he was a supreme pragmatist. Keynesian policies were not dictated by theoretical principles, but by political expediency.

This episode marked the political triumph of the Keynesian commitment to full employment against the orthodox priority of price stability. At first Keynesianism appeared vindicated by its success. The relief of pressure on the pound, followed by a sharp improvement in the terms of trade that strengthened the balance of payments, permitted the return to full convertibility and provided scope for more expansionary policies, which were delayed by fears of inflation until the impact of the US recession began to bite. The removal of restrictions on bank advances, consumer credit and public investment was followed by tax cuts, stimulating the boom that secured the overwhelming victory of the Conservatives in the 1959 election, in which Macmillan's catchphrase, you've 'never had it so good', celebrated the Keynesian victory.

The Radcliffe Committee reported just before the election. Although the report considered only the instruments and not the objectives of policy, it turned out to be an ultra-Keynesian manifesto, concluding that the control of bank credit was both unworkable and ineffective, principally because the high liquidity of the banking system prevented the authorities from contracting credit, while the high liquidity and high profits of the corporate sector meant that companies relied little on external finance so that investment was not sensitive to interest rate changes. The Committee therefore recommended a passive monetary policy directed at the rate of interest rather than the money supply, and reliance on fiscal adjustment as the primary instrument of stabilisation policy.

Although the Radcliffe Report sealed the victory of Keynesianism, it also marked the highest point of its advance. The election boom soon ran up against the familiar constraint of the balance of payments, forcing the government to check expansion after the election by means of monetary controls, raising the bank rate, controlling bank lending and restricting consumer credit. The bank rate rise attracted foreign short-term capital to cover the payments imbalance, but the squeeze on domestic consumption did not lead to the increase in exports predicted by the advocates of deflation. Moreover speculation against the pound in 1961 precipitated a crisis. Substantial borrowing from European central banks and the IMF bolstered the reserves, but to correct the imbalance a deflationary budget raised taxes and cut government spending, while bank rate was raised and credit squeezed, and the government imposed a public sector pay freeze. These measures began to bite just as the downturn set in, pushing the economy into a steep recession. It was clear that neither orthodox deflation nor Keynesian expansionism alone were enough to secure sustained growth. Keynesian macroeconomic policies had to be accompanied by more direct intervention to contain inflation and defend the balance of payments. The key to the reconciliation of full employment with monetary stability came increasingly to be seen as a strategy to foster productivity growth, closely associated with an 'incomes policy' to control wages.

The problem of productivity

The British economy had not been growing slowly by historical standards. However by the middle of the 1950s Britain's performance was looking decidedly lacklustre by comparison with its European neighbours, while Britain's share of world trade was declining rapidly. One explanation for this failure was the structure of Britain's trading relations, that was the result of Labour's strategy of reconstruction on the basis of the Empire and the Sterling Area, confirmed by the Conservatives when they took office. While these had provided the most dynamic markets in the immediate postwar period, and a vital source of dollars, the strong movement of the terms of trade against primary products and the resurgence of Western Europe meant that British exports were directed to the slower growing and less sophisticated markets. Moreover colonial development policies and industrialisation in the dominions meant that indigenous industries were growing up to compete with

British manufactures, while foreign competitors were penetrating Commonwealth and colonial markets. Finally the independence of India and the rise of nationalist movements in the colonies, strongly backed by the US, meant that Britain's privileged political position was under threat.

Although the Suez crisis and the subsequent wave of decolonisation marked the decisive political defeat of the old imperialist strategy, it did not immediately lead to a reorientation of Britain's economic strategy. Although Britain was anxious to gain access to European markets, and so participated in the negotiations around the formation of the EEC, Britain envisaged no more than limited trade liberalisation and refused to make any commitment to the wider ambitions of free trade and economic integration, to say nothing of political union. Thus Britain had not signed the Treaty of Rome that established the EEC. When Britain applied for membership in 1961 its application was eventually vetoed by France on the grounds that Britain's membership was incompatible with its continued global aspirations, so that Britain was forced back, un-reluctantly, on the Commonwealth and the Atlantic partnership. However by 1961 it was also becoming clear that the pattern of Britain's trade was only a symptom of a more fundamental weakness, the low productivity that made British manufactures increasingly uncompetitive on world markets.

There were a number of reasons for the slow growth of productivity. Partly it simply reflected the fact that the low productivity sectors of peasant farming and domestic manufacture had long been eliminated in Britain. However it was also becoming increasingly clear that productivity growth was closely associated with the rate of investment, which in Britain was low by international, if not by historical, standards. The argument that low investment reflected the fact that Britain had inherited a mass of plant, buildings and machinery, to which new equipment was added piecemeal, rather than having built its industries anew after the war, simply begged the question of why Britain had not re-equipped. The problem was not a shortage of capital, for profits had soared in the early stages of the boom, without stimulating a significant increase in domestic investment, surplus capital being absorbed by a growth in liquidity, housing and consumer credit, and overseas investment.

The primary reason for the low rate of investment was that which had lain behind Britain's relative industrial decline since the

1870s, the ability of British productive capital to retreat into the protected markets of the empire in the face of successive world crises. The empire had sustained British capital through the depressions of the late nineteenth century and of the 1930s, and had led the recovery before the First World War and after the Second. Although the imperial relationship had been crucial to Britain's economic, social and political stability, it reduced the pressure to apply new technology, develop new products and introduce new methods of management, and limited the tendency to monopolisation and to the integration of productive and financial capital, in marked contrast to the countries that had more limited access to protected markets, particularly Germany, the US and Japan.

The success of Labour's reconstruction of British imperialism after the Second World War had once more provided the soft markets that enabled British capital to continue in its traditional ways. Even when competitive pressure increased, the low rate of investment meant that British productive capital carried a relatively light burden of external debt and depreciation, and so could continue to make profits so long as revenue covered current costs, further reducing pressure to monopolise industry and to transform methods of production. In most industries monopolisation had still not proceeded nearly as far as in Britain's competitors, leaving fragmented industries with relatively small producers, who resisted competitive pressure through specialisation and product differentiation, and responded to falling profits by cutting back production, rather than by reducing costs through standardisation and mass production. The relative stability of production methods and of corporate organisation meant that British companies still often relied on the most primitive methods of management, with little direct managerial control of the production process. Although the 1950s had seen a considerable increase in the monopolisation of British industry, monopolisation was more concerned with the rationalisation of marketing than of production and had not been accompanied by a significant degree of rationalisation of plants and product ranges, nor by the widespread adoption of the most advanced methods of production. Meanwhile indigenous technical advances were largely confined to the military-related sector, which absorbed a very high proportion of research spending, but which was unable to compete with US producers who enjoyed enormous advantages of scale.

When competitive pressure finally forced managerial and tech-

nical 'rationalisation' on British industry, such rationalisation was
in the context of stagnant or slowly growing markets, involving the
displacement of labour by modern machinery, and the erosion of
the shop-floor workers' control over the production process that had
marked archaic forms of production management. The strength of
union organisation, particularly at plant level, that was a legacy of
the war and immediate post-war period, gave workers the power
to secure reasonable redundancy payments, and to retain an element of control over manning levels, job demarcations and the
intensity of labour, which had long been regarded, particularly by
skilled workers, as rights that were not alienated to the employer
in the wage bargain, and that workers were reluctant to give up
in exchange for wage increases which, all too often, would immediately be eroded by inflation. Although workers' resistance has
frequently been cited as a major cause of low productivity, it was
far more common for employers to milk old plant dry and refuse
new investment demanded by the trades unions than for unions to
resist investment plans outright. However the ability of workers
to prevent the employers from unilaterally dictating the terms of
such investment made re-equipment less attractive, and made even
many modern plants less productive than their equivalents abroad,
where workers had been forced, or persuaded by real and sustained
wage increases, to intensify their labour.

The problem of the slow growth of productivity was one which
appeared directly in the inflationary pressures that resulted from
the attempt of the working class to realise Chancellor Butler's in-
vitation in 1954 to 'aim to double the standard of living in the next
twenty years'.[1] The industrial and political conflicts opened up by
attempts to hold down wages focussed attention on investment and
productivity growth. The failure of restrictive domestic policies to
lead to the expected rise in exports by relieving the pressure of
domestic demand in 1960 finally tipped the balance in favour of
Keynesian arguments that sustained domestic growth was the necessary foundation for investment, productivity growth and rising
exports. The problem was now defined as one of securing such
growth without running into the balance of payments difficulties
that had checked successive recoveries, the 'stop-go' policies that

---

[1] Hastily revised to twenty-five years. Quoted in T. W. Hutchison, *Economics and Economic Policy in Britain, 1964–1966*, Allen and Unwin, London, p. 126

resulted discouraging investment and intensifying the problem of slow productivity growth in a vicious circle of relative decline.

The rise of Keynesian interventionism

The initiative in developing the new interventionist strategy was that of the Federation of British Industries, although it met with an enthusiastic response from the Prime Minister, Harold Macmillan, for it was very much along the lines that he had mapped out twenty years before, and the watchword was 'planning'. However the planning envisaged did not involve any significant extension of the power of the state over private capital, but only a closer co-ordination of the independent investment plans of the private and public sector in which, as far as the FBI was concerned, public investment would be more closely tailored to the needs of the private sector. This was Keynesian planning, not socialist, or even corporatist, planning, aiming to increase investment by stimulating optimistic expectations. On the other hand, planning envisaged a much greater role for the state in the regulation of wages, the higher rates of growth to be achieved by 'indicative' planning reconciling the working class to pay policies that would limit the rate of increase in wages to the rate of growth of productivity, ensuring the stability of prices and profits.

This new strategy was embodied in the National Economic Development Council, the National Incomes Commission and the Public Expenditure Survey Committee. NEDC brought together employers, trades unionists, government representatives and 'independent experts', providing a forum for tripartite debate and for the coordination of plans, but having no executive powers. The idea was that NEDC would arrive at a consensus as to the expected rate of economic growth. The NIC would then promulgate guidelines as to the acceptable rate of pay increases, while PESC would coordinate government expenditure plans over a five-year planning period, within the limit of the resources available.

The political implementation of this collaborationist strategy presupposed the integration of the trades unions into its consultative apparatuses. The trades unions were willing to participate in the NEDC, which provided a channel through which they could press their views on the government, and which gave them increased political legitimacy, without compromising their independence. However the recent pay pause, and the low level initially proposed as the guideline for pay increases, meant that they would have nothing to do with the NIC. Partly in response to such pressure, and partly in a mood of unwarranted optimism, NEDC projected a rate of growth of GDP of 4 per cent, which provoked similarly ambitious pay claims and legitimated increased public expenditure plans, fuelling the by-now traditional pre-election boom.

With the NEDC capital had successfully deflected more radical planning proposals. However the NEDC system suffered from the weakness that all the participants had an interest in making optimistic projections, while there were no means of realising such projections. Thus the planning mechanism institutionalised still further the expansionist tendencies of Keynesianism, without providing any means of significantly increasing the rate of investment to raise output and productivity, while incomes policy institutionalised a generalised expectation of rising wages, without regard to the financial standing of the employer. Even where the government had intervened more directly in the restructuring of capital its success was as limited as its ambition. In the public sector the nationalised industries suffered a decade of underinvestment, prices being kept down by subsidy, while rationalisation exercises in public and private sectors involved plant closures, the liquidation of excess capacity and substantial cuts in employment in the old industries of coal, textiles and the railways, rather than the long overdue programme of reinvestment in the new industries that were coming under growing international competition. The positive encouragement to investment amounted to little more than the fiscal incentives that the government restored in 1953, having abolished them in 1951, which were also used to direct investment to regional pockets of high unemployment from 1963.

Rising wages and planned increases in public expenditure, and an impending election, made it essential that NEDC's promises should be fulfilled, and the 1963 budget accordingly cut taxes substantially in the hope that rapid economic growth would stimulate the investment and productivity increases that would maintain international competitiveness. As the balance of payments deteriorated approaching the election the government did not check the boom, in the hope that the payments imbalance would be merely a transitional problem that would be remedied once domestic production increased to fill the gap. However such hopes were in vain, and Labour took office in the midst of a balance of payments crisis, condemning the Conservative record on investment and productivity, and contrasting private affluence with the 'public squalor' which was the legacy of severe restraint on public expenditure to create space for regular reductions in taxation through the 1950s.

The election of Labour did not mark a break in the strategy of the state, but an extension of the framework of Keynesian planning to compensate for the failure of the market by more actively encouraging investment and productivity growth. Although the new government envisaged a limited nationalisation programme, the main thrust of its strategy was 'rationalisation'. The immediate priority of the government was the balance of payments crisis. The government rejected devaluation, which would increase inflationary pressure while taking some time to have an unpredictable impact on the balance of trade. However, rather than correct the balance of payments by the traditional deflationary measures, the new government imposed import controls and subsidised exports, against international protests. Such measures soon proved insufficient and the government had to raise bank rate and borrow heavily abroad, followed by a package of tax increases to stem speculation against the pound.

Meanwhile short-term crisis measures were accompanied by an expansion of the Conservative's 'planning' apparatus. Battalions of economists were drafted into Whitehall. The Department of Economic Affairs was established to counter the Treasury, charged with drawing up an ambitious National Plan that sought to put the full weight of the government's authority behind optimistic projections of future prosperity, while the new Ministry of Technology was charged with more direct intervention to sponsor industrial rationalisation and technological development, supplemented from 1966 by the Industrial Reorganisation Corporation that sponsored monopolisation schemes as the basis of anticipated rationalisation, and by the increasingly generous provision of subsidies and fiscal incentives for investment. Meanwhile a major programme for the expansion of public education, with a strong emphasis on technical and scientific education, would provide the skilled labour force required by modern technology.

Apart from ambitious plans for the modernisation of the nationalised industries, Labour's programme did not envisage the state direction of investment. The government limited itself to an ideological offensive to instill a growth mentality, and to providing infrastructural support and fiscal incentives to investment. Meanwhile it was recognised that an incomes policy, to contain wages within the limits of productivity growth, could only be implemented with the cooperation of the trades unions. The quid pro quo offered to the trades unions was higher rates of taxation on profits, against which companies could set investment expenditure, and on rentier incomes, to ensure that increased profits were spent productively; the apparatus of planning, that was supposed to co-ordinate the investment plans of the private and public sector; increases in welfare expenditure, particularly in capital spending on the decrepit health service; a continued expansion of the public housing programme, to make up for the decline in private renting; more generous welfare benefits, in line with the expected rise in incomes; and the closer involvement of the trades unions in government. The acceptance of this bargain by the trades union leadership was sealed in a Declaration of Intent in late 1964 and the establishment of the National Board for Prices and Incomes to review pay claims and price increases in 1965.

Although the greater degree of state economic intervention was associated with the closer involvement of employers and trades unions in government, it would be a gross misnomer to describe either the forms of intervention or the political structure of the state as 'corporatist'. However much influence the formal and informal links gave capitalists and trades unions over the formation and implementation of state policy, the state's role, outside agriculture, the nationalised industries and the military sector, was primarily enabling rather than directive, while the state had no mechanisms by which directly to control the rate and allocation of investment. Similarly administrative power remained firmly in the hands of the executive, subject to parliamentary authority, while the participation of capitalists and trades unionists on statutory and advisory bodies was not on a representative basis, and such bodies had few executive powers.

The involvement of capitalists and trades unionists was designed to secure the political and administrative framework for class collaboration within a Keynesian strategy that was very different from the corporatist strategies advocated during the 1930s and implemented under fascist regimes. Thus growing state intervention took place within the framework of the liberal state form in which accumulation remained subject to the law of value imposed by the rule of money and the law, while the regulation of the reproduction of the working class was achieved through the increasingly pervasive system of social administration and the closer involvement of the government in wage regulation and the system of industrial relations. On the other hand, the proliferation of tripartite bodies and of parallel channels of political representation did provide a framework within which political pressures, primarily from the working class, for the state to develop in a corporatist direction mounted as Keynesian interventionism came up against its limits. However such developments would require not only changes in policy, but also fundamental changes in the form of the state, and in the relation between the state and civil society. Any proposals for the state to assume directive powers over capital would provoke strong political resistance from capital, in the name of the sovereignty of Parliament, the limitation of administrative discretion, and the freedom of property under the law, reinforced by the economic pressure of an investment strike and capital flight.

The limits of Keynesian intervention

The contradiction inherent in the Keynesian interventionist strategy was that it sought to restore the profitability of capital by developing institutional forms of regulation of the working class which at the same time strengthened and unified the representation of working class interests. The trades unions were brought into the planning apparatus not on a sectional basis, but as representatives of the working class as a whole. The expectation of a generalised increase in wages, without regard to the profitability of the employer, was institutionalised in the form of incomes policies. The expectation of a generalised increase in the minimum level of subsistence was institutionalised in collective bargaining over the 'social wage'.

The stability of such forms of regulation depended crucially on the ability of capital and the state to accommodate rising wages and public expenditure by transforming methods of production to meet the challenge of international competition. Where such collaborative forms had been developed on the basis of the relative strength of domestic productive capital, as was largely the case in Austria, Sweden and, to a limited extent, Germany, they could provide a framework within which the working class as a whole could be reconciled to the intensification of labour and to substantial structural changes in employment through collaborative incomes policies, 'manpower planning', retraining schemes and generous welfare benefits, at least for as long as capital was able to confine the aspirations of the working class within the limits of profitability. However in Britain such institutions had been developed in response to a deterioration in collaborative class relations, marked by growing working class militancy and a fall in the profitability of domestic productive capital. Thus from its very inception the institutionalisation of the Keynesian class compromise imposed rises in wages and increases in public expenditure that increased the pressure on profits, which was further exacerbated by the deterioration in the terms of trade from the mid–1960s, so undermining the attempt of the state to stimulate investment by encouraging optimistic expectations of profitability on the part of capitalists. The result was to institutionalise the inflationary tendencies of Keynesianism and to increase the amplitude of the 'stop-go' cycle. As the state sought to reconcile the conflicting aspirations of capital and the working class, the institutional forms of the Keynesian Welfare State appeared increasingly as a barrier to both capital, in institutionalising the resistance of the working class, and the working class, in seeking to confine its aspirations within the limits of capital. Thus the class struggle rapidly developed from a struggle within the institutional forms of the Keynesian Welfare State to a struggle over the form of the state itself.

Pressure to increase public expenditure to meet ambitious plans for infrastructural investment was compounded in 1964 by the political need for a government with a small majority that soon sought re-election to respond to the pent-up frustrations of earlier pay restraint in the public sector and to the growing dissatisfaction, on the part of both the public and public sector workers, with the form and scale of provision of public health, housing, education and welfare. The rising tendency of public expenditure was further exaggerated by the fact that large areas of public expenditure were demand-determined and largely outside central control, and by the need to secure the collaboration of the trades unions in the government's incomes policies.

The government was reluctant to raise taxes. Increasing taxation was both politically unpopular and stimulated higher wage demands, despite the attempts of the government to persuade the working class that rising public expenditure constituted an increase in the 'social wage', a claim that lacked conviction since the beneficiaries of increased public expenditure were by and large not those who were called on to meet the cost. Thus the government sought to limit tax increases by increased borrowing, while relieving the pressure on financial markets by easing credit, following the post-Radcliffe strategy of stabilising interest rates rather than the supply of money and credit.

The easing of credit enabled employers to meet wage increases, at the cost of increased indebtedness, in anticipation of being able to restore profitability by raising prices. The government accommodated the growing demand for credit in order to hold down interest rates in the hope of stimulating investment, provoking an inflationary spiral. Incomes policy had only a limited success in containing inflation, primarily because it secured the collaboration of trades unions and employers by promising to maintain both real wages and profitability, a reconciliation that Keynesians believed possible to the extent that inflation was a result of 'money illusion'. In practice trades unions ignored the limits of incomes policies in so far as they were able to secure larger increases by their own efforts, especially through local bargaining, more prosperous employers often being willing to pay such increases as the price of holding on to scarce categories of labour power and intensifying labour. Thus incomes policy tended to increase inflationary pressure as stronger groups of workers set the pace of pay rises while weaker unions used the incomes policy to maintain differentials. As inflation rose the government was forced to reinforce its incomes policies with deflationary measures, which shifted the balance of class forces in favour of employers. While such measures further politicised the class struggle, they also intensified divisions in the working class, particularly between organised and unorganised workers, and between public and private sector workers.

Rising inflation and growing international competition led to a deterioration in the balance of payments, made worse by a strike provoked by the government's decision to to make an example of the seamen, which fuelled the speculation against the pound that led to the crisis of 1966. The government again rejected devaluation as a means of restoring confidence in sterling and increasing international competitiveness, although it was becoming clear that the pound was overvalued. The fear was that a significant devaluation would fuel inflation, while a small devaluation would establish a precedent which would only provoke further speculation. On the other hand, international pressure ruled out more extensive controls on imports. The response to the crisis was therefore a tough deflationary package that increased taxation and cut public expenditure, particularly concentrating on capital spending, which was politically less sensitive than current expenditure, and a blanket wage freeze, to be followed after six months by 'severe restraint'. Nevertheless confidence in sterling was not restored, and a further crisis in 1967, intensified by a bitter dock strike, was met by devaluation, which indeed fuelled inflationary pressure, followed by further tax increases and cuts in public expenditure, which forced up unemployment.

The framework for the government's macroeconomic policy after devaluation was defined by its Letters of Intent to the IMF in 1967 and 1969 which set targets for domestic credit expansion. These targets did not dictate the form of stabilisation policy to be adopted, but they did impose a monetary constraint on policy which implied that the government was committed to pursuing restrictive monetary policies if it failed to correct inflation and the payments imbalance by other means. Thus the targets imposed a modern form of the specie-flow mechanism as the means of disciplining the government.

Although the underlying problem was the lack of competitiveness in the face of the growing overaccumulation of capital on a world scale, the immediate source of the government's difficulties appeared to be inflation and the immediate cause of inflation appeared to be rising wages. Although the trades union leadership reluctantly agreed to successive incomes policies, particular unions frequently broke ranks, while national agreements were increasingly undermined by unofficial action at a local, and even a national level. In the absence of an effective interventionist mechanism for ensuring that productive capital increased investment and raised productivity sufficiently to validate rising wages and public expenditure, incomes policies could only relieve inflationary pressure by forcing down real wages. The result was that incomes policies led to a sharp increase in strikes, and a growing political confrontation between the organised working class and the state, without having more than a temporary impact on wage inflation.

As inflation persisted while unemployment and excess capacity rose, it became clear to the Keynesian mind that inflation could not simply be the result of 'overfull' employment, but could only be the result of the ability of militant trades unions to enforce inflationary pay rises on employers. Thus the government looked for its salvation to trades union reform and the 'reform' of industrial relations, bringing the latter within a legal framework for the first time in Britain. The primary object of the government's offensive was rank and file militancy and unofficial strikes, which were seen as the principal threat to both incomes policies and orderly industrial relations. The Donovan Commission, which emphasised the role of local bargaining and unofficial shop-floor organisation in its 1968 Report, provided the intellectual background to the government's thinking, while the attempts of employers to curb shop-floor organisation in the struggle to wrest control over production from the workers provided an indication of the future direction of industrial relations. However the proposed reforms were unacceptable to the trades unions, in undermining their independence, and the legislation was dropped in exchange for a promise from the TUC to curb unofficial action and demarcation disputes, a promise the TUC had no power to put into effect. Although Labour's legislation was dropped, its proposals, and the implicit agreement of the TUC to its diagnosis, had already pinpointed the scapegoat for the competitive failure of British productive capital.

The government had been forced to abandon its ambitious strategy of expansionism as persistent inflation, rising public expenditure, and a weak balance of payments put it under financial pressure in domestic and international financial markets. Successive deflationary budgets increased unemployment, the cost of welfare benefits tending to neutralise cuts in other areas of public expenditure, but did little to curb inflation as growing shop floor militancy maintained the rising pressure on wages. The Keynesian promise of planned growth with full employment, stable prices, rising wages and improved public services was collapsing into what came to be known as 'stagflation', with both prices and unemployment rising, real wages stagnating, and public expenditure falling at the expense of both services and public sector pay.

Rising unemployment, under the impact of deflationary policies, undermined the apparatus of Keynesian planning. The dilemma was the same as that which had faced the rationalisation movement in the late 1920s, that rationalisation and increased productivity implied the loss of jobs, which was politically unacceptable in the context of rising unemployment. The result was growing resistance from the organised working class to the terms of investment programmes and rationalisation schemes that involved plant closures and job losses, while inflation and successive waves of pay restraint undermined productivity bargaining as inflation eroded negotiated pay increases.

The failure of the state to satisfy the expectations it had aroused led to a rising tide of industrial and political unrest. The trades union movement adopted an increasingly political role, pressing for more radical interventionist measures to stimulate investment and defend jobs. The collaboration of the trades union leadership with the government had led to the rise of a more militant and independent shop stewards' movement, that raised not only questions of pay and the conditions of labour, but of the power of capital and the rights of the direct producers. Meanwhile the expansion of the public sector, the gradual proletarianisation of white collar workers and the growth of higher education was undermining the class identification of sections of the middle class. Middle class radicalism was most dramatically expressed in the student movement, which rejected the paternalistic authoritarianism of the education system, and drew its political strength from opposition to the sycophantic support of the government for US imperialism in Vietnam.

Although the failure of Keynesianism led to growing popular resentment, the identification of the trades union leadership with the government's strategy meant that such resentment lacked a political focus and remained largely unorganised, the lack of organisation being elevated to a political principle by the politics of '68. The divisions between the fragmented grass roots trades union and political struggles were reinforced by government policies. Incomes policies protected unorganised and low paid workers, at the expense of the better paid. Public expenditure cuts benefited taxpayers at the expense of public sector workers and those reliant on welfare and public services. The government's extension of the Conservative's racist immigration policy served to scapegoat black workers for the failings of capital, while its aborted trades union legislation served to scapegoat the unions.

The challenge to Keynesianism

The failure of Keynesian intervention to secure the increases in investment and productivity that could reconcile the sustained accumulation of capital with rising wages and public expenditure led to an intensification of the class struggle, in which the institutional forms of integration of the working class provided a base from which the organised working class could press its claims, regardless of the constraints of profitability. Rank and file militancy inhibited the restructuring of capital by resisting job losses and the intensification of labour, while wage claims increased inflationary pressure. Incomes policies generalised, rather than containing, such pressures. The political assimilation of the trades unions was secured only at the cost of increasing public expenditure and subordinating industrial policies to political priorities. The institutional apparatuses through which the state had sought to resolve the contradictions of liberal Keynesianism had served rather to intensify those contradictions.

The contradictions of Keynesianism were ultimately an expression of the contradictions of the capitalist state form as the growing pressure of overaccumulation undermined the post-war settlement. However the underlying contradiction did not appear immediately as such, but rather appeared in the form of an economic, political and ideological crisis of the Keynesian Welfare State. Thus the limits of Keynesianism did not mark the limits of capitalism, nor even the limits of fiscal regulation, but the limits of the Keynesian political strategy of state-sponsored class collaboration, on the basis of full employment and a generalised expectation of rising living standards, within the framework of the liberal state form. Although the crisis of Keynesianism politicised the class struggle, class polarisation did not appear directly as a struggle for state power, but rather as a progressive erosion of the authority of the state.

Both capital and the working class had an ambivalent relation to the state. Working class economic and political aspirations were channeled by trades unions and political parties through the state. On the other hand, the working class increasingly confronted the state and the industrial relations system as barriers to the realisation of those aspirations, and sought to advance beyond the forms of Keynesian integration. Similarly individual capitals sought the support of the state to maintain profitability in the face of rising costs and more intense international competition, and negotiated wage increases as the price of industrial peace, while at the same time they grew increasingly restive as the economic and political costs of Keynesian intervention mounted. Thus the crisis appeared as a crisis of the liberal form of the Keynesian state, in which class conflict centred not so much on the control of the state apparatus as on the form of the state and, above all, on the relationship between the state and civil society, and between the power of money and the power of the state.

Keynesian interventionism had sought to reconcile the working class to wage 'restraint' and to job losses as the price of industrial 'rationalisation' that would provide future increases in wages and employment. However the bargain was singularly one-sided. While the state sought to increase profitability, at the immediate expense of the working class, and to subsidise investment, it had no means of ensuring that increased profits would be invested to raise domestic investment and productivity. Thus the failure of Keynesian interventionism to realise the aspirations of the working class increasingly raised the question of the democratic accountability of capital and the state, and to growing pressure from sections of the organised working class for the state to bring capital directly under social control, to complement the socialisation of consumption with the socialisation of production, to subordinate the accumulation of capital to the aspirations of the working class. On the other hand, the failure of the state to secure the conditions for sustained accumulation led to growing demands on the part of capital for the subordination of the state to civil society, expressed in the demand for the subordination of the state not to the political rule of capitalists, but to the anonymous power of money. The restoration of the orthodox principles of monetary and fiscal rectitude and the confinement of the working class within the rule of money and the law would confine the reproduction of both capital and the working class within the limits of profitability by bringing both individual capitals and the working class under the rule of the law of value.

The ability of the state to resolve the contradictory pressures to which it was subject was limited not simply by the balance of class forces rooted in civil society, but also by the Keynesian institutional forms that mediated the relation between civil society and the state, and so defined the forms through which the class struggle was expressed politically. The state could not simply dismantle the existing institutional apparatuses, and restore the unfettered rule of money and the law, without provoking economic and political chaos, as the Heath government in Britain found to its cost. Similarly the 1974 Wilson government found that the fear, however remote, that the state might bring capital under a minimal degree of social control provoked threats of an investment strike, the collapse of the pound, and even open talk of a military or royalist coup. Political mobilisation outside the constitution appealed increasingly to both the right and the left, sections of the right pinning their hopes on the repressive apparatus of the state, the left on the strength of the organised working class. However the issue was decided not by a confrontation between revolution and counter-revolution, but by the transformation of the state from within, on the basis of the existing institutional forms provided by the state. Thus the struggles were fought out in and against the Keynesian form of the liberal state.[2]

The attempt to contain these conflicts within the Keynesian political and ideological framework led to the progressive disintegration of the political and ideological forms of the Keynesian Welfare State through the 1970s and early 1980s. The frustration of the aspirations of the working class led to growing rank and file militancy and the rise of 'new social movements' that sought to develop more democratic forms of social and political regulation. However the trades union and political leadership of the working class saw such autonomous movements not as a base on which to build a democratic alternative to the alienated forms of capitalist domination, but as a challenge to their own authority. The Labour Left pressed for an alternative corporatist strategy, but it sought to pursue this strategy by developing the increasingly discredited apparatus of the Keynesian Welfare State, 'planning agreements' marking the limit of its immediate plans to secure the democratic accountability of capital. The trades union leadership sought to preserve its power not by building on popular struggles to construct an organised and united opposition to the capitalist offensive, but by looking to their privileged relation to the state for a strengthening of their legal rights and for an increasing role in the Keynesian consultative apparatus, while pursuing their trades union aims on a sectional basis, through the increasingly antagonistic forms of incomes policy

---

[2]London-Edinburgh Weekend Return Group, *In and Against the State*, Pluto, London, 1979.

and industrial relations. In pinning their faith on the beneficence
of the capitalist state, the trades unions and the Labour Left found
themselves isolated from growing sections of the working class, who
increasingly confronted the bureaucratic and authoritarian forms
of capitalist power not as the instruments of their emancipation,
but as the immediate barriers to their individual and social aspirations. While the working class leadership clung to the tattered
remnants of the Keynesian Welfare State in the deepening crisis,
capital and the state confronted the Keynesian forms of integration as barriers to their own reproduction, and sought to develop
new forms of regulation through which to confine the aspirations
of the working class within the limits of profitability and fiscal constraints. In the course of the ensuing struggles capital developed
new forms of industrial relations, while nominally Keynesian governments adopted an institutional framework appropriate to the
implementation of increasingly 'monetarist' policies. Meanwhile
the ideology of Keynesian interventionism, whether in its more liberal or more radical variants, was progressively eaten away from
within.

The collapse of Keynesian legitimacy marked a decisive ideological and political defeat for the organised working class and opened
the way for the rise of the New Right, whose monetarist ideology
celebrated the failure of Keynesianism and provided a coherent theoretical justification for policies which had increasingly been forced
by circumstance on reluctant governments. Like political economy
and Keynesianism before it, the adoption of monetarism as the official ideology of the state did not initiate a political revolution,
but marked its culmination as the state adopted an ideology appropriate to its emerging form.

The turn to the market

The first moves to dismantle the Keynesian interventionist apparatus in Britain were made by the Conservative government elected
in 1970. The Conservatives in opposition had abandoned their ten-
tative commitment to Keynesian planning to advocate a return to
liberal Keynesianism, making the conquest of inflation their first
priority, with entry into the EEC and the abandonment of Labour's
industrial policy as the means of strengthening market forces; a re-

laxation of taxation to increase incentives; a disengagement of the
state from the system of industrial relations, replacing administrative intervention with legal regulation; and reductions in state
expenditure, trades union 'reform', and a restrictive monetary policy to curb inflation without recourse to an incomes policy.

The government immediately dismantled much of Labour's interventionist apparatus and set about the reform of the financial
system to increase competition and strengthen the instruments of
monetary control. In place of an industrial policy and fiscal regulation the government planned to use the financial sector as the
means of allocating investment funds, and to regulate accumulation
by pursuing a more active monetary policy. Under the new regime
of 'Competition and Credit Control' the control of the money supply would play a more central role in economic policy, while interest
rates and the allocation of funds would be determined by competitive market forces. However this did not imply a monetarist belief
in a direct relation between the money supply and the rate of inflation, monetary policy being seen as a more sensitive instrument
of demand-management rather than having a direct impact on the
rate of inflation, as the monetarists were later to believe.

The greater emphasis on monetary policy, and on the money
supply rather than interest rates as the indicator of the monetary
stance, had already been anticipated by the Labour government.
Although targets for the growth of credit had been imposed by
the IMF in 1967, their introduction accorded with the thinking of
the Bank of England. The interest rate had become an unreliable
indicator of the stance of monetary policy in a period of inflation,
where 'real' interest rates diverged from nominal rates. Thus domestic credit expansion, in the context of fixed exchange rates, or
the money supply, in the context of the flexible exchange rates that
were adopted in the 1970s, became more appropriate indicators of
the monetary stance than the interest rate.

The balance between fiscal and monetary policy had also been
changing. On the one hand, fiscal measures had shown themselves
to be a blunt instrument to deal with inflationary pressures, tax
increases and expenditure cuts being politically unpopular and delayed in their effects. On the other hand, the increased indebtedness of the corporate sector made investment and stockholding
more sensitive to changes in interest rates and the availability of
credit, while increasing interest rates were very effective in checking

speculative investment in stocks, property and financial assets and in attracting a capital inflow. Although soaring public expenditure and pressure on financial markets had forced the Labour government to raise taxes, the government had increasingly relied on monetary measures to reinforce its anti-inflationary policies, higher unemployment undermining the resistance of trades unions, and tighter credit restricting the ability of employers to borrow to finance wage increases. However the liquidity of the banking system meant that measures had to take the form of direct controls that were soon evaded.

Following its rejection of incomes policy the government set about the reform of industrial relations, to replace administrative intervention by legal regulation in the attempt to secure an 'appropriate' balance between trades unions and employers, which necessarily involved an attack on the trades unions, whose excessive power had become the primary scapegoat for the failures of domestic productive capital. However the Conservative reforms fared no better than those of Labour. The system of voluntary registration of trades unions left a space within which the unions could subvert the government's intentions, leading to increasingly militant confrontations in which the government repeatedly backed down to avoid a dangerous political polarisation.

The Conservative's strategy was an unmitigated disaster. The problem was that the Keynesian forms of integration could not simply be dismantled at will. Although they provided channels through which the working class could constitutionally pursue its aspirations, they were not the source of working class strength, but only the institutional form through which that strength was expressed. The attempt to dismantle those forms and subordinate the working class to the immediate authority of money and the law could only lead to a politicisation of the class struggle as long as the organised strength of the working class gave it an autonomous source of power. The Conservatives' failure was compounded by the fact that they sought to dismantle the Keynesian forms of regulation without having developed alternative institutions and policy instruments, so that, far from subordinating accumulation and class relations to the rule of money and the law, the government quite simply lost control.

Continuing wage inflation meant that pay restraint was imposed on the public sector almost immediately. However the manifest arbitrariness and unfairness of the policy, the lack of any effective means of enforcement, and the failure to offer any quid pro quo for union cooperation, meant that the policy was counterproductive, leading to confrontation with the public sector unions, whose new-found militancy enabled them to break through the policy time and again. Meanwhile restrictive policies in the face of growing international competition intensified the rise in unemployment and led to a sharp decline in investment, while leading companies in financial difficulty ran to the government for support. Moreover the instruments of monetary control proved ineffective. In abandoning the economy to the judgement of the market, without any means of regulating either wages or the expansion of credit, the government had unleashed inflationary forces that it had no means of checking.

The new strategy introduced from 1971 marked a return to the Keynesian expansionism of the early 1960s. The government hoped that a massive easing of credit and an increase in state expenditure would stimulate investment and enable accumulation to burst through the barriers that had constrained it over the previous decade. The problem of inflation was to be countered not by a restrictive monetary policy, but by a rigorous incomes policy.

The hope that low interest rates and easy credit would stimulate investment proved to be a vain one. The boom which resulted from the easing of credit was a boom in consumption, much of which was supplied by imports, and in speculative investment in stocks and property. Growing international competition meant that price increases lagged behind money wage increases, further squeezing profits and curtailing domestic investment (and expenditure on research and development). Deteriorating domestic prospects led to a massive increase in overseas investment, to take advantage of more favourable opportunities elsewhere, which was not compensated by the increase in foreign investment that sought a base in the UK from which to take advantage of Britain's entry into the EEC. The outflow of capital, increase in imports, and decline in competitiveness more than offset the positive impact of the world boom on exports. The result was a renewed inflationary surge and a deterioration in the balance of payments, while domestic productive investment stagnated.

A sterling crisis in June 1972 indicated what was to come. Rising commodity prices, culminating in the massive increase in oil prices in late 1973, only served to intensify the pressures. It soon became clear that restrictive policies would have to be reimposed to restore monetary stability. The restriction of the money supply came to the fore again in late 1972, leading to a rise in interest rates, although it was not until a year later that attempts to control the growth of the money supply were effective, when intervention in the market was abandoned in favour of a return to direct controls.

The failure to contain inflation by monetary means meant that the problem of inflation was tackled by a statutory incomes policy, beginning with a blanket freeze. However the policy failed to prevent wages from rising faster than prices, while it set up escalating confrontations between the government and the trades unions, broadened and deepened by the attempt of the government to subject industrial relations to legal regulation, which brought both the government and the law into disrepute.

The class struggle and the crisis of Keynesianism

The Conservative government's policies had managed to unite and radicalise large sections of the working class. Trades union legislation provoked mass opposition, and brought striking workers into direct confrontation with the state. Many public sector workers had taken strike action for the first time. Trades unions, tenants' groups, community groups, welfare rights groups, black and women's groups had begun to come together in struggles that demanded not simply more pay or more government expenditure, but that challenged the bureaucratic and authoritarian forms of capitalist power, challenges that could not be headed off by empty gestures in the direction of 'participation'. Heath's attempt to isolate the miners in 1974 by politicising their strike backfired, the miners coming instead to symbolise a united class confrontation with the government.

In the absence of any realistic alternative this rising tide of struggle looked primarily to the Labour Party to give political form to this symbolic unity. However the Labour Party continued to be dominated by the alliance between a bureaucratic, sectional and economistic trades union leadership and an opportunistic Parliamentary leadership, who were deeply committed to the existing forms of industrial relations and of the state, and for whom the energy, enthusiasm and imagination that had emerged from the grass roots were as much a threat in opposition as they had been in power. Indeed the immediate obstacle to the advance of many women and black workers, as of many shop-floor workers, was the white male-dominated trades union bureaucracy. The immediate obstacle to the aspirations of many tenants' organisations and community groups was bureaucratic Labour local authorities.

The response of the Labour Party to the growing class struggle was to attempt to demobilise popular militancy and contain popular aspirations within the framework of the Keynesian Welfare State by offering a radical Keynesian programme, promising both a major redistribution of wealth and power and an ambitious plan for state intervention in industry. The trades unions were to be reconciled to wage restraint, without a formal incomes policy, by a 'social contract' according to which the government committed itself to expansionism and redistribution. Planning agreements and selective nationalisation would make it possible to secure working class support for an investment-led reflation that would not run into the problems that had beset previous demand-led reflations. For the Left such an industrial policy held out the promise of the democratisation of civil society within an increasingly corporatist political framework, although the Labour leadership had no intention of permitting such a development.

The core of Labour's industrial strategy was not particularly radical, indeed the degree of intervention envisaged was less than was commonplace in many other capitalist countries. The model was not the Soviet Union, but the dynamic capitalist countries, Austria, Sweden, Germany and Japan. The policy would certainly have faced technical problems of implementation, since the state lacked the policy instruments, powers and expertise required to put the strategy into effect. However the major problems were not technical but political. The industrial strategy had been pressed on a reluctant Labour leadership by the Left, and included potentially socialist demands for nationalisation and workers' participation. The fear that any extension of state intervention would be only a prelude to more radical demands led capital to wage a virulent political campaign against it, and even to threaten an investment strike.

In fact no such pressure was necessary. The government took office in the face of a major economic crisis, with a deteriorating balance of payments, worsened by the fall in exports in the world recession, falling profits and investment and accelerating inflation. Moreover the government lacked an overall majority. Thus the industrial strategy was postponed as the government's immediate priority was to tackle the economic crisis and build up support for a second election.

In place of the industrial strategy and investment-led reflation the government sought to buy votes, and buy off the militancy of its supporters, by introducing expansionary budgets, which fulfilled some of its promises of income redistribution, and by conceding substantial public sector pay increases. The effect was, not surprisingly, not to stimulate increases in investment and production, but to lead to accelerating inflation, a further squeeze on profits and investment, and a deteriorating balance of payments. Increases in pay and public expenditure had demobilised the emerging rank and file movement. However the inflationary financing of such increases meant that the price was paid not only by capital, but also by those whose incomes were eroded by inflation. Thus inflation opened up new divisions and unleashed new political forces that enabled capital and the state to move onto the offensive as the crisis deepened. Following the second election the government gave substantial tax concessions to capital and relaxed price controls in the attempt to boost profits and investment. The EEC referendum provided the opportunity for the Labour leadership to inflict a comprehensive and decisive defeat on the Left, which was driven to defend its industrial strategy not on socialist grounds but on the grounds of a narrow chauvinism, as a strategy for national regeneration.

While the British government was still trying to expand the economy, governments elsewhere were imposing deflationary policies in an attempt to eradicate inflation. The result was that soaring inflation in the UK rapidly undermined the competitiveness of domestic production, leading to a collapse in profits, investment and productivity, rising unemployment and a rapid deterioration in the balance of payments. The government's external financial difficulty was compounded by the problem of financing soaring public expenditure, which more than doubled in three years while prices rose by less than 70 per cent, in the face of severely depressed financial markets. Increased domestic borrowing pushed up interest rates and inflated the money supply, while the pound came under growing pressure.

The 1975 budget marked the repudiation of Keynesian expansionism, contracting demand in the face of rising unemployment, and setting targets for the money supply rather than the level of unemployment. Corresponding to the growing emphasis on monetary policy and the control of public expenditure the government was meanwhile developing the instruments required to put such policies into effect. On the one hand, the failure of the Conservative government to control the growth of money and credit, and the need to finance the growing public debt, had led the Bank of England to develop increasingly sophisticated methods of debt management and monetary control. On the other hand, the failure to confine public expenditure within the limits of public revenue led to the development of the system of cash limits. However such methods could not bear the weight of the growing crisis. As the situation deteriorated the government imposed an immediate incomes policy at the end of 1975, with the agreement of the TUC, while the pound was allowed to drift downwards, increasing inflationary pressure, and the control of the money supply brought to the centre of the stage in the 1976 budget, followed by public expenditure cuts to reduce the borrowing requirement. The pound continued to slide, despite a massive loan from the IMF and foreign central banks, as short-term capital flooded out of sterling. In exchange for a further IMF loan the government agreed to a package of spending cuts and monetary restraint, itemised in the Letter of Intent of 1976.

The IMF loan has entered the mythology of the Labour Party as the crucial turning point in the strategy of the Labour government as it capitulated to the demands of foreign bankers. However the terms of the loan imposed no constraints on the government that it had not already adopted voluntarily. The 1975 budget had already repudiated expansionary solutions, cash limits had been introduced to enforce cuts in public expenditure in early 1976, while money supply targets were set in the 1976 budget, and further cuts in public expenditure imposed to reduce the Public Sector Borrowing Requirement in July 1976. Although the Cabinet considered introducing import controls to deal with the crisis, the time for such measures had long past, for the collapse of the pound could only be averted by securing a loan from the IMF, and IMF lending was inconsistent with the adoption of discriminatory trade measures. Far from imposing deflationary policies on a reluctant government, the IMF loan provided an alibi with which to head off mounting political opposition, deflecting criticism of its policies onto foreigners and bankers, while providing the government with the means of supporting sterling through the crisis, and so avoiding a far more destructive deflationary package.

In the event the loan restored confidence in sterling and stabilised financial markets, enabling the government to meet its borrowing requirement with ease and so keep well within the money supply target it had set in the budget. Thus the terms of the IMF loan imposed no effective constraint on the government's economic policy. It was not the IMF that undermined Labour's expansionary strategy, but an increasingly unfavourable international economic situation that arose as Labour sought to head off the radical challenge by pursuing inflationary domestic policies in the face of a world recession.

The episode of 1974–6 represented the death throes of the Keynesian strategy of class collaboration in Britain. The reflation of 1974–5 was imposed primarily by political pressures, but it finally and conclusively undermined the idea that the level of investment is determined by the level of domestic demand, so that demand-management policies could break through the barriers to accumulation. The 'new realism', dating from Callaghan's speech to the 1976 Labour Party conference, reflected a recognition that the driving force of accumulation was not demand but profit, and that henceforth the aspirations of the working class for rising wages and increased public provision had to be confined within the limits of capital. This required not merely a change in economic policy, but a restructuring of the institutional forms of the Keynesian Welfare State.

Keynesianism was undermined as expansionary domestic policies ran up against the barrier of financial crises associated with the deteriorating balance of international payments. For the Labour Left these crises consisted essentially in a confrontation between the money power of capital and the political power of the nation state, to be resolved politically by the subordination of capital to the state through controls on trade and international capital flows, and through the implementation of Labour's radical industrial policy. However the diagnosis of the Left failed to address the critical question of the form of the state. In presuming that the political power of the state could be counterposed to the money power of capital, rather than seeing that the two forms of power were inextricably linked, the Left presumed that the capitalist state could rest on some other power than that of capital.

Successive crises represented not so much a confrontation between the power of capital and the power of the state, as the contradiction inherent in the Keynesian welfare state between the class character of the state and the consensual mechanisms of class collaboration. The Labour leadership was only too aware that for the state to attack the power of capital was to undermine its own foundations. Any attempt to implement the radical strategy of the Left would have collapsed in the face of an investment strike and an international and domestic financial crisis. The only alternative to a resolution of the crisis on capital's terms was the revolutionary transformation of the state form to reintegrate the state and civil society on the basis of the political mobilisation of an organised popular movement that could articulate the democratic aspirations of a united working class, a movement that had begun to emerge in 1974, but that existed in 1976 only in the fantasies of the ultra-Left.

The crisis of Keynesianism and the rise of monetarism

The 1976 crisis saw the burial of the corporatist strategy of the Labour Left, that had been defeated politically in the EEC referendum. Once the Labour government had abandoned its radical industrial strategy, on the grounds of political realism in the face of capitalist opposition, the government had no alternative but to respond to the crisis of 1975–6 by adopting traditional deflationary policies in the attempt to contain inflation so as to restore profitability and the confidence of capital at home and abroad, combined with a 'New Industrial Strategy' based on the well-tried devices of NEDC and its sector working parties. Although the government persisted with incomes policies, these lacked statutory force, and relied increasingly on restrictive monetary policies for their support, the Labour government appealing to popular opposition to inflation to counter the organised strength of the working class and reinforcing sectionalism by proclaiming as forcefully as the classical economists of the nineteenth century that the price of excessive wage increases was rising unemployment, in the vain hope that the threat of such unemployment would be sufficient to moderate wage claims.

The crisis determined the path of the Labour government over the following three years. The priority was to restore the confidence of the financial markets by bringing down inflation, rectifying the imbalance of international payments, and reducing government expenditure. The principal means of achieving this was a rigorous incomes policy, reluctantly supported by the TUC until 1977, backed up by a tight monetary policy and cuts in taxation, and public expenditure cuts (particularly affecting capital spending) substantially larger than those agreed with the IMF. In the event the cuts in spending were outweighed by increases in the cost of unemployment benefit, employment subsidies and temporary employment schemes as unemployment soared; by the continued commitment of the government to increase welfare benefits in line with increases in earnings; by the increasing cost of industrial 'rationalisation' programmes; and by the increased cost of debt service associated with higher interest rates.

Cuts in public expenditure were associated with the development of more rigorous systems of financial and bureaucratic control of public services. This involved the system of cash limits to control expenditure on public services and the increasingly discriminatory provision of welfare benefits. Cash limits were much more than a mechanism of financial control. They had fundamental implications for the form of public administration in subordinating political and administrative discretion to the rule of money, ensuring that the provision of services according to centrally determined bureaucratic and political criteria would be confined within rigorously enforced financial constraints, rather than expanding in response to social need expressed at the point of provision. Thus cash limits ensured that expansion in one branch of provision could only be at the expense of another, and ensured that pay increases could only be secured at the cost of deteriorating services and working conditions and of cuts in employment, thereby opening up divisions between workers within the public sector and between the producers and consumers of public services.

The bureaucratisation of public and welfare services within a framework of financial stringency gave the class struggle a wider base and a broader perspective as public sector workers, welfare recipients and the consumers of public services increasingly challenged not only the scale of public provision, but also its form. Public sector workers resisted not only the erosion of their pay, but also the bureaucratisation of provision, the subordination of provision for social need to financial constraint, and the attempt of the state to enforce the choice between levels of pay and standards of service. Welfare rights groups, tenants organisations, cultural groups, the black and womens' movements, and community groups mobilised a diffuse resentment and confronted the bureaucratic and authoritarian forms of public provision with the collective representation of popular demands for democratic control. Meanwhile resistance to redundancies had led to factory occupations, the establishment of cooperatives, schemes to make socially useful products, and growing demands that capital be brought under social control. However these struggles remained fragmented, lacking a political focus that could unify them around a socialist political programme as the trades unions and the Labour Party, however reluctantly, continued to support the government. Such support was no longer extended in the expectation of any political or economic advance, but out of fear that the return of the Conservatives would unleash an unprecedented assault on the trades unions and the welfare state.

In its own terms Labour's strategy was not unsuccessful. Although a large proportion of the support given to industry was to subsidise the losses of the sectors hardest hit by the crisis, this support was accompanied by a considerable amount of 'rationalisation' and 'restructuring' that resulted in productivity gains for the plants remaining, at the expense of substantial job losses for those made redundant. The share of public expenditure in the national income fell, while the easing of financial markets enabled the government to fund its deficit while remaining within its targets for the money supply. Interest rates fell, while incomes policy was dramatically successful in cutting inflation, until it broke down in 1978–9, while the balance of payments and sterling were restored to vigour. However, much of the improvement was due to the rising contribution of oil revenues to public finances and the balance of payments, not to any improvement in the prospects for domestic accumulation or in manufactured exports, despite the recovery of the world economy.

As its oil revenues rose the government allowed the pound to rise to curb inflation, rather than relax its monetary policy to stimulate growth, putting industrial profits under greater pressure as an appreciating pound was combined with rising real interest rates. Thus industrial profits remained depressed, unemployment kept rising and domestic investment kept falling. Although foreign investment in Britain rose rapidly, the overseas investment of British companies rose even faster, seeking out opportunities abroad that were conspicuously lacking at home. As world inflation began to rise at the end of the decade, in Britain it rose even faster, despite restrictive monetary policies and the appreciation of the pound, and the 'social contract' finally broke down, leading to a massive wave of strikes, particularly in the public sector, in the 'winter of discontent'. Although the social contract was replaced by a hastily patched-up 'Concordat' to present to the electorate, the Concordat had neither teeth nor conviction.

While the Labour government had acknowledged the failure of Keynesian demand-led strategies, most dramatically in Callaghan's famous speech to the 1976 Labour Party Conference, the crisis measures adopted after 1976 showed a new way forward. The government had mobilised popular opposition to inflation and the growing burden of taxation against trades union militancy, and had used its incomes policies to reinforce sectional divisions in the working class opened up by its restrictive monetary policies, resurrecting the archaic wages fund doctrine, now formulated in terms of the 'national cake' rather than the supply of corn, to pin responsibility for both inflation and unemployment onto the trades unions.

Labour had undermined the belief that high levels of unemployment were politically unacceptable, for the impact of unemployment was very uneven and the unemployed presented little political threat, while the trades unions' ability to resist job losses was limited. Labour had similarly undermined the belief that public expenditure must inexorably rise in response to rising public expectations. In this respect Keynesianism had been in some ways a victim of its own success. While the vast majority of the population still relied on public education and public health services, rising wages had enabled a growing proportion of the working class to escape from the bureaucratic and repressive forms of public housing into owner-occupation, while the meagreness of state benefits meant that provision for old-age depended increasingly on private savings, which also topped up state benefits to cover periods of sickness and unemployment. Thus the welfare state, that had been proclaimed as the means of guaranteeing every citizen a right to reasonable standards of health, housing, education and welfare, had increasingly reverted, outside health and education, to being a form of public assistance for the poor. Rising public expenditure had meant that the incidence of taxation had moved progressively down the income scale, so that the welfare state brought a net advantage only to the lowest income earners, the mass of the working class benefiting more from cuts in taxation than from increases in public expenditure. It was the opening up of these divisions in the working class that helps explain the apparent paradox that Labour's standing in the opinion polls had steadily recovered despite cuts in public expenditure, a widespread fall in real wages, and rising unemployment.

Meanwhile the rapid internationalisation of productive capital from the late 1960s, based on the earlier internationalisation of money capital, the merger boom of the 1960s, the increasing unevenness of accumulation on a world scale, and improved international communications, meant that the prospects for capitalists were no longer as closely tied to the state of the domestic economy as they had been in the 1950s, when high profits in a domestic market sheltered from competition provided the basis on which capital could penetrate world markets. Moreover multinational companies raised funds on international financial markets, and so were increasingly insulated from domestic financial restraint. It was no longer the case that a depressed domestic economy depressed the prospects for capital, since the latter planned its production, marketing and finance on a global scale. While backward capitals, and the workers dependent on them, still sought public support and a reflationary solution, the more advanced capitals saw their opportunities within a broader context, their international prospects depending on financial stability and domestic monetary restraint.

Meanwhile rising domestic unemployment and the increased mobility of capital undermined working class resistance to the reorganisation of the labour process, particularly as the introduction of the latest methods of production could only be accomplished by the complete re-equipping of plant, or its rebuilding elsewhere. Thus employers began to take advantage of the demobilisation and demoralisation of the organised working class inflicted by high unemployment, the attacks of successive governments, and the continued collaboration of the trades union leadership with the Labour gov-

ernment, to assert the 'right of management to manage' and to restructure the system of industrial relations to destroy the strength
of shop-floor organisation.

Employers similarly resisted pay claims that sought to preserve
established differentials as they attempted to confine wage increases
within the limits of the profitability of the enterprise, a profitability
that had been considerably reduced on paper by the introduction
of inflation accounting. Existing forms of industrial relations, and
particularly incomes policy and national pay bargaining, presented
a barrier to the attempt to tie pay more closely to results, leading
to the development of new forms of industrial relations based on
pay bargaining at company-level, with payment systems based on
job evaluation and bonus payments that by-passed the shop floor
organisation and extended the scope of personnel management.

The disparity between the costs and the benefits of welfare provision, expressed in a growing resentment at the burden of taxation,
the deterioration of public services, and the bureaucratic and repressive forms of public provision, had progressively undermined
the commitment of the working class to the political institutions of
the welfare state. Although public sector trades unions, and a wide
range of welfare rights, tenants' and community groups, challenged
the alienated forms of state provision, the absence of any political
focus for this fragmented opposition meant that the more typical
response of the employed working class was a privatised rejection
of the state. The aspiration of many, however unrealistic, was not
public provision on the basis of need under democratic control, but
an escape from dependence on the state through private provision
on the basis of adequate wages, private savings and private insurance.

The failure of the trades unions, whether through industrial
action or their relation with the Labour Party, to secure rising living standards and defend jobs on the basis of collective strength
similarly undermined the commitment of the mass of the working class to the existing system of industrial relations and wage-
determination. Although some workers in the public sector and
in declining industries continued fiercely to defend jobs and living standards against the threats of both capital and the state,
the majority of the working class adopted a more fatalistic attitude, taking what they could get, whether in the form of redundancy payments or wage increases negotiated with their immediate

employer, whether through the trades unions or over their heads. The privatisation of working class aspirations, and the resurgence of sectionalism, was expressed politically in popular support, even amongst trades unionists, for the priority accorded by the government to the fight against inflation.

Although the state and capital had established the contours and developed the policy instruments of a monetarist strategy in the regulation of capital and the working class, the Labour government had developed such a strategy within the increasingly discredited ideological and political framework of the institutional forms of Keynesian regulation. Thus the substance of the government's policies had come increasingly into contradiction with their political and ideological forms.

The development of the new systems of personnel management based on the monetary regulation of the working class continued to be undermined by the government's reliance on incomes policies and its systematic involvement in the regulation of industrial relations, through which the trades unions sought to compensate for the rapid erosion of their organised strength by a growing reliance on the state to check the power of capital, guarantee trades union rights, and defend jobs and living standards. The attempt to subordinate industrial policy to the constraints of international competition was undermined by the maintenance of a tripartite apparatus of consultation between government, employers and unions that directed industrial subsidies on the basis of political influence. Attempts to subordinate public expenditure to strict financial control were negated by the demand-determined form of most welfare expenditure, by the lack of control over local-authority spending, and by the political commitment to raise benefits and improve services in line with the growth of wages expressed in the social contract. The full development of new institutional forms of capitalist regulation could not occur until the Keynesian forms had been not only discredited, but dismantled. The remaining barrier to such a dismantlement was the organised strength of the working class, which was manifested in the 'winter of discontent'.

The 1979 election brought the contradiction at the heart of the Labour government's strategy to the fore, the Conservative Party proposing to carry through the logic of Labour's monetarist practice, while the Labour Party proposed to bring its practice back into line with its Keynesian ideology.

The challenge of monetarism

The Conservative turn to monetarism dated from the election of Margaret Thatcher to the leadership in early 1975, anticipating Labour's repudiation of Keynesian expansionism by a matter of months. For Thatcher the destruction of the power of the trades unions, and of the legacy of post-war collectivism, had the force of a moral crusade, to be pursued with all the power at the disposal of the state. Thatcher herself was a gut monetarist, her homilies rarely reaching a level of sophistication greater than that of Victorian popular tracts. However she surrounded herself with advisers who provided the theoretical support for her prejudices, drawing most heavily on the work of Milton Friedman and Friedrich Hayek.

Monetarism embraced a range of different theoretical perspectives, whose common theme was that of the need to maintain monetary stability to ensure the smooth operation of the market and the achievement of a full employment equilibrium. While all monetarists saw price stability as the only means of achieving full employment, and monetary policy as the only means of achieving such stability, they differed as to the appropriate monetary policies to pursue to achieve their goal.

The international monetarists, who had dominated the IMF from the 1960s, remained committed to the classical device of fixed exchange rates and the specie-flow mechanism, monetary policy addressing not the money supply, which could not be controlled in a regime of fixed exchange rates, but 'domestic credit expansion', so that monetary policy was determined by the state of the balance of international payments. However the floating of exchange rates from 1971 freed governments from the balance of payments constraint, enabling them to accommodate domestic inflation by currency depreciation, and moving attention from domestic credit expansion and the balance of payments to the money supply and inflation.

For the simple-minded neo-Keynesian monetarism of Milton Friedman inflation was simply a matter of the excessive expansion of the money supply, which inflated demand and led to generalised inflation. Inflationary pressure might be reinforced by the wage demands of trades unions, but it was the government's expansion of the money supply that created the inflationary expectations that led unions to make such demands, and made employers willing and able to meet them. A gradual reduction in the rate of growth of the money supply would allow expectations to adjust and produce a painless restoration of price stability, while floating exchange rates would ensure that international payments remained in balance.

The neo-Austrians had a more sophisticated monetary over-accumulation theory, according to which inflation arose not solely from the expansion of the money supply, but from the disruption of the market and consequent misallocation of resources that resulted from any government control over the money supply, and more generally from any barriers to the operation of the market. The only solution was the short sharp shock of an immediate restoration of the rule of the market, with either a fixed money supply or a free market in the supply of money. Such a shock would produce bankruptcies and unemployment as overinvestment was liquidated, but the pain would be brief, as long as barriers to the market were removed, the rule of the market ensuring a rapid reallocation of resources.

Rational expectations theorists did not believe that the government could have any impact on the economy, since its interventions would always be discounted by economic agents. For these theorists stability of policy was more important than its substance, and attention was more closely focussed on state restrictions on the freedom of the market than on monetary and fiscal policies.

In Britain it was Friedman's monetarism that initially prevailed, although Hayek's neo-Austrian diagnosis was waiting in the wings. In the United States a more pragmatic approach to policy was associated with the rise of rational expectations theory and the assault on the state with the market dogmatism of the 'supply-siders'.

Friedman's monetarism provided a smooth transition from Keynesianism. At one level monetarism was not inconsistent with Keynesianism. The shift in policy emphasis from fiscal to monetary policy in the fine-tuning of the economy had been under way for a long time, Keynesians largely recognising that they had underestimated the significance of monetary policy. The originality of Milton Friedman, trained as a Keynesian, lay in his reassertion of the principles of classical economics within the framework of the neoclassical synthesis, so that he could present his monetarism as a development of Keynesianism, based on the modification of Keynes's assumptions about expectations, assumptions that were particularly inappropriate in the context of inflation. However the implications of this modification were far-reaching. Whereas Keynesian assumptions, which amounted basically to the idea that expectations were based on past experience, led to the conclusion that speculation destabilised the monetary regulation of accumulation, Friedman's assumption that expectations were essentially anticipatory meant that speculation performed a stabilising role. On this basis Friedman established the impotence of fiscal policy and the power of monetary regulation.

On the one hand, against the Keynesian belief that changes in the money supply would be absorbed by speculative changes in cash balances stimulated by changes in interest rates, with little impact on investment, Friedman argued that changes in interest rates would have a broader impact on spending, not only on investment but also on consumption, as producers and consumers responded to the revaluation of their assets in the wake of a change in the rate of interest. The implication of the argument was that Keynes was wrong to discredit the classical mechanism of adjustment to full employment, according to which the withdrawal of money from circulation in the form of savings would lead to a fall in the rate of interest which would in turn stimulate an equivalent increase in consumption and investment. The massive increase in corporate indebtedness and consumer credit since the 1960s meant that stockholding and consumer demand, if not fixed investment, had become more sensitive to changes in the cost and availability of credit. The increasingly speculative character of inflationary booms had given monetary policy much more leverage on domestic economic activity, while the internationalisation of capital and the pressure of international competition meant that domestic production and investment had become less sensitive to the state of domestic demand, so that there was some empirical justification for Friedman's hypothesis.

On the other hand, where Keynes assumed that consumers would save a fixed proportion of their current incomes, Friedman assumed that spending decisions were related to expected income over a long period, and so would not be sensitive to short-term fluctuations in income, undermining the employment-generating potential of fiscal relaxation. Moreover spending decisions would be made in the light of anticipated price and tax changes, so that any impact of increased income on spending would be neutralised as soon as consumers discounted future price and tax increases. The stabilising effect of welfare benefits, and the post-war tendency for savings to rise as inflation rose, and to fall as price stability was restored, gave some empirical support to Friedman's hypothesis. The implication of his arguments was that Keynesian fiscal policies had little impact on the level of demand, except in so far as the financing of increased public expenditure involved changes in monetary policy. Increased taxation would be discounted by consumers, while increased borrowing would lead to a rise in interest rates, leading in either case to the direct displacement of private by public spending. If the government sought to neutralise the impact of increased borrowing by easing monetary policy, the increase in private spending induced by the fall in interest rates would soon be neutralised as consumers and investors discounted the resulting inflation.

The immediate policy implication of Friedman's argument was that government expenditure policies had little impact on the overall level of demand, but merely displaced private by public expenditure, the precise impact on the former being determined by the methods used to finance increased public expenditure. This did not imply an objection in principle to a budget deficit, but only to the inflationary financing of the deficit. On the other hand, monetary policy had a much greater impact on the real economy than Keynes had anticipated, as changes in the money supply induced changes in spending through their impact on the rate of interest. An easing of monetary policy in conditions of unemployment would lead to increases in spending as the rate of interest fell until full employment was reached, thereafter increases in spending being absorbed by inflation. A restrictive policy in the face of inflation would lead to a fall in spending as interest rates rose. However such a fall would not lead to more than a temporary decline in the level of economic activity as expectations adjusted to the fall in the rate of inflation. If the money supply grew in line with the growing demand for money as means of exchange and means of payment at full employment levels of income, the rate of interest would ensure that full employment was maintained alongside price stability.

Friedman insisted that his monetarism had no necessary implications for the level of state expenditure, but only for the methods of financing. However his theory immediately raised the question of the relation between the market and the state in the allocation of resources, his presumption of the efficiency of the market legitimating the political priorities of the New Right. Against the Keynesian conception of the state as a neutral institution that translates the democratic expression of preferences into a set of economic policies, the New Right proposed a much more cynical conception of the state. For the latter the state offers an alternative system of allocation of goods and services to that provided by money, the primary difference being that the state form of regulation dissociates effort and reward, cost and benefit. This gives rise to the paradox of the fundamentally undemocratic character of the democratic state, proposed by the neo-Austrian critics of the tyranny of the state, who drew heavily on a narrow reading of Adam Smith. The state is undemocratic to the extent that it tries to overrule the judgements of individuals of their own best interests, restricting individual freedom by imposing the ill-informed, opportunistic and dogmatic judgements of vote-seeking politicians on the free choices of sovereign individuals.

State intervention not only undermines the freedom of the individual to decide how best to allocate his or her resources, but also necessarily undermines the incentives on which the dynamism and efficiency of capitalism depends, so that in the end even the beneficiaries of government largesse suffer from the impact of economic decline. Instead of rewarding success and penalising failure, as monetary regulation does, the state will always tend to penalise success and reward failure as those who fall by the wayside seek to secure by political means what they have failed to achieve by their own efforts. Whether through taxation, public borrowing, or inflation, the state appropriates and redistributes resources according to its own political priorities, and to the political pressures to which it is subject, and the more it spends the more it undermines the incentives and the individual freedom of the market. This damage is all the greater if the state resorts to inflationary financing which destroys the integrity of the currency, and so the regulatory role of money. A concern for democracy and for national prosperity alike dictate the subordination of the state and civil society to the rule of money.

Although the monetarist critique of the subversion of the market by the state did not preclude state intervention to redistribute wealth, on the basis of the distinction developed by John Stuart Mill between the historically determined distribution of resources and the market-determined allocation of resources, in practice the redistribution of private wealth was deemed undesirable since it undermined the operation of the market by undermining the security of property. Such constraints did not apply, however, to the transformation of public into private property by the redistribution of public assets. Thus the privatisation of such assets became a central plank of the populism of the New Right.

For the monetarists the economic role of the state was to confine accumulation within the limits of the market by restricting the growth of the money supply. With an appropriate monetary policy changes in the rate of interest would ensure that full employment was maintained alongside price stability. The monetarists, like the classical economists before them, were strongly opposed to granting the government discretion in the determination of its monetary policy, since governments would exploit such discretion to pursue inflationary policies in the expectation of securing short-term political gains. Friedman's belief in the validity of the quantity theory of money, backed up by a mass of somewhat dubious statistical evidence, provided the means of removing government discretion since it implied that the demand for money was directly proportion to the level of money income, the result being that non-inflationary full employment growth would be secured by a fixed rule that kept the growth of the money supply in line with the growth of real national income. The neo-Austrians accorded the government even less discretion, while the rational expectations theorists could allow more, provided that policy was stable and predictable.

The control of the money supply was not as simple a matter as it sounded, for it raised in turn the questions of the definition of money and of the control of its supply that had been at the heart of the 1959 Radcliffe report, which noted that in an advanced credit economy money was simply one among a wide-range of liquid assets, over whose creation the monetary authorities had little control. This control had further been eroded by the internationalisation of money capital, which gave capital access to the money markets of the world. Thus the experience of the monetary authorities had in general been that it was easy to establish control over any particular monetary aggregate, but that capital immediately developed new techniques of credit-creation that by-passed the controls. However Friedman side-stepped such problems in asserting that the stability of the reserve ratios of the banking system ensured that the supply of liquidity would be determined by the supply of the money that served as the reserve base of the banking system.

In the event the instability of reserve ratios and the failure of floating exchange rates to secure stability of the balance of payments soon undermined Friedman's monetarist panacea. Although money supply targets were maintained, and improved techniques of manipulation of financial markets made it possible to adhere to such targets, they soon lost all practical significance, and monetarist governments soon came to pursue discretionary fiscal and monetary policies in the light of domestic inflation and levels of interest and exchange rates. The failure of Friedman's simplistic monetarism led to a turn towards the neo-Austrian and related supply-side doctrines, which focussed on barriers to market regulation and the erosion of incentives presented by high taxation, government intervention, the powers of monopoly, and particularly the supposed monopoly powers of trades unions. Thus the monetarist offensive rapidly broadened from a concern with monetary policy to a frontal assault on the fiscal, legal, and administrative powers of the state, and on the supposed power of the trades unions, providing the ideological rationale for a fundamental restructuring of the Keynesian political and industrial relations apparatuses. However the monetarist offensive by no means implied the abdication of state power in favour of the market that had brought down the Heath government, but rather the systematic exercise of state power to subordinate civil society and the state alike to the rule of money and the law.

The triumph of monetarism

The debate between monetarism and Keynesianism was not resolved in the seminar room, but on the political stage. The strength of monetarism was not intellectual or analytical, for monetarism did little more than reassert the naive classical faith in the efficiency of the market. The strength of monetarism was ideological, for monetarism could articulate, in however mystified a form, growing popular opposition to the bureaucratic and authoritarian forms of the capitalist state, which the Labour Party had failed to mobilise politically, while providing a theory that could explain the failure of both Keynesianism and militant trades unionism, and legitimate the policies that had been forced on reluctant Keynesian governments. The ideological merit of the Conservative's monetarism was that it made a virtue of necessity, representing these crisis measures as the core principles of a new ideology of state regulation. It was not so much its positive merits that gave monetarism its appeal, as the manifest failure of Keynesianism. This was articulated in Thatcher's triumphant refrain that 'there is no alternative'.

The Conservative Party drew its strength from the contradictions between the emerging monetarist practice of the Labour government and the institutional and ideological forms within which that practice was embedded. The Conservative Party hardly mentioned monetary policy in its 1979 manifesto, despite the conversion of the leadership to monetarism over the previous five years, and stood essentially on the Labour government's record, promising to continue the strategy of tight monetary policy, tax cuts financed by cuts in public spending, and the rigorous imposition of cash limits in the public sector, throwing in the sale of public housing at knock-down prices as a vote-winner. The major difference between the manifesto of the Tories and the practice of Labour was that the Tories promised to remove the barriers that had confronted the attempt of the Labour government to realise this programme, the barriers of the discredited institutional forms of Keynesian regulation. Thus the government intended to rely on the tight control of public spending and a restrictive monetary policy to check wage inflation, allowing the state to withdraw from direct intervention in industrial relations, which would be conducted within the framework of a 'reformed' trades union law. Similarly the government proposed to dismantle Labour's apparatus of industrial intervention and return the regulation of accumulation to the tender mercy of the financial markets, which were better able than politicians to judge the viability of an enterprise and its future prospects. Labour, goaded the Tories, had failed to follow the logic of its practice through because of its institutional links with the trades unions.

Labour, meanwhile, stood not on its record, but on the moderate corporatist programme that it had comprehensively rejected in practice, the 'Concordat' replacing its incomes policies, statutory planning agreements replacing its liberal industrial policy and import controls replacing deflation in defence of the balance of payments. Given the manifest inconsistencies between its programme and its practice, most dramatically symbolised in the militant class struggles of the 'winter of discontent' provoked by the government's intransigence, it was hardly surprising that Labour lost the 1979 election.

The first two years of Conservative government saw a change of rhetoric, but not a fundamental change of strategy, lulling the Left into the belief that it had little to fear. The Conservative government took office as the world boom was breaking. Inflation, fuelled by rising wages and import prices, was escalating despite rising unemployment. Soaring oil prices and high interest rates meant that the pound was continuing to rise. The new government faced the same dilemma as the old: Britain's oil production had made the pound a strong currency, although the international competitiveness of manufacturing industry continued to decline. The result was that if the government tightened policy to check inflation, it would drive the pound higher, curbing inflation but further weakening competitiveness, but if it relaxed policy to check the rise in the pound it would stimulate further domestic inflation. Initially the new government followed roughly the same policy as the old, although the effects of such a policy in a growing world recession were rather different from its effects in a world boom, its impact on the exchange rate being further exaggerated by the rapid growth in oil revenues.

The government sought to check inflation primarily by cutting public expenditure rather than tightening monetary policy, imposing rigid cash limits on the public sector in the face of rising inflation, but neutralising the impact on wages by implementing substantial public sector pay increases awarded under a comparability exercise initiated by the previous government. A further boost to inflation was provided by a tax reform that slashed income tax but raised VAT. The pressure on the pound was relieved by freeing capital from exchange controls, stimulating a large capital outflow, but the exchange rate continued to rise, further eroding manufacturing competitiveness, while offering capital the opportunity of securing foreign assets at bargain prices. The increase in VAT, rising wages and import prices, high interest rates, the rising exchange rate and the fall in export demand put an unprecedented squeeze on profits. As stockholdings rose, the indebtedness of the corporate sector mounted, putting upward pressure on bank lending, the money supply and interest rates, while the removal of banking controls meant that the government had no means of regulating the growth of credit, short of draconian monetary contraction. The pressure on financial markets made it difficult for the government to fund its debt, driving interest rates up further. As inflation and unemployment both mounted and profits were slashed a change of policy was imperative.

Although restrictive policies would further increase the pressure on unprofitable capitals, the government's first priority was price stability. The only available means of containing inflation, in the absence of an incomes policy that would have provoked a political confrontation between the government and the organised working class as a whole, was deflationary monetary and fiscal policies. In the face of speculative pressure on financial markets the government could only pursue a restrictive monetary policy, without driving interest rates sky-high, if it could reduce public borrowing. The inflationary pressure and political costs of increased taxation meant that a cut in public borrowing could only be achieved by further reductions in public expenditure.

The 1980 budget introduced the familiar package of crisis measures, centred on cuts in public expenditure, enforced by the rigorous application of cash limits, and a deflationary package. The difference in 1980 was that measures which in the past had been the mark of failure were now proclaimed as the centrepiece of a strategy of regeneration, embodied in the Medium Term Financial Strategy, that set limits to the expansion of the money supply and the Public Sector Borrowing Requirement. For the Conservatives the success of such policies in containing inflation in the past had been undermined by the power of the unions and the lack of determination of both Conservative and Labour governments, which had not been prepared to cut public expenditure or to carry through a sufficiently restrictive monetary policy in the face of growing unemployment and industrial militancy. This time there would be no reversal of policy. The rule of money would play the central role in the regulation of accumulation, replacing the Keynesian political mechanisms of incomes policy, 'planning' and tripartite consultation.

Although the rhetoric of the government stressed the impact of restrictive monetary policy on inflationary expectations, the government also made it clear that if trades unions failed to moderate their wage demands, and employers failed to resist such demands, the result would be rising unemployment and falling profits. In the event expectations did not adjust smoothly. Wages continued to surge ahead. High interest rates and the rise in oil prices drove up the exchange rate. Rising wages and an appreciating pound squeezed profits sharply, while the high cost of credit led companies to slash investment, cut stockholdings, close plant and lay-off workers to maintain their cash flow. The money supply, far from contracting, exploded as companies borrowed heavily to survive the recession.

An emergency budget in the autumn tightened the screw by increasing taxes sharply and further cutting public expenditure, reducing inflationary pressure as unemployment, now rising at a rate of one million per year, strengthened the hand of employers, while falling profits strengthened their determination. Meanwhile, in the face of the crisis, and of the resistance of trades unions to cuts in pay and public expenditure, the government had extended its interventionist role, providing enormous subsidies to coal, steel and British Leyland to maintain wages and employment, expanding the Labour government's make-work schemes, particularly to combat youth unemployment, and extending controls on imports. The cost of such schemes, together with the growing cost of unemployment and debt service, more than outweighed cuts in public expenditure.

The City, whose monetarist inclinations had been reinforced by the government, reacted unfavourably to the explosive growth of the money supply, increasing pressure on financial markets. As the crisis persisted 1981 saw the largest increase in taxation in British history, taking taxes as a proportion of the GDP to the highest level ever recorded, as the government sought to relieve pressure on interest rates by bringing down its borrowing. However the government simultaneously raised interest rates to maintain a grossly overvalued pound, partly in the erroneous belief that a strong currency was a cause rather than a consequence of a strong economy, but primarily to contain inflation. By the autumn of 1981 Margaret Thatcher was the most unpopular Prime Minister since records began, with her monetarist strategy in ruins.

The failure of monetarist economic policies to achieve the miracle cure led to a change in strategy. The 1982 budget effectively abandoned Milton Friedman, raising the supposedly inflexible money supply targets, and adding the exchange rate as a policy consideration. However the government did not reverse its policies, as the previous Conservative government had done in similar circumstances, but rather proposed to carry them further. The rationale of economic policy, insofar as it had one, was now the more pragmatic rational expectations theory. However the rallying cry was that monetarism alone was not enough, it had to be complemented by the systematic eradication of the institutional forms of Keynesianism, and the reconstruction of the state as the means of imposing, with a ruthless impartiality, the rule of money and the law. The task was to wipe all traces of 'socialism' from England's green and pleasant land. The guide was the neo-liberalism of Friedrich Hayek.

Inflation was no longer the result of an excessive increase in the money supply, nor unemployment the result of government policies. Inflation and unemployment were now both the result of the excessive power of the trades unions, reinforced by the indiscriminate generosity of the benefits system that subsidised strikers, reduced competition for jobs, and allowed three million people to choose unemployment rather than engaging in productive work. Labour had sown the wind, the unions were to reap the whirlwind. For Hayek the 'legalised powers of the unions have become the biggest obstacle to raising the living-standards of the working class as a whole. They are the chief cause of the unnecessarily big differences between the best- and worst-paid workers. They are the prime source of unemployment. They are the main reason for the decline of the British economy in general'.[3]

The government's approach to the unions was the one aspect of its policy that displayed a systematic approach from the beginning, picking off unions in the public sector one by one, and progressively tightening its anti-union laws. The 1980 Act was relatively modest, doing little more than give legal force to the terms of the TUC's Concordat with the Labour Party, curtailing the right to strike by withdrawing traditional legal immunities and weakening the 'closed shop', while reducing social security benefits payable to strikers and their families. The Act provoked a limited response from the TUC, which was hamstrung by its own pacifist rhetoric. The 1982 Act went much further, severely limiting the right of unions to strike and to picket, while the 1984 Act sought to tie the unions down

---

[3] Friedrich Hayek, *Unemployment and the Unions*, IEA, London, 1980, p. 52.

completely by imposing ballots before industrial action. The laws on their own were not sufficient to defeat the trades unions, as the 1970 government had discovered, but the greater willingness of employers to use the law; the draconian penalties imposed on unions who broke the law; the willingness of the judiciary to expedite proceedings against unions and to apply such penalties to the full; the systematic use of the police in support of employers; the more aggressive attitudes of management; and the determination of the government to defeat the unions, whatever the cost, provided an environment that was hardly favourable to the pursuit of even the most modest of trades union aims.

Although the TUC was committed to opposing the law, in practice its opposition was muted by the devastating consequences of violating the new legislation, and the knowledge that it had little hope of calling on mass support from a trades union movement decimated by unemployment and divided and demoralised by successive defeats. Thus the government was able to pick off individual unions in a systematic campaign that culminated in the defeat of the miners in 1985, in which the TUC and the Labour leadership stood aside. The willingness of the unions to act within the law was given a positive thrust by the 'new realism', which involved accommodation with government and employers, while the unions pinned their hopes for improvement not on rebuilding an organised mass movement, but on the election of a Labour government. Meanwhile the government appealed over the heads of the trades union leadership to the members, exploiting the divisions that were a legacy of the demobilisation of the rank and file as the leadership had sought to advance through collaboration with the Labour Party, and expressing, in a mystified form, the growing disillusionment of the membership with a bureaucratic, and increasingly ineffectual, trades union leadership. This populist appeal of the government to the mass of the working class reflected and reinforced a parallel transformation in the system of industrial relations as employers sponsored consultation exercises and continued to develop new forms of personnel management and new payments systems.

The attack on the unions provided a scapegoat for the government's own failure, and aroused the enthusiasm of its supporters, but did little for its standing in the polls. The government's popularity only rose when it turned its attention from the enemy within to the enemy without, suddenly discovering an enthusiasm for a forgotten outpost of the empire, which led it to launch a war with Argentina over the latter's occupation of the Malvinas Islands. The Labour Party's craven support, reflecting the glory of its own impe-rialist tradition, which had had its most farcical moment in Harold Wilson's invasion of Anguilla with a detachment of the Metropoli-tan Police, only strengthened the government's blood-lust, and en-abled Margaret Thatcher to raise her approval rating from 36 to 59 per cent at the modest cost of a couple of thousand lives.

By 1983 the worst of the recession had passed as the world econ-omy moved into the recovery phase of the cycle, under the impact of expansionist policies in the US. Although incomes had barely risen, consumer expenditure surged forward, financed by a fall in personal savings as inflation moderated and by a rapid growth of consumer credit. The unions were in full retreat, employers asserting their 'right to manage' and confining wage rises within the limits of prof-itability. Although the multinational companies had closed plant at an unprecedented rate, the removal of exchange controls and the overvalued pound provided them with the opportunity to acquire overseas assets on very favourable terms, more than making up for the devaluation of capital through the liquidation of unprofitable domestic operations. The new aggressiveness of employers resulted in a sharp fall in wage inflation, while a substantial improvement in the terms of trade and high productivity growth, as outdated plant was scrapped and labour intensified, meant that the government could allow the pound to fall by 14 per cent, relieving the pressure on profits and interest rates, without the fall stimulating renewed inflation. The government had conquered inflation, and brought production within the limits of profitability, at the cost of cutting a swathe through manufacturing industry and increasing registered unemployment to three million.

The stabilisation of prices, the rapid growth of productivity, and the recovery from 1982, with private sector wages rising once again, enabled the government to present its strategy as a success story. Although manufacturing investment showed no signs of re-covering, rising productivity, soaring profits and a healthy stock market enabled the government to argue that British industry was 'leaner and fitter' as a result of its experience, while the determi-nation of the government and employers had checked the power of the trades unions, and the strong pound and the Malvinas War had re-established Britain as a world power. Success was marked by large tax cuts in the 1983 budget, which fuelled a Keynesian pre-election boom.

The Labour Party, meanwhile, had split, the right having left to form the Social Democratic Party, which offered Thatcherism with a genial face, whose grin became a leer with the replacement of Jenkins by Owen as leader after the election. The Labour Party entered the election on the programme of the Alternative Economic Strategy, a development of the radical industrial strategy on which it had fought the 1974 and 1979 elections. While the programme had had some plausibility in 1974, the subsequent destruction of the power of the organised working class and the massive internationalisation of productive capital had made it politically unrealistic by 1983.[4] It became clear in the course of the election campaign that the leadership was positively opposed to the strategy, while even its advocates were unconvinced. The election campaign reinforced Thatcher's cry that 'there is no alternative', and the government was re-elected with a substantially increased majority in 1983.

In its second term the government built on its success in the first. However the defeat of the miners in 1985, the government's greatest triumph, also deprived it of its alibi. Trades union power had been so reduced that it could no longer be plausibly blamed for anything. Thus the focus of the government's offensive shifted once again, from the trades unions to the state itself. The bitter dispute with the teachers, and the policies of a few radical education authorities, offered the government a new scapegoat. Unemployment and economic decline were no longer the result of Keynesian policies, nor of the trades unions, but of the failure of the education system to provide appropriate training, and of the barriers to reform presented by the 'educational establishment'. However the attack on education emerged as a part of a broader offensive against the forms of public provision.

Despite the government's anti-state rhetoric, it had presided over a steady rise in the level of state expenditure, both absolutely and as a proportion of the GNP. This was not for want of trying to cut expenditure. The system of cash limits had been reinforced by a drive for 'efficiency', which involved the introduction of new forms of administrative and financial control, and the move to pri-

---

[4] I have discussed this more fully in Simon Clarke, 'Capitalist Crisis and the Rise of Monetarism', *Socialist Register 1987*, Ralph Miliband et al. , eds, Merlin, London, 1987.

vatisation and competitive tendering which was a means of breaking the power of the public sector unions, forcing down wages and
intensifying and casualising labour on an enormous scale. The government had also progressively tightened its grip on local authority
spending, which had previously escaped central government control by virtue of the revenue-raising powers of local authorities and
the system of block grants. Welfare benefits had been squeezed,
and the subsidisation of public housing eliminated, although the
savings on the latter were more than neutralised by the increased
subsidisation of private home ownership. Nevertheless there were
limits to which public expenditure could be reduced by these methods. Although the government defeated the organised opposition
of trades unions and local authorities to its policies, the latter were
able to mount effective political campaigns in the face of deteriorating public services, which forced the government to commit itself
to maintaining standards of provision. Similarly, generalised cuts
in welfare benefits provoked widespread electoral dissatisfaction.
Meanwhile the massive increase in unemployment had led to an
enormous increase in the cost of welfare provision, despite the reduction in rates, the increasingly repressive administration of the
system, and its more selective application. The government was
only able to reconcile rising expenditure with its aim of reducing
both taxes and public borrowing by selling off public housing and
public monopolies.

The attack on public expenditure had not only been directed
at the cost but also at the form of provision. In the area of social
security this involved a return to the repressive principles of se-
lectivity and means-testing that had lain at the heart of the Poor
Law. This was particularly used to force the unemployed onto
make-work schemes that increasingly provided cheap labour, particularly to the service sector, under the guise of 'training'. Elsewhere the strategy was one of privatisation. The privatisation of
public monopolies was achieved, despite the concerted opposition
of the trades unions, with little difficulty. Privatisation promised
to free management from restrictions on the diversification and
internationalisation of the enterprise imposed by legislative, administrative and financial constraints. The public was promised
higher standards of service and lower costs as a result of increased
competition, although there is little evidence that such promises
carried much conviction. More importantly the floatation of public

corporations offered windfall profits to subscribers, and fuelled the stock market boom.

In relation to public services and social insurance the government's unspoken strategy was to force a shift from public to private provision by reducing the standards of public services to such an extent that individuals would take out private pensions, private health insurance and move into private housing and private education. This strategy proved extremely successful in forcing a shift from public to private housing by pushing up public sector rents, and selling off public housing at knock-down prices. It also had some success in the area of pensions, although the public expenditure implications would take decades to work through. However the strategy was a dismal failure in the areas of health and education, where political opposition to the extension of charging for public services and growing unrest at the rapid deterioration of services mounted. The government responded to such pressures by introducing financial and administrative reforms, ostensibly to increase efficiency and democratic accountability, but in fact as an attempt to deflect popular dissatisfaction with the government's parsimony, and to fragment and divide popular unrest. This was to be achieved by the radical decentralisation of finance and administration within the public sector. The expectation was that decentralisation would lead to growing resentment, on the part of both producers and consumers of public services, at the continued confinement of decentralised units within the straightjacket of central financial and bureaucratic constraints, and so for growing popular pressure for the piecemeal privatisation of individual hospitals, health centres, schools, colleges and universities (and the principle could be extended to all public services, such as sport and leisure facilities, children's and old people's homes, and even the prison service). It was this strategy of creeping privatisation that was presented to the electorate in the margins of the 1987 election manifesto, and that was made the centrepiece of the programme for the government's third term.

The programme of social security 'reform' and of privatisation of public services, the massive restructuring of production, employment, and industrial relations and payment systems in the public and private sectors, led to a growing polarisation between the beneficiaries of these changes and the vast majority of the population who were, in one way or another their victims. However the form

of these economic, social and political changes exploited and reinforced the divisions within the working class that had been opened
up by the crisis over the previous decade, leaving the opposition in
disarray.

There is no evidence that the government's programme enjoyed
enthusiastic popular support, even on the part of the minority of
the population who regularly voted for the Conservative Party.
The government had owed its re-election in 1983 almost entirely to
the Malvinas War and to the absence of any effective opposition.
It owed its re-election in 1987 primarily to the sustained boom
of the previous five years, that had been fed by easy credit and
tax reductions, made possible by enormous oil revenues, within
the context of a world boom led by the United States. Although
the government had a low approval rating on the issues that the
electorate regarded as central, the issues of health, education and
unemployment, all that the divided opposition could offer in 1987
was a small increase in public spending on health and education,
and an extension of the make-work schemes to create more jobs,
without being able to explain how it would meet the costs of such
a programme without raising taxes or generating inflation. In the
absence of any coherent alternative the government was able to
exploit old fears of Keynesian chaos and secure its re-election, once
more on a minority vote.

Paradoxically the recovery that secured the re-election of the
Conservatives in 1983, and carried them through to their third victory in 1987, was not based on monetarist policies, but on Keynesian fiscal expansion within a tight monetary framework, although
the government maintained the priority of price stability over full
employment, as Keynes himself might well have done in similar circumstances. International financial pressures continued to dictate
a tight monetary policy. Despite the rapid growth of the money
supply, real interest rates rose sharply as inflation fell. However
economic recovery in Britain, combined with sales of public assets and healthy oil revenues, enabled the government to boost
consumption by cutting taxes. Although investment and manufacturing production barely increased, and the deficit on trade
in manufactured goods continued to deteriorate, the government
could sustain such an expansion without running into the customary crisis because of the stimulus given to accumulation on a world
scale by a classic Keynesian deficit-financed boom, accompanied

by an increasingly overvalued dollar, in the United States. The triumph of monetarism, no less than the crisis of Keynesianism, was not a specifically British phenomenon, but was conditioned by the dynamics of accumulation on a global scale.

Overaccumulation and the world crisis of Keynesianism

The crisis of Keynesianism was precipitated by the domestic impact of a global crisis of overaccumulation, and its development conditioned by the pace of global accumulation. Although the crisis unfolded in different countries with a different rhythm and in the context of different social and political institutions, the different national experiences were determined primarily by the uneven development of capital in the context of the overaccumulation of capital on a world scale. The contradictions of Keynesianism appeared most acutely in Britain, where the systematic socialisation of working class reproduction was combined with increasingly backward domestic productive capital and an exceptional exposure to foreign competition, but the same contradictions opened up around the world as the pressure of overaccumulation became more acute.

Despite the wishful thinking of Keynes and Adam Smith, the post-war boom had not been driven by domestic consumption but by profits. The boom had been initiated by the high domestic profits of the post-war decade, and had been sustained to the extent that capital could overcome the barrier of the limited domestic market by conquering world markets on the basis of increases in productivity and the development of new products.

The ultimate limit to the pursuit of Keynesian policies at a national level was set by the balance of international payments. The limit to their pursuit on a world scale was set by the supply of international credit to finance growing payments imbalances. The growth of international liquidity from the 1950s had accommodated imbalances in international payments and increased the latitude available to national governments. However the pursuit of expansionary domestic policies only intensified the overaccumulation and uneven development of capital on a global scale, accumulation being sustained through the 1960s by the explosion of international credit and rising world inflation. The limits to Keynesianism on a world scale appeared in the form of the growing instability of the international monetary system associated primarily with the weakening of the dollar.

As the world role of sterling declined with the emergence of a multilateral payments system at the end of the 1950s the growth of international liquidity had been dominated by the growing supply of dollars held outside the US, that corresponded in the first instance to the cumulative US balance of payments deficit, but which was soon augmented by credit-creation by the international banks. While the US deficit corresponded to growing US overseas investment, overseas dollar holdings were ultimately validated by the profitability of such investment. However from the late 1960s the deficit increasingly corresponded to US military expenditure overseas and to a deteriorating balance of trade. International credit was increasingly extended to the US not to serve as capital but as revenue, secured not against US overseas investment but against the dwindling US gold reserves.

The British devaluation of 1967 dented confidence in the stability of the gold-exchange standard, precipitating a rush into gold and bringing the dollar into the speculative front line. The Vietnam War, on top of the Keynesian inflationism of the Great Society programme, had led to a severe deterioration in the external position of the US as increased overseas military expenditure and the resort to inflationary financing to support an unpopular War led to a growing outflow of dollars. Pressure on the dollar threatened not only to provoke a US recession, that would have world-wide repercussions, but also to undermine the international monetary system that sustained the accumulation of capital on a world scale. Armed with the lessons of the 1930s, central bank cooperation was able to stem the speculative tide through currency swaps and the parity of the dollar was maintained, although only by confining its convertibility to official transactions so that a two-tier gold market developed with the market price rising steadily against the official price.

Pressure on sterling and the dollar was eased as governments around the world reacted to the upsurge of industrial militancy and political unrest (partly provoked by attempts to contain the domestic impact of US inflationism), and to the threat of a US-led recession, by pursuing expansionary policies in their turn. Restrictive monetary policies in the US were soon reversed as they threatened to provoke a recession in the run-up to the 1970 congressional elections, and the US external position continued to deteriorate rapidly as domestic inflation undermined the balance of trade and low interest rates stimulated a capital outflow. The US government began actively to use the power of the dollar to export US inflation and secure a realignment of exchange rates. European governments had no option but to support the dollar, but official purchases of dollars increased domestic liquidity, further fuelling the inflationary boom that was rapidly assuming global proportions. The attempt to contain domestic credit expansion and relieve the pressure on the dollar led to the revaluation or floating of the major non-dollar currencies in early 1971. However this was not sufficient to stem speculation against the dollar, which went off gold with a 10 per cent devaluation. The Smithsonian agreement between the major powers stabilised their currencies within narrow limits, but the agreement soon broke down as the dollar was further devalued in 1973 and the regime of fixed exchange rates was abandoned to inaugurate the new era of the 'managed float'.

The breakdown of the gold-exchange standard did not lead to the collapse of the international monetary system, as it had in the 1930s. The dollar offensive had undermined Keynesian hopes of an internationalist solution to the problems of world liquidity, but Keynesians and monetarists alike believed that floating exchange rates would provide an alternative answer. The expectation was that floating exchange rates would free national governments to pursue domestic economic policies without running into constraints imposed by speculation against the currency, while the smoother adjustment of currencies would reduce the demand for international liquidity, facilitating the stabilisation of the international system, and allow other currencies to join the dollar in a world role, reducing the burden on the US authorities and the vulnerability of the international system to the vagaries of US economic policy.

In the event all these hopes proved false. Although there was a growth in multi-currency borrowing, and in international invoicing in domestic currencies, the dollar continued to be pre-eminent in world financial markets, with futures markets providing a hedge against depreciation. The internationalisation of money capital gathered pace, fuelled by growing payments imbalances, on the one hand, and the increasing use of international financial markets as sources of funds by multinational companies and national governments, on the other, further increasing the vulnerability of national currencies to speculation. Speculation, far from being stabilising, proved to be destabilising, currency adjustments regularly 'overshooting'. This meant that national authorities needed larger, not smaller, reserves to defend floating currencies, while the latitude to pursue domestic policies independently of external considerations was reduced, not increased. The result was that the cyclical pattern of accumulation in the various different countries, which had previously been dominated by domestic political and economic conditions, was overridden by the cyclical pattern of accumulation on a world scale, dominated by the US.

Floating exchange rates considerably reduced the ability of national governments to pursue expansionary policies against the trend of accumulation on a world scale. If a government pursued an unduly expansionary domestic policy, fears of inflation would soon lead to speculation against the currency. If the government allowed the currency to depreciate, the result would be increased inflationary pressure, which would fuel further speculation and a further depreciation in a downward spiral, which could only be checked by the adoption of restrictive policies.

The one major exception to this remained the United States. The demonetisation of gold, the oil crisis, and the scarcity of the strong currencies reinforced the dominance of the dollar, and so enabled the US to force a growing supply of dollars onto world markets. The relatively low propensity of the US to import meant that a depreciation of the dollar strengthened the competitive position of the exposed sectors of the US economy without having a major impact on US domestic inflation, while the flood of dollars onto the world market stoked inflationary pressures in the rest of the world. Although the US balance of payments deficit provoked speculation against the dollar, the danger of an uncontrolled depreciation was averted because the dependence of the world monetary system on the dollar meant that international and national monetary authorities had little option but to support the dollar by official interventions in the foreign exchange markets and by adjusting domestic monetary policies to accommodate the flow of dollars. Only when speculative flows of private capital exceeded the willingness and ability of foreign governments to support the dollar, as in 1973, 1979 and 1987, did a threatened collapse of the dollar finally put the pressure on the US authorities. In general, however, the US government could pursue policies motivated by domestic considerations, with little regard for the external position. Meanwhile, faced with the weakening international position of the US economy; the growing domestic unevenness of US accumulation, and the conflicting political pressures of financial conservatism and populist expansionism, US governments pursued increasingly erratic policies, which further destabilised accumulation on a world scale.

Expansionary US policies stimulated accumulation on a world scale, and so increased the latitude available to governments pursuing Keynesian policies. However the result was that the world economy moved into a synchronised, and increasingly inflationary, world boom that by 1973 was assuming speculative dimensions, inflation sustaining profits in the face of growing overproduction in manufacturing on a world scale, and surplus capital being diverted into speculative channels, particularly on commodity markets as accumulation in manufacturing began to run ahead of the supply of raw materials. The boom was finally brought to a halt by the rapid increase in commodity prices, above all oil, in 1973–4, which led to massive international transfers of surplus value, primarily between oil producers and oil importers, disrupted the system of international payments, and threatened to drive world inflation into an uncontrollable upward spiral.

The oil price rise confronted all the industrial countries with the prospect of large balance of payments deficits. The recycling of petrodollars through the international banking system provided the increase in international liquidity that made it possible to accommodate the pressure on the system of international payments and to finance the immediate payments deficits. However the rise in import prices increased inflationary pressure and further eroded profits, while the instability of the international financial system, associated with floating exchange rates and the weakness of the dollar, increased the vulnerability of national currencies to speculation. Thus the crisis of 1974 precipitated an unprecedented crisis of profitability, and presented national governments with the pressures of domestic and international monetary instability, bringing the crisis of Keynesianism to a head.

The alternatives facing national governments were to pursue restrictive policies, in the attempt to neutralise the impact of rising import prices on domestic inflation, or to pursue expansionary policies, in the attempt to counter the impact of the rise in import prices on profitability. While the former strategy would squeeze domestic profits further, provoking a sharp recession with rising unemployment and the liquidation of weaker capitals, the latter strategy threatened to precipitate an inflationary spiral. The policies adopted were determined primarily by the financial and political pressures to which the various national governments were subject. The outcome of such policies depended not so much on the policies adopted, as on the course of the industrial and political struggles that it unleashed.

A restrictive policy contained inflationary pressure by provoking a sharp domestic recession. In Germany, where political opposition to inflation had already been mounting, capital responded to such a recession with a determined offensive against the working class, the brunt of which was borne by immigrant workers. Profitability was restored by the massive liquidation of unprofitable plant, laying off large numbers of workers, holding down wages, transforming methods of production, and investing in the more advanced branches of production. New investment, low inflation, strong demand for German exports, particularly of advanced means of production, and an undervalued mark enabled German capital to expand exports rapidly to eliminate the balance of payments deficit, and to pay rising wages, although unemployment remained high. The relative success of such policies confirmed the commitment of the German authorities to monetary conservatism, and their diagnosis of the crisis of 1974 as a classic overaccumulation crisis stimulated by monetary laxity. In the United States, on the other hand, restrictive policies led to a rapid increase in unemployment, major financial failures, a collapse of confidence on the stock exchange, and widespread political and industrial unrest, with no signs of a revival, forcing the government rapidly to reverse its policy in favour of a Keynesian expansionary strategy.

Most countries initially responded to the crisis by adopting expansionary policies, tapping world markets for balance of payments finance and, with the exception of the US, accommodating rising inflation by regular devaluation. Japan was hardest hit by the rise in oil and raw material prices, which accelerated the decline in profits and led to a sharp fall in investment, although employers continued to produce at a loss and to hoard labour. The government responded to the recession with a devaluation, which increased international competitiveness, and a large increase in the budget deficit, which absorbed surplus capital. Capital responded by exploiting the collaborative system of labour relations, that had been established on the basis of the destruction of militant trades unionism in the difficult period of the 1950s, to hold down wages, and to increase productivity by reorganising production and intensifying labour. The result of the capitalist offensive was that profits recovered, inflation fell sharply and accumulation was sustained as capital sought new outlets for its surplus product on world markets, particularly in the United States.

In Britain the government pursued a similar expansionary policy, as we have seen, with very different results. Although pressure on profits led to an intensification of class struggle, neither capital nor the state were able to hold down wages or to intensify labour, and far from British capital penetrating world markets to restore the balance of international payments, the balance of payments deteriorated as imports poured in and capital flooded abroad, forcing a reversal of policy in 1976. The non-OPEC developing countries followed similar policies, with very similar results, while France and Italy, which also responded initially with expansionary policies, stood somewhere between the British and Japanese examples. Only the US, once it had reversed its deflationary policy in 1975, was able to sustain an expansionary policy throughout the recession as the deteriorating balance of trade was compensated by rising overseas dollar holdings and growing foreign investment in the US.

Increasing OPEC imports and the expansionary policies of the weaker countries dragged the world economy out of the recession of 1973–5, although recovery was limited by the collapse of investment and the reversal of expansionary policies outside the US. Thus the recession gave way to a period of 'stagflation', marked by the persistence of inflation alongside rising rates of unemployment.

As governments around the world were forced to reverse expansionary policies in the face of escalating inflation they increasingly followed the examples of Germany and Switzerland of using restrictive monetary policies not simply as crisis measures but as active instruments in the attempt to contain inflation. Such policies were effective not in restricting the money supply, as monetarists believed, for capitalists were adept at tapping new sources of credit, but primarily by forcing up the exchange rate, which led to an immediate improvement in the terms of trade, but which above all increased the pressure of international competition on domestic productive capitals, forcing them to hold down wages and to transform methods of production, such pressure being reinforced where high interest rates sustained an overvalued currency. Although such policies were effective in containing inflation, at the cost of a massive increase in unemployment, they further increased the instability of the international monetary system as national governments pushed up exchange rates, to combat inflation, and pulled them down, to restore international competitiveness.

Despite the increasing strength of Germany and Japan, the pace of accumulation on a world scale continued to be dominated by the US, through its impact on world trade and on world liquidity and interest rates, and to be restricted by the persistence of overproduction on a world scale. Between 1975 and 1977 the US dollar appreciated relative to the currencies of its trading partners as the growing demand for international liquidity and rising foreign investment in the US, associated with the rapid internationalisation of productive capital, sustained the US deficit. However this led to a serious overvaluation of the dollar in relation to the US's foremost competitors, Japan and Germany, which were rapidly increasing their penetration of the US market. Thus the US engineered a sharp devaluation against the yen and the mark over the next two years, stimulating a mini world boom. The continued pursuit of expansionary policies in the US allowed a degree of latitude to national governments that persisted with Keynesian policies, albeit in increasingly difficult circumstances. However the boom at the end of the 70s was brought to an abrupt halt by rising commodity prices and speculation against the dollar. The US responded to the crisis by adopting severely restrictive monetary policies from late 1979 that drove up US interest rates, leading to a massive inflow of short-term capital and a rapid appreciation of the dollar, to which other national governments could only respond, sooner or later, by pursuing equally restrictive policies. The result was an even sharper world recession than that of 1974–5, in which governments had even less latitude to pursue independent policies than they had enjoyed five years earlier.

The period from 1974–9 marked a transitional phase in which national governments pursued divergent, and often unstable, domestic policies in response to the conflicting pressures of working class aspirations, expressed primarily through the organised labour movement and the institutional forms of the Keynesian Welfare State, which were accommodated by expansionary policies, and the growing political and financial pressures generated by inflation, which governments were increasingly able to harness to check working class aspirations and pursue restrictive policies. The transitional phase was brought to an end by the crisis at the end of the decade, as the sharp world recession turned stagflation into deflation, marking the end of the Keynesian road, completing a decisive shift in the balance of class forces in favour of capital. The recession of 1979–81 accentuated class divisions, critically undermined the political and industrial strength of the organised working class, and destroyed the weaker productive capitals, while opening the way to a renewed capitalist offensive, involving the accelerated restructuring of capitalist social relations and development of new institutional forms within which to regulate class relations, associated politically with the rise of the New Right, and the 'new realism' of a social democratic 'politics of austerity'. However, the removal of the barrier to accumulation presented by working class aspirations did not resolve the crisis of overaccumulation.

International financial pressures dictated tight monetary policies to contain inflationary pressure throughout the 1980s. However restrictive monetary policies by no means implied that accumulation was confined within the limits of the market. Recovery from the depression of 1979–81 led to the longest continuous boom since the war, despite persistent unemployment and growing pauperisation for those whom it passed by. Accumulation was sustained through the boom by expansionary fiscal policies, primarily in the United States, and by the massive expansion of domestic and international credit, which absorbed surplus capital and accommodated the growing unevenness and overaccumulation of capital on a world scale. Whereas the governments of the Left in the 1970s had pursued monetarist macroeconomic policies within a Keynesian ideological and political framework, the governments of the New Right increasingly adopted Keynesian macroeconomic policies within a monetarist ideological and political framework.

While recession turned to acute depression in the third world in the wake of the crisis of 1979–80, the election of Reagan led to the emergence of a new strategy in the US. The Reagan strategy involved a tight monetary policy, with a consequent overvalued dollar, combined with tax cuts and a huge increase in military

spending to stimulate accumulation, particularly in the technologically advanced military and military-related sectors. In theory
the soaring budget deficit was to be eliminated by cuts in non-
military government spending, but such cuts never materialised,
while tax cuts were supposed to stimulate increased revenues as
the restoration of incentives stimulated a recovery of the 'supply-
side', although the supply side barely recovered, and the boom was
based on the usual growth of consumption, financed by soaring
private and public debt, and met by rising imports.

In practice Reaganomics was a combination of an extremely
expansionary fiscal policy with a restrictive monetary policy and
an overvalued exchange rate that accelerated the domestic restructuring of US capital, with widespread closures and mass unemployment in the old industrial heartland, and a boom, centred on
military-related industries, in the sun-belt states and the West.
High unemployment and an offensive against the trades unions,
inspired by the state and backed up by tight monetary policy,
combined with a readiness of productive capital to relocate in the
largely non-unionised sun-belt states, limited the ability of trades
unions to secure wage increases or resist plant closures, and so
checked inflationary pressures. However soaring imports were not
matched by rising exports, the result being an escalating balance
of payments deficit, which was financed, together with the growing
budget deficit, by a sustained capital inflow attracted by high US
interest rates and a booming stock market.

The initial impact of this policy was a rapid rise in unemployment and a fall in inflation as the tight money policy began to bite
in the context of the world recession. However towards the end of
1982 the fiscal stimulus was beginning to take effect, monetary policy was eased, interest rates fell, and the uneven US recovery was
under way. US expansion, combined with the growing overvaluation of the dollar, provided a rapidly growing market for the more
advanced capitals in the rest of the world, stimulating a similarly
uneven recovery of the world economy. While the more advanced
capitals on a world scale prospered, high interest rates and tight
credit kept the pressure on weaker capitals and high unemployment and aggressive management eroded the bargaining position
of the working class. High interest rates and cuts in taxation and
public expenditure secured a massive redistribution of income and
wealth in favour of the rich domestically and on a world scale,

inflating profits and rapidly expanding the market for the more advanced consumer products. The redistribution of income reinforced the boom, but also reinforced the uneven development of accumulation on a world scale by shifting demand in favour of the most advanced producers, particularly in Germany, Japan and the Newly Industrialising Countries.

By 1985 the appreciation of the dollar had led to a substantial deterioration of the US balance of trade. Despite increasingly desperate US pleas, Germany and Japan had refused more than token measures to relieve the pressure on the US by restricting their exports or by reflating their domestic economies, for fear of stimulating renewed domestic inflation. From late 1985 the US was compelled to respond to growing speculative pressure, that drove up interest rates and threatened to halt the US boom, by engineering a devaluation of the dollar. As the dollar fell, and the US trade and budget deficits continued to increase, there was a growing danger that speculation would plunge the dollar into an uncontrolled slide, threatening the stability of the international monetary system. The Louvre accord in early 1987 sought to stabilise world exchange rates, but did nothing to correct the underlying imbalances that derived from the growing unevenness of accumulation on a world scale. Although the monetary authorities managed to contain speculative pressure on the dollar, with increasing difficulty, fears that the boom would be brought to a halt, whether by a renewed surge of speculation against the dollar, which national monetary authorities would be unable or unwilling to check, by US deflationary policies, or by a wave of protectionism, led in October 1987 to the collapse of the speculative boom on world stock markets that had gathered momentum over the previous two years, followed by the slide of the dollar.

Chapter 12

Conclusion

Money, the market and the state

It is easy to dismiss monetarism as no more than an ideological cloak for the political rise of the New Right, that expresses the decline of the old working class and the rise of the yuppie, but that has little practical significance. Despite its anti-state rhetoric monetarism did not lead to a fall in state expenditure nor in the level of taxation. Despite its attack on welfarism, it has not destroyed the central institutions of the welfare state, and has not reduced levels of welfare expenditure. Despite its attack on the trades unions, it has not presided over a decline in collective bargaining. Despite its rhetoric of democracy, it has massively increased the powers of the executive and shown contempt for democratically elected bodies. Despite its attack on state support for industry, it has continued to pour in money. Despite its attack on Keynesianism, it has continued to rely on fiscal instruments and soon abandoned the attempt to rely on control of the money supply. Despite its attack on incomes policies, it has applied rigid, if unilateral, control over public sector wages. Despite its eulogies to competition, it has presided over an unprecedented wave of monopolisation. Despite its emphasis on the rewards of enterprise, it has fed an orgy of speculation. Despite its emphasis on sound finance, it has presided over an explosion of debt. Despite its emphasis on law and order, it has presided over a mounting crime wave. Despite its emphasis on the family, families have been split up by the pressures of unemployment, poverty and homelessness at a growing rate. The changes that have taken place, particularly in the structure of public expenditure, the structure of employment and the level of unemployment, have largely continued trends that were well-established by the mid 1970s, exaggerated by the crisis of 1980–2. Even the dramatic fall in trades union membership is largely the result of unemployment and structural changes in employment. Thus social democratic governments in France, Southern Europe, Australia and New Zealand had to introduce similar monetarist policies in the face of the crisis. In short it might seem that the significance of monetarism is largely rhetorical, its practical results the product of economic crisis rather than of any fundamental political changes, its rhetoric contradicted by its practice at every turn.

There is no doubt that the rise of monetarism did not inaugurate any fundamental changes, but marked the culmination of well-established trends, which had already secured the New Right a political base and an ideological appeal. It is true that monetarism does not represent a frontal assault on the welfare state, on which expenditure has continued to rise, or on the working class, sections of which have enjoyed an unprecedented growth in living standards, even if they have paid the price in insecurity of employment and the intensification of labour. There is also no doubt that monetarism, like all state ideologies that have preceded it, is a fundamentally contradictory ideology. Nevertheless there is also no doubt that the rise of monetarism is the ideological expression of fundamental changes in the form of the state, that have reflected, and reinforced, the massive political defeat of the working class.

The crisis of Keynesianism and the rise of monetarism were neither a reflection of political and ideological changes, nor merely the result of economic crisis, but reflected the contradictory form of the capitalist state in the face of the global crisis of overaccumulation, the development of the contradiction being determined by the outcome of a pervasive class struggle. The Keynesian Welfare State was constructed on the basis of the systematic rationalisation of the institutions of industrial relations, social administration and electoral representation that had been evolving over the previous century. However the force behind this rationalisation was the industrial and political strength of the organised working class at the end of the Second World War, while its political stability rested on the dynamism of the post-war boom. Keynesianism expressed the belief that the contradictory form of the liberal state could be overcome, as a generalised rise in wages and public expenditure would both maintain the dynamism of the boom and integrate the working class into advanced capitalism, subordinating the power of money to the power of the state. However Keynesianism provided no means of securing the sustained accumulation of capital by overcoming the tendency to the overaccumulation and uneven development of capital. Indeed, far from overcoming the contradictory form of capital accumulation, Keynesian policies accentuated its crisis tendencies.

As profits fell in the face of the growing pressure of overaccumulation the institutions of the Keynesian welfare state appeared as a barrier to capital in institutionalising a generalised expectation of rising wages and increasing public expenditure, and in providing the institutional forms through which the working class could seek to realise such expectations. However neither capital nor the state could simply launch a frontal assault on the working class, while the limits of the national form of the state in the face of a global overaccumulation crisis progressively narrowed the freedom of manoeuvre of social democratic governments. Nevertheless the institutions of the Keynesian welfare state were progressively eroded from within as pressure on profitability forced capitalists to resist wage claims and the state to hold down public expenditure. The result was to open up divisions within the working class. The emerging class unity institutionalised in the Keynesian Welfare State was undermined as the pressure of the crisis intensified trades union sectionalism, while increasingly restrictive incomes policies politicised such sectionalism, and as rising public expenditure imposed a growing burden of taxation and led to escalating inflation. Meanwhile rising unemployment progressively undermined the bargaining position of the trades unions, repeated crises dampened working class expectations, and the state diverted popular resentment at rising taxation and inflation against the trades unions and welfare expenditure.

As employers successfully asserted 'management's right to manage', and as the state successfully diverted responsibility for rising unemployment, inflation and rising taxation onto the extravagance of working class aspirations, it became increasingly clear that the basis of the post-war settlement had dissolved. On the one hand, capital and the state could not satisfy the aspirations of the whole of the working class. On the other hand, political stability did not require them to do so. The integration of the trades unions into the Keynesian Welfare State had led to a demobilisation of the rank and file, while the deepening crisis had undermined trades union unity and opened a gulf between the trades union leadership and its members. Although pockets of militancy remained, they could no longer provide a focus for working class unity as they had in the late 1960s and early 1970s. The internationalisation of capital had rapidly undermined the possibility of social democratic governments pursuing radical interventionist strategies, that had been a real danger in the 1940s, and that were still a threat in the early 1970s.

The triumph of monetarism did not involve the dismantling of the systems of industrial relations and social administration, nor, in the metropolitan centres, the abolition of electoral representation. However it did involve fundamental changes in the political form of the Keynesian welfare state, as governments of the Left and Right responded to the crisis by exploiting and intensifying the divisions within the working class on the basis of the progressive reimposition of the rule of money, so that by the 1980s the political institutions of Keynesian class collaboration, through which the working class had been able to pursue its collective aspirations, had become an empty shell, and their dismantling almost a formality.

The reimposition of the rule of money, despite the monetarist rhetoric, certainly does not involve a withdrawal of the state in favour of the rule of the market, a strategy pursued by the Heath government with disastrous consequences. The rule of money is no longer mediated primarily by the market. The market defines only the ultimate barrier to accumulation. The rule of money is directly imposed on capitals and on the state by the banks and financial institutions. Within the capitalist corporation the rule of money is imposed on the various subsidiaries, divisions and branches of the conglomerate with the development of decentralised financial management and accounting systems, so that the corporation takes on the form of the holding company. The corporation relates to many of its formally independent suppliers not through the market, but through long-term contracting and sub-contracting arrangements. It protects itself against price and currency fluctuations in competitive markets by buying futures.

The rule of the market is not imposed on the working class

through the 'labour market', which has long been relegated to the fantastic world of the economist, but through systems of industrial relations and personnel management. The rise of monetarism has corresponded with the transition from an industrial relations system based on a generalised expectation of increasing wages, regardless of financial constraints, to systems of 'human resource management' and the development of payment systems that tie pay at all levels directly to financial results.

The monetarist political revolution has primarily amounted to the attempt to transform the form of the state by the introduction of similar systems of management, accounting, subcontracting and 'human resource management' as the means of subordinating the state apparatus, and the provision of welfare benefits and public services, to the rule of money, and so systematically confining the provision of public services within the limits of the financial resources put at their disposal according to the political priorities of the state, without regard for social need. The increasingly ruthless subordination of civil society and the state to the power of money has accordingly led to the progressive erosion of the legitimacy of representative and democratic bodies, which are reduced to the fora within which particular interests press their partisan claims, and against which monetarism asserts the primacy of the general interest embodied in the disinterested rule of money. The authoritarianism of monetarist regimes is not a quirk of the personality of their political leaders, but is inherent in the monetarist project.

The limits of monetarism

Monetarism has sought to secure the rigorous subordination of civil society and the state to the rule of money, against all popular, democratic and bureaucratic resistance. It has attempted to overcome democratic resistance by by-passing and dissolving democratic bodies or by eroding their powers. It has attempted to overcome bureaucratic resistance to its political reforms by introducing managers from the private sector and trades union resistance by the threat of privatisation. It has attempted to overcome civil resistance by strengthening the repressive apparatus of the state. However, the result of the monetarist revolution in government has been not efficiency but chaos. The drive to impose rigid financial controls and to cut costs in the public sector has disrupted well-established planning mechanisms and managerial procedures to create administrative chaos, economic irrationality, and a collapse of morale that threatens the breakdown of public services, epitomised in Britain by the crises in housing, education, transport and the health service. Despite the political collapse of the Left, monetarist policies have faced widespread opposition and determined resistance, both in and against the state apparatus. Nevertheless monetarism has been able to prevail politically, partly because of the fragmented character of the opposition, but primarily because of the sustained world boom.

Although monetarist policies effected the massive devaluation of capital and destruction of productive capacity, particularly in the recessions of 1974-6 and 1979-82, they have not removed the tendency to the overaccumulation of capital or confined accumulation within the limits of the market. Indeed the sharpening of international competition and the rapid pace of technical change through the 1980s intensified the overaccumulation and uneven development of capital, which was accommodated only by the explosion of domestic and international debt. While the boom was sustained governments were able to isolate working class resistance to restrictive economic and social policies and aggressive managerial strategies, while capital was able to concede a steady rise in the wages of large sections of the working class. The political stability of monetarism, no less than that of Keynesianism, depended on the sustained, if uneven, accumulation of capital on a world scale.

The crash of 1987 dramatically brought home how precarious were the foundations of the apparent success of monetarism. Although the international financial system survived the crises of 1974 and 1979, and absorbed the debt crisis of the third world from 1982, the 1987 crash has further undermined the pyramid of debt, and it is unlikely that it could survive another severe blow. The stock market crash and the decline of the dollar are not in themselves a threat, and government intervention could probably cope with isolated failures, but a renewed world recession, precipitated by a sharp US contraction, would be likely to lead to major defaults which would reverberate through the Eurodollar and inter-bank money markets, turn recession into depression, and threaten global collapse. In such an event Latin America gives us a foretaste of the domestic politics of monetarism in a crisis, while its global politics do not bear thinking about.

In the face of the looming crisis the US is no longer in a position to sustain global accumulation by pursuing expansionary policies, and its attempts to persuade Germany and Japan to do so have a negligible chance of success. In principle the US could continue to cover its deficit, if necessary borrowing in foreign currencies and attracting an inflow of foreign direct investment, although such measures would be likely to provoke growing domestic political opposition. In principle international co-operation could continue to shore up the international financial system and maintain the expansion of credit required to sustain accumulation in the hope that the devaluation of the dollar, increased US exports of military hardware, and increased European and Japanese payments against US overseas military expenditure might restore the US external balance without requiring a domestic recession, but such measures imply the ability of the US government to impose the costs of domestic adjustment onto the working class and of external adjustment onto its allies. Thus the most likely outcome is that the system will stagger on, interrupted by monetary and financial crises, while the world economy slides into recession and domestic and international political tensions mount.

The historical precedents are not encouraging. The previous phases of global overaccumulation resulted in the rise of protectionism and imperialism, as nation states sought to insulate domestic productive capital from the impact of the crisis, which led to rapid changes in international alliances, and the formation of blocks which culminated in global war. Despite the massive internationalisation of capital the possibilities of such a development are very real. The tendencies to protectionism are already strong, the economic and political appeal of militarism is growing fast, and the areas of conflict are already mapped out. It is not difficult to imagine Europe turning to the Soviet block, and Japan confirming its subordination to the US, with Britain stuck in the middle. It is not difficult to imagine arms-length military confrontations in the Middle East, Southern Africa or Latin America that could flare up into major wars. However there is no inevitability in such developments. Protectionism and imperialism arose in the previous crises of overaccumulation as the outcome of the domestic conflicts unleashed by the crisis, as desperate measures through which the state sought to confine the domestic class struggle within the limits of its capitalist form. Barbarism is capital's alternative to socialism.

The crisis of social democracy and the future of socialism

The necessity of socialism has never been more urgent. The objective conditions for a democratic socialist society have never been more fully developed. The concentration and centralisation of capital has socialised production to an unprecedented degree. The computer, through which monetarism has been able to perfect the subordination of society to the alienated rule of money, provides the instrument that makes it possible to bring the complex apparatus of social production under democratic control.

The subjective conditions for socialism are also more fully developed than in any previous period of history. Despite political defeats, workers continue to express their resentment and their frustration, individually and collectively, and seek to realise their hopes and aspirations through trades unions and through the 'new social movements'. Moreover monetarism has politicised these struggles to an unprecedented degree as effective trades unionism brings workers into direct confrontation with the state; as public sector trades unions and elected authorities mobilise popular opposition to the collapse of public services; as welfare claimants confront the increasingly repressive administration of social security; as the middle class faces the erosion of its professional and managerial autonomy; and as the police abandon the fight against crime to become an instrument of civil repression.

Nevertheless the fact remains that the working class has suffered a massive political defeat, and the forces of popular resistance to monetarism are fragmented, demoralised and disorganised. The crisis of Keynesianism was not only a crisis of the state, it was also a crisis of socialism, in both its social democratic and its more radical variants. Monetarism provided a provisional resolution of the crisis of the state. Socialism has only just begun to address its crisis.

There is no reason why socialism should not put itself back on the historical agenda, if only it can learn the lessons of its defeats. The fundamental lessons are three. First, the basis of socialism can only be the socialisation of production. Only by bringing social production under social control can the contradictory tendencies of capitalist accumulation, that lead to the pauperisation of growing masses of the world population, to the intensification of class struggle, to wars and to recurrent crises, be overcome. Second, socialism has to be internationalist. This is not dictated simply by the internationalisation of capital, for the crisis is unleashing nationalist political and ideological forces that counter such internationalisation. It is more fundamentally a political imperative. Nationalism is the supreme expression of the alienated form of the capitalist state, fetishising the 'illusory community' of the nation against the emerging unity of the 'real community' embodied in the collective organisation of the working class. Third, socialism has to be democratic. This does not mean that socialism should confine itself within the limits of the formal democracy of the capitalist state. The experience of state socialism and social democracy alike shows that the attempt to build socialism from above, on the basis of the illusory community of the capitalist state and the formalism of its democratic processes, soon leads the state to confront the real community of the democratic organisations of the working class as a barrier to socialism. The socialisation of production cannot be divorced from the question of the political forms of such socialisation.

It is too easy to pin responsibility for the triumph of the New Right on the bankruptcy of social democracy and betrayal by its leadership. The failure of social democracy is as much a failure of the Left to have offered a credible alternative. The underlying dilemma is the perennial one of the relation between the social and political struggles of the working class, the relation between revolution and reform. However this is a false dilemma, imposed on the socialist movement by its failure to confront the fundamental political issue of the contradictory form of the capitalist state, which dictates that the class struggle is necessarily a struggle at one and the same time in and against the state. The failure to confront this issue underlies the polarisation of the social and political struggles of the working class, separating these two moments of the class struggle and setting them in conflict with one another, such conflict appearing on the one hand in divisions within the working class movement, between those workers able to secure their sectional interests on the basis of their industrial strength and those who look to the state for support, and on the other hand in the polarisation of revolutionary socialism and social democracy.

Social democracy fetishises the democratic form of the state, and ignores its class character, which leads it to confront the social struggles of the working class as a barrier to socialism, rather than as its social foundation. In the face of such a confrontation the revolutionary left has tended to make the opposite error, seeking to develop the social struggles of the working class into a revolutionary confrontation with the class state, without realising that the unity of the fragmented social struggles of the working class can only be constructed politically, and such a political unity can only be constructed through the state. Thus revolutionary politics has tended to degenerate into sectarianism, as contending parties seek to present themselves as the authentic expression of the working class, and into ultra-leftism, as such parties seek to validate their claims by proposing revolutionary programmes devoid of any political substance.

From the 1890s to the 1930s social democratic politics was underpinned by a belief in the inevitability of socialism. The failure of the market to secure the coordination of production, and the inherent tendency to underconsumption, meant that successive capitalist crises could only be resolved by the monopolisation of the commanding heights of the economy, and the socialisation of the reproduction of the working class. Thus reform and revolution were reconciled as the state progressively extended its command over civil society, and reformist and revolutionary socialists could maintain an uneasy alliance within the framework of social democracy. However this alliance, which was already being undermined by the political advance of the working class before the First World War, was broken by the outbreak of war, the character of the war raising in the starkest terms the issue of the character of the state, as a class state or a national state.

With the political assimilation of the reformist leadership in the course of the war the separation of reformist from revolutionary socialism became a direct antagonism, as the reformist leadership saw the war as an opportunity to constitute the state as a national state, and to extend its power over civil society as a stage in the transition to socialism, while revolutionary socialists sought to build on popular struggles to construct a revolutionary movement that would overthrow the class state. Yet behind this antagonism was a paradoxical complementarity. The political character of the revolutionary movement was determined primarily by the extensive wartime intervention of the state in civil society which gave the social struggles of the working class an immediately political content, while the political advance of reformism was determined primarily by the strength of the revolutionary opposition which reforms sought to demobilise and defuse. The political advance of reformism brought this contradiction to a head in the wave of revolution and counter-revolution, in which the defeat of the revolutionary movement, outside Russia, prepared the political ground for the reversal of the war-time gains of reformism and the reconstruction of the liberal state form.

The depression of the 1930s and the rise of fascism undermined the social democratic belief that socialism would be the inevitable outcome of capitalist crises, while strengthening its commitment to Parliamentarism. Although social democrats continued to pay lip-service to nationalisation and planning, Keynesianism promised to abolish capitalist crises, while reconciling rising wages and growing welfare expenditure with the sustained accumulation of capital. If Keynesianism could resolve the contradictions of the capitalist mode of production, the question of the ownership of the means of production became secondary, inequality to be dealt with by the taxation of inherited wealth and rentier incomes, poverty to be eradicated by the welfare state, and the power of employers to be counterbalanced by trades unionism and protective legislation. Thus social democrats played a leading role in the post-war reconstruction of the liberal state form.

The failure of liberal Keynesianism in the face of the global overaccumulation of capital led to a growth of the interventionist apparatuses of the state in the attempt to reconcile the class character of the state with its democratic form. As in the First World War growing state intervention and the institutionalisation of class collaboration progressively politicised the social struggles of the working class. However such struggles remained trapped within the existing forms of working class politics, which reproduced the contradictory form of the capitalist state. The institutional forms of the Keynesian welfare state provided channels through which the working class could pursue its aspirations through trades unionism and electoral politics. As such institutions appeared increasingly as a barrier to popular aspirations, the social struggles of the working class presented a challenge to the social and political power of capital, and pressed beyond the limits of the liberal state form. However social democracy failed to harness the progressive moment of the struggle against the state to the conservative moment of the struggle within the state, seeing the emerging challenge to the state as a barrier to its own reformist ambitions. Thus the political struggle of the working class, far from overcoming the contradictory form of the capitalist state on the basis of everyday struggles in and against the state, reproduced that contradiction within its own ranks, dividing and fragmenting the social and political struggles of the working class. The failure of the Left to give a progressive political form to the struggle against the state meant that working class aspirations were increasingly privatised, expressed not by socialism, but by the anti-state rhetoric of the New Right.

The response of the organised left in Britain to the crisis of socialism does not augur well for the future. While the ultra-left sects saw every display of militancy as a stage in the building of a revolutionary confrontation of the working class with the state, and the libertarian left celebrated the fragmentation and disorganisation of these struggles as a political virtue, the majority of the Left continued to look to the state as the agent of socialism. However the Left saw the failure of social democracy not as a failure to address the issue of the form of the state, but as a failure on the part of the opportunistic political and trades union leadership. The resulting struggle for control of the Labour Party further eroded the ability of the Labour Party to present a coherent alternative to monetarism.

The temporary victory of the Left in the Labour Party proved a debacle, its programme resoundingly rejected by the electorate in the 1983 election, while radical local authorities found themselves increasingly isolated in the face of the central government's offensive, on the one hand, and working class resistance to their plans, on the other. Thus the Left split in its turn, the 'hard Left' denouncing the 'soft Left' for its opportunism, the 'soft Left' condemning the 'hard Left' for its utopian failure to recognise the limits of political reality imposed by the liberal form of the state.

The resounding failure of the Left brought home the limits of the liberal state form. However it also brought home the failure of the left to confront the issue of the forms of working class political organisation. The limits of the liberal state form cannot be overcome from within, but only by building on the collective strength of an organised socialist movement. The limits of social democracy are not simply a matter of its leadership or its political programme, they are reproduced in its own institutional and political forms. The separation of the state from civil society is reproduced within the social democratic party in the separation of its trades union from its political wings. The formal character of bourgeois democracy is reproduced in the formalism of internal party democracy. The alienated form of capitalist state power is reproduced in the subordination of the party to its political leadership, which expresses the unity of the movement against the sectionalism and fragmentation of its component parts. Thus the opportunism of social democracy, whatever the character of its leadership, is institutionalised in the duplication of the political forms of the liberal state within the social democratic party.

The way forward for socialism cannot be provided by the 'new Realists', who seek to paper over the divisions within the working class opened up by monetarism by redefining socialism as monetarism tempered with humanity. Nor can it be provided by an ultra-Left whose revolutionary rhetoric expresses only the frustrations of political impotence. If socialism is to be more than an empty rhetoric it can only be based on a socialist movement. Thus the socialist agenda is not a matter of developing policies and a programme for the 1990s, nor is it a matter of an opportunistic or insurrectionary struggle for state power. Building socialism means building socialist democracy and socialist internationalism within the working class movement, so that differences of sectional interest, of gender, of race and of nation can be confronted and resolved self-consciously, to build a united movement which expresses the 'real community' of co-operative social relations.

This is no utopian project. Its real foundations lie in the frustrations of the working class in the face of the alienated forms of capitalist domination and in the democratic forms of collective organisation through which the working class seeks to overcome its divisions in day-to-day struggles in every sphere of social life. The socialist project is a matter of building on the solidarity, spontaneity and imagination developed in such fragmented struggles. Such a project is never easy, for the differences of interest within the working class are real differences, which are constantly reproduced and reinforced by the continued separation of civil society and the state, through which human social power confronts humanity as an external force in the alienated forms of money and the state. However the task of socialism is not to mimic the alienated forms of capitalist power by imposing unity on these fragmented struggles from above, but to challenge the division between civil society and the state by giving the emerging unity of working class struggles a political form which will express not the illusory community of the liberal state, but the real community of human social life, and so transform formal democracy into social democracy.

Index